Er. D.C. Gupta

disha
Nurturing Ambitions

Modern Physics

for JEE Main & Advanced

(Study Package for Physics)

Fully Solved

Includes Past JEE & KVPY Questions

Useful for Class 12, KVPY & Olympiads

- **Head Office :** B-32, Shivalik Main Road, Malviya Nagar, New Delhi-110017
- **Sales Office :** B-48, Shivalik Main Road, Malviya Nagar, New Delhi-110017
  Tel. : 011-26691021 / 26691713

Page Layout : Prakash Chandra Sahoo

Typeset by Disha DTP Team

Printed at: **Repro Knowledgecast Limited, Thane**

DISHA PUBLICATION

For further information about the books from DISHA,

Log on to **www.dishapublication.com** or email to **info@dishapublication.com**

STUDY PACKAGE IN PHYSICS FOR JEE MAIN & ADVANCED

Contents

Study Package Booklet 12 - Modern Physics

Chapter 5

Electron, Photon, Atom, Photoelectric Effect and X-rays (245- 300)

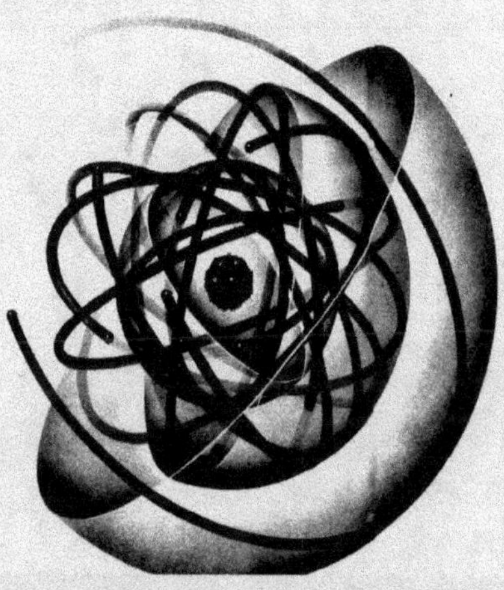

5.1 DISCHARGE THROUGH GASES AT LOW PRESSURE

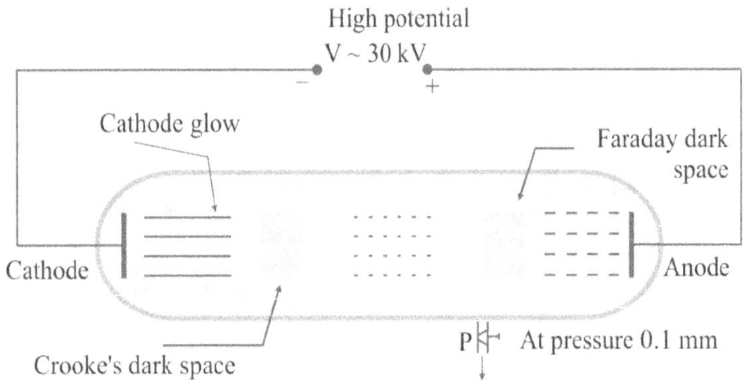

*Fig.*5.1 **Discharge tube.**

At normal pressure, gases are poor conductor of electricity because they have very few charged particles for conduction. These charged particles are produced due to cosmic rays. When a potential difference is applied across the discharge tube, the charged particles start accelerating. At low pressure these charged particles can move a considerable distance and aquire enough energy to ionise the other molecules after collisions. The free electrons and positive ions are produced inside the discharge tube, and conduction starts between electrodes fitted in the tube.

When pressure inside the discharge tube decreases gradually from 10 mm of mercury to 0.1 mm of mercury, Crookes dark space, Cathode glow, Faraday dark space and then alterate dark and bright bands are observed.

5.2 CATHODE RAYS

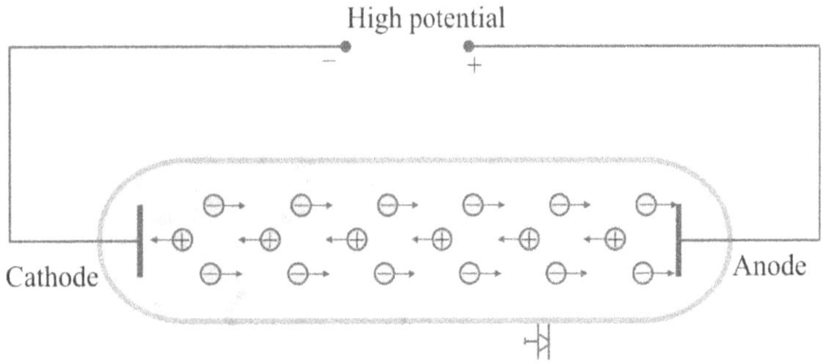

Fig. **5.2**

At the pressure of 10^{-3} mm of mercury, the molecules of the gas ionise and the free electrons move towards anode. The positive ions hit the cathode and cause emission of electrons from cathode. These emitted electrons also move towards anode. Thus cathode rays in the discharge tube are the stream of electrons produced due to collisions. Cathode rays were discovered by **Sir William Crookes**.

Properties of cathode rays

1. Cathode rays are the stream of electrons, and so they carry negative charge.
2. The cathode rays are independent of the nature of the gas and material of the electrode used in the discharge tube. Therefore e/m of cathode rays is a universal constant. It is 1.759×10^{11} C/kg.
3. They can be deflected by electric and magnetic fields.
4. Cathode rays can penetrate thin foils of metals.
5. Cathode rays ionise the gas through which they pass.
6. Cathode rays exert mechanical force on the object they strike.
7. They produce heat when allowed to fall on material surface.
8. Cathode rays produce fluorescence when they strike a number of crystals, minerals etc.
9. On striking to the target of high atomic weight and high melting point, they produce X-rays.
10. They travel in straight lines and so cast shadow of objects placed in their path.

5.3 DISCOVERY OF ELECTRON

The discovery of electron was done by **J.J. Thomson.** He called them as cathode corpuscles. He studied the properties of electrons and suggest that electrons are the necessary constituents of all the atoms. He measured charge-to-mass ratio of an electron e/m in 1897. This ratio is also called the specific charge of the electron. Fifteen years after Thomson's experiment of determination of e/m, Millikan succeeded in measuring the charge of the electron with his famous oil-drop experiment. He found the charge of an electron as 1.602×10^{-19} C. Thus the mass of the electron can be obtained as :

$$m_e = \frac{e}{(e/m)} = \frac{1.602\times10^{-19}}{1.759\times10^{11}} = 9.1\times10^{-31} \text{ kg.}$$

Thomson's measurement of e/m

Thomson's apparatus consisted of highly evaluated glass tube with a cathode C and an anode A. With this arrangement a narrow beam of electrons all having the same speed can be obtained by adopting a high potential difference between A and C. If V is the potential difference, then kinetic energy attained by each electron will be eV. Thus, if v is the speed of the electron, then

$$\frac{1}{2}mv^2 = eV$$

or $$v = \sqrt{\frac{2eV}{m}}. \quad ...(i)$$

Now this accelerated beam of electrons passes through a region, having perpendicular electric $\vec{\mathbf{E}}$ and magnetic $\vec{\mathbf{B}}$ field. The value of $\vec{\mathbf{E}}$ and $\vec{\mathbf{B}}$ are so adjusted that an undeflected beam of electrons is obtained on the screen S. Thus if E and B are their magnitudes, then for undeflected beam; electric force and magnetic force on each electron must be equal in magnitude and opposite in direction. So

$$eE = evB$$

or $$v = \frac{E}{B}. \quad ...(ii)$$

On simplifying equations (i) and (ii), we get

$$\frac{e}{m} = \frac{E^2}{2VB^2}. \quad ...(1)$$

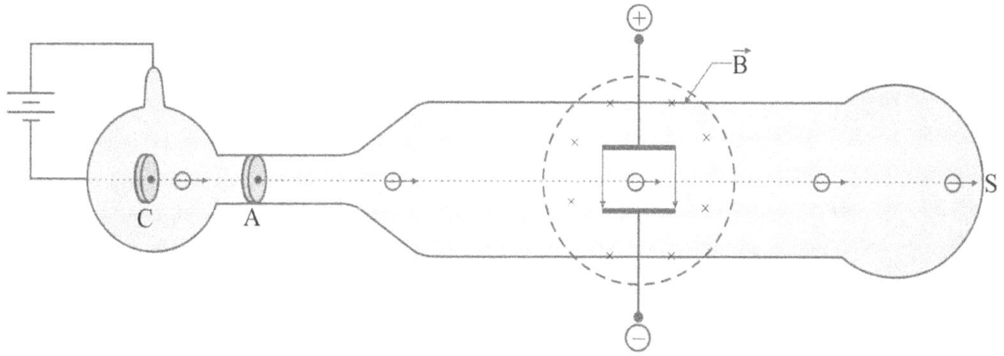

Fig **5.3. Cathode ray oscilloscopes (CRO).**

5.4 PHOTON

Several phenomenon like, interference, diffraction and polarisation have been explained on the bases of wave nature of light. Photoelectric effect, Comptons effect can be only explained on the basis of particle nature of light. Einstein forwarded the Plank's quantum theory of light to explain photoelectric effect. According to quantum theory, light propagates in the form of small energy particles, called **photons**.

Energy of photon : The kinetic energy of the photon of frequency f is given by, $E = hf$. Here h is the Plank's constant whose value is 6.6×10^{-34} J-s. If λ is the wavelength associated with the photon, then $E = \frac{hc}{\lambda}$, where c is the speed of light, which is 3×10^8 m/s.

Energy of photon is not continuous but is in packets, called **quanta** (plural of quantum). It is like quantum of money ; one rupia, two rupees, three rupees not one and half rupee.

Mass of photon

Photon is the energy particle and so has no meaning at rest. Its rest mass is zero. The kinetic mass of the photon can be obtained from, $E = mc^2$,

$$\therefore \quad m = \frac{E}{c^2}. \qquad ...(1)$$

Momentum of photon

It is defined as :

$$p = mc = \frac{E}{c^2}c = \frac{E}{c}$$

$$= \frac{hc/\lambda}{c}$$

$$\therefore \quad P = \frac{h}{\lambda}. \qquad ...(2)$$

Intensity of light : Intensity of radiation is the energy crossing unit area in unit time. Thus if E energy crosses area A in time t, then

$$I = \frac{E}{At}.$$

As

$$\frac{E}{t} = \text{power and so } I = \left[\frac{\text{Power}}{A}\right]$$

At a distance r from a point source of power P, intensity is given by

$$I = \frac{\text{Power}}{4\pi r^2} \Rightarrow I \propto \frac{1}{r^2}.$$

For a line source at a distance r,

$$I = \frac{\text{Power}}{2\pi r \ell} \Rightarrow I \propto \frac{1}{r}.$$

Number of photons

If P is the power of the source, and E is the energy of each photon, then number of photons emitted by a source in one second

$$n = \frac{\text{Power}}{E}.$$

Radiation force

We know that radiation (visible or other) possesses momentum and so exerts force on the object on which it strikes. Suppose radiation of intensity I strikes the plane object of area A. If ΔP is the change in momentum of the object after collision with the radiation, then force exerted on the object

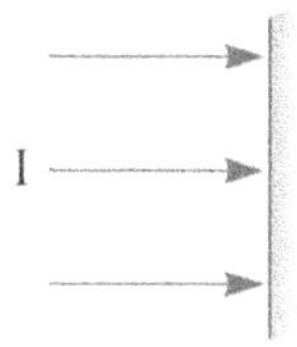

Fig. 5.4

$$F = \frac{\Delta p}{\Delta t}.$$

(i) If radiation is absorbed by the object, then $\Delta P = P$. Momentum $P = \frac{E}{c}$ and

$E = IA\Delta t$, $\therefore$ $P = \frac{IA\Delta t}{c}$,

and $$F = \frac{\frac{IA\Delta t}{c}}{\Delta t} = \frac{IA}{c} = \frac{\text{Power}}{c} \quad ...(3)$$

(ii) If surface of the object is perfectly reflecting, then

$$\Delta P = 2P = \frac{2IA\Delta t}{c},$$

and $$F = \frac{2IA}{c} = \frac{2\ \text{Power}}{c}. \quad ...(4)$$

(iii) If r is the coefficient of reflection, then

$$F = \frac{(1+r)\ \text{Power}}{c}.$$

Ex. 1 **A stream of electrons each of mass m, charge e and velocity 3×10^7 m/s is deflected 2 mm in passing 10 cm through an electric field of 1800 V/m perpendicular to their path, calculate e/m for electrons.**

Sol. Suppose electron beam is going along x-axis and electric field is acting along –ve y-axis. Acceleration of the electron

$$a_y = \frac{Ee}{m}.$$

Fig. 5.5

If t is the time taken to move x distance, then

$$t = \frac{x}{v},$$

$$\therefore \quad y = \frac{1}{2}a_y t^2$$

$$= \frac{1}{2}\frac{Ee}{m}\left(\frac{x}{v}\right)^2$$

or $$\frac{e}{m} = \frac{2yv^2}{Ex^2}$$

$$= \frac{2\times(2\times10^{-3})(3\times10^7)^2}{1800\times(0.10)^2}$$

$$= 2 \times 10^{11}\ \text{C/kg}.$$ ***Ans.***

Ex. 2 **How many photons are emitted per second by a 5 mW laser source operating at 632.8 nm ?**

Sol. The energy of each photon

$$E = \frac{hc}{\lambda}$$

$$= \frac{(6.63\times10^{-34})\times(3\times10^8)}{632.8\times10^{-9}}$$

$$= 3.14 \times 10^{-19}\ \text{J}.$$

The number of photons emitted per second is given by

$$n = \frac{Power}{E}$$

$$= \frac{5\times10^{-3}}{3.14\times10^{-19}}$$

$$= 1.6 \times 10^{16}.$$ ***Ans.***

Ex. 3 **A small plane perfectly reflecting mirror of area A and mass M is hanging vertically with the help of a massless tring of length ℓ. Light of intensity I is incident normally on it. Find the angle made by the string with the vertical.**

Sol. The force exerted by the light on the mirror $F = \frac{2IA}{c}$.

If T is the tension in the string, then for equilibrium of the mirror

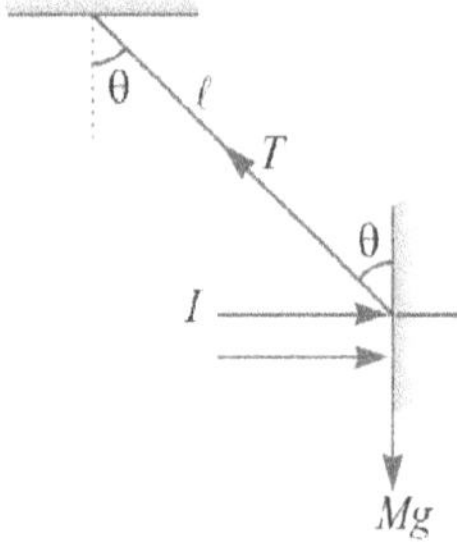

Fig. 5.6

$$T \sin\theta = F,$$

and $$T \cos\theta = Mg.$$

$$\therefore \quad \tan\theta = \frac{F}{Mg}$$

or $$\tan\theta = \frac{2IA}{cMg}. \qquad \textbf{Ans.}$$

Ex. 4 **A perfectly reflecting solid sphere of radius *r* is kept in the path of a parallel beam of light of large aperture. If the beam carries an intensity *I*, find the force exerted by the beam on the sphere.**

Sol. If P is the momentum of the incident beam, then change in momentum of the sphere (along normal of the sphere)

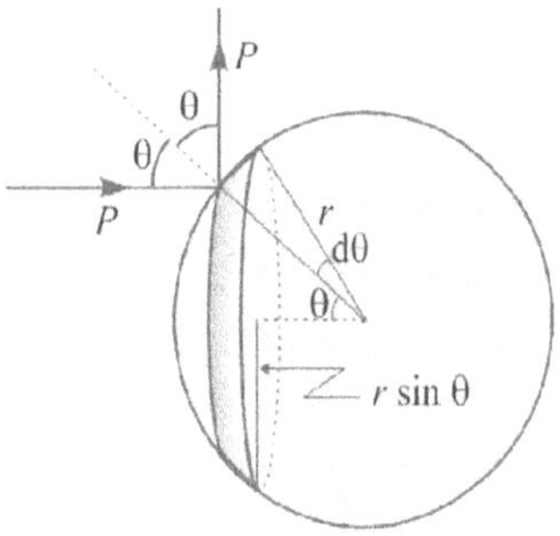

Fig. 5.7

$$\Delta P = 2P\cos\theta$$

As $$P = E/c,$$

$$\therefore \quad \Delta P = \frac{2E}{c}\cos\theta \qquad \text{...(i)}$$

If ΔA is the area of the element, then area perpendicular to the incident beam becomes $\Delta A \cos\theta$,

where $\Delta A = 2\pi(r\sin\theta)(r\,d\theta) = = 2\pi r^2 \sin\theta\, d\theta$.

The energy incident on this area in time Δt

$$E = I(\Delta A\cos\theta)\Delta t$$

Substituting this value in equation (i), we have

$$\Delta P = \frac{2(I\,\Delta A\cos\theta\Delta t)\cos\theta}{c}$$

$$= \frac{2I(\Delta A)\Delta t\cos^2\theta}{c}$$

The force on the element, $$= \frac{\Delta P}{\Delta t},$$

or $$dF = \frac{2I(\Delta A)\cos^2\theta}{c}$$

The effective force on the element

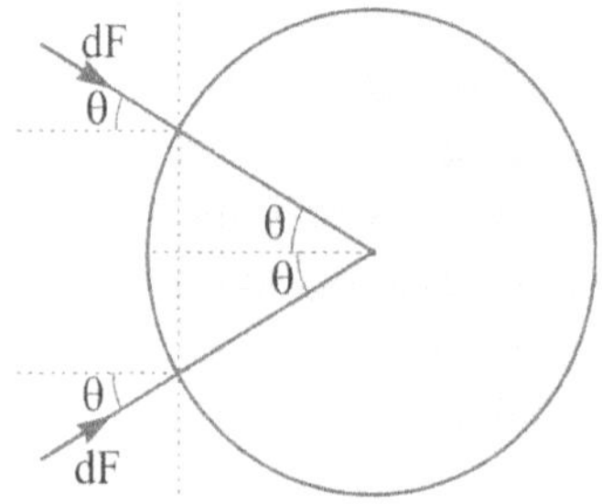

Fig. 5.8

$$dF\cos\theta = \frac{2I(\Delta A)\cos^3\theta}{c}$$

$$= \frac{2I}{c}(2\pi r^2 \sin\theta\, d\theta)\cos^3\theta$$

The net force on the sphere

$$F = \int_0^{\pi/2} dF\cos\theta$$

$$= \frac{2I}{c}(2\pi r^2)\int_0^{\pi/2} \cos^3\theta\sin\theta\, d\theta$$

$$= \frac{-4\pi r^2 I}{c}\int_0^{\pi/2} \cos^3\theta(d\cos\theta)$$

$$= -\frac{4\pi r^2 I}{c}\left|\frac{\cos^4\theta}{4}\right|_0^{\pi/2}$$

$$= \frac{\pi r^2 I}{c}. \qquad \textbf{Ans.}$$

5.5 PHOTO-ELECTRIC EFFECT

When light of certain frequency is incident on a metal surface, electrons are ejected from the metal. This phenomenon is called **photoelectric effect (PEE)**. Electrons ejected from the metal are called photoelectrons. The photoelectric effect was first observed by **Heinrich Hertz in 1887**. The effect was investigated in details by **Hallwachs and Lenard**.

Work function

We know that metals have large number of free electrons. These electrons move freely inside the metal but can not come out from it due to attraction of the positive ions. Some energy is needed to liberate the electrons from the bondage of the attraction of the ions. The minimum energy required to liberate the electrons from the metal surface, is called **work function,** and is represented by W_0.

Work functions of some photometals

Metal	Work function (ev)	Metal	Work function (eV)
Cesium	1.9	Calcium	3.2
Potassium	2.2	Copper	4.5
Sodium	2.3	Silver	4.7
Lithium	2.5	Platinum	5.6

Threshold frequency

The minimum frequency of the radiation which is just enough to liberate the electrons from the metal surface is called threshold frequency. Thus is f_0 is the threshold frequency, then work function

$$W_0 = hf_0, \qquad ...(1)$$

where h is called Plank's constant, whose value is 6.626×10^{-34} J-s.

Threshold wavelength

We know that the product of frequency and corresponding wavelength of any radiation is a constant and equal to c. Thus if λ_0 is the threshold wavelength, then

$$\lambda_0 = \frac{c}{f_0}. \qquad ...(2)$$

Hence threshold wavelength is the longest wavelength which can cause photoelectric effect. Thus photoelectric effect takes place only if $\lambda \leq \lambda_0$, or $f \geq f_0$.

Kinetic energy of the photoelectrons

When light is incident on a metal surface, photons collide with the free electrons at or just within the surface of a metal, they transfer their energy to the electrons. Only some electrons will get this energy. In a particular collision, the photon may give all of its energy to the free electrons. If the energy of the photon is more than the work function W_0, the electron may come out of the metal. It is not necessary that if energy transfer to an electron is more than W_0, then the electron will come out from the metal surface. The electron after getting the energy, may lose its energy due to collisions with the atoms of the metal. Only an electron near the surface gets the extra energy and comes out from the metal surface.

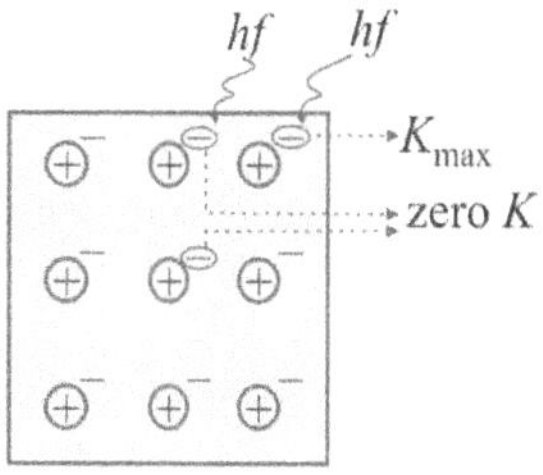

Fig. 5.9

Thus the kinetic energy of the photoelectrons emitted from the metal surface ranges from zero to a maximum value (K_{max}). If E is the energy of incident photons, then the maximum kinetic energy of any electron can be;

$$K_{max} = E - W_0. \qquad ...(3)$$

Equation (3) is called Einstein's photoelectric equation.

Experimental set-up of PEE

The experimental set-up to study the photoelectric effect is shown in *fig.* 5.10.

When monochromatic light of frequency greater than f_0 is incident on the cathode,

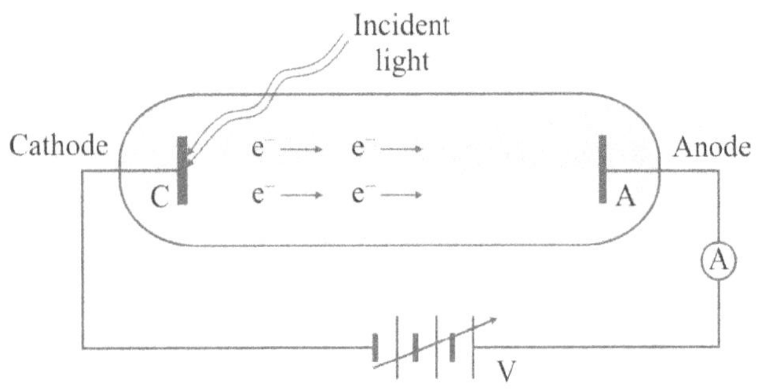

Fig. **5.10**

photoelectrons are emitted from it and they move towards anode *A*. Initially, the space between the cathode and the anode contains a number of electrons making up electron cloud. This negative charge repels the fresh electrons coming from the cathode. The electrons of maximum kinetic energy are able to reach the anode and constitutes a photocurrent. If anode is made positive with respect to the cathode, the emitted electrons are attracted by the anode and the photoelectric current increases. With the increase in anode potential, the photoelectric current increases and becomes maximum. Thereafter current will not increase with the increase in anode potential. This maximum value of current is called the **saturation current** (i_s). This will happen when all the emitted electrons by the cathode in any time interval are attracted by the anode . *Fig.* 5.11 shows the photoelectric current *i* with anode potential *V.*

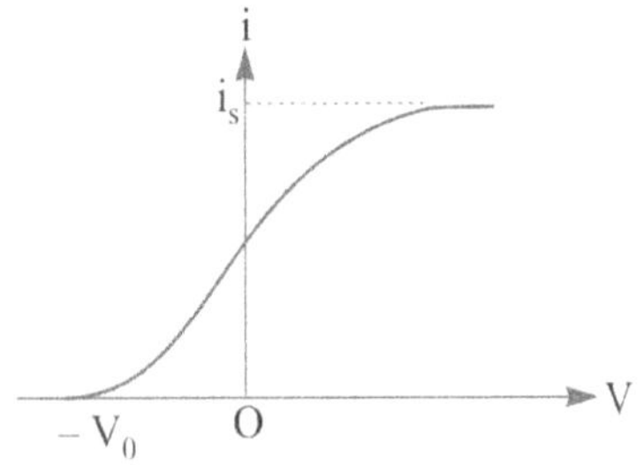

Fig. **5.11**

Stopping potential

When anode is given negative potential with respect to the cathode, the photoelectric current decreases. For a particular value of anode potential, the photoelectric current becomes zero. The minimum negative anode potential at which photoelectric current becomes zero is called stopping or **cut off potential** V_0. To stop the photoelectric current, we must ensure that even the fastest electron will not reach the anode. Thus stopping potential is related to the maximum kinetic energy of the ejected electrons. If V_0 is the stopping potential, then

$$K_{max} = eV_0. \qquad ...(4)$$

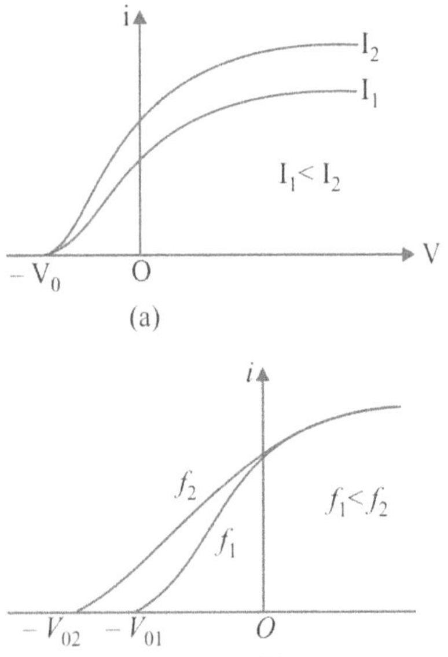

Fig. **5.12**

5.6 CHARACTERISTICS OF PEE

1. Effect of intensity of incident light

When the intensity of the light increases, more number of photons strike with the photometal and thereby liberate more number of electrons. Because of this, photo current increases. As the frequency of the incident light is same, so maximum kinetic energy and hence slopping potential remains same.

2. Effect of frequency of incident light

When the intensity of incident light is kept constant and its frequency increases, the number of photons remains same but their kinetic energy increases. Therefore the emitted electrons are same in number but of greater kinetic energy and hence stopping potential also increases. *Fig.* 5.12 shows the variation of photocurrent with frequency of light *f.*

3. Effect of photometal

When intensity and frequency of incident light are kept constant and photo-metal is changed, the stopping potential V_0 versus frequency *f* are parallel straight lines. This shows that the slope V_0/f is same for all metals and is equal to universal constant (h/e). If the graph is plotted between K_{max} and *f*, then there is straight line. Slope of which gives the value of *h* (*Fig.* 5.13 b).

4. Effect of time

Metal starts emitting electrons as soon as light is incident on it and so there is no time lag between incident light and emitted electrons.

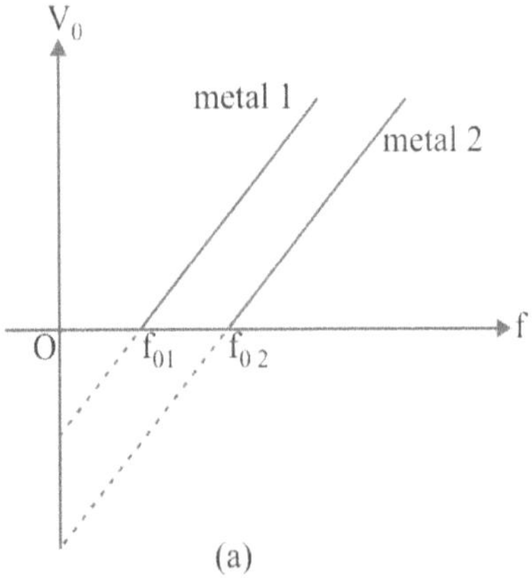

(a)

5.7 EINSTEIN EXPLANATION OF PEE

Einstein forwarded the Plank's quantum theory to explain photoelectric effect. According to him light is made of small energy bundles, called photons. The energy of photon is proportional to the frequency *f.* That is

$$E = hf,$$

where h is a universal constant, called Plank's constant. He made the following assumptions :

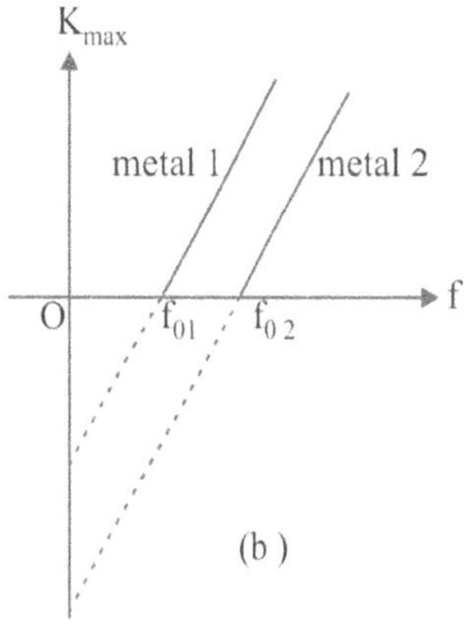

Fig. 5.13

1. The photoelectric effect is the result of collisions between photons of incident light and free electrons of the metal.
2. The electrons of metal are bound with the nucleus by attractive forces. The minimum energy required to liberate an electron from this binding is called work function W_0.
3. The incident photon interacts with a single electron and spend energy in two parts :
   (i) in liberating the electron from the metal surface,
   (ii) and imparting kinetic energy to emitted electrons. Thus if hf is the energy of incident photons, then

$$hf = W_0 + K_{max} \quad ...(i)$$

As
$$f = \frac{c}{\lambda} \text{ and } W_0 = \frac{hc}{\lambda_0},$$

$$\therefore \quad \frac{hc}{\lambda} = \frac{hc}{\lambda_0} + \frac{1}{2}mv_{max}^2 . \quad ...(ii)$$

Above equation is known as **Einstein photo-electric equation.** It should be remembered that photoelectric effect will occur only if $\lambda \leq \lambda_0$.

4. The efficiency of photoelectric effect is less than 1%, i.e., only less than 1% of photons are capable of ejecting electrons from the metal surface. The rest 99% of the photon energy will convert into thermal energy.
5. If V_0 is the stopping potential, then $K_{max} = eV_0$ and so

$$hf = W_0 + eV_0$$

or
$$\frac{hf}{e} = \frac{W_0}{e} + V_0$$

or
$$V_0 = -\frac{W_0}{e} + \left(\frac{h}{e}\right)f. \quad ...(iii)$$

The equation (iii) is a straight line between V_0 and f, whose slope is $\left(\frac{h}{e}\right)$, which is a universal constant.

5.8 COMPTON'S EFFECT

When radiation of short wavelength (like X-rays) is incident on target of electron, the wavelength of scattered X-rays becomes longer than the wavelength of incident X-rays. This was first studied by Compton and therefore is known as **Compton's effect.**

According to him if λ and λ' are the wavelengths of incident and scattered X-rays, then shift in wavelength $\Delta\lambda$ is given by

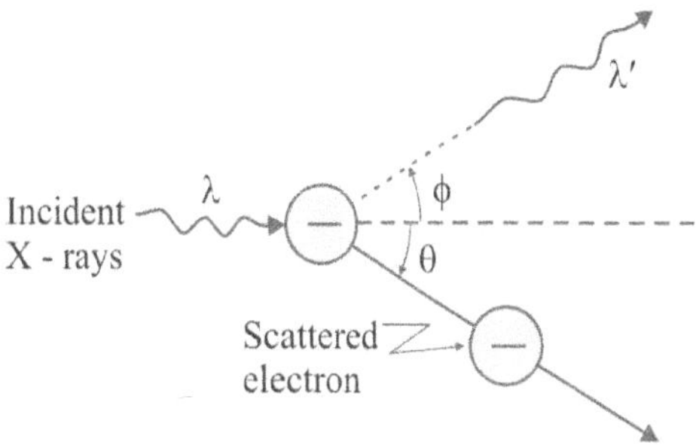

Fig. 5.14

$$\Delta\lambda = \lambda' - \lambda = \frac{h}{mc}(1 - \cos\phi),$$

where ϕ is the scattering angle.

$\Delta\lambda$ is known as Compton's shift and $\frac{h}{mc}$ is a constant, called the Compton wavelength.

Compton shift depends only on the scattering angle. This phenomenon supported the view that both momentum and energy are transferred via photons.

5.9 Matter Waves

The idea of matter waves was introduced by **Louis de Broglie** in 1924. According to him; a beam of light is a wave, but it transfers energy and momentum to matter via photons. Why can't a beam of particles have the same properties ? That is particle, like electron should be associated with a wave. He told that the wavelength associated with a particle of momentum P is given by :

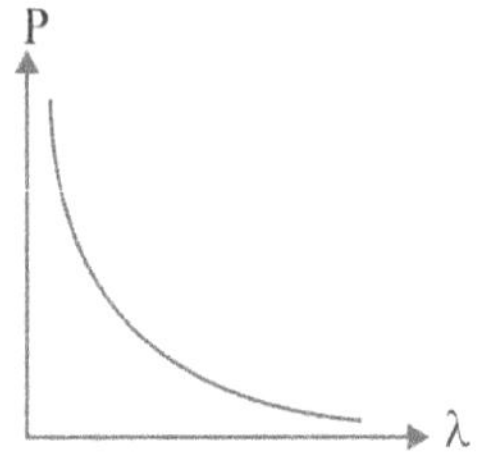

Fig. **5.15**

$$\lambda = \frac{h}{P}. \quad ...(1)$$

The wavelength calculated from this equation is called de Broglie wavelength of the moving particle. For a particle of kinetic energy K, $P = \sqrt{2mK}$,

$$\therefore \quad \lambda = \frac{h}{\sqrt{2mK}}. \quad ...(2)$$

For charged particle accelerated through potential difference V, $K = qV$, and so

$$\lambda = \frac{h}{\sqrt{2mqV}}. \quad ...(3)$$

(i) For an electron m = 9.1×10^{-31} kg, $q = e = 1.6 \times 10^{-19}$C.

$$\therefore \quad \lambda = \frac{12.27}{\sqrt{V}} \text{Å}.$$

(ii) For thermal neutron, $K = \frac{3}{2}kT,$

$$\therefore \quad \lambda = \frac{h}{\sqrt{3mkT}}.$$

For neutron $m = 1.67 \times 10^{-27}$ kg

$$\therefore \quad \lambda = \frac{25.17}{\sqrt{T}} \text{Å}.$$

Davisson and Germer Experiment :

1. The wave nature of electrons was first experimentally verified by C. J. Davisson and L. H. Germer in 1927 and independently by G. P. Thomson in 1928, who observed diffracted effects with beams of electrons scattered by crystals. **Davisson and Thomson shared the Nobel Prize in 1937 for their experimental discovery of diffraction of electrons by crystal.**
2. Electrons of devised velocity falls on the nickel crystal and the intensity of the electron beam scattered in a given direction, is measured by the electron detector (collector).
3. The experiment was performed by varrying the accelerating voltage from 44 V to 68 V.
4. It was noticed that a strong peak appeared in the intensity of the scattered electron of a voltage of 54 V at an scattering angle $\theta = 50^0$.
5. The appearance of the peak in a particular direction is due to the constructive interference of electrons scattered from different layers of the regularly spaced atoms of the crystals. From the measurement, the wavelength of matter waves was found to be 0.165 nm.

   The de Broglie wavelength λ associated with electrons, using V = 54 V is given by

$$\lambda = \frac{1.27}{\sqrt{V}} = \frac{1.27}{\sqrt{54}} = 0.167\text{nm}.$$

Thus there is an excellent agreement between the theoritical value and experimentally obtained value of de Broglie wavelength.

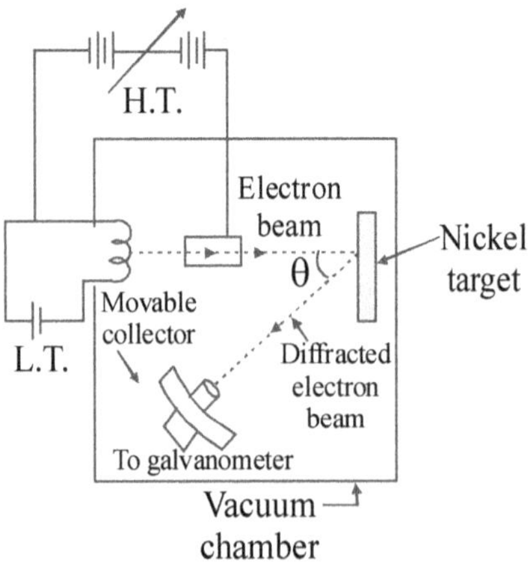

Davisson - Germer electron diffraction arrangement

Ex. 5 **With what velocity must an electron travel so that its momentum is equal to that of photon of wavelength λ = 5200 Å ?**

Sol. Momentum of the photon

$$P = \frac{h}{\lambda} = \frac{6.626\times10^{-34}}{5200\times10^{-10}} = 1.27\times10^{-27}\ N\text{-}s$$

If v is the required velocity of the electron, then

$$mv = 1.27 \times 10^{-27}$$

or $$v = \frac{1.27\times10^{-27}}{m} = \frac{1.27\times10^{-27}}{9.1\times10^{-31}} = 1395 \text{ m/s.} \textit{Ans.}$$

Ex. 6 **(i) A stopping potential of 0.82 volt is required to stop the emission of photoelectrons from the surface of a metal by light of wavelength 4000 Å. For light of wavelength 3000 Å, the stopping potential is 1.85 volt. Find the value of Plank's constant. 1 eV = 1.6 × 10⁻¹⁹ J.**

(ii) At stopping potential, if the wavelength of the incident light is kept fixed at 4000 Å, but the intensity of light increased two times, will photoelectric current be obtained ? Give reasons for your answer.

Sol.

(i) For two wavelengths λ_1 and λ_2, we have

$$\frac{hc}{\lambda_1} = W_0 + eV_1 \quad ...(i)$$

and $$\frac{hc}{\lambda_2} = W_0 + eV_2 \quad ...(ii)$$

Subtracting equation (i) from (ii), we have

$$hc\left(\frac{1}{\lambda_2}-\frac{1}{\lambda_1}\right) = e(V_2 - V_1)$$

or $$h\times(3\times10^8)\left[\frac{1}{3\times10^{-7}}-\frac{1}{4\times10^{-7}}\right] = 1.6\times10^{-19}[1.85-0.82]$$

On solving, we get $h = 6.592 \times 10^{-34}$ J-s. *Ans.*

(ii) With the increase in intensity of incident light there will no change in the energy of the electrons and so no electron will reach the anode.

Ex. 7 **Calculate the value of the retarding potential needed to stop the photo-electrons ejected from a metal surface of work function 1.2 eV with light of frequency 5.5 × 10¹⁴ Hz.**

Sol. If V_0 is the stopping potential, then by Einstein photoelectric equation, we have

$$eV_0 = hf - W_0$$

$$\therefore \quad V_0 = \frac{hf - W_0}{e}$$

$$= \frac{6.62\times10^{-34}\times5.5\times10^{14} - 1.2\times1.6\times10^{-19}}{1.6\times10^{-19}}$$

$$= 1.07\text{ V} \quad \textit{Ans.}$$

Ex. 8 **Find the frequency of light which ejects electrons from a metal surface, fully stopped by a retarding potential of 3V. The photoelectric effect begins in this metal at a frequency of 6 × 10¹³ Hz. Find the work function for this metal. Given h = 6.63 × 10⁻³⁴ J-s.**

Sol. Work function

$$W_0 = hf_0 = 6.63 \times 10^{-34} \times 6 \times 10^{13} = 3.98 \times 10^{-20}\text{ J.}$$

If f is the required frequency, then

$$hf = W_0 + eV_0$$

$$\therefore \quad f = \frac{W_0 + eV_0}{h} = \frac{3.98\times10^{-20} + 1.6\times10^{-19}\times3}{6.63\times10^{-34}}$$

$$= 1.324 \times 10^{15}\text{ Hz } .\textit{Ans.}$$

Ex. 9 **When a beam of 10.6 eV photons of intensity 2.0 W/m² falls on a platinum surface of area 1.0 × 10⁻⁴ m² and work function 5.6 eV, 0.53 of the incident photons eject photoelectrons. Find the number of photoelectrons, emitted per second and their minimum and maximum energies (in eV). Take 1eV = 1.6 × 10⁻¹⁹ J.**

Sol. Energy incident on the platinum surface per second or

$$\text{power} = IA = 2.0 \times 1 \times 10^{-4} = 2 \times 10^{-4}\text{ J/s}$$

The energy of each photon E = 10.6 eV

$$= 10.6 \times 1.6 \times 10^{-19}\text{ J}$$

The number of photons incident on the surface

$$= \frac{2\times10^{-4}}{10.6\times1.6\times10^{-19}} \text{ per sec.}$$

As only 53% can eject electrons, and so photo electrons ejected per second

$$= 0.53\left[\frac{2\times10^{-6}}{10.6\times1.6\times10^{-19}}\right] = 6.25 \times 10^{11}. \textit{ Ans.}$$

According to Einstein photoelectric equation

$$K_{max} = E - W_0 = 10.6 - 5.6$$
$$= 5\text{ eV.}$$

The minimum kinetic energy of photoelectrons will be zero.

Ex. 10 **A beam of white light in incident normally on a plane surface absorbing 70% of the light and reflecting the rest. If the incident beam carries 10 W of power, find the force exerted by it on the surface.**

Sol. If P is the momentum of the incident beam, then momentum after reflection becomes 0.3 P. Thus change in momentum is 1.3 P. In this case force exerted by the light is given by

$$F = \frac{1.3\ Power}{c} = \frac{1.3\times10}{3\times10^8} = 4.3 \times 10^{-8}\text{ N } \textit{Ans.}$$

Ex. 11 **In an arrangement on photoelectric effect, the emitter and the collector plates are placed at a separation of 10 cm and are connected through an ammeter without any cell (*fig.* 5.16). A magnetic field *B* exists parallel to the plates. The work function of the emitter is 2.39 eV and the light incident on it has wavelengths between 400 nm and 600 nm. Find the minimum value of *B* for which the current registered by the ammeter is zero. Neglect any effect of space charge.**

Sol.

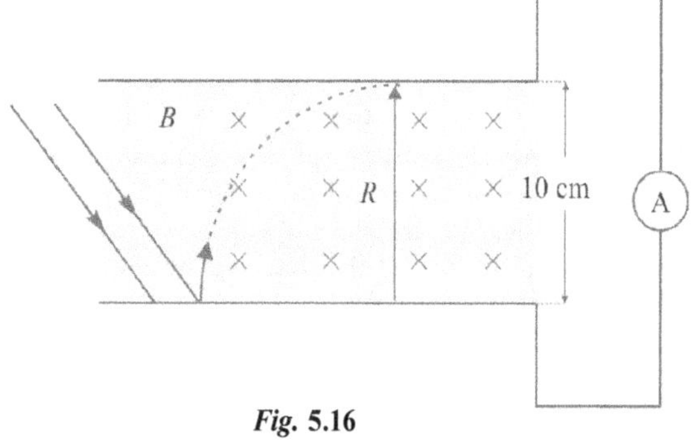

Fig. 5.16

The photocurrent will be zero, if electrons after emitted from lower plate will miss the upper plate. Because of the magnetic field, electrons will follow circular path. If v is the velocity of the electrons, then radius of the path must not be greater than 10 cm.

As $$R = \frac{mv}{eB}$$

$$\therefore \quad B = \frac{mv}{eR}. \qquad ...(i)$$

The energy of the incident light corresponding to λ = 600 nm is;

$$E = \frac{hc}{\lambda} = \frac{6.63\times10^{-34}\times3\times10^{8}}{600\times10^{-9}} J$$

$$= 2.07 \text{ eV}.$$

Since work function is 2.39 eV, and so no photo electric effect will occur. Now if v is the velocity of the emitted electrons corresponding to λ = 400 nm, then

$$\frac{hc}{\lambda} = W_o + \frac{1}{2}mv^2$$

$$\frac{6.63\times10^{-34}\times(3\times10^{8})}{400\times10^{-9}} = 2.39\times1.6\times10^{-19} + \frac{1}{2}\times(9.1\times10^{-31})v^2$$

$$\therefore \quad v = 5.02 \times 10^6 \text{ m/s}$$

From equation (i), we have

$$B = \frac{9.1\times10^{-31}\times5.02\times10^{6}}{1.6\times10^{-19}\times0.10}$$

$$= 2.85 \times 10^{-5} T. \qquad \textit{Ans.}$$

Ex. 12 **In a photoelectric experiment, photons with kinetic energy = 5 eV are incident on a metal surface having work function 3 eV. For intensity of incident photons $I_A = 10^5$ W/m², saturation current of 4 μA is obtained. Sketch the graph between i and voltage for I_A and $I_B = 2I_A$.**

Sol. The stopping potential $V_o = E - W_0$

$$= 5 - 3 = 2\text{eV}.$$

The stopping potential remains same for I_A and I_B. But saturation current becomes double for I_B in comparison to the current due to I_A. The graph between i and V is shown in *fig.* 5.17.

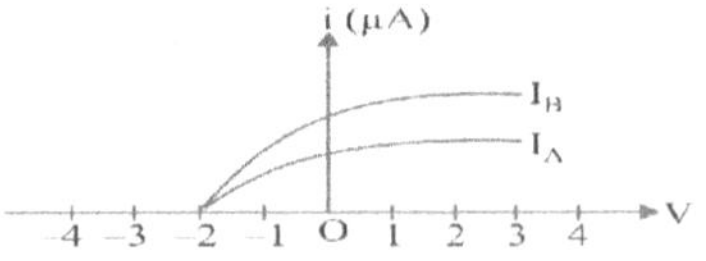

Fig. 5.17

Ex. 13 **A monochromatic point source S radiating wavelength 6000 Å, with power 2 watt, an aperture A of diameter 0.1 m and a large screen are placed as shown in *fig.* 5.18. A photo emissive detector D of surface area 0.5 cm² is placed at the centre of the screen. The efficiency of the detector for the photo electron generation per incident photon is 0.9.**

(a) Calculate the photon flux at the centre of the screen and the photo current in the detector.

(b) If a concave lens L of focal length 0.6m is inserted in the aperture as shown, find the new values of photon flux and photocurrent. Assume uniform average transmission of 80% from the lens.

(c) If the work function of the photon emissive surface is 1 eV, calculate the value of the stopping potential in the two cases (without and with the lens in the aperture).

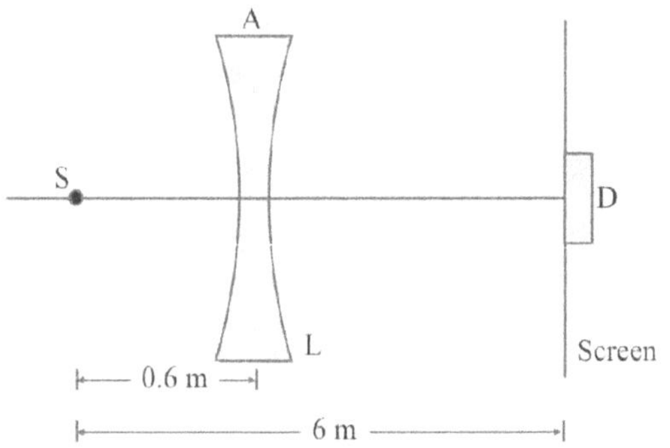

Fig. 5.18

Sol. (a) Energy of photon $E = \frac{hc}{\lambda}$

$$= \frac{6.63\times10^{-34}\times3\times10^{8}}{6000\times10^{-10}}$$

$$= 3.315 \times 10^{-19} \text{ J}$$

The number of photons emitted per second

$$n = \frac{\text{Power}}{E}$$

$$= \frac{2}{3.315\times10^{-19}}$$

$$= 6.033 \times 10^{18} \text{ per second}$$

Photon flux =number of photons per unit area per second

$$= \frac{n}{4\pi r^2} = \frac{6.033\times10^{18}}{4\pi(6.0)^2}$$

$$= 1.33 \times 10^{16} \text{ photons/m}^2\text{–s}$$

The number of electrons emitted per second

$$= 0.9 \times 1.33 \times 10^{16}$$

Photo current = $\left[0.9\times1.33\times10^{16}\right]\times$ area of detector $\times e$

$$= 0.9 \times 1.33 \times 10^{16}\times 0.5 \times 10^{-4}\times 1.6 \times 10^{-19}$$

$$= 0.096 \ \mu A \qquad \textit{Ans.}$$

(b)

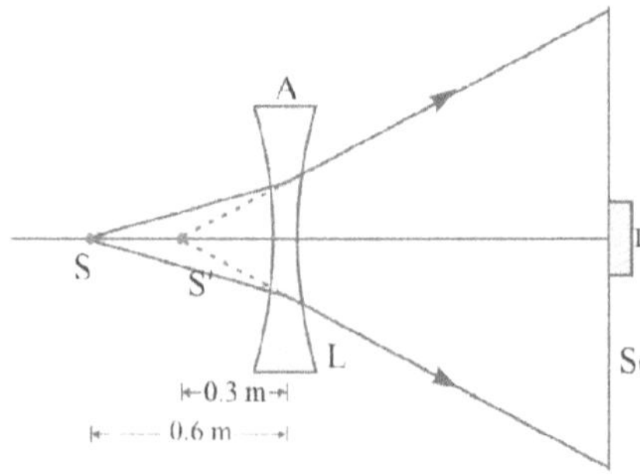

Fig. 5.19

For concave lens $u = -0.6$ m

$f = -0.6$ m

Using lens formula, $\frac{1}{v} - \frac{1}{u} = \frac{1}{f}$, we have

$$\frac{1}{v} - \frac{1}{-0.6} = \frac{1}{-0.6}$$

$\therefore \quad v = -0.3$ m

It shows that S′ becomes the source of photons and it is at a distance of 5.7 m from the screen.

The number of photons reaching the detector

$$n' = [0.80 \times \text{photon flux}] \times \left[\frac{\text{solid angle subtended by detector}}{\text{solid angle subtended by lens}}\right]$$

$$= 0.8 \times 1.33 \times 10^{16} \times \frac{\left(\frac{0.5 \times 10^{-4}}{5.7^2}\right)}{\left(\frac{\pi(0.05)^2}{(0.3)^2}\right)}$$

$$= 1.88 \times 10^{13}$$

Now photon flux $= \frac{n'}{\text{area of detector}}$

$$= \frac{1.88 \times 10^{13}}{0.5 \times 10^{-4}} = 3.76 \times 10^{17} / \text{m}^2\text{-s}$$

$\therefore$ Photo current $i' = 0.9 \times \text{photon flux} \times e$

$= 0.9 \times 3.76 \times 10^{17} \times 1.6 \times 10^{-19}$

$= 0.0541\ \mu A$ **Ans.**

(c) By Einstein photoelectric equation

$$E = W_0 + eV_0$$

$$\therefore \quad V_0 = \frac{E - W_0}{e}$$

$$= \frac{3.315 \times 10^{-19} - 1.6 \times 10^{-19}}{1.6 \times 10^{-19}}$$

$= 1.03\ V$ **Ans.**

The stopping potential in the two cases is same because it does not depend on the intensity of the electrons.

5.10 THE ATOM

Observations and experiments have concluded that atom is the basic constituent of each substance; which is neutral and stable. In Vedas, references are given about the basic constituent of the substances. It is called atom. After the Rutherford experiments, it has been accepted that positive nucleus is the centre of the atom and electrons are revolving around the nucleus in different orbits. In last hundred years, scientists have discovered the following facts regarding with the atom. These are :

1. The atom as a whole is neutal.
2. The atom is stable.
3. The size of the atom is order of 10^{-10} m.
4. The atom emits discrete radiations etc.

Rutherford α-scattering experiment

Rutherford and his students performed an experiment to know about the atom. In the experiment α-particles are allowed to fall on gold foil and following observations are made :

Most of the α-particles pass through the foil without deviation and some of them are deflected through small angles. Few (1 in thousand) are deflected through the angle more than 90°, and very few retraces its path. By the calculations they concluded that number of α-particles scattered at an angle θ is given by

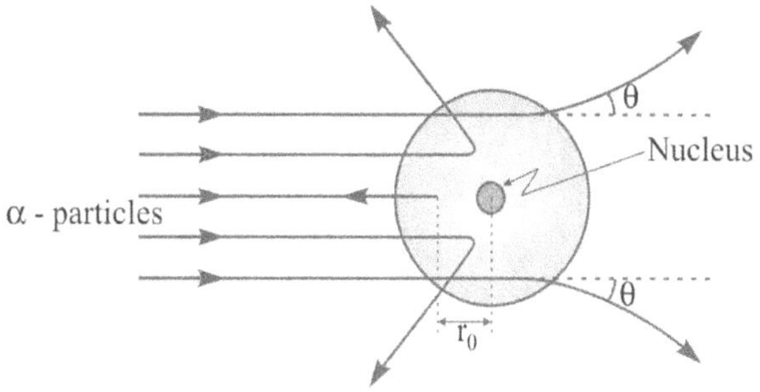

$$N \propto \frac{1}{\sin^4 \frac{\theta}{2}}. \quad ...(1)$$

Fig. **5.20**

Distance of closest approach

The minimum distance from the centre of atom upto which α-particle can go is called distance of closest approach r_0. It is nearly equal to the radius of the nucleus. If an α-particle of kinetic energy K is projected towards the atom, then at closest approach, the entire kinetic energy of the α-particle will convert into potential energy. Thus at closest approach

$$K = \frac{1}{4\pi \epsilon_0} \frac{(Ze)(2e)}{r_0}$$

$$\therefore \quad r_0 = \frac{Ze^2}{2\pi \epsilon_0 K}. \qquad ...(2)$$

Rutherford's atomic model

On the basis of α-scattering experiment, Rutherford proposed an atomic model. According to this model :

(i) Most of the mass and entire positive charge is concentrated at the centre of the atom, which is called nucleus.

(ii) The electrons revolve round the nucleus in different circular orbits.

Causes of failure of Rutherford's model

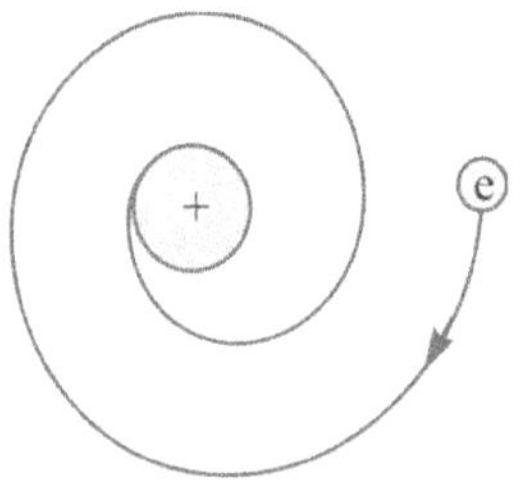

Fig. 5.21

1. It could not explain the stability of the atom. According to Maxwell, accelerated charge particle (circulating electron) radiates energy. Thus an electron moving on a circular path around nucleus should also radiate energy. As a result the electron should go on the path of decreasing radius and ultimately falls into the nucleus. But actually this not happens.
2. It could not explain the distribution of electrons outside the nucleus.
3. It could not explain the line spectrum of the atom.

The model has experimental base and so could not be discarded. The model was modified by his student **Neils Bohr.**

5.11 BOHR'S ATOMIC MODEL

Bohr modified Rutherford's atomic model and gave three postulates on the bases of early quantum concepts. These postulates are :

1. An electron in an atom could revolve around nucleus (as proposed by Rutherford) in certain stable orbits without the emission of energy.

The Coulomb's force provides the required centripetal force to the revolving electrons. Thus for an electron in an orbit of radius r with a speed v,

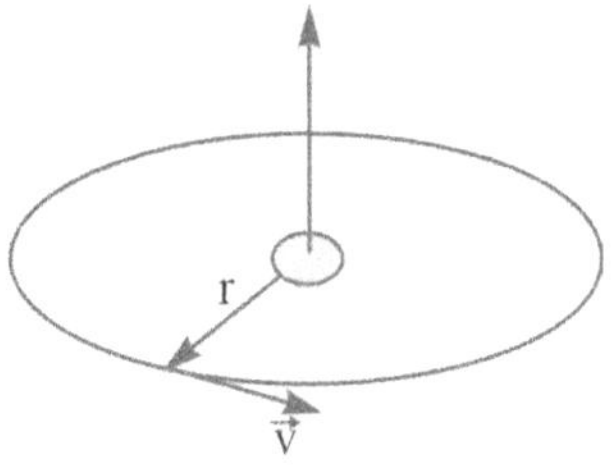

Fig. 5.22

$$\frac{mv^2}{r} = \frac{1}{4\pi \epsilon_0} \frac{(Ze)e}{r^2}. \qquad ...(1)$$

According to postulate, each atom has certain definite stable states in which it can exist, and each possible state has definite energy. These are called the stationary states of the atoms.

2. Electrons can revolve only in those orbits for which the angular momentum is some integral multiple of $\frac{h}{2\pi}$. Thus we can write

$$mvr = n\frac{h}{2\pi}, \text{ where } n = 1, 2, ... \qquad ..(2)$$

According to this postulate electron orbital momentum is quantised.

3. The radiation of energy occurs when an electron jumps from one permitted orbit to other. When it does so, a single photon is emitted having energy equal to the energy difference between the initial and final states. The frequency of the emitted photon is given by;

$$hf = E_i - E_f. \qquad ...(3)$$

This postulate shows the quantisation of the radiation.

Deductions (for hydrogen like atom)

(i) **Radius of nth orbit :**

From equation (2), we have

$$v = \frac{nh}{2\pi mr} \qquad ...(i)$$

Substituting this value in equation (1), we get

$$r_n = \left(\frac{\epsilon_o h^2}{\pi me^2}\right)\frac{n^2}{Z} = 0.53\frac{n^2}{Z}\,\text{Å} \qquad ...(4)$$

(ii) **Speed of electron :**

Now substituting the value of r_n in equation (i), we get

$$v_n = \left(\frac{e^2}{2\epsilon_o h}\right)\frac{Z}{n} = \left(\frac{c}{137}\right)\frac{Z}{n}. \qquad ...(5)$$

(iii) **Kinetic energy :**

From equation (1), $$mv_n^2 = \frac{1}{4\pi\epsilon_0}\frac{Ze^2}{r_n}$$

∴ Kinetic energy, $$K = \frac{1}{2}mv_n^2 = \frac{1}{8\pi\epsilon_0}\frac{Ze^2}{r_n}$$

(iv) **Potential energy :**

The potential energy of charged nucleus (+ Ze) and election (– e) is given by

$$U = \frac{1}{4\pi\epsilon_0}\frac{(Ze)(-e)}{r_n} = -\frac{1}{4\pi\epsilon_0}\frac{Ze^2}{r_n}$$

(v) **Total energy :**

$$E = K+U$$

$$= \frac{1}{8\pi\epsilon_0}\frac{Ze^2}{r_n} - \frac{1}{4\pi\epsilon_0}\frac{Ze^2}{r_n}$$

or $$E = -\frac{1}{8\pi\epsilon_0}\frac{Ze^2}{r_n}. \qquad ...(6)$$

Thus it can be concluded that

$$K = -\frac{U}{2} = -E \qquad ...(7)$$

On substituting the value of r_n in equation (6), we get

$$E = -\left(\frac{me^4}{8\epsilon_0^2 h^2}\right)\frac{Z^2}{n^2}$$

$$= -\left(\frac{me^4}{8\epsilon_0^2 ch^3}\right)ch\frac{Z^2}{n^2}.$$

Here $\left(\frac{me^4}{8\epsilon_0^2 ch^3}\right)$ is constant and called **Rydberg's constant**. It is denoted by R and its value is 1.09×10^7 per m. Thus we can write

$$E = -Rhc\frac{Z^2}{n^2}. \quad ...(8)$$

On substituting the values of constants, we have

$$E = -13.6\frac{Z^2}{n^2}\,eV. \quad ...(9)$$

For hydrogen atom, Z = 1

	For $n = 1$
$r_n = 0.53\,n^2$ Å,	$r_1 = 0.53$ Å
$v_n = \frac{c}{137\,n}$ m/s	$v_1 = \frac{c}{137}$ m/s
$E = \frac{-13.6}{n^2}$ eV	$E_1 = -13.6$ eV

$$n = 1, E_1 = -13.6\text{ eV}$$
$$n = 2, E_2 = -3.4\text{ eV}$$
$$n = 3, E_3 = -1.51\text{ eV}$$
$$n = 4; E_4 = -0.85\text{ eV}$$

Ionisation energy and potential

The energy required to liberate the electron from the bondage of nucleus is called ionisation energy. For ionisation, $n = \infty$,

$\therefore$ $$E_\infty = 0.$$

Thus $$E_\infty - E_1 = 0-(-13.6) = 13.6\text{ eV.}$$

The corresponding potential is called ionisation potential. For hydrogen atom it is 13.6 V.

Excitation energy and potential

When energy is given to the atom, it goes to the electron. So electron jumps to the higher energy level. This is called excitation. For first excited state electron jumps from $n = 1$ to $n = 2$. Thus

$$E_2 - E_1 = -3.4-(-13.6) = 10.2\text{ eV},$$

and first excitation potential is 10.2 V.

For second excited state; $n = 1$ to $n = 3$

$$E_3 - E_1 = -1.51-(-13.6) = 12.1\text{ eV},$$

and excitation potential is 12.1 V.

Transition of electron

When energy is given to any electron, it jumps into higher energy level. It stays there for 10^{-8}s and returns back into lower energy levels by emitting radiations in the form of photons. If E_i and E_f are the initial and final energy levels and f is the frequency of the emitted photons, then

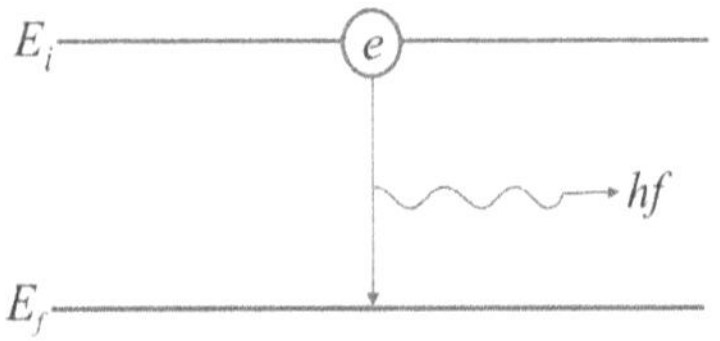

Fig. 5.23

$$E_i - E_f = hf$$

or $$hf = RhcZ^2\left[\frac{1}{n_f^2} - \frac{1}{n_i^2}\right]$$

or $$f = RcZ^2\left[\frac{1}{n_f^2} - \frac{1}{n_i^2}\right] \quad ...(10)$$

Wave number

It is the number of waves in unit length. If λ is the wavelength, then wave number is given by $1/\lambda$. Equation (10) can be written as

$$\frac{c}{\lambda} = RcZ^2\left[\frac{1}{n_f^2} - \frac{1}{n_i^2}\right]$$

or
$$\frac{1}{\lambda} = RZ^2\left[\frac{1}{n_f^2} - \frac{1}{n_i^2}\right]. \qquad ...(11)$$

Number of spectral lines

If electron falls from n^{th} state to ground state, then number of spectral lines emitted are given by :

$$\frac{n(n-1)}{2}.$$

5.12 SPECTRAL LINES OF HYDROGEN ATOM

The spectrum of hydrogen atom consists of a set of isolated parallel lines. The wavelengths of the lines are characteristics of the element emitting the radiations. The experiments show that the frequencies of the radiation emitted by particular element would exhibit some regular pattern. In 1885, Johann **Jakob Balmer** found a simple formula, which can be used to get the frequencies or wavelengths of spectral lines of hydrogen atom. Balmer found that the wavelength of spectral lines can be obtained by;

$$\frac{1}{\lambda} = R\left[\frac{1}{2^2} - \frac{1}{n^2}\right] \quad ; \quad n = 3, 4, 5, ..., \infty$$

where R is a constant, called Rydberg's constant.

This series is known as Balmer series.

Series limit :

Longest wavelength emitted is corresponding to $n = 3$.

or
$$\frac{1}{\lambda_{max}} = R\left[\frac{1}{2^2} - \frac{1}{3^2}\right] = \frac{5R}{36}$$

$$\therefore \quad \lambda_{max} = \frac{36}{5R} = 6563 \text{ Å}$$

The shortest wavelength emitted is corresponding to $n = \infty$. Thus

$$\frac{1}{\lambda_{min}} = R\left[\frac{1}{2^2} - \frac{1}{\infty^2}\right]$$

$$\therefore \quad \lambda_{min} = \frac{4}{R} = 3646 \text{ Å}.$$

Other series

Other series of spectra for hydrogen atom have been discovered after Balmer series. These are :

Lyman series

When electron jumps from any higher energy state to ground state ($n = 1$), the series of spectral lines is called Lyman series. Thus for Lyman series

$$\frac{1}{\lambda} = R\left[\frac{1}{1^2} - \frac{1}{n^2}\right]; n = 2, 3, ..., \infty.$$

Series limit :

For longest wavelength, $n = 2$

$$\frac{1}{\lambda_{max}} = R\left[\frac{1}{1^2} - \frac{1}{2^2}\right]$$

or $$\lambda_{max} = \frac{4}{3R} = 1216\,\text{Å}.$$

Shortest wavelength is corresponding to $n = \infty$.

$$\therefore \quad \frac{1}{\lambda_{min}} = R\left[\frac{1}{1^2} - \frac{1}{\infty^2}\right]$$

or $$\lambda_{min} = \frac{1}{R} = 912\,\text{Å}.$$

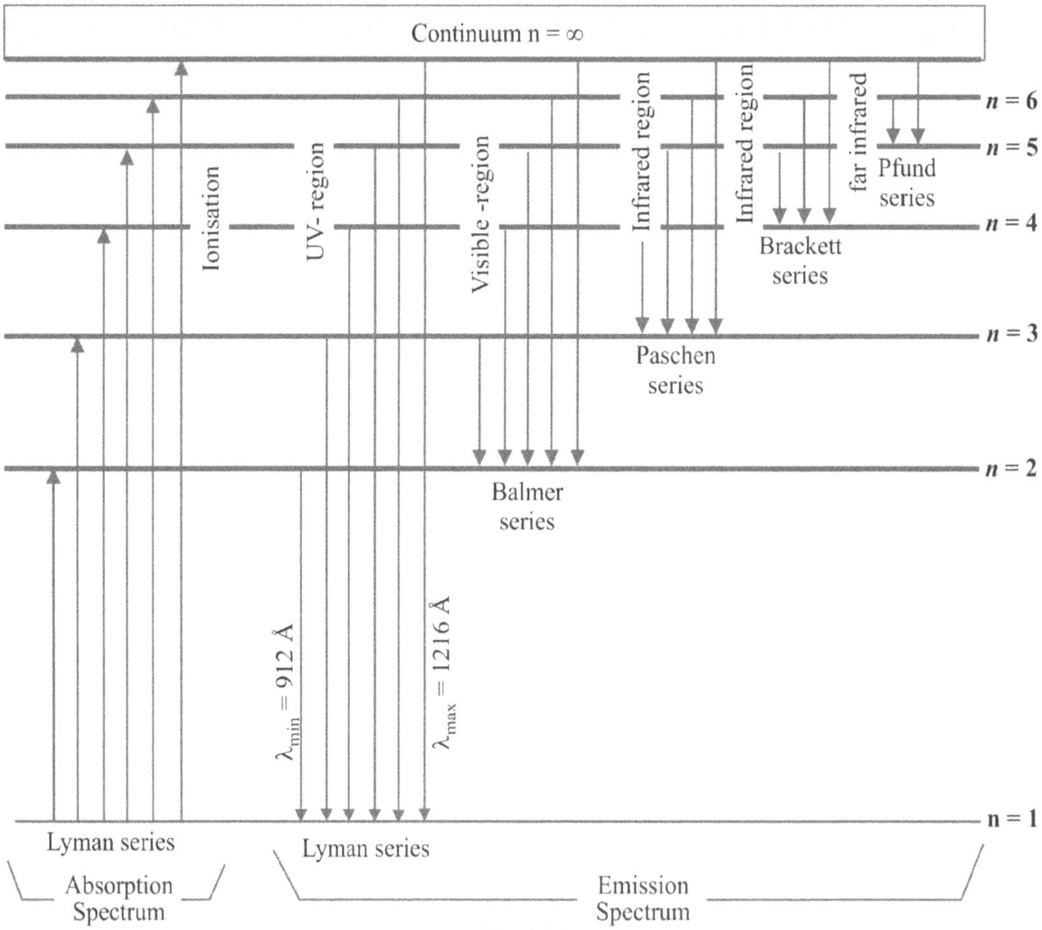

Fig. **5.24**

Paschen series

When electron jumps from any higher every state to $n = 3$ state, the series of spectral lines is called Paschen series. Thus for Paschen series

$$\frac{1}{\lambda} = R\left[\frac{1}{3^2} - \frac{1}{n^2}\right]; n = 4, 5, \ldots\ldots, \infty.$$

Brackett series

When electron jumps from any higher energy state to n = 4 state, the series of spectral lines is called Brackett series. Thus for Brackett series

$$\frac{1}{\lambda} = R\left[\frac{1}{4^2}-\frac{1}{n^2}\right]; n = 5, 6, ..., \infty.$$

Pfund series

When electron jumps from any higher energy state to $n = 5$ state, the series of spectral lines is called Pfund series. Thus for Pfund series

$$\frac{1}{\lambda} = R\left[\frac{1}{5^2}-\frac{1}{n^2}\right]; n = 6, 7, ..., \infty.$$

Absorpsion spectrum

The absorption spectrum of hydrogen atom consists only the Lyman series and the lines are obtained when electron jumps from ground state to any higher state.

Note:

1. For $n = 4$, the number of spectral lines emitted be 6. These six lines can be emitted at least by four atoms.
2. If E is the energy of electron in $n = 4$ state, then

$$E = \frac{hc}{\lambda_1}+\frac{hc}{\lambda_2}+\frac{hc}{\lambda_3}$$

$$= \frac{hc}{\lambda_4}+\frac{hc}{\lambda_3} = \frac{hc}{\lambda_6}.$$

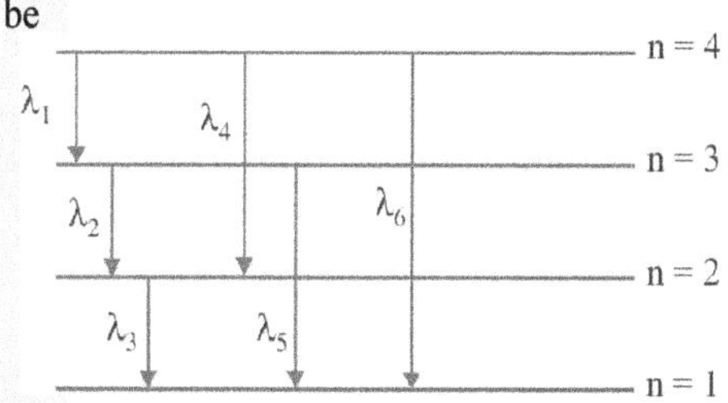

Fig. 5.25

3. According to de-Broglie, only those orbits are possible for which circumference of orbit is equal to the integral multiple of de-Broglie wavelength. Thus for linear momentum P

$$2\pi r = n\frac{h}{P}$$

or $$Pr = n\frac{h}{2\pi}$$

or $$mvr = n\frac{h}{2\pi}.$$

4. Student should remember the value of $\frac{1}{R}$, instead of R. The value is :

$$\frac{1}{R} = 912\,\text{Å}.$$

5.13 SHORT COMINGS OF BOHR'S ATOMIC MODEL

Bohr's theory about atomic model can explain a number of experimental observed facts and has correctly predicted the spectral lines of hydrogen atom and singly ionised helium atom. However the theory could not explain the following facts:

(i) The theory could not account the spectra of atoms having more than one electron.

(ii) This theory fails to explain fine spectral lines of hydrogen atom.

(iii) The theory fails to give correct results when an atom is placed in electric or magnetic field. It is found that when electric or magnetic field is applied to the atom, each spectral line splits into several lines. The former is called as **Stark effect** and the later as **Zeeman effect**.

5.14 CORRECTION FOR THE FINITE MASS OF THE NUCLEUS

In Bohr's theory of atomic model, it was assumed that nucleus remains at rest at the centre of the atom and electron revolve around it. This can only true when the nucleus has infinite mass. On account of the finite mass of the nucleus both the electron and nucleus rotate about a common centre of mass. Suppose mass of electron and nucleus are m and M respectively. If r_e and r_n are the respective distances of electron and nucleus from centre of mass, then

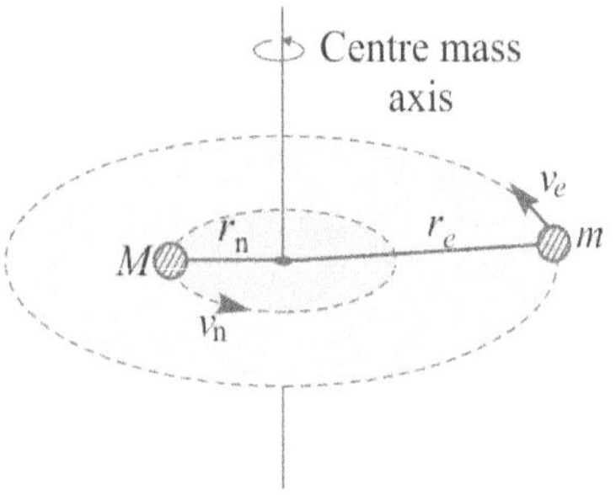

Fig. 5.26

$$r_e + r_n = r \quad ...(i)$$

and
$$m r_e = M r_n \quad ...(ii)$$

On solving above equations, we get

$$r_e = r\left[\frac{M}{m+M}\right]$$

and
$$r_n = r\left[\frac{m}{m+M}\right]$$

If ω be the angular velocity about the centre mass axis, then

$$v_e = \omega r_e \text{ and } v_n = \omega r_n$$

The kinetic energy of the electron-nucleus system

$$E = \frac{1}{2}mv_e^2 + \frac{1}{2}Mv_n^2$$

$$= \frac{1}{2}m\omega^2 r_e^2 + \frac{1}{2}M\omega^2 r_n^2$$

On substituting the values of r_e and r_n and simplifying, we have

$$E = \frac{1}{2}\left[\frac{mM}{m+M}\right]r^2\omega^2.$$

Here $\frac{mM}{m+M} = \mu$, is called reduced mass of the system and $\omega r = v$ is the velocity of electron with respect to nucleus. Therefore

$$E = \frac{1}{2}\mu v^2.$$

In the pre assumed model we can get the related quantities by replacing m from μ.

Rydberg constant

The value of Rydberg constant R obtained earlier is for a nucleus of infinite mass. Thus we can write

$$R_\infty = \frac{me^4}{8\epsilon_0^2 ch^3}.$$

For nucleus of finite mass (M), its value can be written as :

$$R_{\text{finite}} = \frac{\mu e^4}{8\epsilon_0 ch^3} = \frac{me^4}{\left(1+\frac{m}{M}\right)8\epsilon_0^2 ch^3}$$

or
$$R_{\text{finite}} = \frac{R_\infty}{1+\frac{m}{M}}.$$

It shows that Rydberg constant increases with increase of mass of nucleus.

Ex. 14 **How time period of revolution of an electron depends on principal quantum number *n* ?**

Sol. The time taken to complete the circle

$$= \frac{\text{Circumference}}{\text{speed}}$$

For an electron on a path of radius r, time period

$$T = \frac{2\pi r}{v}.$$

As $r \propto n^2$ and $v \propto \frac{1}{n}$,

$$\therefore \quad T \propto n^3. \qquad \textit{Ans.}$$

Ex. 15 **What is the angular momentum of an electron in Bohr's hydrogen atom whose energy is – 3.4 eV ?**

Sol. We know that,

$$E = -\frac{13.6}{n^2} eV$$

$$\therefore \quad -3.4 = -\frac{13.6}{n^2}$$

$$\text{or} \quad n = 2.$$

The angular momentum L of an electron is given by $\frac{nh}{2\pi}$.

For $n = 2$, $L = \frac{h}{\pi}$. *Ans.*

Ex. 16 **Suppose the potential energy between electron and proton at a distance *r* is given by – $Ke^2/3r^3$. Use Bohr's theory to obtain energy levels of such a hypothetical atom.**

Sol. Given, $U = -\frac{Ke^2}{3r^3}$

Force $F = -\frac{dU}{dr} = \frac{Ke^2}{r^4}$

By Newton's second law

$$\frac{mv^2}{r} = \frac{Ke^2}{r^4} \qquad \text{...(i)}$$

Also $mvr = \frac{nh}{2\pi}$ ...(ii)

On solving equations (i) and (ii), we get

$$v = \frac{nh}{2\pi mr}$$

and

$$r = \frac{4\pi^2 K e^2 m}{h^2 n^2}. \textit{Ans.}$$

Ex. 17 **A hydrogen atom moves with a velocity u, and makes a head on inelastic collision with another stationary hydrogen atom. Both atoms are in ground state before collision. What is the minimum value of n, if one of them is to be given a minimum excitation energy ? The ionisation energy is 13.6 eV. Mass of hydrogen atom is 1.0078 × 1.66 × 10^{-27} kg.**

Sol. By conservation of linear momentum for the two hydrogen atoms, we have

$$mu = (m + m)\, v$$

$$\text{or} \quad v = \frac{u}{2}.$$

The energy of excitation = loss in kinetic energy of the atoms

$$\Delta E = \frac{1}{2}mu^2 - 2\times\frac{1}{2}mv^2$$

$$= \frac{1}{2}mu^2 - m\left(\frac{u}{2}\right)^2 = \frac{mu^2}{4} \qquad \text{...(i)}$$

The minimum excitation energy $= 13.6\left[\frac{1}{1^2} - \frac{1}{2^2}\right] = 10.2$ eV. ...(ii)

Thus from (i) and (ii), we have

$$\frac{mu^2}{4} = 10.2 \text{ eV}$$

$$\text{or} \quad \frac{1}{4}\times\left(1.0078\times 1.66\times 10^{-27}\right)u^2 = 10.2 \times 1.6 \times 10^{-19}$$

$$\therefore \quad u = 6.24 \times 10^4 \text{ m/s.} \qquad \textit{Ans.}$$

Ex. 18 **An electron in the ground state of hydrogen atom is revolving in anti-clockwise direction in the circular orbit of radius *R* (*fig.* 5.27).**

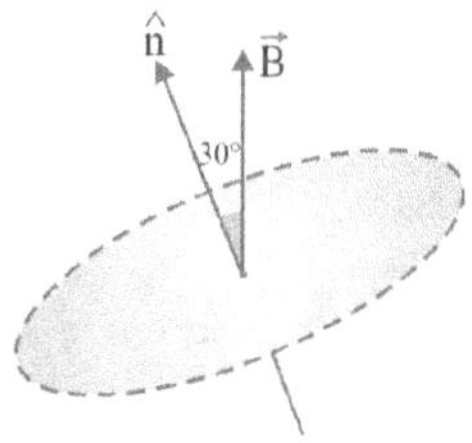

Fig. **5.27**

(i) **Obtain an expression for the orbital magnetic dipole moment of the electron.**

(ii) **The atom is placed in a uniform magnetic induction $\vec{B}$ such that the plane normal of the electron orbit makes an angle 30° with the magnetic induction. Find the torque experienced by the orbiting electron.**

Sol. (i)According to Bohr's theory

$$mvr = \frac{nh}{2\pi}.$$

For $n = 1$, $mvr = \frac{h}{2\pi}$

$$\therefore \quad v = \frac{h}{2\pi mr}$$

Current

$$i = \frac{q}{T} = \frac{e}{\left(\frac{2\pi r}{v}\right)}$$

$$= \frac{ev}{2\pi r} = \frac{e}{2\pi r}\times\frac{h}{2\pi mr}$$

$$= \frac{eh}{4\pi^2 mr^2}.$$

The magnetic moment, $M = iA$

$$= \frac{eh}{4\pi^2 mr^2} \times \pi r^2$$

$$= \frac{eh}{4\pi m}. \qquad \textit{Ans.}$$

(ii) Torque on dipole in magnetic field is given by

$$\tau = MB \sin 30^\circ$$

$$= \frac{eh}{4\pi m} \times B \times \frac{1}{2}$$

$$= \frac{ehB}{8\pi m}. \qquad \textit{Ans.}$$

Ex. 19 The stopping potential for the photoelectrons emitted from a metal surface of work function 1.7 eV is 10.4 V. Find the wavelength of the radiation used. Also identify the energy levels in hydrogen atom which will emit this wavelength.

Sol. Given $W_0 = 1.7$ eV, $V_0 = 10.4$ V.

By Einstein's photoelectric equation, we have

$$\frac{hc}{\lambda} = W_0 + eV_0$$

or $$\frac{(6.63\times10^{-34})\times(3\times10^8)}{\lambda} = 1.7\times1.6\times10^{-19} + 1.6\times10^{-19}\times10.4$$

After solving, we get $\lambda = 1.026 \;\; 10^{-7} \, m = 1026$ Å

This wavelength lies in ultraviolet region, so the series must be Lyman. Thus

$$\frac{1}{\lambda} = R\left[\frac{1}{1^2} - \frac{1}{n^2}\right]$$

or $$\frac{1}{1.026\times10^{-7}} = 1.1\times10^7\left[1 - \frac{1}{n^2}\right]$$

After solving, we get $n = 3$.

Hence the energy levels involved are from $n = 3$ to $n = 1$.

Ex. 20 The radius of first orbit of hydrogen atom is 0.53 Å. Calculate;

(i) radius of third orbit of Li^{++},

(ii) speed of electron in fourth orbit of He^+.

Sol.

(i) The radius of nth orbit of atom of atomic number Z is given by :

$$r_n = 0.53\frac{n^2}{Z} \text{ Å}$$

For Li^{++}, $Z = 3$ and for $n = 3$, we have

$$\therefore \quad r_3 = 0.53\frac{(3)^2}{3} = 1.59 \text{ Å}$$

(ii) The speed $v_n = \frac{c}{137} \times \frac{Z}{n}$

For H_e^+, $Z = 2$ and for $n = 4$, we have

$$v_4 = \frac{c}{137} \times \frac{2}{4} = \frac{c}{274} \text{ m/s. } \textit{Ans.}$$

Ex. 21 The wavelength of the first line of Lyman series for hydrogen is identical to that of the second line of Balmer series for some hydrogen-like ion *X*. Calculate energies of the four levels of *X*. Also find its ionisation potential (Given : Ground state binding energy of hydrogen atom 13.6 eV).

Sol.

For first line of Lyman series in hydrogen atom

$$\frac{1}{\lambda_1} = R\left[\frac{1}{1^2} - \frac{1}{2^2}\right] = \frac{3R}{4}. \quad ...(i)$$

For second line of Balmer series of hydrogen like ion X

$$\frac{1}{\lambda_2} = Z^2 R\left[\frac{1}{2^2} - \frac{1}{4^2}\right]$$

$$= \frac{3Z^2R}{16}$$

According to given condition

$$\lambda_1 = \lambda_2$$

or $$\frac{3R}{4} = \frac{3Z^2R}{16}$$

$$\therefore \quad Z = 2.$$

Thus the ion X is singly ionised helium atom. The energy of the nth state is given by

$$E = -13.6\frac{Z^2}{n^2}$$

$$\therefore \quad E_1 = -13.6\frac{2^2}{1^2} = -54.4 \text{ eV}$$

$$E_2 = -13.6\frac{2^2}{2^2} = -13.6 \text{ eV}$$

$$E_3 = -13.6\frac{2^2}{3^2} = -6.04 \text{ eV}$$

$$E_4 = -13.6\frac{2^2}{4^2} = -3.40 \text{ eV} \textit{ Ans.}$$

Ex. 22 A 100 eV electron collides with a stationary helium ion (He^+) in its ground state and excites it to a higher level. After collision, He^+ ion emits two photons in succession with wavelengths 1085 Å and 304 Å. Find the quantum number of the excited state. Also calculate the energy of the electron after collision.

Sol. The energy of the excited state

$$E = \frac{hc}{\lambda_1} + \frac{hc}{\lambda_2}$$

$$= 6.63\times10^{-34}\times3\times10^{8}\left[\frac{1}{1085\times10^{-10}} + \frac{1}{304\times10^{-10}}\right]$$

$$= 8.38 \times 10^{-18}\ \text{J}$$

or $E = 52.3$ eV ...(i)

For He^{+} ion, this energy is equal to

$$E = 13.6\times Z^2\left[1-\frac{1}{n^2}\right] \quad ...(ii)$$

Thus $52.3 = 13.6\times2^2\left[1-\frac{1}{n^2}\right]$

On solving, $n = 5$.

Thus energy lost by electron; from equation (ii)

$$= 13.6\times\left[1-\frac{1}{5^2}\right]$$

$$= 52.32\ \text{eV}$$

Energy of electron after collision

$$= 100\ \text{eV} - 52.32$$

$$= 47.68\ \text{eV}. \qquad \textit{Ans.}$$

Ex. 23 **A hydrogen-like atom (described by the Bohr model) is observed to emit six wavelengths, originating from all possible transitions between a group of levels. These levels have energies between – 0.85 eV and – 0.544 eV (including both these values).**

(a) Find the atomic number of the atom.

(b) Calculate the smallest wavelength emitted in these transitions.

Take hc = 1240 eV – nm, ground state energy of hydrogen atom = –13.6 eV.

Sol. (a) For the emission of six spectral lines, there must be four energy levels. Thus two more levels are in between – 0.85 eV and –0.544 eV.

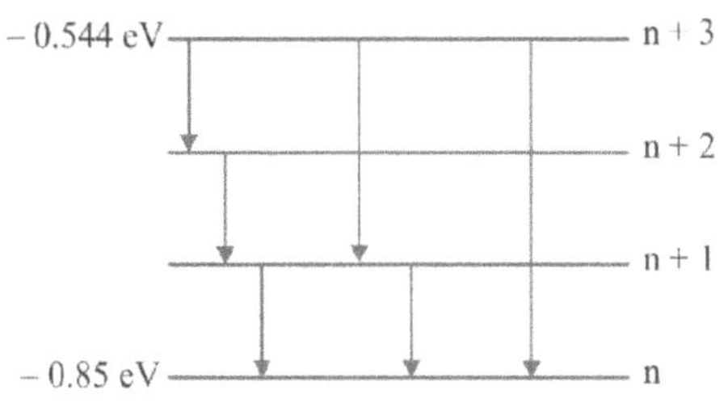

Fig. 5.28

If n represents the energy levels of energy – 0.85 eV, then (n + 3) will represent the energy levels of energy –0.544 eV. Thus

$$-13.6\frac{Z^2}{n^2} = -0.85\ \text{eV} \quad ...(i)$$

and

$$\frac{-13.6\,Z^2}{(n+3)^2} = -0.544\ \text{eV} \quad ...(ii)$$

Solving equations (i) and (ii), we get

$$Z = 3, n = 2.$$

(b) The smallest wavelength is corresponding to maximum energy transition. Thus

$$\lambda_{min} = \frac{hc}{\Delta E}$$

$$= \frac{6.63\times10^{-34}\times3\times10^{8}}{[-0.544-(-0.85)]\times1.6\times10^{-19}}$$

$$= 4052\ nm. \qquad \textit{Ans.}$$

Ex. 24 **A double ionised lithium atom is hydrogen-like with atomic number 3 :**

(i) Find the wavelength of the radiation required to excite that electron in Li^{++} from the first to the third Bohr orbit. (Ionisation energy of hydrogen atom equals 13.6 eV).

(ii) How many spectral lines are observed in the emission spectrum of the above excited state?

Sol. (i) We know that

$$E = -13.6\frac{Z^2}{n^2}$$

For $n = 1$ $\quad E_1 = -13.6\frac{3^2}{1^2} = -122.4\ eV$

and $\quad E_3 = -13.6\frac{3^2}{3^2} = -13.6\ eV$

The energy required to send the electron from $n = 1$ to $n = 3$ state is, $\Delta E = E_3 - E_1$

$$= E_3 - E_1$$

$$= -13.6 - (-122.4)$$

$$= 108.8\ \text{eV}.$$

If λ is the required wavelength, then

$$\frac{hc}{\Delta E} = \Delta E$$

$$\therefore \quad \lambda = \frac{hc}{\Delta E} = \frac{12375}{108.8}$$

$$= 113.74\ \text{Å}. \qquad \textit{Ans.}$$

(ii) As $n = 3$, and so there are three possible spectral lines.

Ex. 25 **Hydrogen atom in its ground state is excited by means of monochromatic radiation of wavelength 975 Å. How many different lines are possible in the resulting spectrum? Calculate the longest wavelength amongst them. You may assume the ionisation energy for hydrogen atom as 13.6 eV.**

Sol. The energy of an electron in n^{th} orbit in hydrogen atom is given by;

$$E = -\frac{13.6}{n^2}\ \text{eV}$$

Energy of electron in its ground state is

$$E_1 = \frac{-13.6}{1^2} = -13.6\,eV.$$

The energy of excitation $\Delta E = \frac{hc}{\lambda} = \frac{\left[6.63\times10^{-34}\right]\times3\times10^8}{975\times10^{-10}}$

$$= 12.75 \text{ eV}$$

If electron jumps into n^{th} orbit, then

$$E_1 + \Delta E = E_n$$

or $$-13.6 + 12.75 = -\frac{13.6}{n^2}$$

On solving, we get $n = 4$.

The longest wavelength is corresponding to $n = 4$ to $n = 3$. Thus

$$E_3 = \frac{-13.6}{3^2} = -1.51\,eV$$

and $$E_4 = \frac{-13.6}{4^2} = -0.85 \text{ eV}$$

$$\therefore \quad \Delta E = E_4 - E_3 = -0.83 - (-1.51)$$

$$= 0.661 \text{ eV}$$

The corresponding wavelength λ is given by

$$\lambda = \frac{hc}{\Delta E} = \frac{12375}{0.661}$$

$$= 18721 \text{ Å}$$ ***Ans.***

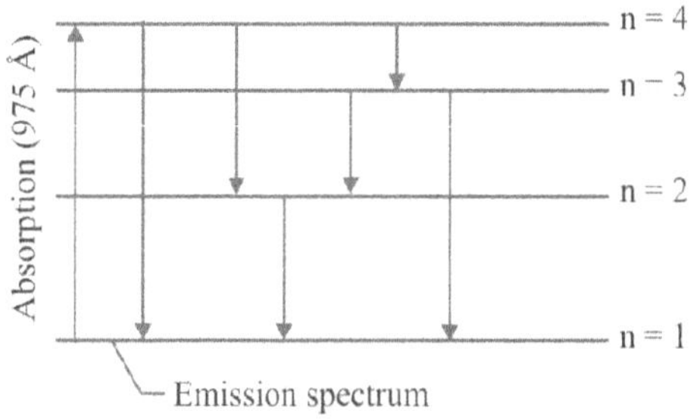

Fig. **5.29**

5.15 X-RAYS

X-rays are produced when fast moving electrons of energy order of 10^3eV to 10^6 eV are allowed to strike the target of high atomic mass. They were first observed by Wilhelm K. Rontgen in 1895 and so called Rontgen rays. X-rays are the electromagnetic waves, and they are governed by quantum relation $E = hf$.

Coolidge tube

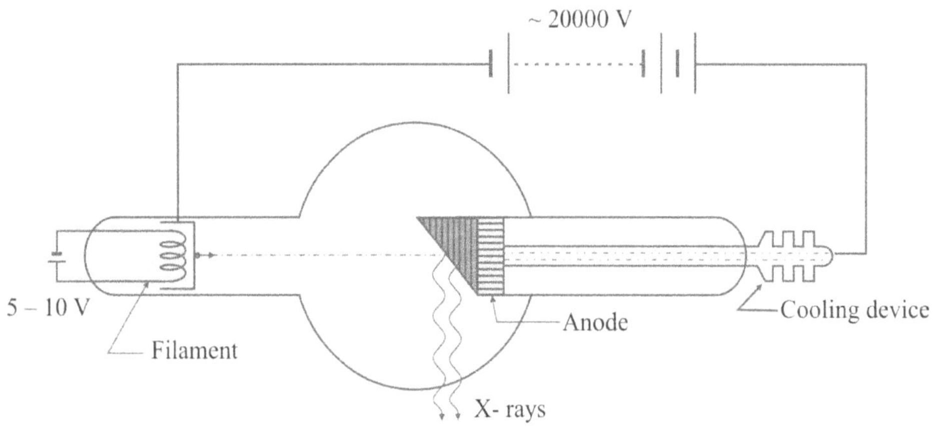

***Fig.* 5.30.** Coolidge, X-ray tube.

The modern X-ray tube was designed by Coolidge in 1913. A Coolidge tube is shown in *fig.* 5.30.

It consists of evacuated glass tube containing a filament in the form of cathode and a metal target in the form of anode. Filament is heated from a low tension battery of 5 to 10 V. The target is made of tungsten or molybdenum, which has high atomic mass and melting point. The target is cooled by flowing cold water. A high potential difference of about 20000 V is applied between target and filament. The electrons emitted by the filament are accelerated by this potential difference. When these high energetic electrons strike the target, X-rays are produced. The X-rays energy is small percentage of the electrons energy while rest is dissipated as heat energy. X-rays of wavelength range 0.1 Å to 4 Å are called hard X-rays and from 4 Å to 100 Å are called soft X-rays.

Control of intensity of X-rays

The intensity of X-rays means the number of photons emitted from the target. The intensity of photons and hence X-rays is directly proportional to the electrons emitted from the filament and this can be increased by increasing the filament current. So intensity of X-rays is proportional to filament current.

Control of penetration power of X-rays

The penetration power of the X-rays depends on their kinetic energy, which depends on potential difference between target and filament. Thus peneration power of X-rays is proportional to potential difference between target and filament.

5.16 ORIGIN OF X-RAYS

When energetic electrons strike the target, they penetrate the target. They loss their kinetic energy and comes to rest inside the metal. The electron before finally being stopped makes several collisions with the target atoms. At each collision one of the following two types of X-rays are produced.

1. Continuous X-rays

When an electron passes close to the nucleus of the target atom, it decelerates. The loss in kinetic energy of electron during deceleration is emitted in the form of X-rays. As electrons make collisions at all angles; right from glancing to the direct hit, they suffer varying decelerations and hence radiations of all possible wavelengths. This forms continuous X-rays. The minimum wavelength of the X-rays is corresponding to the maximum loss of kinetic energy of the striking electron. Thus if an electron of kinetic energy E loses its entire kinetic energy in the collision, then wavelength λ_{min} is given by;

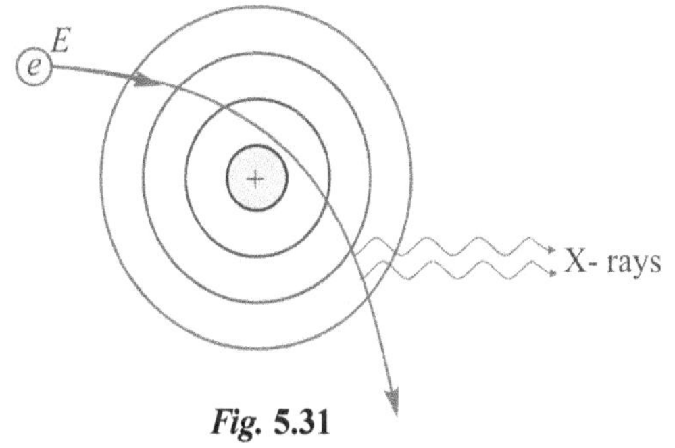

Fig. 5.31

$$\frac{hc}{\lambda_{min}} = \Delta E$$

or $$\lambda_{min} = \frac{hc}{E}$$

If V is the accelerating potential, then

$$E = eV, \text{ and}$$

$$\lambda_{min} = \frac{hc}{eV} = \frac{12375}{V} \text{ Å}.$$

The X-rays consist of mixture of wavelengths ranges from λ_{min} to ∞. Their intensity with wavelength is shown in *fig.* 5.32.

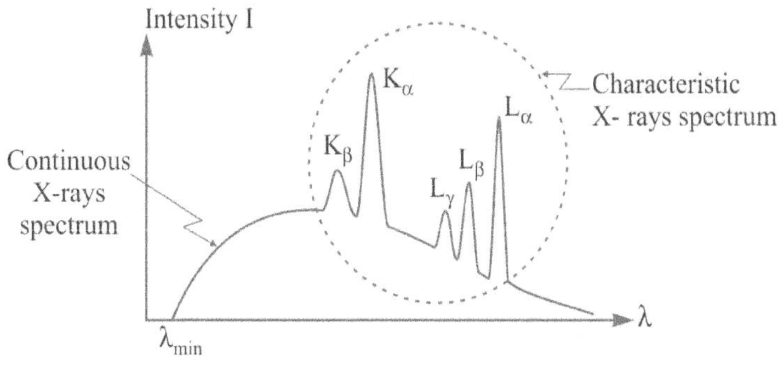

Variation of intensity of X-rays with emitted wavelength.

Fig. 5.32

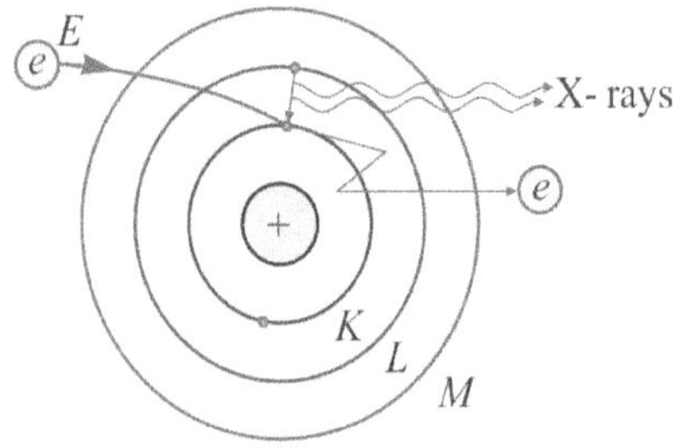

*Fig.*5.33. **Characteristic X-rays.**

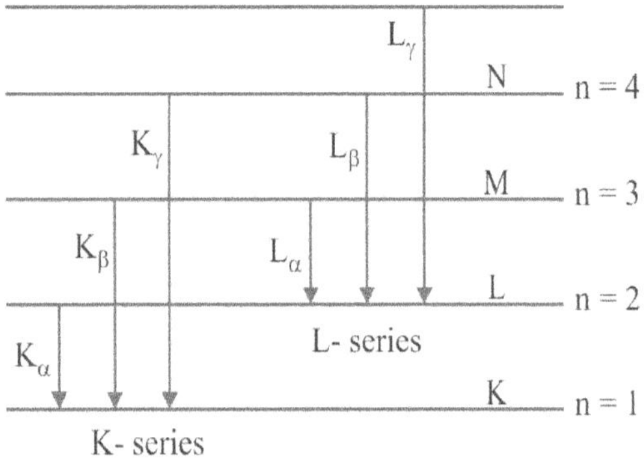

***Fig.* 5.34**

2. Characteristic X-rays

Some of the striking electrons penetrate the surface atoms of the target material and knock out the tightly bound electrons even from the inner most shells of the atom. Thus a vacancy gets created at that place. This vacancy cannot remain vacant and is filled by the electrons from higher shell. In these transitions X-rays of certain wavelengths are produced. These are called characteristic X-rays. For the transition of electron from E_1 to E_2, the frequency or wavelength of emitted photons (X-rays) can be written as :

$$E_1 - E_2 = hf = \frac{hc}{\lambda}.$$

If the striking electron knocks off an atomic electron from K shell and the vacancy is filled by electrons from $L, M,$ ....shells, then the emitted radiation is called X-rays of K-series.

For K_α – line; $\quad E_L - E_K = \frac{hc}{\lambda_{K_\alpha}}.$

For K_β –line; $\quad E_M - E_K = \frac{hc}{\lambda_{K_\beta}}$

Both these transitions are highly probable. Similarly if striking electron knocks off atomic electron from L-shell and the vacancy is filled by electrons from $M, N,$ ....shells, then the emitted radiation is called X-rays of L-series and so on.

For L_α – line; $\quad E_M - E_L = \frac{hc}{\lambda_{L_\alpha}}$

For L_β – line; $\quad E_N - E_L = \frac{hc}{\lambda_{L_\beta}}$

5.17 MOSELEY'S LAW

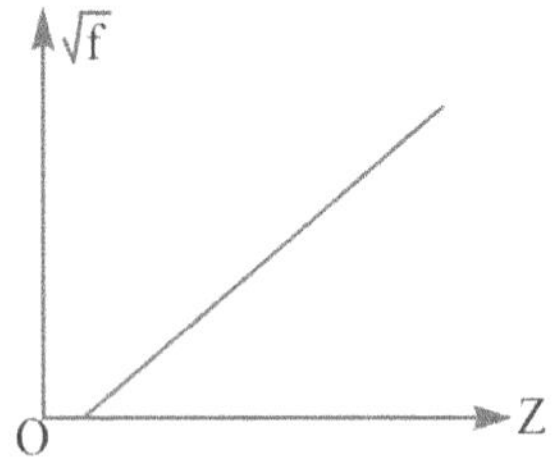

***Fig.* 5.35**

Moseley in 1913 studied the characteristic X-rays emitted by different elements and he associated them with their atomic numbers. He found that square root of characteristic frequency is linearly related with atomic number Z of the element. Moseley's observations for K_α X-rays can be mathematically expressed as :

$$\sqrt{f} = a(Z - b) \qquad ...(1)$$

where a and b are constants. This relation is known as **Moseley's law**. Moseley's law qualitatively can be understood as follows :

Consider an atom of atomic number Z from which an electron from its K shell has been knocked out. Let the vacancy so created is filled by the electron from L shell. The knocked off electron is associated with the nucleus and so the electron making the transition finds a charge $(Z–1)e$ at the centre. In Bohr's model if Z is replaced by $(Z–b)$ with $b \simeq 1$, then we have

$$\Delta E = hf = Rhc(Z-b)^2\left[\frac{1}{1^2} - \frac{1}{2^2}\right] = Rhc(Z-b)^2 \times \frac{3}{4}$$

or
$$\sqrt{f} = \sqrt{\frac{3Rc}{4}}\,(Z-b). \qquad ...(2)$$

On comparing equations (1) and (2), we find

$$a = \sqrt{3Rc/4}.$$

5.18 PROPERTIES OF X-RAYS

1. X-rays are electromagnetic waves of short wavelength of order of 1Å, and travel with the speed $c = 3\times10^8$ m/s in vacuum.
2. They can exhibit the phenomenon of reflection, refraction, diffraction and interference.
3. X-rays can be used for crystal study.
4. They are electrically neutral, and hence can not be deflected by electric and magnetic fields.
5. They have ionising power and therefore can ionise the gases.
6. They can penetrate substances like; flash, thick paper thin metal sheets etc.
7. They can cause photoelectric effect when incident on metals.
8. They cause fluorescence in many substances like barium, cadmium, zinc sulphate etc.
9. They have destructive effect on living tissues.
10. X-rays get absorbed when they are incident on substance. When X-rays of intensity I_0 is incident on a medium of thickness x, the intensity of emerging X-rays is given by, $I = I_0\, e^{-\mu x}$, where μ is the coefficient of absorption.

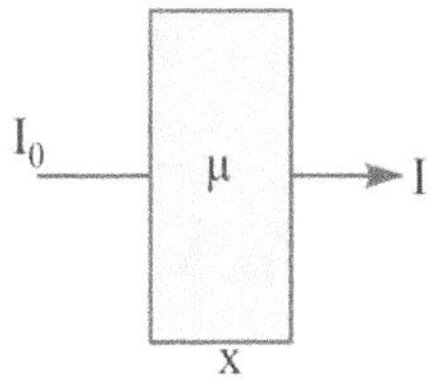

Fig. 5.36

5.19 BRAGG'S LAW

Bragg used X-rays for crystal study. He observed that when X-rays falls on a crystal such as NaCl, X-rays are scattered in all directions by crystal structure. The scattered X-rays interfere constructively in some directions, resulting intensity maxima; in other directions the interference is destructively, resulting in intensity minima. This process of scattering and interference is a form of diffraction. He found that when X-rays are incident on a crystal at an angle θ, then the intensity of diffracted X-rays is maximum, if

$$2d\sin\theta = n\lambda \qquad \text{for } n = 1, 2, \ldots\ldots$$

Here d is the spacing between crystal planes. The above equation is known as **Bragg's law**.

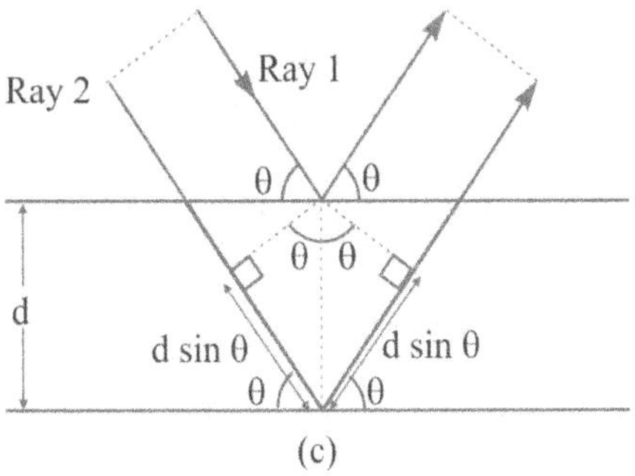

Fig. 5.38

Ex. 26 **A cobalt target is bombarded with electron, and the wavelengths of its characteristic X-ray spectrum are measured. There is also a second, fainter characteristic spectrum, which is due to an impurity in the cobalt. The wavelengths of the K_α lines are 178.9 pm (cobalt) and 143.5 pm (impurity), and the proton number for cobalt is Z_{Co} = 27. Determine the impurity using only these data.**

Sol. By Moseley's law, we have

$$\sqrt{f} = a(Z-1).$$

As $f = \dfrac{c}{\lambda}$, so we can write

$$\sqrt{\frac{c}{\lambda}} = a(Z-1)$$

For cobalt, $$\sqrt{\frac{c}{\lambda_{Co}}} = a(Z_{Co} - 1) \quad ...(i)$$

For X impurity, $$\sqrt{\frac{c}{\lambda_X}} = a\,(Z_x - 1) \quad ...(ii)$$

From equations (i) and (ii), we get

$$\sqrt{\frac{\lambda_{Co}}{\lambda_x}} = \frac{Z_x - 1}{Z_{Co} - 1}$$

or $$\sqrt{\frac{178.9}{143.5}} = \frac{Z_x - 1}{27 - 1}$$

On solving, we get $Z_x = 30.0$ ***Ans.***

Thus impurity atom is zinc.

Ex. 27 **Find the shortest wavelength of the X-rays emitted by an X-ray tube operating at 30 kV.**

Sol. We know that,

$$\frac{hc}{\lambda_{min}} = eV$$

$$\therefore \quad \lambda_{min} = \frac{hc}{eV} = \frac{12375}{V} \text{ Å}$$

$$= \frac{12375}{30 \times 10^3} = 0.4125 \text{ Å}. \quad \textit{Ans.}$$

Ex. 28 **Show that the wavelength of K_β of a material and wavelength of K_α and L_α X-rays of the same material are related as :**

$$\frac{1}{\lambda_{K\beta}} = \frac{1}{\lambda_{K\alpha}} + \frac{1}{\lambda_{L\alpha}}.$$

Sol. The energy levels diagram of an atom with one electron knocked out is shown in *fig.* 5.37.

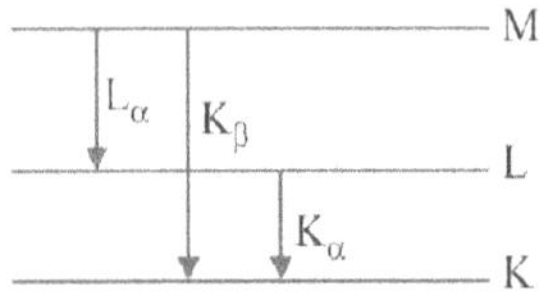

***Fig.* 5.37**

For K_α, X-ray, $$E_L - E_K = \frac{hc}{\lambda_{K\alpha}} \quad ...(i)$$

For K_β, X-ray, $$E_M - E_K = \frac{hc}{\lambda_{K\beta}} \quad ...(ii)$$

For $K\gamma$, X-ray, $$E_M - E_L = \frac{hc}{\lambda_{L\alpha}} \quad ...(iii)$$

From above equations, we get

$$\frac{1}{\lambda_{K\beta}} = \frac{1}{\lambda_{K\alpha}} + \frac{1}{\lambda_{L\alpha}}.$$

Ex. 29 **The wavelength of the characteristic X-ray K_α line emitted by a hydrogen-like element is 0.32 Å. Calculate the wavelength of K_β line emitted by the same element.**

Sol. For hydrogen like atom

$$\frac{1}{\lambda} = Z^2 R\left[\frac{1}{n_f^2} - \frac{1}{n_i^2}\right].$$

For K_α – line, $$\frac{1}{\lambda_{K\alpha}} = Z^2 R\left[\frac{1}{1^2} - \frac{1}{2^2}\right]$$

$$= \frac{3Z^2R}{4}. \quad ...(i)$$

For K_β – line, $$\frac{1}{\lambda_{K\beta}} = Z^2 R\left[\frac{1}{1^2} - \frac{1}{3^2}\right]$$

$$= \frac{8Z^2R}{9}. \quad ...(ii)$$

From equations (i) and (ii), we have

$$\frac{\lambda_{K\beta}}{\lambda_{K\alpha}} = \frac{3/4}{8/9} = \frac{3 \times 9}{4 \times 8} = \frac{27}{32}$$

$$\therefore \quad \lambda_{K\beta} = \frac{27}{32}\lambda_{K\alpha} = \frac{27}{32} \times 0.32 \text{ Å}$$

$$= 0.27 \text{ Å}. \quad \textit{Ans.}$$

Ex. 30 **Characteristic *X*-rays of frequency 4.2×10^{18} Hz are produced when transition from *L* shell to *K* shell take place in a certain target material. Use Moseley's law to determine the atomic number of target material. Given Rydberg constant $R = 1.1 \times 10^7 \text{ m}^{-1}$.**

Sol. We know that,

$$\sqrt{f} = \sqrt{\frac{3Rc}{4}}\,(Z - 1)$$

or $$\sqrt{4.2 \times 10^{18}} = \sqrt{\frac{3 \times 1.1 \times 10^7 \times 3 \times 10^8}{4}}\,(Z - 1)$$

On solving, we get $Z = 42.$ ***Ans.***

Review of Formulae & Important Points

1. Cathode rays :

*Gases starts conducting at low pressure (order of 10^{-3} mm of Hg).

The e/m of cathode rays was determined by Thomson using mutually perpendicular electric field and magnetic field.

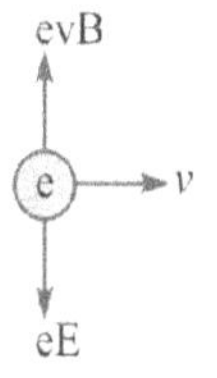

$$evB = eE$$

or $$v = (E / B)$$

If an electron is accelerated by potential V then

$$eV = (1/2)\, mv^2$$

or $$\frac{e}{m} = \frac{v^2}{2V} = \frac{(E/B)^2}{2V}.$$

* e/m of cathode rays is = 1.76×10^{11} C/kg and is independent of nature of gas in the tube.

* e/m of positive rays depend on nature of gas.

2. Plank's hypothesis :

Light propagate in small packets of energy, called photon. Each photon having energy

$$E = hf = hc/\lambda.$$

* Rest mass of photon is zero.

Momentum of photon = $h\nu/c = h/\lambda$

Number of photon per second emitted by a source of power P is

$$N = \frac{P}{(hc/\lambda)}$$

3. Photoelectric effect :

The emission of electron from metal surface by light is called photo electric effect (PEE).

Einstein's photo - electric equation

$$E = W_0 + K.E_{max}$$

or $$hf = hf_0 + (1/2)mv_{max}^2$$

$$\frac{hc}{\lambda} = \frac{hc}{\lambda_0} + \frac{1}{2}mv_{max}^2$$

* With increase in intensity of incident light, photoelectric current increase but maximum K.E. of electron remains same.

* With increase in frequency of incident light, photo electric current will not change but maximum K.E. of photo-electrons increases.

4. Compton's effect :

$$\text{Compton shift } \Delta\lambda = \frac{h}{m_0 c}(1-\cos\phi).$$

de Brogile Waves : If a particle of m is moving with a speed v then corresponding wavelength

$$\lambda = \frac{h}{mv}$$

$$= \frac{h}{\sqrt{2mK.E.}}$$

5. Rutherford α - scattering formulae

Atomic Model

(1) **Size of nucleus :** Distance of closest approach

$$E_k = \frac{1}{4\pi \in_0}\frac{(Ze)(2e)}{r_0}$$

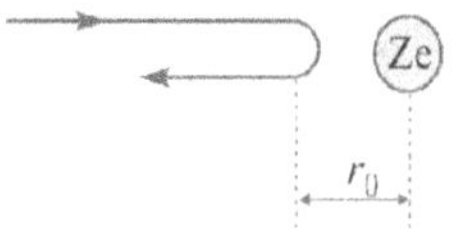

$$\Rightarrow \quad r_0 = \frac{1}{4\pi \in_0}\frac{2Ze^2}{E_k}.$$

(ii) The number of α-particles scattered at an angle φ by a nucleus is $N_\varphi \propto \dfrac{1}{\sin^4 \dfrac{\varphi}{2}}$.

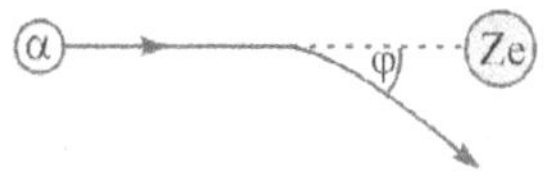

6. Bohr's Model

(i) Electrons revolve around the certain circular orbits without radiating energy, such that

$$\frac{1}{4\pi \in_0}\frac{Ze^2}{r} = \frac{mv^2}{r}$$

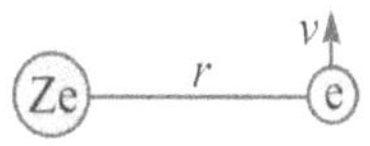

(ii) Quantization of orbit

$$mvr = \frac{nh}{2\pi},\ n = 1, 2, \ldots\ldots\ldots$$

(iii) Quantization of energy $hf = E_2 - E_1$.

(iv) Mass of revolving electron remains constant.

$$r_n = (0.53/Z)n^2 Å$$

$$V_m = \frac{c}{137}\frac{Z}{n} \text{ m/s}$$

$$-\text{T. E.} = \text{K.E.} = (-\text{P.E.}/2)$$

$$E_n(\text{T. E}) = (-13.6\ Z^2/n^2)\text{eV}$$

7. **Wave number :** $\frac{1}{\lambda} = RZ^2\left[\frac{1}{n_1^2} - \frac{1}{n_2^2}\right]$.

Spectrum of hydrogen atom :

1. Lymen Ultraviolet $n_1 = 1,\ n_2 \geq 2$
2. Balmer Visible $n_1 = 2,\ n_2 \geq 3$
3. Paschen Infrared $n_1 = 3,\ n_2 \geq 4$
4. Brackett Infrared $n_1 = 4,\ n_2 \geq 5$
5. Pfund Infrared $n_1 = 5,\ n_2 \geq 6$.

8. **Limitations of Bohr's theory**

1. It can only explain the structure of hydrogen like atom.

2. It is unable to explain the fine spectral lines.

Phosphorescence and fluorescence :

Certain substance emit visible light when high frequency radiation incident on it. If the emission continues after the source of excitation is removed then it is called phosphorescence. If not, is called fluorescence.

First excitation potential $V_1 = [(E_2 - E_1)/e]$

Ionisation potential $= [(E_\infty - E_1)/e]$

$= 13.6$ V for hydrogen

9. **X-rays** (1Å to 100 Å)

When fast moving electrons strike to a target of high melting point and atomic mass, X-rays are produced.

* Intensity of X-rays is proportional to filament current.
* Penetrating power is proportional to potential difference across filament & target.
* X-rays of $\lambda > 4Å$ are called soft and X-rays $\lambda \leq 4Å$ are called hard X-rays.

10. **X-rays Spectra :**

1. Continuous spectrum are produced due to deceleration of electrons.
2. Characteristic spectrum are produced due to knock of bound electrons from the inner orbit and the vacancy so caused is filled by either free electron or electrons from higher orbits.

$$E_L - E_k = h f_{k\alpha}$$

$$E_M - E_k = h f_{k\alpha}$$

Energy of X-ray $= hf = \frac{hc}{\lambda}$.

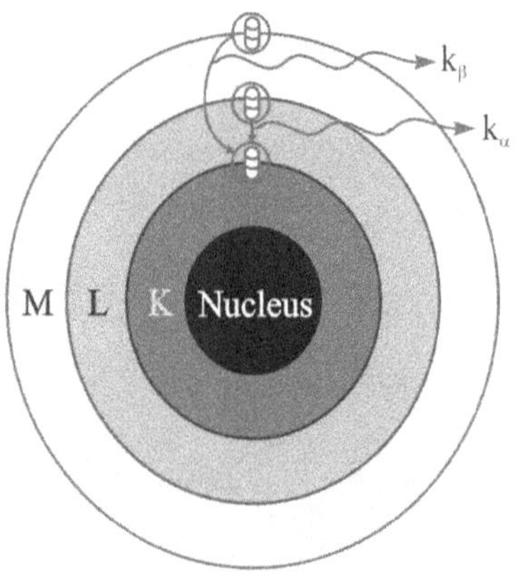

Dynamic mass of X-ray $= \frac{hf}{c^2} = \frac{h}{c\lambda}$.

Minimum wavelength of continuous X-rays

$$\lambda_{min} = \frac{hc}{eV}.$$

Bragg's law $2d\sin\theta = n\lambda$ (n = 1, 2, ...)

Intensity of X-rays after passing through a medium of thickness x is $I = I_0 e^{-kx}$.

★★★

Modern Physics

MCQ Type 1

Exercise 5.1

LEVEL - 1

Only one option correct

1. The cathode rays have particle nature because of the fact that
   (a) they can propagate in vacuum
   (b) they are deflected by electric and magnetic fields
   (c) they produced fluorescence
   (d) they cast shadows

2. In a Thomson set-up for the determination of e/m, electrons accelerated by 2.5 kV enter the region of crossed electric and magnetic fields of strengths 3.6×10^4 Vm^{-1} and 1.2×10^{-3} T respectively and go through undeflected. The measured value of e/m of the electron is equal to
   (a) 1.0×10^{11} C-kg^{-1} (b) 1.76×10^{11} C-kg^{-1}
   (c) 1.80×10^{11} C-kg^{-1} (d) 1.85×10^{11} C-kg^{-1}

3. In an electron gun, the electrons are accelerated by the potential V. If e is the charge and m is the mass of an electron, then the maximum velocity of these electrons will be
   (a) $\frac{2eV}{m}$ (b) $\sqrt{\frac{2eV}{m}}$
   (c) $\sqrt{\frac{2m}{eV}}$ (d) $\frac{V^2}{2em}$

4. A bullet of mass 40 g travels at a speed 1000 m/s, its de-Broglie wavelength is ;
   (a) 500×10^{-10} m (b) 1225×10^{-20} m
   (c) 1667×10^{-30} m (d) none of these

5. An electron of mass m when accelerated through a potential difference V has de-Broglie wavelength λ. The de-Broglie wavelength associated with a proton of mass M accelerated through the same potential difference will be
   (a) $\lambda\frac{m}{M}$ (b) $\lambda\sqrt{\frac{m}{M}}$
   (c) $\lambda\frac{M}{m}$ (d) $\lambda\sqrt{\frac{M}{m}}$

6. What will be the ratio of de-Broglie wavelengths of proton and α-particle of same energy
   (a) 2 : 1 (b) 1 : 2
   (c) 4 : 1 (d) 1 : 4

7. If the kinetic energy of a free electron doubles, its de-Broglie wavelength changes by the factor
   (a) $\frac{1}{\sqrt{2}}$ (b) $\sqrt{2}$
   (c) $\frac{1}{2}$ (d) 2

8. A particle of mass M at rest decays into two particles of masses m_1 and m_2, having non-zero velocities. The ratio of the de-Broglie wavelengths of the particles, λ_1 / λ_2 is
   (a) m_1 / m_2 (b) m_2 / m_1
   (c) 1.0 (d) $\sqrt{m_2} / \sqrt{m_1}$

9. The number of photo-electrons emitted per second from a metal surface increases when
   (a) the energy of incident photons increases
   (b) the frequency of incident light increases
   (c) the wavelength of the incident light increases
   (d) the intensity of the incident light increases

10. Energy conversion in a photoelectric cell takes place from
   (a) chemical to electrical (b) magnetic to electrical
   (c) optical to electrical (d) mechanical to electrical

11. As the intensity of incident light increases
   (a) photoelectric current increases
   (b) photoelectric current decreases
   (c) kinetic energy of emitted photoelectrons increases
   (d) kinetic energy of emitted photoelectrons decreases

12. Ultraviolet radiations of 6.2 eV falls on an aluminium surface (work function 4.2 eV). The kinetic energy in joules of the fastest electron emitted is approximately
   (a) 3.2×10^{-21} (b) 3.2×10^{-19}
   (c) 3.2×10^{-17} (d) 3.2×10^{-15}

13. The work function of a substance is 4.0 eV. The longest wavelength of light that can cause photoelectron emission from this substance is approximately
   (a) 540 nm (b) 400 nm
   (c) 310 nm (d) 220 nm

14. The maximum kinetic energy of photoelectrons emitted from a surface when photons of energy 6 eV fall on it is 4 eV. The stopping potential in volts is
   (a) 2 (b) 4
   (c) 6 (d) 10

Answer Key	1	(b)	2	(c)	3	(b)	4	(c)	5	(b)	6	(a)	7	(a)
Sol. from page 177	8	(c)	9	(d)	10	(c)	11	(a)	12	(b)	13	(c)	14	(b)

15. What is the stopping potential when the metal with work function 0.6 eV is illuminated with the light of 2 eV
(a) 2.6 V (b) 3.6 V
(c) 0.8 V (d) 1.4 V

16. When yellow light is incident on a surface, no electrons are emitted while green light can emit. If red light is incident on the surface, then
(a) no electrons are emitted
(b) photons are emitted
(c) electrons of higher energy are emitted
(d) electrons of lower energy are emitted

17. The work functions of metal A and B are in the ratio 1 : 2. If light of frequencies f and $2f$ are incident on the surfaces of A and B respectively, the ratio of the maximum kinetic energies of photoelectrons emitted is (f is greater than threshold frequency of A, $2f$ is greater than threshold frequency of B)
(a) 1 : 1 (b) 1 : 2
(c) 1 : 3 (d) 1 : 4

18. Light of two different frequencies whose photons have energies 1eV and 2.5eV respectively, successively illuminates a metal of work function 0.5eV. The ratio of maximum kinetic energy of the emitted electron will be
(a) 1 : 5 (b) 1 : 4
(c) 1 : 2 (d) 1 : 1

19. The cathode of a photoelectric cell is changed such that the work function changes from W_1 to W_2 $(W_2 > W_1)$. If the current before and after changes are I_1 and I_2, all other conditions remaining unchanged, then (assuming $hf > W_2$)
(a) $I_1 = I_2$ (b) $I_1 < I_2$
(c) $I_1 > I_2$ (d) $I_1 < I_2 < 2I_1$

20. When a metal surface is illuminated by light of wavelengths 400 nm and 250 nm, the maximum velocities of the photoelectrons ejected are v and $2v$ respectively. The work function of the metal is (h - Planck's constant, c = velocity of light in air)
(a) $2\text{ hc} \times 10^6$ J (b) $1.5\text{ hc} \times 10^6$ J
(c) $\text{hc} \times 10^6$ J (d) $0.5\text{ hc} \times 10^6$ J

21. Two identical photo-cathodes receive light of frequencies f_1 and f_2. If the velocities of the photo electrons (of mass m) coming out are respectively v_1 and v_2, then
(a) $v_1 - v_2 = \left[\frac{2h}{m}(f_1 - f_2)\right]^{1/2}$ (b) $v_1^2 - v_2^2 = \frac{2h}{m}(f_1 - f_2)$
(c) $v_1 + v_2 = \left[\frac{2h}{m}(f_1 + f_2)\right]^{1/2}$ (d) $v_1^2 + v_2^2 = \frac{2h}{m}(f_1 + f_2)$

22. When ultraviolet rays are incident on metal plate, then photoelectric effect does not occurs. It occurs by the incidence of
(a) X-rays (b) radio wave
(c) infrared rays (d) green house effect

23. Molybdenum is used as a target element for production of X-rays because it is
(a) a heavy element and can easily absorb high velocity electrons
(b) a heavy element with a high melting point
(c) an element having high thermal conductivity
(d) heavy and can easily deflect electrons

24. The shortest wavelength of X-rays emitted from an X-ray tube depends on the
(a) current in the tube
(b) voltage applied to the tube
(c) nature of gas in the tube
(d) atomic number of target material

25. If f_1, f_2 and f_3 are the frequencies of corresponding K_α, K_β and L_α X-rays of an element, then
(a) $f_1 = f_2 = f_3$ (b) $f_1 - f_2 = f_3$
(c) $f_2 = f_1 + f_3$ (d) $f_2^2 = f_1 f_3$

26. In X-ray spectrum wavelength λ of line K_α depends on atomic number Z as
(a) $\lambda \propto Z^2$ (b) $\lambda \propto (Z-1)^2$
(c) $\lambda \propto \frac{1}{(Z-1)}$ (d) $\lambda \propto \frac{1}{(Z-1)^2}$

27. For the structural analysis of crystals, X-rays are used because
(a) X-rays are highly penetrating radiations
(b) X-rays are highly penetrating radiations
(c) Wavelength of X-ray is of order of nuclear size
(d) X-rays are coherent radiations

28. For production of characteristic K_β X-rays, the electron transition is
(a) $n = 2$ to $n = 1$ (b) $n = 3$ to $n = 2$
(c) $n = 3$ to $n = 1$ (d) $n = 4$ to $n = 2$

Answer Key														
Sol. from page 289	15	(d)	16	(a)	17	(b)	18	(b)	19	(a)	20	(a)	21	(b)
	22	(a)	23	(b)	24	(b)	25	(c)	26	(d)	27	(a)	28	(c)

29. The intensity distribution of X-rays from two colllidge tubes operated on different voltages V_1 and V_2 and using different target materials of atomic numbers Z_1 and Z_2 is shown in the figure. Which one of the following inequalities is true

(a) $V_1 > V_2,\ Z_1 < Z_2$

(b) $V_1 > V_2,\ Z_1 > Z_2$

(c) $V_1 < V_2,\ Z_1 < Z_2$

(d) $V_1 = V_2,\ Z_1 < Z_2$

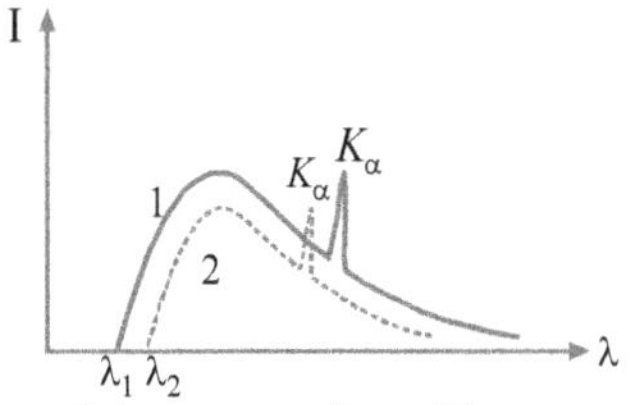

30. In producing X-rays a beam of electrons accelerated by a potential difference V is made to strike a metal target. For what value of V, X-rays will have the lowest wavelength of 0.3094 Å

(a) 10 kV (b) 20 kV

(c) 30 kV (d) 40 kV

31. The X-ray beam coming from an X-ray tube will be

(a) monochromatic

(b) having all wavelengths smaller than a certain maximum wavelength

(c) having all wavelengths larger than a certain minimum wavelength

(d) having all wavelengths lying between a minimum and a maximum wavelength

32. The potential difference applied to an X-ray tube is increased. As a result, in the emitted radiation

(a) the intensity increases

(b) the minimum wavelength increases

(c) the intensity decreases

(d) the minimum wavelength decreases

33. The binding energy of the innermost electron in tungsten is 40 keV. To produce characteristic X-rays using a tungsten target in an X-rays tube the potential difference V between the cathode and the anti-cathode should be

(a) V < 40 kV (b) $V \le 40\ kV$

(c) $V > 40\ kV$ (d) $V > / < 40\ kV$

34. The wavelength of most energetic X-rays emitted when a metal target is bombarded by 40 KeV electrons, is approximately ($h = 6.62 \times 10^{-34}$ J-sec; 1 eV = 1.6×10^{-19} J; $c = 3\times10^8$ m/s)

(a) 300 Å (b) 10 Å

(c) 4 Å (d) 0.31 Å

35. The potential difference applied to an X-ray tube is 5kV and the current through it is 3.2 mA. Then the number of electrons striking the target per second is

(a) 2×10^{16} (b) 5×10^{16}

(c) 1×10^{17} (d) 4×10^{15}

36. The wavelength of K_α X-rays produced by an X-ray tube is 0.76 Å. The atomic number of the anode material of the tube is

(a) 20 (b) 60

(c) 40 (d) 80

37. The K_α X-ray emission line of tungsten occurs at λ = 0.021 nm. The energy difference between K and L levels in this atom is about

(a) 0.51 MeV (b) 1.2 MeV

(c) 59 KeV (d) 13.6 eV

38. K_α wavelength emitted by an atom of atomic number Z = 11 is λ. Find the atomic number for an atom that emits K_α radiation with wavelength 4λ

(a) Z = 6 (b) Z = 4

(c) Z = 11 (d) Z = 44

39. The figure shows the variation of photocurrent with anode potential for a photo-sensitive surface for three different radiations. Let I_a, I_b and I_c be the intensities and f_a, f_b and f_c be the frequencies for the curves *a*, *b* and *c* respectively

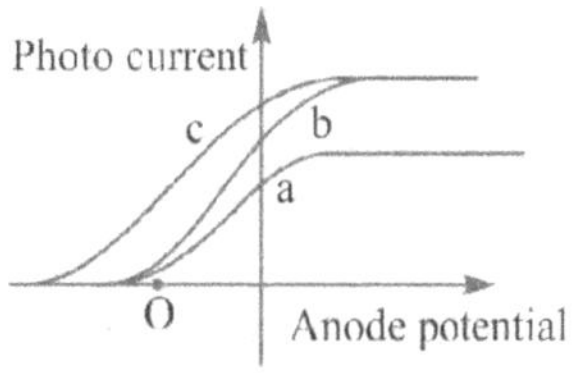

(a) $f_a = f_b$ and $I_a \ne I_b$ (b) $f_a = f_c$ and $I_a = I_c$

(c) $f_a = f_b$ and $I_a = I_b$ (d) $f_a = f_b$ and $I_a = I_b$

40. According to Einstein's photoelectric equation, the graph between the kinetic energy of photoelectrons ejected and the frequency of incident radiation is

(a) 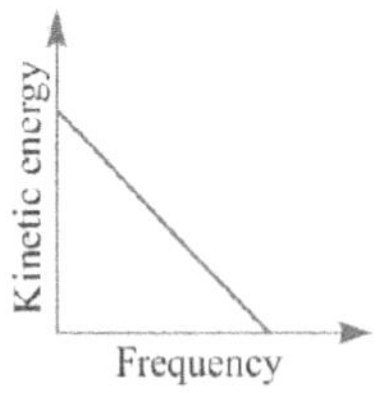

(b) 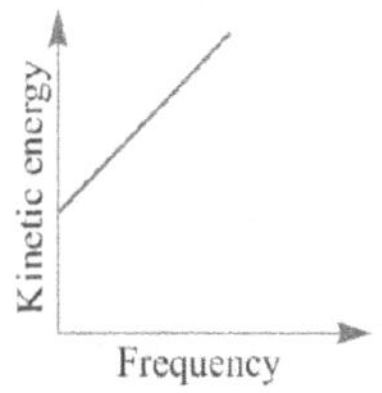

(c) 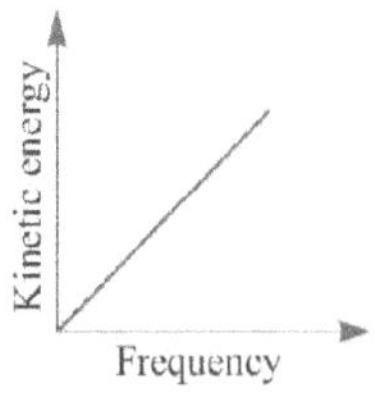

(d) 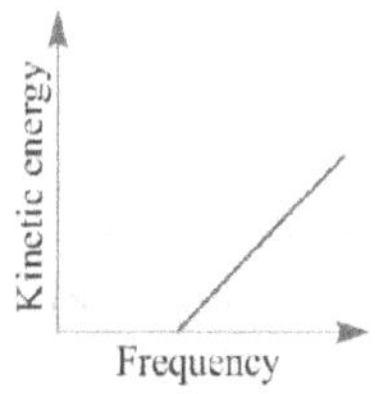

41. The stopping potential V for photoelectric emission from a metal surface is plotted along Y-axis and frequency *f* of incident light along X-axis. A straight line is obtained as shown. Planck's constant is given by

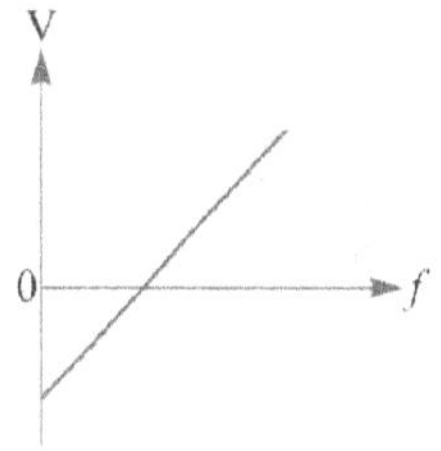

(a) slope of the line

(b) product of slope on the line and charge on the electron

(c) product of intercept along Y-axis and mass of the electron

(d) product of Slope and mass of electron

Answer Key	29	(a)	30	(d)	31	(c)	32	(d)	33	(c)	34	(d)	35	(a)
Sol. from page 289	36	(c)	37	(c)	38	(a)	39	(a)	40	(d)	41	(b)		

42. According to Einstein's photoelectric equation, the plot of the kinetic energy of the emitted photo electrons from a metal versus the frequency, of the incident radiation gives a straight line whose slope
   (a) is the same for all metals and independent of the intensity of the radiation
   (b) depends on the intensity of the radiation
   (c) depends both on the intensity of the radiation and the metal used
   (d) depends on the nature of the metals used

43. If in nature there may not be an element for which the principal quantum number n > 4, then the total possible number of elements will be
   (a) 60 (b) 32
   (c) 4 (d) 64

44. The kinetic energy of the electron in an orbit of radius r in hydrogen atom is (e = electronic charge, $k = \frac{1}{4\pi \epsilon_0}$)
   (a) $k\frac{e^2}{r^2}$ (b) $k\frac{e^2}{2r}$
   (c) $k\frac{e^2}{r}$ (d) $k\frac{e^2}{2r^2}$

45. The velocity of an electron in the second orbit of sodium atom (atomic number = 11) is v. The velocity of an electron in its fifth orbit will be
   (a) v (b) $\frac{22}{5}v$
   (c) $\frac{5}{2}v$ (d) $\frac{2}{5}v$

46. Which of the following statements are true regarding Bohr's model of hydrogen atom?
   (I) Orbiting speed of electron decreases as it shifts to discrete orbits away from the nucleus
   (II) Radii of allowed orbits of electron are proportional to the principal quantum number
   (III) Frequency with which electrons orbit around the nucleus in discrete orbits is inversely proportional to the cube of principal quantum number
   (IV) Binding force with which the electorn is bound to the nucleus increases as it shits to outer orbits
   Select correct answer using the codes given below

Codes.
   (a) I and III (b) II and IV
   (c) I, II and III (d) II, III and IV

47. In the following atoms and molecules for the transition from n = 2 to n = 1, the spectral line of minimum wavelength will be produced by
   (a) hydrogen atom (b) deuterium atom
   (c) uni-ionized helium (d) di-ionized lithium

48. Which one of the series of hydrogen spectrum is in the visible region?
   (a) Lyman series (b) Balmer series
   (c) Paschen series (d) Bracket series

49. In a beryllium atom, if a_0 be the radius of the first orbit, then the radius of the second orbit will be in general
   (a) na_0 (b) a_0
   (c) n^2a_0 (d) $\frac{a_0}{n^2}$

50. If the wavelength of the first line of the Balmer series of hydrogen is 6561 Å, the wavelength of the second line of the series should be
   (a) 13122 Å (b) 3280 Å
   (c) 4860 Å (d) 2187 Å

51. When a hydrogen atom is raised from the ground state to an excited state
   (a) P.E. increases and K.E. decreases
   (b) P.E. decreases and K.E. increases
   (c) both kinetic energy and potential energy increase
   (d) both K.E. and P.E. decrease

52. The ratio of the kinetic energy to the total energy of an electron in a Bohr orbit is
   (a) –1 (b) 2
   (c) 1 : 2 (d) none of these

53. Ratio of the wavelengths of first line of Lyman series and first line of Balmer series is
   (a) 1 : 3 (b) 27 : 5
   (c) 5 : 27 (d) 4 : 9

54. As per Bohr model, the minimum energy (in eV) required to remove an electron from the ground state of doubly ionized Li atom (Z = 3) is
   (a) 1.51 (b) 13.6
   (c) 40.8 (d) 122.4

55. The ionisation energy of hydrogen atom is 13.6 eV. Following Bohr's theory, the energy corresponding to a transition between the 3rd and the 4th orbit is
   (a) 3.40 eV (b) 1.51 eV
   (c) 0.85 eV (d) 0.66 eV

Answer Key	42	(a)	43	(a)	44	(b)	45	(d)	46	(a)	47	(d)	48	(b)
Sol. from page 189	49	(c)	50	(c)	51	(a)	52	(a)	53	(c)	54	(d)	55	(d)

56. The wavelength of radiation emitted is λ_0 when an electron jumps from the third to the second orbit of hydrogen atom. For the electron jump from the fourth to the second orbit of the hydrogen atom, the wavelength of radiation emitted will be

(a) $\frac{16}{25}\lambda_0$ (b) $\frac{20}{27}\lambda_0$

(c) $\frac{27}{20}\lambda_0$ (d) $\frac{25}{16}\lambda_0$

57. If the binding energy of the electron in a hydrogen atom is 13.6 eV, the energy required to remove the electron from the first excited state of Li^{++} is

(a) 122.4 eV (b) 30.6 eV

(c) 13.6 eV (d) 3.4 eV

58. The ground state energy of hydrogen atom is – 13.6 eV. What is the potential energy of the electron in this state

(a) 0 eV (b) – 27.2 eV

(c) 1 eV (d) 2 eV

59. The diagram shows-the energy levels for an electron in a certain atom. Which transition shown represents the emission of a photon with the most energy

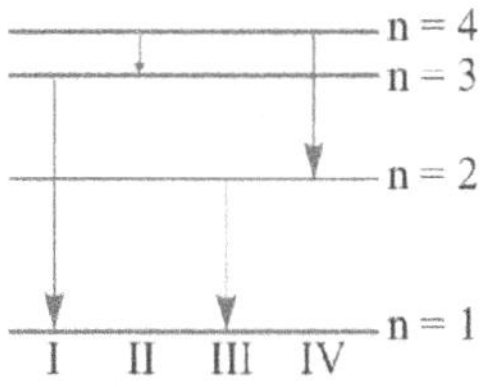

(a) I (b) II

(c) III (d) IV

60. An α-particle of 5 MeV energy strikes with a nucleus of uranium at stationary at an scattering angle of 180°. The nearest distance upto which α-particle reaches the nucleus will be of the order of

(a) 1 Å (b) 10^{-10} cm

(c) 10^{-12} cm (d) 10^{-15} cm

61. For the Bohr's first orbit of circumference $2\pi r$, the de-Broglie wavelength of revolving electron will be

(a) $2\pi r$ (b) πr

(c) $\frac{1}{2\pi r}$ (d) $\frac{1}{4\pi r}$

62. The energy of a photon is $E = hf$ and the momentum of photon $p = \frac{h}{\lambda}$, then the velocity of photon will be

(a) E/p (b) Ep

(c) $\left(\frac{E}{p}\right)^2$ (d) 3×10^8 m/s

63. There are n_1 photons of frequency f_1 in a beam of light an equally emergetic beam, there are n_2 photons of frequency f_2. *Then* the correct relation is

(a) $\frac{n_1}{n_2} = 1$ (b) $\frac{n_1}{n_2} = \frac{f_1}{f_2}$

(c) $\frac{n_1}{n_2} = \frac{f_2}{f_1}$ (d) $\frac{n_1}{n_2} = \frac{f_1^2}{f_2^2}$

64. Photoelectric effect supports quantum nature of light because

(i) there is minimum frequency of light below which no photoelectrons are emitted

(ii) electric charge of photoelectrons is quantized

(iii) maximum kinetic energy of photoelectrons depends only on the frequency of light and not on its intensity

(iv) even when metal surface is faintly illuminated the photoelectrons leave the surface immediately

(a) (i), (ii), (iii) (b) (i), (ii), (iv)

(c) (ii), (iii), (iv) (d) (i), (iii), (iv)

65. The transition from the state n = 4 to n = 3 in a hydrogen like atom results in ultraviolet radiation. Infrared radiation will be obtained in the transition from :

(a) 2 → 1 (b) 3 → 2

(c) 4 → 2 (d) 5 → 4

66. When light of wavelength 300 nm falls on a photoelectric emitter photoelectrons are liberated . For another emitter, however light of 600 nm wavelength is sufficient for creating photoemission. What is the ratio of the work functions of the two emitters :

(a) 1 : 2 (b) 2 : 1

(c) 4 : 1 (d) 1 : 4

67. The time taken by a photoelectron to come out after the photon strikes is approximately :

(a) 10^{-10} s (b) 10^{-16} s

(c) 10^{-1} s (d) 10^{-4} s

Answer Key	56	(b)	57	(b)	58	(b)	59	(a)	60	(c)	61	(a)
Sol. from page 289	62	(a)	63	(c)	64	(d)	65	(d)	66	(b)	67	(a)

LEVEL -2

1. A photo cell is receiving light from a source placed at a distance of 1 m. If the same source is to be placed at a distance of 2 m, then the ejected electron
   (a) moves with one-fourth energy as that of the initial energy
   (b) moves with one-fourth of momentum as that of the initial momentum
   (c) will be half in number
   (d) will be one-fourth in number

2. The frequency of the incident light falling on a photosensitive metal plate is doubled, the kinetic energy of the emitted photoelectrons is
   (a) double the earlier value (b) unchanged
   (c) more than doubled (d) less than doubled

3. When a point source of monochromatic light is at a distance of 0.2 m from a photoelectric cell, the cut-off voltage and the saturation current are 0.6 volt and 18 mA respectively. If the same source is placed 0.6 m away from the photoelectric cell, then
   (a) the stopping potential will be 0.2 V
   (b) the stopping potential will be 0.6 V
   (c) the saturation current will be 6 mA
   (d) the saturation current will be 18 mA

4. Electrons with energy 80 keV are incident on the tungsten target of an X-ray tube. K shell electrons of tungsten have ionization energy 72.5 keV. X-rays emitted by the tube contain only
   (a) a continuous X-ray spectrum with a minimum wavelength of ~ 0.155 Å
   (b) a continuous X-ray spectrum with all wavelengths
   (c) the characteristic X-rays spectrum of tungsten
   (d) a continuous X-ray spectrum with a minimum wavelength of ~ 0.155 Å and the characteristic X-ray spectrum of tungsten

5. An electron of mass 'm' and charge 'e' initially at rest gets accelerated by a constant electric field E. The rate of change of de-Broglie wavelength of this electron at time t, ignoring relativistic effects is :
   (a) $\dfrac{-h}{eEt^2}$ (b) $\dfrac{-eht}{E}$
   (c) $\dfrac{-mh}{eEt^2}$ (d) $\dfrac{-h}{eE}$

6. The potential energy of a particle of mass m is given by
$$U(x)=\begin{cases}E_0; & 0\le x\le 1\\ 0; & x>1\end{cases}$$
λ_1 and λ_2 are the de-Broglie wavelengths of the particle, when $0\le x\le 1$ and $x>1$ respectively. If the total energy of particle is $2E_0$, the ratio $\dfrac{\lambda_1}{\lambda_2}$ will be
   (a) 2 (b) 1
   (c) $\sqrt{2}$ (d) $\dfrac{1}{\sqrt{2}}$

7. A photon collides with a stationary hydrogen atom in ground state inelastically. Energy of the colliding photon is 10.2 eV. After a time interval of the order of micro second another photon collides with same hydrogen atom inelastically with an energy of 15 eV. What will be observed by the detector ?
   (a) 2 photon of energy 10.2 eV
   (b) 2 photon of energy of 1.4 eV
   (c) one photon of energy 10.2 eV and an electron of energy 1.4 eV
   (d) one photon of energy 10.2 eV and another photon of 1.4 eV

8. The intensity of X-rays from a Coolidge tube is plotted against wavelength as shown in the figure. The minimum wavelength found is λ_c and the wavelength of the K_α line is λ_k. As the accelerating voltage is increased

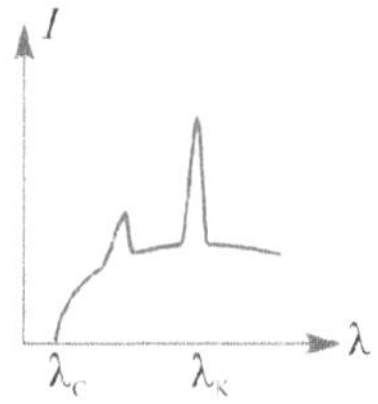

   (a) $(\lambda_k-\lambda_c)$ increases (b) $(\lambda_k-\lambda_c)$ decreases
   (c) λ_k increases (d) λ_k decreases

9. The energy levels of the hydrogen spectrum is shown in figure. There are some transitions A, B, C, D and E. Transition A, B and C respectively represent

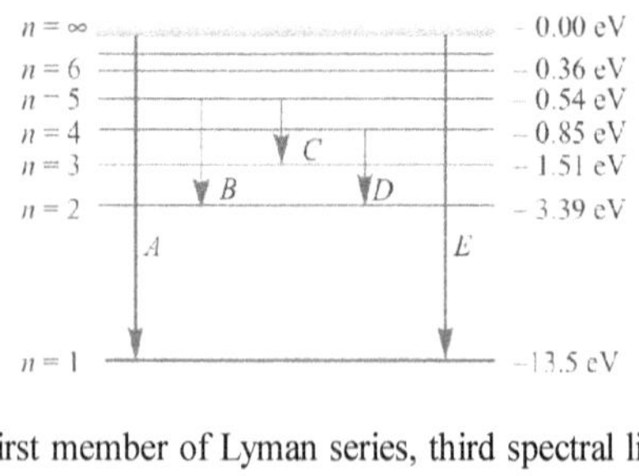

   (a) first member of Lyman series, third spectral line of Balmer series and the second spectral line of Paschen series
   (b) ionization potential of hydrogen, second spectral line of Balmer series and third spectral line of Paschen series
   (c) series limit of Lyman series, third spectral line of Balmer series and second spectral line of Paschen series
   (d) series limit of Lyman series, second spectral line of Balmer series and third spectral line of Paschen series

Answer Key	1	(d)	2	(c)	3	(b)	4	(d)	5	(a)
Sol. from page 292	6	(c)	7	(c)	8	(a)	9	(c)		

10. Ionization potential of hydrogen atom is 13.6 V. Hydrogen atoms in the ground state are excited by monochromatic radiation of photon energy 12.1 eV. The spectral lines emitted by hydrogen atoms according to Bohr's theory will be

(a) one (b) two
(c) three (d) four

11. An energy of 24.6 eV is required to remove one of the electrons from a neutral helium atom. The energy (in eV) required to remove both the electrons from a neutral helium atom is

(a) 79.0 (b) 51.8
(c) 49.2 (d) 38.2

12. Imagine an atom made up of a proton and a hypothetical particle of double the mass of the electron but having the same charge as the electron. Apply the Bohr's atom model and consider all possible transitions of this hypothetical particle to the first excited level. The longest wavelength photon that will be emitted has wavelength λ (given in terms of the Rydberg constant R for the hydrogen atom) equal to

(a) 9 / (5R) (b) 36 / (5R)
(c) 18 / (5R) (d) 4 / R

13. A hydrogen atom and a Li^{++} ion are both in the second excited state. If J_H and J_{Li} are their respective electronic angular momenta, and E_H and E_{Li} their respective energies, then

(a) $J_H > J_{Li}$ and $|E_H| > |E_{Li}|$

(b) $J_H = J_{Li}$ and $|E_H| < |E_{Li}|$

(c) $J_H = J_{Li}$ and $|E_H| > |E_{Li}|$

(d) $J_H < J_{Li}$ and $|E_H| < |E_{Li}|$

14. The electric potential between a proton and an electron is given by $V = V_0 \,\ell n \dfrac{r}{r_0}$, where r_0 is a constant. Assuming Bohr's model to be applicable, write variation of r_n with n, n being the principal quantum number

(a) $r_n \propto n$ (b) $r_n \propto 1/n$

(c) $r_n \propto n^2$ (d) $r_n \propto 1/n^2$

15. Electrons with de-Broglie wavelength λ fall on the target in an X-ray tube. The cut-off wavelength of the emitted X-rays is

(a) $\lambda_0 = \dfrac{2mc\lambda^2}{h}$ (b) $\lambda_0 = \dfrac{2h}{mc}$

(c) $\lambda_0 = \dfrac{2m^2c^2\lambda^3}{h^2}$ (d) $\lambda_0 = \lambda$

16. Suppose an electron is attracted towards the origin by a force $\dfrac{k}{r}$ where k is a constant and r is the distance of the electron from the origin. By applying Bohr model to this system, the radius of the nth orbital of the electorn is found to be 'r_n' and the kinetic energy of the electron to be 'K_n'. Then which of the following is true

(a) K_n independent of n, $r_n \propto n$ (b) $K_n \propto \dfrac{1}{n}$, $r_n \propto n$

(c) $K_n \propto \dfrac{1}{n}$, $r_n \propto n^2$ (d) $K_n \propto \dfrac{1}{n^2}$, $r_n \propto n^2$

17. Hydrogen (H), deuterium (D), singly ionized helium (He^+) and doubly ionized lithium (Li^{++}) all have one electron around the nucleus. Consider n = 2 to n = 1 transition. The wavelengths of emitted radiations are λ_1, λ_2, λ_3 and λ_4 respectively. Then approximately :

(a) $\lambda_1 = \lambda_2 = 4\lambda_3 = 9\lambda_4$
(b) $4\lambda_1 = 2\lambda_2 = 2\lambda_3 = \lambda_4$
(c) $\lambda_1 = 2\lambda_2 = 2\sqrt{2}\lambda_3 = 3\sqrt{2}\lambda_4$
(d) $\lambda_1 = \lambda_2 = 2\lambda_3 = 3\sqrt{2}\lambda_4$

18. Photoelectric effect experiments are performed using three different metal plates p, q and r having work functions $\phi_p = 2.0$ eV, $\phi_q = 2.5$ eV and $\phi_r = 3.0$ eV respectively. A light beam containing wavelengths of 550 nm, 450 nm and 350 nm with equal intensities illuminates each of the plates. The correct I-V graph for the experiment is [take hc = 1240 eV nm] :

(a)
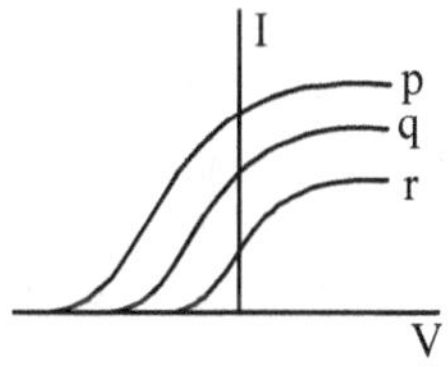

(b)
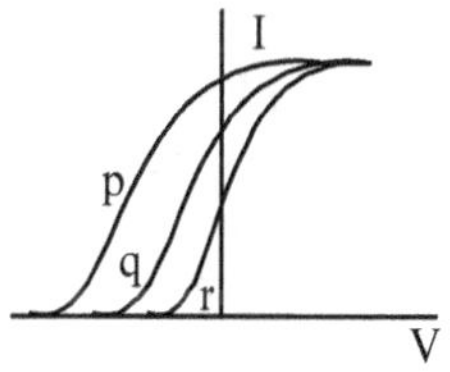

(c)
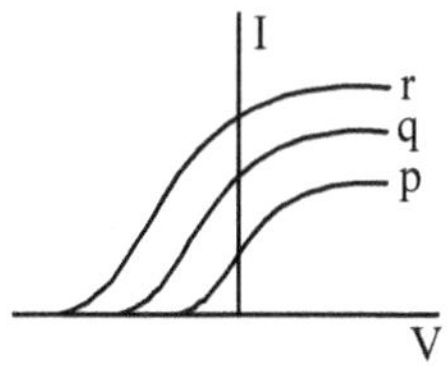

(d)
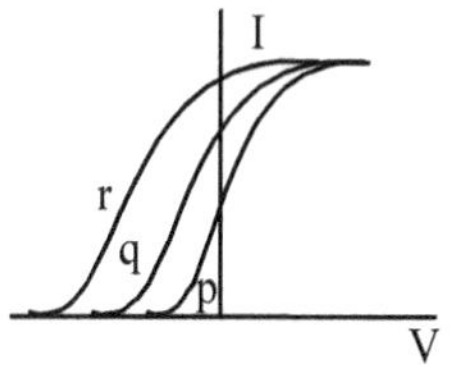

19. In a hydrogen like atom electron makes transition from an energy level with quantum number n to another with quantum number $(n-1)$. For $n >> 1$, the frequency of radiation emitted is :

(a) $f \propto \dfrac{1}{n}$ (b) $f \propto \dfrac{1}{n^2}$

(c) $f \propto \dfrac{1}{n^3}$ (d) $f \propto \dfrac{1}{n^{3/2}}$

Answer Key	10	(c)	11	(a)	12	(c)	13	(b)	14	(a)	15	(a)
Sol. from page 292	16	(a)	17	(a)	18	(a)	19	(c)				

Modern Physics

MCQ Type 2

Exercise 5.2

1. The threshold wavelength for photoelectric emission from a material is 5200 Å. Photo-electrons will be emitted when this material is illuminated with monochromatic radiation from a
   (a) 50 watt infrared lamp (b) 1 watt infrared lamp
   (c) 50 watt ultraviolet lamp (d) 1 watt ultraviolet lamp

2. When photon of energy 4.25 eV strike the surface of a metal A, the ejected photoelectrons have maximum kinetic energy T_A eV and de-Brolie wavelength λ_A. The maximum kinetic energy of photoelectrons liberated from another metal B by photon of energy 4.70 eV is $T_B = (T_A - 1.50)eV$. If the de-Broglie wavelength of these photoelectrons is $\lambda_B = 2\lambda_A$, then
   (a) the work function of A is 2.25 eV
   (b) the work function of B is 4.20 eV
   (c) $T_A = 2.00$ eV
   (d) $T_B = 2.75$ eV

3. The electron in a hydrogen atom makes a transition $n_1 \rightarrow n_2$, where n_1 and n_2 are the principal quantum numbers of the two states. Assume the Bohr model to be valid. The time period of the electron in the initial state is eight times that in the final state. The possible values of n_1 and n_2 are
   (a) $n_1 = 4, n_2 = 2$ (b) $n_1 = 8, n_2 = 2$
   (c) $n_1 = 8, n_2 = 1$ (d) $n_1 = 6, n_2 = 3$

4. An X-ray tube is operating at 50kV and 20 mA. The target material of the tube has a mass of 1.0 kg and specific heat 95 J kg^{-1} C^{-1}. One percent of the supplied electric power is converted into X-rays and the entire remaining energy goes into heating the target. Then :
   (a) A suitable target material must have a high melting temperature
   (b) A suitable target material must have low thermal conductivity
   (c) The average rate of rise of temperature of target would be 2°C/s
   (d) The minimum wavelength of the X-rays emitted is about 0.25×10^{-10} m

5. The graph between $1/\lambda$ and stopping potential (V) of three metals having work functions W_1, W_2 and W_3 in an experiment of photo-electric effect is plotted as shown in the figure. Which of the following statement (s) is/are corret? [Here λ is the wavelength of the incident ray]

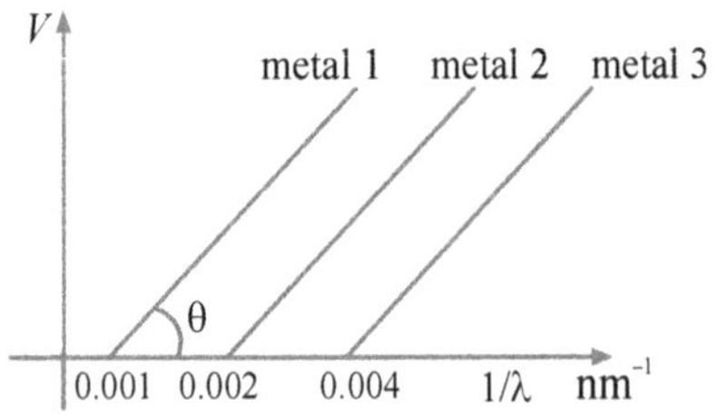

   (a) Ratio of work functions $W_1 : W_2 : W_3 = 1 : 2 : 4$
   (b) Ratio of work functions $W_1 : W_2 : W_3 = 4 : 2 : 1$
   (c) $\tan\theta$ is directly proportional to hc/e, where h is Planck's constant and c is the speed of light.
   (d) The violet colour light can eject photoelectrons from metals 2 and 3.

Answer Key	1	(c, d)	2	(a, b, c)	3	(a, d)	4	(a, c, d)
Sol. from page 293	5	(a, c)						

Modern Physics

Statement Questions

Exercise 5.3

Read the two statements carefully to mark the correct option out of the options given below. Select the right choice.

(a) If both the statements are true and the ***Statement* - 2** is the correct explanation of ***Statement* - 1**.

(b) If both the statements are true but ***Statement* - 2** is not the correct explanation of the ***Statement* - 1**.

(c) If ***Statement* - 1** true but ***Statement* - 2** is false.

(d) If ***Statement* - 1** is false but ***Statement* - 2** is true.

1. ***Statement* -1 :** When the speed of the electron increases, its specific charge decreases.

   ***Statement* -2 :** With the increase in speed of electron, its mass increases.

2. ***Statement* -1 :** Two sources of equal intensity always emit equal number of photons in any time interval.

   ***Statement* -2 :** Two sources of equal intensity may emit equal number of photons in any time interval.

3. ***Statement* -1 :** Two photons of equal wavelength must have equal linear momentum.

   ***Statement* -2 :** Two photons of equal linear momentum will have equal wavelength.

4. ***Statement* -1 :** In an experiment on photoelectric effect, a photon is incident on an electron from one direction and the phtoelectron is emitted almost in the opposite direction. It violate the principle of conservation of linear momentum.

   ***Statement* -2 :**It does not violate the principle of conservation of linear momentum.

5. ***Statement* -1 :** The kinetic energy of photoelectrons emitted from metal surface does not depend on the intensity of incident photon.

   ***Statement* -2 :** The ejection of electrons from metallic surface is not possible with frequency of incident photons below the threshold frequency.

6. ***Statement* -1 :** The photon behaves like a particle.

   ***Statement* -2 :** If E and P are the energy and momentum of the photon, then $p = E/c$.

7. ***Statement* -1 :** The de-Broglie wavelength of a molecule varies inversly as the square root of temperature.

   ***Statement* -2 :** Root mean square speed of a molecule depends on temperature.

8. ***Statement* -1 :** Standard optical diffraction can not be used for discriminating between different X-ray wavelengths.

   ***Statement* -2 :** The grating spacing is not of the order of X-ray wavelengths.

9. ***Statement* -1 :** The phtoelectrons produced by a monochromatic light beam incident on a metal surface have a spread in their kinetic energies.

   ***Statement* -2 :** The work function of the metal is its characteristics property.

10. ***Statement* -1 :** The specific charge of positive rays is not universal constant.

    ***Statement* -2 :** The mass of ion varies with speed.

11. ***Statement* -1 :** The first excited energy of a He^+ ion is the same as the ground state energy of hydrogen.

    ***Statement* -2 :** It is always true that one of the energies of any hydrogen-like ion will be the same as the ground state energy of a hydrogen atom.

12. ***Statement* -1:** The minimum orbital angular momentum of the electron in a hydrogen atom is $\frac{h}{2\pi}$.

    ***Statement* -2 :** The angular momentum for any stable orbit in hydrogen atom is equal to $nh/2\pi$.

13. ***Statement* -1 :** For a hydrogen atom with principal quantum number *n*, speed *v*, the product of *v* and *n* is a constant.

    ***Statement* -2 :** If *E* is the total energy of an electron in an orbit of radius *r* in hydrogen atom, then the product of *E* and *r* is a constant.

14. ***Statement* -1 :** The visible light and X-ray travel at the same speed in vacuum.

    ***Statement* -2 :** They travel with the same speed in glass.

15. ***Statement* -1 :** K, X-ray is emitted when a hole makes a jump from the K shell to some other shell.

    ***Statement* -2 :** The wavelength of *K* X-ray is smaller than the wavelength of L X-ray of the same material.

16. ***Statement* -1 :** Continuous X-rays can be used to identify the element.

    ***Statement* -2 :** Characteristic X-rays can be used to identify the element.

17. ***Statement* -1 :** Moseley's law for characteristic X-ray is $\sqrt{f} = a(z-b)$. In this equation *a* and *b* are independent of the material.

    ***Statement* -2 :** *a* is independent but *b* depends on the material.

Answer Key	1	(a)	2	(d)	3	(d)	4	(d)	5	(b)	6	(a)	7	(a)	8	(a)	9	(b)
Sol. from page 194	10	(b)	11	(c)	12	(a)	13	(b)	14	(c)	15	(b)	16	(d)	17	(c)		

Modern Physics

Passage & Matrix

Exercise 5.4

PASSAGES

Passage for (Qs. 1 - 3) :

A tungsten (Z = 74) target is bombarded by electrons in an X-ray tube.

1. The minimum value of the accelerating potential that will permit the production of the characteristic k_α and k_β lines of tungsten is (the K, L, and M energy levels for tungsten have 69.5, 11.3 and 2.30 keV respectively)

(a) 49.5 kV (b) 69.5 kV
(c) 75.3 kV (d) none of these

2. For this accelerating potential V, the λ_{min} is

(a) 17.9 pm (b) 24.8 pm
(c) 27.3 pm (d) none of these

3. The wavelength of K_β is

(a) 18.5 pm (b) 24.8 pm
(c) 27.3 pm (d) none of these

Passage for (Qs. 4 - 6) :

When a particle is restricted to move along x-axis between $x = 0$ and $x = a$, where a is of nanometer dimension, its energy can take only certain specific values. The allowed energies of the particle moving in such a restricted region, correspond to the formation of standing waves with nodes at its ends $x = 0$ and $x = a$. The wavelength of this standing wave is related to the linear momentum p of the particle according to the de-Broglie relation. The energy of the particle of mass m is related to its linear momentum as $E = \frac{p^2}{2m}$. Thus, the energy of the particle can be denoted by a quantum number 'n' taking values 1, 2, 3, ... (n = 1, called the ground state) corresponding to the number of loops in the standing wave.Use the model described above to answer the following three questions for a particle moving in the line $x = 0$ to $x = a$. Take $h = 6.6 \times 10^{-34}$ J s and $e = 16 \times 10^{-19}$ C.

4. The allowed energy for the particle for a particular value of n is proportional to

(a) a^{-2} (b) $a^{-3/2}$
(c) a^{-1} (d) a^2

5. If the mass is m = 1.0×10^{-30} kg and a = 6.6 nm, the energy of the particle in its ground state is closest to :

(a) 0.8 meV (b) 8 meV
(c) 80 meV (d) 800 meV

6. The speed of particle, that can take discrete values, is proportional to :

(a) $n^{-3/2}$ (b) n^{-1}
(c) $n^{1/2}$ (d) n

MATRIX MATCHING

7. Consider Bohr's model to be valid for a hydrogen like atom with atomic number Z. Match quantities given in **Column -I** to those given in **Column II.**

Column – I	Column – II
A. $\frac{Z^3}{n^5}$	(p) Angular speed
B. $\frac{Z^2}{n^2}$	(q) Magnetic field at the centre due to revolution of electron
C. $\frac{Z^2}{n^3}$	(r) Potential energy of an electron in n^{th} orbit
D. $\frac{Z}{n}$	(s) Speed of an electron in n^{th} orbit
	(t) Frequency of revolution of electron

Answer Key	1	(b)	2	(a)	3	(a)	4	(a)	5	(b)
Sol. from page 294	6	(d)	7	(A-(q) ; B-(r) ; C-(p, t) ; D-(s)						

8. Four physical quantities are listed in **Column I.** Their values are listed in **Column II** in a random order:

Column I		Column II
(A) Thermal energy of air molecules at room temp.	(p)	0.02 eV
(B) Binding energy of heavy nuclei per nucleon.	(q)	2 eV
(C) X-ray photon energy	(r)	1K eV
(D) Photon energy of visible light	(s)	7 MeV

9. In the following, **Column I** lists some physical quantities and the **Column II** gives approximate energy values associated with some of them. Choose the appropriate value of energy from **Column II** for each of the physical quantities in **Column I** and write the corresponding letter p, q, r, etc. against the number (A), (B), (C), etc. of the physical quantity in the answer book. In your answer, the sequence of **Column I** should be maintained.

Column I		Column II
(A) Energy of thermal neutrons	(p)	0.025 eV
(B) Energy of X-rays	(q)	0.5 eV
(C) Binding energy per nucleon	(r)	3 eV
(D) Photoelectric threshold of a metal	(s)	20 eV
	(t)	10 ke V
	(u)	8 Me V

10 This question contains statements given in two columns which have to be matched. Statements (A, B, C, D) in **Column I** have to be matched with statements (p, q, r, s) in **Column II**. The answers to this question have to be appropriately bubbled as illustrated in the following example.

If the correct matches are A-p, A-s, B-q, B-r, C-p, C-q and D-s, then the correctly bubbled 4 × 4 matrix should be as follows :

Some laws / processes are given in **Column I**. Match these with the physical phenomena given in **Column II** and indicate your answer by darkening appropriate bubbles in the 4 × 4 matrix given in the ORS.

Column I		Column II
(A) Transition between two atomic energy levels	(p)	Characteristic X-rays
(B) Electron emission from a material	(q)	Photoelectric effect
(C) Mosley's law	(r)	Hydrogen spectrum
(D) Change of photon energy into kinetic energy of electrons	(s)	β-decay

11. Match the following Column II gives nature of image formed in various cases given in column I

Column – I		Column – II
A. $n = 5$ to $n = 2$	(p)	Lyman series
B. $n = 8$ to $n = 4$	(q)	Brackett series
C. $n = 3$ to $n = 1$	(r)	Paschen
D. $n = 4$ to $n = 3$	(s)	Balmer
	(t)	Infrared region

12. Match the following

Column -I		Column -II
A. Radiation pressure	(p)	particle nature of radiation
B. Threshold wavelength	(q)	Stopping potential
C. Maximum kinetic energy of photoelectron	(r)	Maximum wavelength of incident photons for photoelectric effect
D. Quantisation of angular momentum of electron	(s)	de Broglie hypothesis
	(t)	Principal quantum number

Answer Key						
Sol. from page 294	8	A-(p) ; B-(s) ; C-(r) ; D- (q)	9	A-(p) ; B-(t) ; C-(u) ; D-(r)	10	A-(p, r); B-(q,r) ; C-(p); D - (q)
	11	A-(s) ; B-(q, t) C-(p) ; D(r, t)	12	A-(p) ; B-(r) ; C-(q) ; D-(s, t)		

Modern Physics

Subjective Integer Type

Exercise 5.5

Solution from page 295

1. A molecule of a gas, filled in a discharge tube, gets ionized when an electron is detached from it. An electric field of 5.0 kV/m exists in the vicinity of the event. (a) Find the distance travelled by the free electron in 1 μs assuming no collision. (b) If the mean free path of the electron is 1.0 mm, estimate the time of transit of the free electron between successive collisions.

Ans. (a) 440 m (b) 1.5 ns.

2. A monochromatic source of light operating at 200W emits 4×10^{20} photons per second. Find the wavelength of the light.

Ans. 400 nm.

3. A totally reflecting a small plane mirror placed horizontally faces a parallel beam of light as shown in figure. The mass of the mirror is 20g. Assume that there is no absorption in the lens and that 30% of the light emitted by the source goes through the lens. Find the power of the source needed to support the weight of the mirror. Take g = 10 m/s^2

Ans. 100 MW

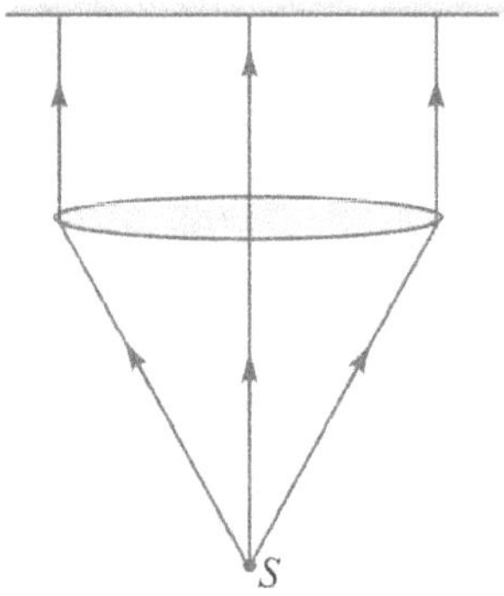

4. In the arrangement shown in figure, $y = 1.0$ mm, $d = 0.24$ mm and $D = 1.2$ m. The work function of the material of the emitter is 2.2 eV. If photocurrent is $0.3x$, then value. of x is ?

Ans. x =3 V

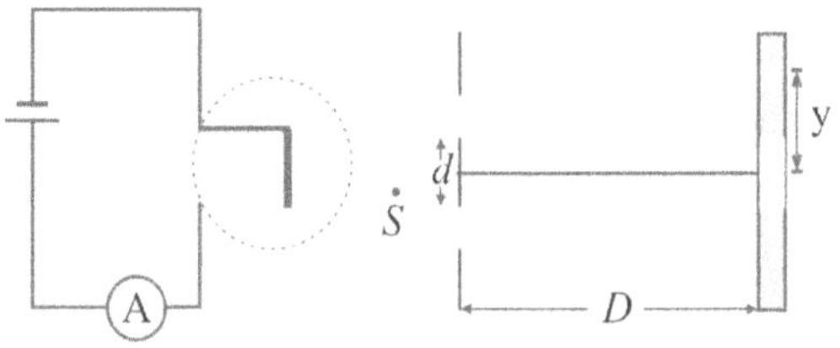

Modern Physics

Subjective

Exercise 5.6

Solution from page 296

1. An electron gun with its anode at a potential of 100 V fires out electrons in a spherical bulb containing hydrogen gas at low pressure (10^{-2} mm of Hg). A magnetic field of 2.83×10^{-4} T curves the path of electrons in a circular orbit of radius 12.0 cm. (The path can be viewed because the gas ions in the path focus the beam by attracting electrons and emitting light by electron capture, this method is known as 'fire beam tube' methods). Determine e/m from the data.

Ans. 1.73×10^{11} C/kg.

2. A 100 W point source emits monochromatic light of wavelength 6000 Å. (a) What is the total number of photons emitted by the source per second? (b) The photon flux at a distance of 5 m from the source.

Ans. (a) 3×10^{20} photons/ s (b) 10^{18} photons / m^2-s.

3. A parallel beam of monochromatic light of wavelength 500 nm is incident normally on a perfectly absorbing surface. The power through any cross-section of the beam is 10 W. Find (a) the number of photons absorbed per second by the surface and (b) the force exerted by the light beam on the surface.

Ans. (a) 2.52×10^{19} (b) 3.33×10^{-8} N.

4. An electrons, in a hydrogen-like atom is in excited state. It has a total energy of –3.4 eV. Calculate (i) the kinetic energy and (ii) the de-Broglie wavelength of the electron.

Ans. (i) 3.4 eV (ii) 6.63 Å.

5. Find the frequency of light which ejects electrons from a metal surface fully stopped by a retarding potential of 3V. The photo electric effect begin in this metal at frequency of 6×10^{14} per second.

Ans. 1.32×10^{15} Hz.

6. Light of wavelength 180 nm ejects photoelectron from a plate of a metal whose work function is 2 eV. If a uniform magnetic field of 5×10^{-5} T is applied parallel to plate, what would be the radius of the path followed by electrons ejected normally from the plate with maximum energy ?

Ans. 0.149 m.

7. When a surface is irradiated with light of wavelength 4950 Å, a photocurrent appears which vanishes if a retarding potential greater than 0.6 V is applied across the photo tube. When a different source of light is used, it is found that the critical retarding potential is changed to 1.1 V. Find the work function of the emitting surface and the wavelength of second source. If the photoelectrons (after emission from the surface) are ejected to a magnetic field of 10 T, what changes will be observed in the above two retarding potentials..

Ans. 3.12×10^{-19} V, 4077 Å, No change in speed.

8. A beam of light has three wavelengths 4144 Å, 4972 Å and 6216 Å with a total intensity of 3.6×10^{-3} W/m^2 equally distributed amongst the three wavelengths. The beam falls normally on an area 1.0 cm^2 of a clean metallic surface of work function 2.3 eV. Assume that there is no loss of light by reflection and that each energetically capable photon ejects one electron. Calculate the number of photo electrons liberated in two seconds.

Ans. 1.09×10^{12}

9. A monochromatic light source of frequency f illuminates a metallic surface and ejects photoelectrons. The photo electrons having maximum energy are just able to ionize the hydrogen atoms in ground state. When the whole experiment is repeated with an incident radiation of frequency $\frac{5f}{6}$, the photoelectrons so emitted are able to excite the hydrogen atom beam which then emit a radiation of wavelength 1215Å. Find the work function of metal and the frequency f.

Ans. 6.875 eV, 5×10^{15} Hz

10. Electrons in hydrogen -like atoms (Z = 3) make transitions from the fifth to the fourth orbit and from the fourth to the third orbit. The resulting radiations are incident normally on a metal plate and eject photoelectrons. The stopping potential for the photoelectrons ejected by the shorter wavelength is 3.95 V. Calculate the work function of the metal and the stopping potential for the photoelectrons ejected by the longer wavelength. (Rydberg constant $R = 1.094 \times 10^7$ m^{-1}).

Ans. 2eV, 0.75 V.

11. A cylindrical rod of some laser material 5×10^{-2} m long and 10^{-2} m in diameter contains 2×10^{25} ions per m^3. If on excitation all the ions are in the upper energy level and de-excite simultaneously emitting photons in the same direction, calculate the maximum energy contained in a pulse of radiation of wavelength 6.6×10^{-7} m. If the pulse lasts for 10^{-7}s. Calculate the average power of the laser during the pulse.

Ans. 23.55 J, 235 MW.

12. In an experiment on photoelectric emission following observations are made :

(i) Wavelength of incident light $\lambda = 1.98 \times 10^{-7}$ m

(ii) stopping potential $V_0 = 2.5$ V. Find (a) energy of photo electrons with maximum speed (b) threshold frequency (c) work function.

Ans. (a) 4.0×10^{-19} J (b) 9.1×10^{14} Hz (c) 6.0×10^{-19} J .

13. A small plate of a metal (work function $W_0 = 1.17$ eV) is placed at a distance of 2m from a monochromatic light source of wavelength 4.8×10^{-7} m and power 1W. The light falls normally on the plate. Find the number of photons striking the metal plate per square metre per second. If a constant magnetic field of strength is 10^{-4}T is applied parallel to the metal surface, find the radius of the largest circular path followed by the emitted photo electrons.

Ans. 4.82×10^{16}, 4 cm.

14. The energy of an excited hydrogen atom is –3.4 eV. Calculate the angular momentum of the electron according to Bohr's theory.

Ans. 2.11×10^{-34} **J.**

15. A lithium atom has three electrons. Assume the following simple model of the atom. Two electrons move close to the nucleus making up a spherical cloud around it and the third moves outside this cloud in a circular orbit. Bohr's model can be used for the motion of this third electron but n = 1 states are not allowed to it. Calculate the ionisation energy of lithium in ground state using the above model.

Ans. 3.4 eV.

16. A small particle of mass m moves in such a way that the potential energy $U = \frac{1}{2}m^2\omega^2r^2$ where ω is a constant and r is the distance of the particle from the origin. Assuming Bohr's model of quantization of angular momentum and circular orbits, find radius of the nth allowed orbit.

Ans. $r = \left(\frac{nh}{2\pi m\omega}\right)^{1/2}$.

17. Monochromatic radiation of wavelength λ is incident on a hydrogen sample in ground state. Hydrogen atoms absorb a fraction of light and subsequently emit radiation of six different wavelengths. Find the value of λ.

Ans. 97.5 nm

18. How many different wavelengths may be observed in the spectrum from a hydrogen sample if the atoms are excited to states with principal quantum number n?

Ans. $\frac{n(n-1)}{2}$

19. Suppose a moving hydrogen atom makes a head on inelastic collision with a stationary hydrogen atom. Before collision both atoms are in the ground state and after collision they move together. What is the minimum velocity of the moving hydrogen atom if one of the atom is given the minimum excitation energy after the collision ?

Ans. 6.24×10^4 **m/s.**

20. Using Bohr model of quantisation of energy, determine;

(a) the excitation energy of n = 3 level of He^+ atom

(b) the ionisation potential of ground state of Li^{++} atom.

Ans. (a) 48.4 eV (b) 122.7 eV.

21. A gas of hydrogen like ions is prepared in such a way that the ions are only in the ground state and the first excited state. A monochromatic light of wavelength 1216 Å is absorbed by the ions. The ions are lifted to higher excited states and emit radiation of six wavelengths, some higher and some lower than the incident wavelength. Find the principal quantum number of all the excited states. Identify the nuclear charge on the ions . Calculate values of the maximum and minimum wavelengths.

Ans. 4700 Å, 245Å.

22. An X-ray tube operated at dc potential difference of 40 kW produces heat at the target at the rate 720 W. Assuming that 0.5% of the energy of the incident electrons is converted in X-radiation. Calculate (i) number of electron per second striking the target (ii) the velocity of incident electrons. Given e/m of electron = 1.8×10^{11} C/kg.

Ans. (i) 11.3×10^{16} **(ii)** 1.2×10^8 **m/s.**

23. An electron in hydrogen like atom makes a transition from n^{th} orbit and emits radiation corresponding to Lyman series. If de-Broglie wavelength of electron in n^{th} orbit is equal to the wavelength of radiation emitted, find the value of n. The atomic number of atom is 11.

Ans. $n \simeq 25$.

24. If K_α radiation of Mo (Z = 42) has a wavelength of 0.71Å. Calculate the wavelength of the corresponding radiation of Cu (Z = 29).

Ans. 1.52 Å.

★★★

Hints & Solutions

Solutions EXERCISE 5.1 LEVEL - 1

1. (b)

2. (c) $\frac{e}{m} = \frac{(E/B)^2}{2V}$

$= \frac{(3.6\times10^4/1.2\times10^{-3})^2}{2\times2.5\times10^3}$

$= 1.80\times10^{11}$ C/kg

3. (b) $\frac{1}{2}mv^2 = eV$

or $v = \sqrt{\frac{2eV}{m}}$.

4. (c) $P = mv = \frac{40}{1000}\times1000 = 40$ N-s

Wavelength, $\lambda = \frac{h}{p} = \frac{6.67\times10^{-34}}{40}$

$= 1667\times10^{-30}$ m

5. (b) $\lambda = \frac{h}{\sqrt{2meV}}$

$\therefore$ $\frac{\lambda_1}{\lambda_2} = \sqrt{\frac{m_2}{m_1}}$, for same potential

or $\lambda_2 = \lambda\sqrt{\frac{m}{M}}$.

6. (a) $\lambda = \frac{\lambda}{\sqrt{2mK}}$

$\therefore$ $\frac{\lambda_p}{\lambda\alpha} = \sqrt{\frac{m_\alpha}{m_p}}$, for same kinetic energy.

or $= \sqrt{\frac{4}{1}} = 2$.

7. (a) As $\lambda = \frac{\lambda}{\sqrt{2mK}}$, so $\lambda_2 = \frac{h}{\sqrt{2m(2k)}} = \frac{\lambda}{\sqrt{2}}$.

8. (c) $0 = \vec{P}_1 + \vec{P}_2$

or $\vec{P}_1 = -\vec{P}_2$

or $P_1 = P_2$

Now $\frac{\lambda_1}{\lambda_2} = \frac{P_2}{P_1}$

$= 1$.

9. (d)

10. (c)

11 (a)

12. (b) Einstein equation

$hf = W_0 + k$

or $6.2 = 4.2 + k$

or $K = 2$ eV

$= 2\times1.6\times10^{-19}$

$= 3.2\times10^{-19}$ J

13. (c) $W_0 = \frac{hc}{\lambda_{max}}$

or $\lambda_{max} = \frac{hc}{w_0} = \frac{6.67\times10^{-34}\times3\times10^8}{4\times1.6\times10^{-19}}$

$= 310$ nm.

14. (b) $K = 4$eV

$\therefore$ $eV_s = 4$ eV

or $V_s = 4$V.

15. (d) $hf = W_0 + k$

or $2 = 0.6 + eV_s$

$\therefore$ $V_s = 1.4$ V.

16. (a) $\lambda_g < \lambda_y$. The wavelength of green light is the longest to cause PEE, and so red light cannot cause PEE.

17. (b) $hf = W_0 + K_1 \Rightarrow K_1 = hf - W_0$

and $2hf = 2W_0 + K_2 \Rightarrow 2hf - 2W_0$

$\therefore$ $\frac{K_1}{K_2} = \frac{hf - W_0}{2(hf - W_0)} = \frac{1}{2}$

18. (b) We have

$E = W_0 + K$

or $1 = 0.5 + K_1 \Rightarrow K_1 = 0.5$

and $2.5 = 0.5 + K_2 \Rightarrow K_2 = 2.0$

$\therefore$ $\frac{K_1}{K_2} = \frac{0.5}{2.0} = \frac{1}{4}$

19. (a) With the increase in work function, the kinetic energy of ejected electrons decreases, but intensity remains same and so $I_1 = I_2$.

20. (a) We have, $E = W_0 + K$

or $\frac{hc}{400\times10^{-9}} = W_0 + \frac{1}{2}mv^2$ ... (i)

and $\frac{hc}{250\times10^{-9}} = W_0 + \frac{1}{2}(2m)v^2$ ... (ii)

On simplifying above equations, we get

$W_0 = 2hc\times10^6 J$.

21. (b) $hf_1 = W_0 + \frac{1}{2}mv_1^2$

and $hf_2 = W_0 + \frac{1}{2}mv_2^2$

$\therefore$ $\frac{2h}{m}(f_1 - f_2) = v_1^2 - v_2^2$.

22. (a) The wavelength of X-ray is shorter than ultraviolet rays so PEE can possible with X-rays.

23. (b)

24. (b) $$\lambda_{min} = \frac{12375}{V} Å$$

25. (c) $$E_L - E_k = hf_1,$$
$$E_m - E_k = hf_2,$$
and $$E_m - E_L = hf_3.$$
$$\therefore \quad f_2 = f_1 + f_2$$

26. (d) $$\sqrt{f} = a(Z-b)$$
or $$\sqrt{\frac{c}{\lambda}} = a(Z-1)$$
or $$\lambda \propto \frac{1}{(Z-1)^2}.$$

27. (a)

28. (c)

29. (a) $\lambda_{min} \propto \frac{1}{V}$ and $\lambda \propto \frac{1}{(Z-1)^2}$.

Wavelength of k_α is greater for 1 and so Z of it is smaller.

30. (d) We have,
$$\lambda_{min} = \frac{12375}{V}$$
or $$V = \frac{12375}{\lambda_{min}} = \frac{12375}{0.3094}$$
$$= 20000 \text{ V}$$

31. (c)

32. (d) As $\lambda_{min} = \frac{12375}{V}$, so with increase in V, λ will decrease.

33. (c)

34. (d) $$\lambda_{min} = \frac{12375}{V} = \frac{12375}{40 \times 10^3} = 0.31 Å$$

35. (a) $$q = it = 3.2 \times 10^{-3} \times 1 = 3.2 \times 10^{-3} \text{ C}$$
$$\therefore \quad n = \frac{q}{e} = \frac{3.2 \times 10^{-3}}{1.6 \times 10^{-19}} = 2 \times 10^{16}.$$

36. (c) We know that,
$$\sqrt{f} = a(z-b)$$
or $$\sqrt{\frac{c}{\lambda}} = \sqrt{\frac{3RC}{4}}(Z-1)$$
On substituting the values of constant and simplifying, we get $z = 40$.

37. (c) $$E_L - E_k = \frac{hc}{\lambda}$$
$$= \frac{6.6 \times 10^{-34} \times 3 \times 10^8}{0.021 \times 10^{-9}}$$
$$= 59 \text{ keV}.$$

38. (a) $$\sqrt{f} = a(z-b) \ ; \ b = 1$$
or $$\sqrt{\frac{\lambda_1}{\lambda_2}} = \frac{(Z_2 - b)}{(Z_1 - b)}$$
or $$\sqrt{\frac{\lambda}{4\lambda}} = \frac{Z_2 - 1}{11 - 1}$$
or $$\frac{1}{2} = \frac{Z_2 - 1}{10}$$
$$\therefore \quad Z_2 = 6.$$

39. (a)

40. (d)

41. (b) We know that
$$E = W_0 + k_{max}$$
or $$hf = W_0 + eV$$
or $$h = \frac{W_0}{f} + \frac{eV}{f}.$$
Clearly (b) is the correct answer.

42. (a)

43. (a) For $n = 4$, electronic configuration is : 1, 8, 18, 32. Total number of elements = 2 + 8 + 18 + 32 = 60.

44. (b) For hydrogen atom
$$\text{Centripetal force} = \frac{mv^2}{r}$$
or $$\left(\frac{1}{4\pi \epsilon_0}\right)\frac{e \times e}{r^2} = \frac{mv^2}{r}$$
$$\therefore \quad \frac{1}{2}mv^2 = \left(\frac{1}{4\pi \epsilon_0}\right)\frac{e^2}{2r} = \frac{ke^2}{2r}.$$

45. (d) We know that $$v_n = \left(\frac{c}{137}\right)\frac{Z}{n}$$
$$\therefore \quad \frac{v_2}{v_5} = \frac{5}{2}$$
$$v_5 = \frac{2}{5}v_2$$
$$= \frac{2}{5}v.$$

46. (a) Speed of the electron,
$$v = \frac{1}{137}\frac{C}{n}.$$
So speed of electron decreases with n.

Time period, $$T = \frac{2\pi r}{v}$$
Also $r \propto n^2$, and $v \propto \frac{1}{n}$
$$\therefore \quad T \propto n^3$$
and $$f \propto \frac{1}{n^3}.$$

47. (d) $$\frac{1}{\lambda} = Z^2 R\left(\frac{1}{1^2} - \frac{1}{2^2}\right).$$
The atomic number of lithium is largest and so spectral line wavelength is minimum.

48. (b)

49. (c)

50. (c) Balmer series, $\frac{1}{\lambda} = R\left(\frac{1}{2^2} - \frac{1}{n^2}\right)$; $n = 3, 4, ...$

$$\frac{1}{\lambda_1} = R\left(\frac{1}{2^2} - \frac{1}{3^2}\right) = \frac{5R}{36}$$

and $$\frac{1}{\lambda_2} = R\left(\frac{1}{2^2} - \frac{1}{4^2}\right) = \frac{3R}{16}$$

$$\therefore \quad \frac{\lambda_2}{\lambda_1} = \frac{20}{27}$$

or $$\lambda_2 = \frac{20}{27}\lambda_1 = \frac{20}{27} \times 6561 = 4860 \text{ Å}$$

51. (a) $K = \frac{1}{8\pi \in_0} \frac{Ze^2}{r}$ and $U = \frac{-1}{4\pi \in} \frac{Ze^2}{r}$, so with increase in r K decreases while U increases.

52. (a)

53. (c) Wavelength of first line of Lyman series

$$\frac{1}{\lambda} = R\left(\frac{1}{1^2} - \frac{1}{2^2}\right)$$

or $$\frac{1}{\lambda_1} = \frac{3R}{4}$$

or $$\lambda_1 = \frac{4}{3R}.$$

and $$\frac{1}{\lambda_2} = R\left(\frac{1}{2^2} - \frac{1}{3^2}\right) = \frac{5R}{36}$$

or $$\lambda_2 = \frac{36}{5R}$$

$$\therefore \quad \frac{\lambda_1}{\lambda_2} = \frac{5}{27}$$

54. (d) $$E = 13.6 Z^2 \text{ eV} = 13.6 \times (3)^2 = 122.4 \text{ eV}$$

55. (d) $$E_3 = \frac{-13.6}{3^2} = -1.51 eV$$

and $$E_4 = \frac{-13.6}{4^2} = -0.85 eV$$

$$\therefore \quad E_4 - E_3 = 0.66 \text{ eV}$$

56. (b) $$\frac{1}{\lambda_0} = R\left(\frac{1}{2^2} - \frac{1}{3^2}\right)$$

or $$\frac{1}{\lambda_0} = \frac{5R}{36} \quad \dots (1)$$

and $$\frac{1}{\lambda} = R\left(\frac{1}{2^2} - \frac{1}{4^2}\right) = \frac{3R}{16}$$

Dividing equation (i) and (ii) we get

$$\lambda = \frac{20}{27}\lambda_0.$$

57. (b) For lithium, $$E_2 = -13.6\frac{z^2}{n^2} = -\frac{13.6 \times 3^2}{2^2} = -30.6 \text{ eV}$$

So energy needed to remove the electron $= 30.6$ eV.

58. (b) Potential energy
$= 2 \times$ total energy
$= 2 \times (-13.6)$
$= -27.2$ eV.

59. (a)

60. (c) $$K = \frac{1}{4\pi \in_0} \frac{2Ze^2}{r_0}$$

$$\therefore \quad r_0 = \frac{2Ze^2}{4\pi \in_0 K}.$$

61. (a) We have, $$mvr = \frac{nh}{2\pi}$$

For $n = 1$, $$mv = \left(\frac{h}{2\pi r}\right)$$

Now wavelength,

$$\lambda = \frac{h}{p} = \frac{h}{mv} = \frac{h}{(h/2\pi r)} = 2\pi r.$$

62. (a) Given $E = hf$ and $P = \frac{h}{\lambda}$.

If v is the velocity of photon, then

$$E = \frac{hv}{\lambda}, \text{ and so } v = E/P$$

63. (c) For equal energy, we have

$$n_1 \times hf_1 = n_2 \times hf_2$$

$$\therefore \quad \frac{n_1}{n_2} = \frac{f_2}{f_1}.$$

64. (d)

65. (d)

66. (b) $$\frac{W_1}{W_2} = \frac{hc/\lambda_1}{hc/\lambda_2} = \frac{\lambda_2}{\lambda_1} = \frac{600}{300} = \frac{2}{1}.$$

67. (a)

Solutions EXERCISE 5.1 LEVEL - 2

1. (d) Intensity of source, $I \propto \frac{1}{r^2}$, and so with doubling the distance, intensity and hence number of ejected electrons becomes one fourth in number.

2. (c)
$$hf = W_0 + K_1$$
$$\therefore \quad K_1 = hf - W_0 \quad \ldots \text{(i)}$$
$$\text{and } 2hf = W_0 + K_2$$
$$\therefore \quad K_2 = 2hf - W_0$$
$$\text{or } K_2 = 2hf - 2W_0 + W_0$$
$$= 2(hf - W_0) + W_0$$
$$= 2K_1 + W_0.$$

3. (b) With the change in distance, the intensity of source decreases $\left(I \propto \frac{1}{r^2}\right)$, and so saturation current will change. Stopping potential remains same.

4. (d)
$$\lambda_{min} = \frac{12375}{V} \mathring{A}$$
$$= \frac{12375}{80 \times 10^3} = 0.155 \mathring{A}$$

5. (a) Acceleration, $a = \frac{Ee}{m}$

Velocity of electron, $v = at = \frac{Eet}{m}$.

Wavelength, $\lambda = \frac{h}{mv} = \frac{h}{Eet}$.

Now $\frac{d\lambda}{dt} = -\frac{h}{eEt^2}$.

6. (c) For $0 \le x \le 1$, $K_1 = E - U = 2E_0 - E_0 = E_0$

For $x > 1$, $K_2 = E - U = 2E_0 - 0 = 2E_0$

$$\text{Now } \frac{\lambda_1}{\lambda_2} = \frac{h/\sqrt{2mK_1}}{n/\sqrt{2mK_2}} = \sqrt{\frac{K_2}{K_1}}$$
$$= \sqrt{2}.$$

7. (c) 13.6 eV energy needed to liberate the electron form hydrogen atom. So electorn will liberate with kinetic energy. = 15 – 13.6 = 1.4 eV.

8. (a) As $\lambda_e = \frac{12375}{V}$, so with increase in V, λ_e decreases. $(\lambda_k - \lambda_e)$ will increases.

9. (c)

10. (c) $-13.6 + 12.1 = \frac{-13.6}{n^2}$

or $n = 3$.

The spectral lines corresponding to $n = 3$ will be

$$\frac{n(n-1)}{2} = \frac{3(3-1)}{2} = 3$$

11. (a) The ionisation energy of helium atom

$= 13.6\, Z^2 = 13.6 \times 2^2 = 54.4$ eV

So total energy needed to remove both the electrons from helium atom = 24.6 + 54.4 = 79 eV.

12. (c) With mass 2m Rydberg constant becomes,

$$R' = \frac{(2m)e^4}{8 \epsilon_0^2 ch^3} = 2R.$$

For longest wavelength, transition to first executed level.

$$\frac{1}{\lambda'} = R'\left(\frac{1}{2^2} - \frac{1}{3^2}\right)$$
$$\text{or } \frac{1}{\lambda'} = 2R \times \frac{5}{36}$$
$$\text{or } \lambda' = \frac{18}{5R}.$$

13. (b) Angular momentum of revolving electron does not depend on atomic number, while energy depends on Z. i.e., $E_n = -\frac{13.6Z^2}{n^2}$. So $(E_H) < |E_{Li}|$.

14. (a) Electric field,

$$E = -\frac{dV}{dr}$$
$$= -\frac{d}{dr}\left[V_0 \ln \frac{r}{r_0}\right]$$
$$= -\frac{V_0}{r}.$$

Centripetal force,

$$Ee = \frac{mv^2}{r}$$
$$\text{or } \frac{V_0}{r} e = \frac{mv^2}{r}$$
$$\text{or } v = cr^{\circ}$$
$$\text{Now } mvr = \frac{nh}{2\pi}$$
$$\therefore \quad r = \frac{nh}{2\pi mv}$$
$$\text{or } r \propto n.$$

15. (a)
$$\lambda = \frac{h}{p} = \frac{h}{\sqrt{2mK}} \Rightarrow K = \frac{h^2}{2m\lambda^2}$$

Wavelength,

$$\lambda_0 = \frac{hc}{K}$$
$$= \frac{hc}{(h^2/2m\lambda^2)} = \frac{2mc\lambda^2}{h}$$

16. (a)
$$\frac{mv^2}{r} = \frac{K}{r}$$
$$\text{or } v = \sqrt{\frac{K}{m}} = cr^{\circ}$$

Now $mvr = \frac{nh}{2\pi}$

or $r = \frac{nh}{2mmv}$

$\therefore \quad r \propto n.$

Also kinetic energy

$$K = \frac{mv^2}{2}$$

$$= \frac{m}{2} \times \frac{K}{m}$$

$$= \frac{K}{2}.$$

17. (a) $Z_1 = 1, Z_2 = 1, Z_3 = 2$ and $Z_4 = 3$.

$$\frac{1}{\lambda} = RZ^2\left(\frac{1}{1^2} - \frac{1}{2^2}\right)$$

or $\lambda = \frac{4}{3RZ^2}$

or $\lambda Z^2 = \text{constant}$

So $\lambda_1(1)^2 = \lambda_2(1)^2 = \lambda_3(2)^2 = \lambda a(3^2)$

or $\lambda_1 = \lambda_2 = 4\lambda_3 = 9\lambda_4$.

18. (a) $E_{\lambda_1} = \frac{hc}{\lambda}$

$$= \frac{1240}{550} eV = 2.25\ eV$$

$$E_{\lambda_2} = \frac{1240}{450} eV = 2.8 eV$$

and $E_{\lambda_3} = \frac{1240}{250} eV = 3.5\ eV$

For metal r, λ_3 is able to generate photoelectron

For metal q, λ_2, λ_3 are able to generate electron.

For metal p, all wavelength are able to generate electrons. Hence photoelectric current will be maximum for P and minimum for r.

19. (c) $hf = Rhc\left[\frac{1}{(n-1)^2} - \frac{1}{n^2}\right]$

or $f = RC\left[\frac{n^2 - (n-1)^2}{(n-1)^2 n^2}\right]$

$$= RC\frac{(2n-1)}{(n-1)^2 n^2}$$

For n >> 1, $2n - 1 \simeq 2n$ and $n - 1 \simeq n$.

$$f \propto \frac{1}{n^3}$$

Solutions EXERCISE 5.2

1. (c, d)
Any wavelength less than 5200 Å can cause PEE. So ultraviolet light of any wattage can cause PEE.

2. (a, b, c)

$4.25 = W_1 + T_A$ ... (i)

and $4.70 = W_2 + (T_A - 1.50)$ ... (ii)

Also $\frac{\lambda_A}{\lambda_B} = \frac{P_B}{P_A} = \frac{\sqrt{2mk_B}}{\sqrt{2mk_A}} = \sqrt{\frac{k_B}{k_A}} = \sqrt{\frac{T_B}{T_A}}$

or $\frac{\lambda_A}{2\lambda_A} = \sqrt{\frac{T_B}{T_A}}$

$\therefore \quad T_A = 4\ T_B$.

By doing hit and trial in (ii) equation, we get $W_2 = 4.20$ eV, $T_A = 2.0$ eV.

3. (a, d)

$T \propto n^3$, and so

$$\frac{T_1}{T_2} = \left(\frac{4}{2}\right)^3 = 8 \text{ and } \frac{T_1}{T_2} = \left(\frac{6}{3}\right)^3 = 8.$$

4. (a, c, d)

$0.99(Vit) = mc\Delta T$

or $0.99 \times 50 \times 10^3 \times 20 \times 10^{-3} = 1 \times 95 \times \left(\frac{\Delta T}{t}\right)$

or $\left(\frac{\Delta T}{t}\right) = 10.42$ C/s

$$\lambda_{min} = \frac{12375}{V}$$

$$= \frac{12375}{50 \times 10^3} = 0.25 Å.$$

5. (a, c)
Work function,

$$W = \frac{hc}{\lambda}$$

$\therefore W_1 : W_2 : W_3 = 0.001 : 0.002 : 0.004$

$= 1 : 2 : 4$

Also $E = W + k$

or $\frac{hc}{\lambda} = W + eV$

$$V = \frac{W}{e} - \frac{hc}{e\lambda}$$

$$= \left(\frac{W}{e} - \frac{hc}{e\lambda}\right)$$

So $\tan\theta$ is proportional to $\frac{hc}{e}$.

Solutions EXERCISE 5.3

1. (a) Specific charge of electron = e/m.

As $m = \frac{m_0}{\sqrt{1-\frac{v^2}{c^2}}}$, so with increase in speed, mass of electron also increases; e/m decreases.

2. (d) Total number of emitted photons depends on energy of each photon. The energy of photons of two sources may be different.

3. (d) To photons of equal wavelength will have equal momentum (magnitude), but direction of momentum may be different.

4. (d)

5. (b)

6. (a)

7. (a) $\lambda = \frac{h}{P} = \frac{h}{mv_{rms}}$

Also $v_{rms} = \sqrt{\frac{3kT}{m}}$

$\therefore \quad \lambda = \frac{h}{\sqrt{3mkT}}$.

8. (a)

9. (b) The kinetic energy of emitted photoelectrons varies from zero to a maximum value. Work function depends on metal used.

10. (b) Specific charge of positive rays is given by

$= \frac{q}{m}$.

As m is different for different ion. So q/m will be different for different ions. Also $m = \frac{m_0}{\sqrt{1-\frac{v^2}{c^2}}}$

11. (c) For helium ion,

$$E = \frac{-13.6Z^2}{n^2} eV = \frac{-13.6(2)^2}{2^2} = -13.6\,eV.$$

For hydrogen atom,

$$E = \frac{-13.6}{1^2} = -13.6eV.$$

12. (a) The angular momentum of any stable orbit is given by,

$$L = \frac{nh}{2\pi}.$$

For its minimum value, $n = 1$, and so $L = \frac{h}{2\pi}$.

13. (b) Speed $v = \frac{c}{137n}$

$\therefore \quad vn = \text{constant}$

Also, $E = -\frac{13.6}{n^2}$

and $r = 0.53\,n^2$

$\therefore \quad E_r = \text{constant}$

14. (c) The speed of visible light and X-rays are same in vacuum, but different in glass $\left(v = \frac{c}{\mu}\right)$.

15. (b)

16. (d) Characteristic X-rays depends on atomic number, so they can be used to identify the element.

17. (c)

Solutions EXERCISE 5.4

1. (a) 2. (a) 3 (a)

4. (a) $\lambda = \frac{h}{p}$ and $E = \frac{p^2}{2m}$

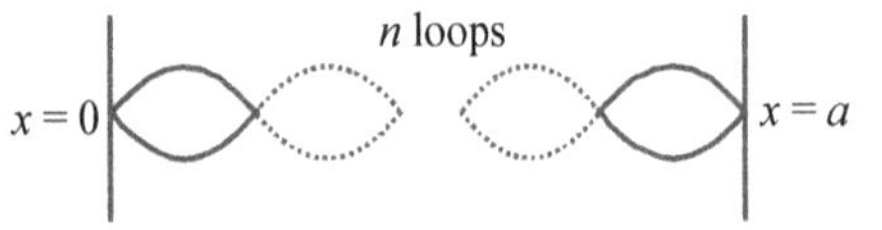

$\Rightarrow \quad E = \frac{h^2}{2m\lambda^2}$

The length in which the particle is restricted to move is a.

This length is a multiple of $\frac{\lambda}{2}$.

Now, $n\frac{\lambda}{2} = a \Rightarrow \lambda = \frac{2a}{n}$

$\Rightarrow \quad E = \frac{h^2n^2}{2m \times 4a^2} = \frac{n^2h^2}{8ma^2}$

$\Rightarrow \quad E \propto a^{-2}$ for a particular value of n.

5. (b) For ground state $n = 1$,

Given $m = 1.0 \times 10^{-30}$ kg, $a = 6.6 \times 10^{-9}$ m

$$\therefore \quad E = \frac{1^2 \times (6.6 \times 10^{-34})^2}{8 \times 1 \times 10^{-30} \times (6.6 \times 10^{-9})^2} \text{J} = \frac{10^{-68}}{8 \times 10^{-48}} \text{J}$$

$$= \frac{10^{-20}}{8} \text{J} = \frac{10^{-20}}{8 \times 1.6 \times 10^{-19}} \text{eV} = \frac{100}{8 \times 1.6} \text{meV} \simeq 8\,\text{meV}$$

6. (d) $\lambda = \frac{h}{p} \Rightarrow \lambda = \frac{h}{mv} \Rightarrow mv = \frac{h}{\lambda}$

But $\frac{n\lambda}{2} = a \Rightarrow \lambda = \frac{2a}{n}$

$\therefore \quad mv = \frac{nh}{2a} \Rightarrow v = \frac{nh}{2am} \Rightarrow v \propto n$

7. A-(q); B-(r) ; C-(p, t); D-(s)
8. (A) - (p); (B) -(s) ; (C) - (r) ; (D) - (q)
9. (A) - (p); (B) - (t) ; (C) - (u) ; (D) - (r)
10. (A) - (p, r); (B) - (q, r) ; (C) - (p) ; (D) - (q)
11. A-(s); B-(q, t) ; C-(p); D-(r, t)
12. A - (p), B - (r), C- (q), D - (s, t)

Solutions EXERCISE 5.5

1. (a) The acceleration of the electron is given by

$$a = \frac{Ee}{m} = \frac{(5\times10^3)\times(1.6\times10^{-19})}{9.1\times10^{-31}}$$

$$= 8.8\times10^{14}\ \text{m/s}^2$$

The distance travelled by electron is given by

$$s = \frac{1}{2}at^2 = \frac{1}{2}\times(8.8\times10^{14})(10^{-6})^2$$

$$= 4.4 \times 10^2 = 440\ \text{m} \qquad \textbf{\textit{Ans.}}$$

(b) The time between two successive collision.

$$t = \sqrt{\frac{2s}{a}} = \sqrt{\frac{2\times1\times10^{-3}}{8.8\times10^{14}}} = 1.5ns$$

2. If E is the energy of each photon, then

$$nE = P$$

$$\therefore \quad E = \frac{P}{n} = \frac{200}{4\times10^{20}} = 50\times10^{-20}J$$

If λ is the wavelength of light, then

$$E = \frac{hc}{\lambda}$$

$$\therefore \quad \lambda = \frac{hc}{E} = \frac{(6.63\times10^{-34})\times(3\times10^8)}{500\times10^{-20}}$$

$$\simeq 400\ \text{nm} \qquad \textbf{\textit{Ans.}}$$

3. For perfectly reflecting mirror, the force exerted by the light of power P is,

$$F = \frac{2\ \text{Power}}{c}$$

For the equilibrium of the mirror

$$F = mg$$

$$\text{or} \quad \frac{2\ \text{Power}}{c} = mg$$

$$\therefore \quad \text{Power} = \frac{mg\times c}{2}$$

$$= \frac{(20\times10^{-3}\times10)\times(3\times10^8)}{2}$$

$$= 30\times10^6\ \text{W}$$

As only 30% of the power of the source is given to the mirror, so power of source needed

$$= \frac{30}{0.30} = 100MW \qquad \textbf{\textit{Ans.}}$$

4. If λ is the wavelength emitted by the source S, then fringe width,

$$\beta = 2y = \frac{D\lambda}{d}$$

$$\therefore \quad \lambda = \frac{2yd}{D}$$

$$= \frac{2\times(1\times10^{-3})\times(0.24\times10^{-3})}{1.2}$$

$$= 0.4\times10^{-6}\ \text{m}$$

By Einstein equation,

$$hf = W_0 + \text{eV}$$

$$\text{or} \quad \frac{hc}{\lambda} = W_0 + eV$$

$$\therefore \quad V = \frac{hc}{e\lambda} - \frac{W_0}{e}$$

$$= \frac{(6.63\times10)^{-34}\times(3\times10^8)}{(1.6\times10^{-19})\times(0.4\times10^{-6})} - \frac{2.2\times1.6\times10^{-19}}{1.6\times10^{-19}}$$

$$= 0.9\ \text{V} \qquad \textbf{\textit{Ans.}}$$

Solutions EXERCISE 5.6

1. If V id the accelerating potential, then kinetic energy of the electron is given by

$$eV = \frac{1}{2}mv^2 \quad \text{... (i)}$$

As each electron moves in circular path due to magnetic field, so

$$evB = \frac{mv^2}{r} \quad \text{... (ii)}$$

After solving above equations, we get

$$\frac{e}{m} = \frac{2V}{r^2B^2}$$

$$= \frac{2\times 100}{(12\times 10^{-2})^2\times(2.83\times 10^{-4})^2}$$

$$= 1.73 \times 10^{11} \text{ C/kg.}$$ ***Ans.***

2. (a) The energy of each photon

$$E = \frac{hc}{\lambda} = \frac{(6.6\times 10^{-34})\times(3\times 10^8)}{6000\times 10^{-10}}$$

$$= 3.3 \times 10^{-19} \text{ J.}$$

The number of photon emitted per second

$$n = \frac{\text{Power}}{E} = \frac{100}{3.3\times 10^{-19}} = 3\times 10^{20}$$

(b) Photon flux is the total number of photons passing normally per unit area per second. Thus

$$\text{Photon flux} = \frac{3\times 10^{20}}{4\pi(5)^2} \simeq 10^{18}.$$ ***Ans.***

3. (a) The energy of each photon

$$E = \frac{hc}{\lambda} = \frac{(6.63\times 10^{-34})\times(3\times 10^8)}{500\times 10^{-9}}$$

$$= 3.978 \times 10^{-19} \text{ J}$$

The number of photons absorbed (the number of photons emitted) per second

$$n = \frac{\text{Power}}{E} = \frac{10}{3.978\times 10^{-19}}$$

$$= 2.50 \times 10^{19}$$ ***Ans.***

(b) The force exerted on the surface is given by

$$F = \frac{\text{Power}}{c} = \frac{10}{3\times 10^8}$$

$$= 3.33 \times 10^{-8} \text{ N}$$ ***Ans.***

4. (i) Kinetic energy = – total energy

or $K = -(-3.4) = 3.4$ eV.

(ii) The de-Broglie wavelength is given by

$$\lambda = \frac{h}{P} = \frac{h}{\sqrt{2mK}}$$

$$= \frac{6.63\times 10^{-34}}{\sqrt{2\times(9.1\times 10^{-31})\times(3.4\times 1.6\times 10^{-10})}}$$

$$= 6.63 \text{ Å}$$ ***Ans.***

5. The work function of the metal

$$W_0 = hf_0 = (6.63 \times 10^{-34})\times (6\times 10^{14})$$

$$= 3.98 \times 10^{19} \text{ J}$$

If f is the frequency of the light, then

$$hf = W_0 + eV_0$$

$$\therefore \quad f = \frac{W_0 + eV_0}{h}$$

$$= \frac{3.98\times 10^{-19} + 1.6\times 10^{-19}\times 3}{6.63\times 10^{-34}}$$

$$= 1.32\times 10^{15} \text{ Hz}$$ ***Ans.***

6. If v_{max} is the speed of the fastest electron emitted from the metal surface, then

$$\frac{hc}{\lambda} = W_0 + \frac{1}{2}mv_{max}^2$$

$$\frac{(6.63\times 10^{-34})\times(3\times 10^8)}{(180\times 10^{-9})} = 2\times(1.6\times 10^{-19}) + \frac{1}{2}(9.1\times 10^{-31})v_{max}^2$$

$$\therefore \quad v = 1.31 \times 10^6 \text{ m/s}$$

The radius of the electron is given by

$$r = \frac{mv}{qB} = \frac{(9.1\times 10^{-31})\times(1.31\times 10^6)}{(1.6\times 10^{-19})\times(5\times 10^{-9})}$$

$$= 0.149 \text{ m}$$ ***Ans.***

7. (i) By Einstein equation

$$hf = W_0 + eV_0.$$

$$W_0 = \frac{hc}{\lambda} - eV_0$$

$$= \frac{(6.63\times 10^{-34})\times(3\times 10^8)}{4950\times 10^{-10}} - (1.6\times 10^{-19})\times 0.6$$

$$= 3.12 \times 10^{-19} \text{ J}$$ ***Ans.***

(ii) For the second surface

$$hf' = W_0 + eV_0'$$

or $\frac{hc}{\lambda'} = 3.12\times10^{-19}+1.6\times10^{-19}\times1.1$

$\therefore \lambda' = 4077$ Å

As magnetic force is always acts perpendicular to the direction of motion, so its speed remains constant.

8. The threshold wavelength

$$\lambda_0 = \frac{hc}{W_0}$$

$$= \frac{(6.63\times10^{-34})\times(3\times10^8)}{2.3\times(1.6\times10^{-19})}$$

$= 5404$ Å.

Thus the only wavelengths 4144Å and 4972Å can emit electrons from metal surface.

As intensity of each wavelength is equal

$$I_1 = I_2 = \frac{3.6\times10^{-3}}{3} = 1.2\times10^{-3}\ \text{W/m}^2$$

The power of each of these wavelength

$P_1 = P_2 = 1.2\times10^{-3}\times10^{-4}$

$= 1.2\times10^{-7}$ W

The energy of photons are

$$E_1 = \frac{hc}{\lambda_1} = \frac{(6.63\times10^{-34})\times(3\times10^8)}{4144\times10^{-10}}$$

$= 4.8\times10^{-19}$ J

and $$E_2 = \frac{hc}{\lambda_2} = \frac{(6.63\times10^{-34})\times(3\times10^8)}{4972\times10^{-10}}$$

$= 4.02\times10^{-19}$ J

The number of photons incident =number of electrons emitted

Thus emitted electrons in two second

$$n_1 = \frac{P_1}{E_1}\times2 = \frac{1.2\times10^{-7}}{4.8\times10^{-19}}\times2 = 0.5$$

$$n_2 = \frac{P_2}{E_2}\times2 = \frac{1.2\times10^{-7}}{4.02\times10^{-19}}\times2 = 0.59\times10^{12}$$

The total number of electrons emitted

$n = n_1 + n_2 = 1.09\times10^{12}$ ***Ans.***

9. By Einstein equation, we can write

$hf = W_0 +$ Ionisation energy

or $hf = W_0 + 13.6\times(1.6\times10^{-19})$ ...(i)

For the radiation of frequency $\frac{5f}{6}$, we have

$$h\left(\frac{5f}{6}\right) = W_0 + \frac{hc}{\lambda}$$

$$= W_0 + \frac{(6.63\times10^{-34})\times(3\times10^8)}{3\times10^8} \quad \text{... (ii)}$$

On simplifying equation (i) and (ii), we get

$W_0 = 11.0\times10^{-19}$ J $= 6.87$ eV

and $f = 5\times10^{15}$ Hz. Ans

10. According to Bohr's model for hydrogen atom, we can write

$$\frac{1}{\lambda_1} = Z^2R\left(\frac{1}{n_f^2}-\frac{1}{n_i^2}\right)$$

$$= 3^2\times(1.094)\left(\frac{1}{4^2}-\frac{1}{5^2}\right)$$

$\therefore \lambda_1 = 4.514\times10^{-7}$ m

and $$\frac{1}{\lambda_2} = 3^2\times1.094\times10^7\left(\frac{1}{3^2}-\frac{1}{4^2}\right)$$

$\therefore \lambda_2 = 2.089\times10^{-7}$ m.

Out of these, the shorter wavelength is λ_2

$$\therefore \frac{hc}{\lambda_2} = W_0 + eV_0$$

or $$W_0 = \frac{hc}{\lambda_2} - eV_0$$

$$= \frac{(6.63\times10^{-34})\times(3\times10^8)}{2.089\times10^{-7}} - (1.6\times10^{-19})$$

$= 3.2\times10^{-19}$ J $= 2$eV

For λ_1, $$\frac{hc}{\lambda_1} = W_0 + eV_0'$$

$$\therefore V_0' = \frac{hc}{e\lambda_1} - \frac{W_0}{e}$$

$$= \frac{(6.63\times10^{-34})\times(3\times10^8)}{(1.6\times10^{-19})\times(4.514\times10^{-7})} - \frac{3.2\times10^{-19}}{1.6\times10^{-19}}$$

$= 0.75$ V ***Ans.***

11. Total number of ions in the rod

$$N = (2\times10^{25})\times\left[\frac{\pi}{4}\times(10^{-2})^2\right]\times(5\times10^{-2})$$

$= 7.85\times10^{19}$

The energy of excitation

$$E = N\times\frac{hc}{\lambda}$$

$$= (7.85\times10^{19})\times\frac{(6.6\times10^{-34})\times(3\times10^8)}{6.6\times10^{-7}}$$

$= 23.55$ J

Average power $$P = \frac{E}{t} = \frac{23.55}{10^{-7}} = 23.55\times10^7 W$$

$\simeq 235$ MW ***Ans.***

12. (a) Maximum kinetic energy of the photoelectrons

$$K_{max} = eV_0$$

$$= (1.6\times10^{-19})\times(2.5)$$

$$= 4.0 \times 10^{-19}\ J$$

(b) By Einstein equation

$$hf = W_0 + K_{max}$$

$$\therefore\quad W_0 = \frac{hc}{\lambda} - K_{max}$$

$$= \frac{(6.63\times10^{-34})\times(3\times10^8)}{1.98\times10^{-7}} - 4.0\times10^{-19}$$

$$= 6.0\times10^{-19} J$$

(c) Threshold frequency

$$f_0 = \frac{W_0}{h} = \frac{6.0\times10^{-19}}{6.63\times10^{-34}}$$

$$= 9.1\times10^{14} Hz$$ ***Ans.***

13. Energy of each photon

$$E = \frac{hc}{\lambda} = \frac{19.9\times10^{-26}}{4.8\times10^{-7}}$$

$$= 4.125\times10^{-19} J$$

The rate of emission of photons from the source

$$= \frac{1}{4.125\times10^{-19}} = 2.422\times10^{18}$$

Number of photons striking per square metre per second on the plate

$$= \frac{2.422\times10^{18}}{4\pi(2)^2} = 4.82\times10^{18}$$

If v_0 is the speed of the fastest electrons

$$\frac{hc}{\lambda} = W_0 + \frac{1}{2}mv_0^2$$

$$4.125\times10^{-19} = (1.17 \times 1.6 \times 10^{-19}) + \frac{1}{2}\times9.1\times10^{-31}\times v_0^2$$

$$\therefore\quad v_0 = 7.04 \times 10^5\ m/s$$

The radius $$r = \frac{mv}{qB} = \frac{(9.1\times10^{-31})\times(7.04\times10^5)}{(1.6\times10^{-19})\times10^{-4}}$$

$$= 4\ cm$$ ***Ans.***

14. If given energy is corresponding to the nth state of the atom, then

$$E = -\frac{13.6}{n^2}$$

or $$-3.4 = \frac{-13.6}{n^2}$$

$$\therefore\quad n = 2$$

The angular momentum, for $n = 2$

$$L = 2\left(\frac{h}{2\pi}\right) = \frac{h}{\pi}$$

$$= \frac{6.63}{\pi}\times10^{-34} = 2.11\times10^{-34} J-s$$ ***Ans.***

15. In the given model third electron moves in the field of charge +3e – 2e = e. Thus the energies of the electron are same as that in hydrogen atom. Thus energy of ground state (n = 2) will be

$$E = -\frac{13.6}{n^2}eV$$

$$= -\frac{13.6}{2^2} = -3.4\ eV$$

Thus ionisation energy will be $= 0-(-3.4)$

$= 3.4$ eV ***Ans.***

16. The force

$$F = -\frac{dU}{dr} = -\frac{d}{dr}\frac{(m\omega^2r^2)}{2} = -m\omega^2 r$$

For the motion of the particle in a circle of radius

$$m\omega^2 r = \frac{mv^2}{r}$$

$$\therefore\quad v = \omega r \qquad \text{... (i)}$$

According to Bohr's model

$$mvr = \frac{nh}{2\pi}$$

or $$v = \frac{nh}{2\pi mr} \qquad \text{... (ii)}$$

From equations (i) and (ii), we get

$$r = \left[\frac{nh}{2\pi m\omega}\right]^{1/2}$$ ***Ans.***

17. For six different wavelength the atom must be excited from $n = 4$. Thus

$$E_4 = -\frac{13.6}{4^2} = -0.85\ eV.$$

The energy imparted to the atom

$$E = E_4 - E_1 = -0.85-(-13.6) = 12.75 eV.$$

If λ is the wavelength of incident photos, then

$$\frac{hc}{\lambda} = 12.75 \times (1.6 \times 10^{-19})$$

$$\therefore\quad \lambda = 97.5\ nm$$ ***Ans.***

18. From the nth state, the atom may go to $(n-1)^{th}$, ..., 2th or 1st state. There are (n – 1) possible transitions corresponding to n^{th} state. The atom reaching $(n-1)^{th}$ state may have $(n-2)$ transitions and so on. Therefore the total possible transitions are

$$N = (n-1)+(n-2)+.....+2+1$$

$$= \frac{n(n-1)}{2}. \qquad \textbf{Ans}$$

19. Suppose u is the velocity of the hydrogen atom before collision. By principle of conservation of linear momentum, we have

$$mu + 0 = (m+m)\,v$$

$$\therefore \quad v = \frac{u}{2}$$

If ΔK is the loss of kinetic energy in the collision, then

$$\frac{1}{2}mu^2 + 0 = \frac{1}{2}mv^2 + \frac{1}{2}mv^2 + \Delta K$$

$$\text{or} \quad \Delta K = \frac{mu^2}{4}.$$

The minimum energy needed to execute the hydrogen atom

$$\Delta E = E_2 - E_1 = -\frac{13.6}{2^2} - \left(-\frac{13.6}{1^2}\right)$$

$$= \frac{3}{4} \times 13.6\ eV$$

Thus

$$\Delta K = \Delta E$$

$$\frac{1}{4}mu^2 = \frac{3}{4} \times (13.6 \times 1.6 \times 10^{-19})$$

$$\text{or} \quad \frac{1}{4}\left(1.0078 \times 1.66 \times 10^{-27}\right)u^2$$

$$= \frac{3}{4}(13.6 \times 1.6 \times 10^{-19})$$

$$\therefore \quad u = 6.24 \times 10^4 \text{ m/s.} \qquad \textbf{Ans.}$$

20. (a) The energy of hydrogen like atom is given by

$$E = -13.6Z^2\left(\frac{1}{n_f^2} - \frac{1}{n_i^2}\right).$$

The energy required to excite the electron from n = 1 to n = 3 level of He^+ atom is

$$\Delta E = E_3 - E_1 = -13.6 \times 2^2 \times \left(\frac{1}{3^2} - \frac{1}{1^2}\right)$$

$$= 48.4 \text{ eV.} \qquad \textbf{Ans.}$$

(b) For lithium atom, z = 3, ionisation energy

$$\Delta E = E_\infty - E_1 = -13.6(3)^2\left(\frac{1}{\infty^2} - \frac{1}{1^2}\right)$$

$$= 122.7 \text{ eV.}\textbf{Ans.}$$

Thus ionisation potential is 122.7 V

21. The energy of the photon of wavelength $\lambda = 1216\,\text{Å}$ is

$$E = \frac{hc}{\lambda} = \frac{19.6 \times 10^{-24}}{1216 \times 10^{-10}}$$

$$= 10.2 \text{ eV}$$

The ions after absorbing this energy, emit the radiations of six possible wavelengths . These are shown in figure.

We know that $E_n = -13.6\dfrac{Z^2}{n^2}eV$

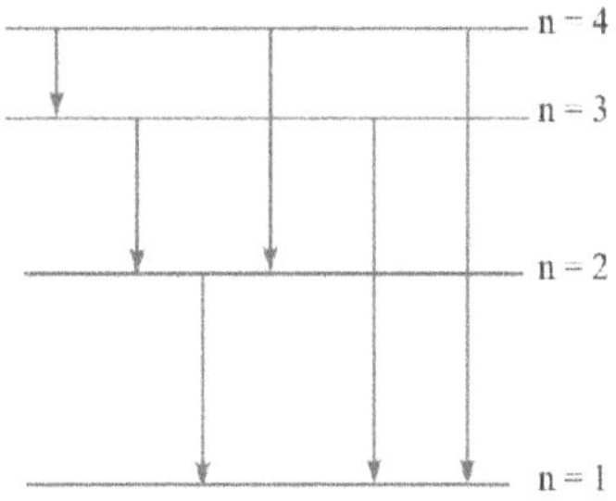

$$\therefore \quad 10.2 = E_4 - E_2$$

$$= -13.6Z^2\left(\frac{1}{4^2} - \frac{1}{2^2}\right)$$

$$\therefore \quad Z = 2 \qquad \text{(gas is helium ions)}$$

Now

$$E_1 = -13.6\frac{Z^2}{1^2} = -54.4 \text{ eV}$$

$$E_2 = -13.6\frac{2^2}{2^2} = -13.6\ eV$$

$$E_3 = -6.04 \text{ eV}$$

$$E_4 = -3.4 \text{ eV}$$

Thus

$$\Delta E_{max} = 54.4 - 3.4 = 51.0\ eV$$

$$\therefore \quad \lambda_{min} = \frac{hc}{\Delta E_{max}} = \frac{19.9 \times 10^{-26}}{51 \times 1.6 \times 10^{-19}} = 245\text{Å}$$

Similarly

$$\lambda_{max} = \frac{hc}{\Delta E_{min}} = \frac{19.9 \times 10^{-26}}{2.64 \times 1.6 \times 10^{-19}} = 4700\text{Å}.$$

Ans.

22. (i) If P is the power of the source, then

$$0.995\,P = 720$$

$$\therefore \quad P = \frac{720}{0.995} = 723.5W$$

As

$$P = Vi$$

$$\therefore \quad i = \frac{P}{V} = \frac{723.5}{40 \times 10^3} = 18.08 \times 10^{-3}\,\text{Å}$$

The number of electrons strike per second

$$n = \frac{i}{e} = \frac{18.08 \times 10^{-3}}{1.6 \times 10^{-19}} = 11.3 \times 10^{16}$$

Ans

(ii) If v is the velocity of the electrons, then

$$\frac{1}{2}mv^2 = eV$$

$$\therefore \quad v = \sqrt{2\left(\frac{e}{m}\right)V}$$

$$= \sqrt{2 \times 1.8 \times 10^{11} \times 40 \times 10^3}$$

$$= 1.2 \times 10^8 \text{ m/s}$$ ***Ans.***

23. If λ is the de-Broglie wavelength, then for n^{th} orbit

$$2\pi r_n = n\lambda$$

where $$r_n = \frac{\epsilon_0 h^2 n^2}{\pi m e^2 Z}$$

$$\therefore \quad \frac{1}{\lambda} = \frac{me^2 Z}{2\epsilon_0 h^2 n} \quad \text{... (i)}$$

For Lyman series

$$\frac{1}{\lambda} = Z^2 R\left(\frac{1}{1^2} - \frac{1}{n^2}\right) \quad \text{... (ii)}$$

From equations (i) and (ii), we have

$$Z^2 R\left(1 - \frac{1}{n^2}\right) = \frac{me^2}{2\epsilon_0 h^2}\frac{Z}{n} \quad \text{... (iii)}$$

where $$R = \frac{me^4}{8\epsilon_0^2 ch^3} \quad \text{... (iv)}$$

After substituting the values in (iii) & (iv), we get

$$n = 25.$$ ***Ans***

24. By Mosley's law, we have

$$\sqrt{f} = a(Z - b)$$

For K_α radiation, b = 1, also $f = \dfrac{c}{\lambda}$

$$\therefore \quad \frac{1}{\lambda} \propto (Z-1)^2$$

Now $$\frac{\lambda_{cu}}{\lambda_{Mo}} = \frac{(Z_{mo}-1)^2}{(Z_{Cu}-1)^2} = \frac{(42-1)^2}{(29-1)^2}$$

On substituting $\lambda_{Mo} = 0.71 Å$ and solving, we get

$$\lambda_{Cu} = 1.52 \text{ Å}.$$ ***Ans.***

Chapter 6

Nuclear Physics

(301- 336)

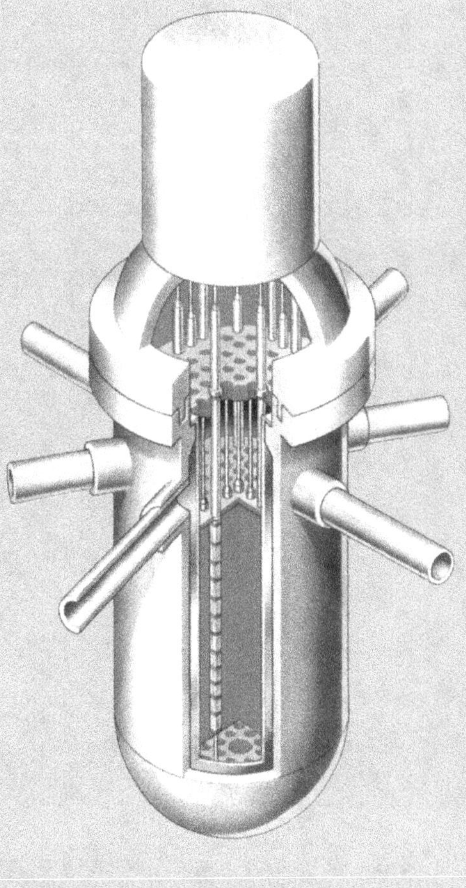

6.1 THE NUCLEUS

The idea of nucleus was first introduced by Rutherford after his experiment; α-scattering experiment. The experiments were carried out by Sir Ernest Rutherford and two of his students , Ernest Marsden and Hans Geizer in 1910 in England. According to him almost the mass of the atom and entire positive charge is concentrated inside the nucleus. The nucleus was supposed to consist of two types of particles; protons and neutrons. Their masses are :

$$\text{mass of the proton} = 1.672 \times 10^{-27}\ \text{kg}$$

$$\text{mass of the neutron} = 1.675 \times 10^{-27}\ \text{kg.}$$

The charge on the proton is 1.6×10^{-19}C, while neutron has no charge. The total number of the protons inside the nucleus is called **atomic number** and is represented by Z. The total number of protons and neutrons inside the nucleus is known as **mass number** and represented by A.

6.2 PROPERTIES OF NUCLEUS

Some of the important properties of the nucleus are :

(i) Nuclear radius

By his experiments, Rutherford concluded that the distance of the closest approach of the α-particle to the nucleus can be regarded as the measure of size of the nucleus. He found the nucleus size of the order of 10^{-14}m. The radius of an atomic nucleus can be determined by the empirical formula;

$$r = r_0 A^{1/3}, \qquad \ldots(1)$$

where r_0 is a constant equal to 1.2×10^{-15} m, which is same for all nuclei and A is the mass number.

The volume of the nucleus

$$V = \frac{4}{3}\pi r^3$$

$$= \frac{4}{3}\pi\left(r_0 A^{1/3}\right)^3$$

or

$$V = \frac{4}{3}\pi r_0^3 A.$$

It shows that the volume of a nucleus is proportional to A.

(ii) Nuclear density

We know that density of nucleus

$$\rho = \frac{\text{mass of nucleus}}{\text{volume of the nucleus}}$$

$$\text{Mass of the nucleus is} \simeq \text{mass number} \times \text{mass of proton}$$

$$= A \times 1.672 \times 10^{-27}$$

$$\text{Volume of the nucleus} = \frac{4}{3}\pi r^3$$

$$= \frac{4}{3}\pi r_0^3 A$$

$$\therefore \quad \text{Density of nucleus} = \frac{A \times 1.672 \times 10^{-27}}{\frac{4}{3}\pi r_0^3 A}$$

or $$\rho = \frac{3\times 1.672\times 10^{-27}}{4\pi(1.2\times 10^{-15})^3}$$

$$\approx 2.31\times 10^{17}\ \text{kg/m}^3$$

This shows that the nuclear density is very large as compared to the density of ordinary matter. Also the density of nuclear matter is independent of the size of the nucleus as the density of a matter is independent of the size of the ordinary matter.

(iii) Nuclear spin

We have studied that an electron has an angular momentum due to its spin motion. It is given by

$\vec{M}_{spin} = -\frac{e}{m}\vec{S}$. Similarly proton and neutron each has a spin momentum

$= \frac{1}{2}\left(\frac{h}{2\pi}\right)\vec{S}$. Each contributes a spin to the nucleus and combine to give it a spin angular momentum.

Isotopes

These are the atoms which have same atomic number but different mass numbers. The isotopes of element have same number of protons but unequal number of neutrons. Few examples are :

(i) Isotopes of uranium : ${}_{92}U^{234}$, ${}_{92}U^{235}$, ${}_{92}U^{238}$.

(ii) Isotopes of radium : ${}_{88}Ra^{223}$, ${}_{88}Ra^{224}$, ${}_{88}Ra^{225}$, ${}_{88}Ra^{226}$, ${}_{88}Ra^{228}$.

(iii) Isotopes of thorium : ${}_{90}Th^{227}$, ${}_{90}Th^{228}$, ${}_{90}Th^{229}$, ${}_{90}Th^{230}$, ${}_{90}Th^{231}$, ${}_{90}Th^{232}$, ${}_{90}Th^{234}$.

Isotones

The atoms whose nuclei have same number of neutrons are called isotones. For example ${}_1H^3$ and ${}_2He^4$ are isotones because each one has 2 neutrons. Similarly ${}_8O^{16}$ and ${}_6C^{14}$ are isotones.

Isobars

Atoms having same mass number but different atomic numbers are called isobars. They have different number of protons and neutrons. Few examples are :

(i) ${}_{30}Zn^{92}$ and ${}_{42}Mo^{92}$.
(ii) ${}_{24}Cr^{54}$ and ${}_{26}Fe^{54}$.
(iii) ${}_{90}Th^{234}$, ${}_{91}Pa^{234}$ and ${}_{92}U^{234}$.

6.3 THE ATOMIC MASS UNIT

In 1960, carbon ${}_6C^{12}$ has been accepted internationaly as the reference of atomic mass unit. One atomic mass unit abbreviated as **amu** is taken as the 1/12 the mass of carbon atom.

$$\text{The mass of one carbon atom} = \frac{12}{6.023\times 10^{23}}\ \text{gram}$$

$$\therefore \quad 1\ \text{amu} = \frac{1}{12}\times\frac{12}{6.023\times 10^{23}}\ \text{gram}$$

$$\text{or} \quad 1\ \text{amu} = 1.66\times 10^{-27}\ \text{kg.}$$

Mass-energy equivalence

According to Einstein, mass can be converted into energy by $E = mc^2$, where c is the speed of light. The energy E is called as mass energy. Thus energy equivalent 1 amu mass is :

$$= (1.66 \times 10^{-27}) \times (3 \times 10^8)^2$$

$$= 1.49 \times 10^{-10} \text{ J}$$

$$= \frac{1.49 \times 10^{-10}}{1.6 \times 10^{-13}} \text{ MeV}$$

or $\quad 1 \text{amu} = 931 \text{ MeV.}$

The energy equivalence of mass of ;

(i) an electron = 0.51 MeV

(ii) a proton = 938.2 MeV

(iii) a neutron = 969.5 MeV

6.4 MASS DEFECT AND BINDING ENERGY

It is observed that the mass of a nucleus is always less than the mass of the constituent nucleons (sum of protons and neutrons). This difference in mass is known as **mass defect.** Let M be the mass of a nucleus of atomic number Z. If m_p and m_n be the masses of proton and neutron respectively, then mass defect,

$$\Delta m = \text{mass of nucleons - mass of nucleus}$$

or $\quad \Delta m = Z m_p + (A - Z) m_n - M \qquad \ldots(2)$

This mass defect will appear in the form of binding energy of nucleus, which is responsible for binding the nucleons into a small nucleus. Thus

$$\text{binding energy, } \Delta E = \Delta mc^2 \qquad \ldots(3)$$

and binding energy per nucleon

$$\Delta e = \frac{\Delta mc^2}{A}.$$

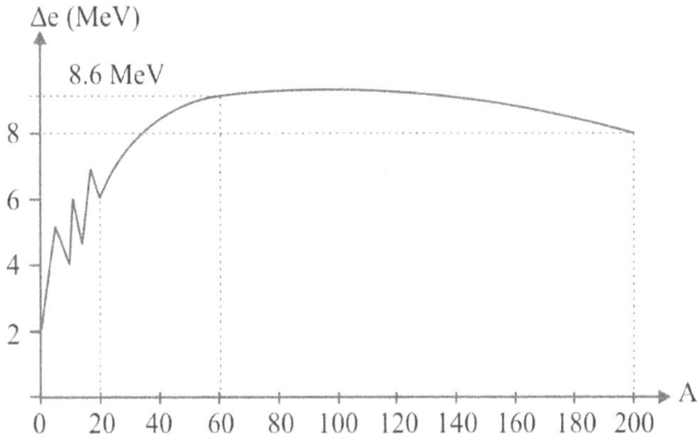

Fig. 6.1

Variation of binding energy per nucleon with mass number A

Figure shows the average binding energy per nucleon Δe against mass number A. It is observed that Δe rises first sharply and reaches a maximum value 8.6 MeV at $A = 60$, and then falls slowly, decreasing to 7.6 MeV for elements of higher mass number $A = 240$, the value of Δe are unusual for $_2He^4$, $_6C^{12}$ and $_8O^{16}$ (see *fig.* 6.1)

Ex. 1 Calculate the energy released when three alpha particles combine to form a $_6C^{12}$ nucleus. The atomic mass of $_2He^4$ is 4.002608 amu.

Sol. The process of formation of carbon nucleus is as ;

$$3\,_2H^4 \longrightarrow {}_6C^{12} + E$$

The mass defect,

Δm = mass of three α particles – mass of carbon nucleus

$$= 3 \times 4.002608 - 12$$

$$= 0.007824 \text{ amu}$$

The energy released $\quad E = 0.007824 \times 931 \text{ MeV}$

$$= 7.28 \text{ MeV.}$$ ***Ans.***

Ex. 2 Calculate the binding energy of an α - particle. Given mass of proton = 1.0073 amu, mass of neutron = 1.0087 amu, mass of α-particle = 4.0015 amu.

Sol. The mass defect in the process of formation of α-particle,

$$\Delta m = (2m_p + 2m_n) - m_\alpha$$
$$= (2\times 1.0073 + 2\times 1.0087) - 4.0015$$
$$= 0.0307 \text{ amu}$$

The binding energy $E = 0.0307 \times 931$
$$= 28.58 \text{ MeV.}$$ ***Ans.***

Ex. 3 The binding energy of $_{17}Cl^{35}$ is 298 MeV. Find its atomic mass. The mass of hydrogen atom $_1H^1$ is 1.008143 amu and that of a neutron is 1.008976 amu. Given 1 amu = 931 MeV.

Sol. There are 17 protons and 18 neutrons in the nucleus of $_{17}Cl^{35}$. Their total mass

$$= 17 \times 1.008143 + 18 \times 1.008986$$
$$= 35.300179 \text{ amu.}$$

Mass defect $\Delta m = \dfrac{E}{c^2} = \dfrac{298}{931} = 0.320085 \text{ amu}$

The atomic mass of $_{17}Cl^{35} = 35.00179 - 0.320085$
$$= 34.980094 \text{ amu.}$$ ***Ans.***

6.5 NUCLEAR STABILITY

The stability of a nucleus can be understood by neutron-proton ratio; $\frac{N}{Z}$. This ratio lies from little less than 1 for lighter nuclei to 1.6 for heavy nuclei. It has been observed that the nuclei with $\frac{N}{Z}$ ratio nearly one are more stable. Heavy nuclei in which neutrons are greater than protons are also stable. Figure shows a plot of N versus Z for the stable nuclei.

The stability of nucleus can be understood on the basis of competition between the attractive nuclear force and the repulsive electrical force. For $\frac{N}{Z}$ less than one. i.e., with larger value of Z, the electrical repulsion between protons becomes greater than attractive force between them and so nucleus no long remains stable.

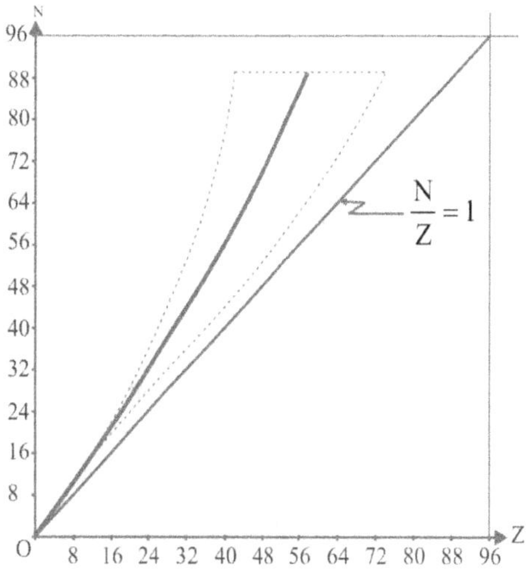

Fig. **6.2**

Heavy nuclei with $\frac{N}{Z}$ ratio greater than one, i.e., nuclei with large number of neutrons have strong attractive forces between them, necessary to keep the nucleus stable.

6.6 RADIOACTIVITY

The spontaneous disintegration of nucleus, is called radioactivity. This phenomenon was discovered by Henry Becquerel in 1896. Some radioactive elements are ; uranium, radium, thorium, polonium etc. **Madam Curie** discovered radium which is 10^6 times more radioactive than uranium. Radioactivity is the nuclear phenomenon which does not depend on any physical or chemical changes.

Nuclear radiations

Rutherford discovered that radioactive elements emit two types of particles : α and β-particles. Each parent nucleus changes into daughter nucleus after emitting α and β particles until it changes into stable nucleus. Later, Villard discovered γ-radiations along with α and β radiations. When radiations from any radioactive element enter into electric or magnetic field, they split into three parts : α-rays, β-rays and γ-rays.

Properties of α, β and γ- rays

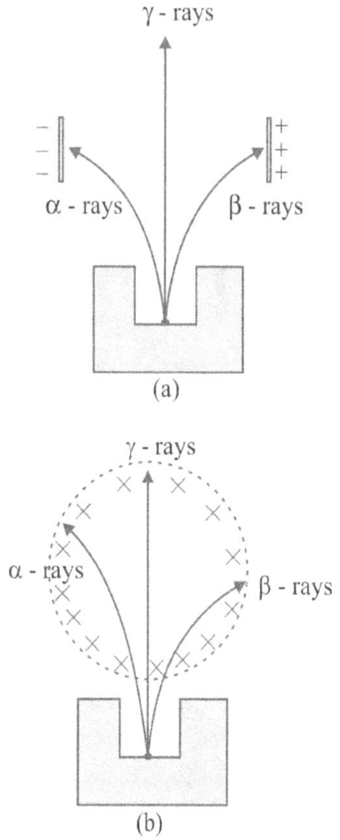

Fig. **6.3. Deflection of α, β and γ-rays in electric and magnetic fields.**

	Feature	α- rays	β -rays	γ - rays
1	Identity	Helium nucleus $_2He^4$	Fast moving electron $_{-1}\beta^0$	Photon
2	Charge	+2e	–e	Zero
3	Mass	$4m_p$ ($m_p = 1.87 \times 10^{-27}$ kg)	$m_e = 9.1 \times 10^{-31}$ kg	rest mass zero
4.	Speed	$\simeq 10^7$ m/s	1 to 99% of speed of light	speed of light 3×10^8 m/s
5	Effect of electric and magnetic field	Deflected	Deflected	Not deflected
6	Ionisation power in comparison to γ -rays	10000	100	1
7	Penetration power	less (can be stopped by paper)	100 times α	10000 times α
8	Equation of decay	$_ZX^A \xrightarrow{-\alpha} {}_{Z-2}Y^A + {}_ZHe^A$	$_ZX^A \longrightarrow {}_{Z+1}Y^A + {}_{-1}e^0 + \bar{\nu}$	$_ZX^A \longrightarrow {}_ZX^A + \gamma$

6.7 Laws of Radioactive Disintegration

Rutherford and Soddy discovered the following laws :

(i) Radioactive disintegration is random. It is the matter of chance to disintegration any of the atom first.

(ii) During disintegration, either α-particle or β- particle is emitted at a time. Both the particles are never emitted simultaneously.

(iii) When an α-particle is emitted, a new atom is formed whose atomic number is decreased by two and mass number by four. Thus for an atom X of atomic number Z and mass number A,

$$_ZX^A \longrightarrow {}_{Z-2}Y^{A-4} + {}_2He^4 + \gamma - \text{rays.}$$

(iv) Similarly, when a β-particle is emitted, a new atom is formed whose atomic number is increased by one but mass number remains the same. Thus for an atom X,

$$_ZX^A \longrightarrow {}_{Z+1}Y^A + {}_{-1}\beta^0 + \gamma - \text{rays.}$$

(v) The rate of decay of atoms is proportional to the number of undecayed atoms present at any instant. Thus if N is the number of atoms at any instant, then rate of disintegration $\left(-\frac{dN}{dt}\right)$ is ;

$$\left(-\frac{dN}{dt}\right) \propto N$$

or

$$\left(-\frac{dN}{dt}\right) = \lambda N \qquad \ldots(i)$$

where λ is a constant and is called **decay or disintegration constant.**

From equation (i), we have

$$\frac{dN}{N} = -\lambda dt$$

If N_0 and N are the number of atoms at $t = 0$ and at any time t, then

$$\int_{N_0}^{N} \frac{dN}{N} = \int_0^t -\lambda dt$$

or $$|\ln N|_{N_0}^{N} = -\lambda t$$

or $$\ln\frac{N}{N_0} = -\lambda t$$

or $$N = N_0 e^{-\lambda t}. \qquad \ldots(1)$$

This shows that the number of atoms of a radioactive substance decreases exponentially with time.

Note:

1. The life time of atoms of radioactive substances are from zero to infinity.
2. If a radioactive substance decays simultaneously α and β-particles with disintegration constants λ_1 and λ_2 respectively, then effective value of λ is :

$$\lambda = \lambda_1 + \lambda_2$$

and $$N = N_0 e^{-(\lambda_1+\lambda_2)t}.$$

3. The β-particle is not present initially in the nucleus but it is produced by the disintegration of neutron into a proton. Thus

$${}_0n^1 = {}_1H^1 + {}_{-1}\beta^0 + \bar{\nu} \text{ (antineutrino)}.$$

When a proton is converted into neutron, a positron is emitted. Thus

$${}_1H^1 \longrightarrow {}_0n^1 + {}_1\beta^0 + \nu \text{ (neutrino)}$$

4. When a nucleus emits a γ- particle, neither the atomic number nor the mass number changes.

6.8 HALF LIFE

The half life period of a radioactive substance is defined as the time in which one-half of the radioactive substance is disintegrated. If N_0 is the initial number of radioactive atoms, then after a half life $t_{1/2}$, the number of atoms present are $\frac{N_0}{2}$. Thus at $t = t_{1/2}$

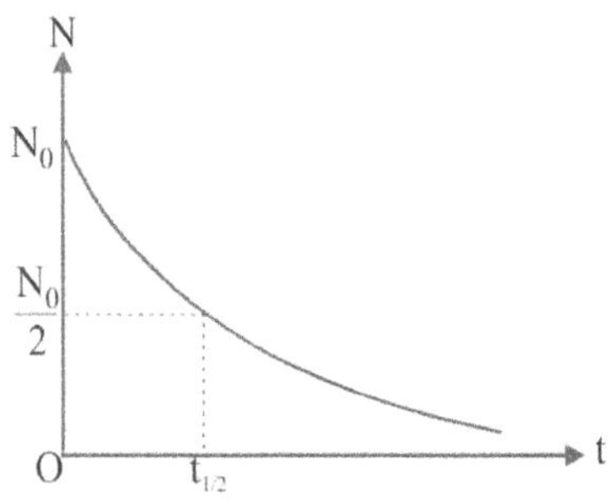

Fig. 6.4

$$N = \frac{N_0}{2}$$

$$= N_0 e^{-\lambda t_{1/2}}$$

or $$e^{\lambda t_{1/2}} = 2$$

∴ $$\lambda t_{1/2} = \ln 2$$

or $$t_{1/2} = \frac{\ln 2}{\lambda} = \frac{0.693}{\lambda}$$

We can form a working formula line as follows :

After $t = t_{1/2}$, $N = \frac{N_0}{2} = N_0(1/2)^1$

$t = 2t_{1/2}$, $N = \frac{N_0}{4} = N_0(1/2)^2$

- -

$t = nt_{1/2}$, $N = N_0(1/2)^n$. ...(1)

Average or mean life

The life time of radioactive atoms ranges from zero to infinity. The average life of all the atoms of a radioactive substance can be defined as :

$$T = \frac{\text{sum of the life times of all the atoms}}{\text{total number of atoms}}$$

If dN are the number of atoms with life time t, then

$$T = \int_0^\infty \frac{(dN)t}{N_0}.$$

As $N = N_0 e^{-\lambda t}$, $\therefore$ $dN = N_0 \lambda e^{-\lambda t} dt$. Thus

$$T = \int_0^\infty \frac{(N_0 \lambda e^{-\lambda t} dt)t}{N_0}$$

$$= \lambda \int_0^\infty e^{-\lambda t} t dt$$

After integrating, we get

$$T = \frac{1}{\lambda}. \qquad \text{...(2)}$$

As $\lambda = \frac{0.693}{t_{1/2}}$

$$\therefore \qquad T = \frac{1}{(0.693/t_{1/2})} = 1.44 t_{1/2}$$

Activity of radioactivity substance

The disintegration of radioactive atoms per unit time is called **activity**. Thus activity A is:

$$A = \left|\frac{dN}{dt}\right|$$

$$= \left|\frac{dN_0 e^{-\lambda t}}{dt}\right|$$

$$= \left|(-\lambda) N_0 e^{-\lambda t}\right|$$

or $$A = \lambda N. \qquad \text{...(4)}$$

If A_0 is the initially activity, so

$$A_0 = \lambda N_0.$$

$$\therefore \qquad \frac{A}{A_0} = \frac{N}{N_0}$$

As $N/N_0 = e^{-\lambda t}$, $\therefore$ $$\frac{A}{A_0} = e^{-\lambda t}.$$

Units of activity

The SI unit of activity is becquerel.

$$1 \text{ becquerel} = 1 \text{ disintegration /s}$$
$$1 \text{ curice} = 3.7 \times 10^{10} \text{ disintegration/s}$$
$$1 \text{ rutherford} = 10^{6} \text{ disintegration /s}$$

6.9 RADIOACTIVE EQUILIBRIUM

Suppose a parent nuclide A with disintegration constant λ_A decay into daughter nuclides B with disintegration constant λ_B which changes into nuclide as follows :

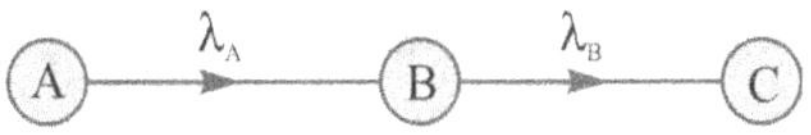

Fig. 6.5

Let at $t = 0$, the number of atoms of *A* are N_0 and that of *B* are zero. After time *t*, there are N_A atoms of *A* and N_B atoms of B.
At any time *t*,
the net rate of formation of *B* = rate of disintegration of *A* – rate of disintegration of *B*

Thus $$\frac{dN_B}{dt} = \lambda_A N_A - \lambda_B N_B$$

As $$N_A = N_0 e^{-\lambda_A t}$$

∴ $$\frac{dN_B}{dt} = \lambda_A N_0 e^{-\lambda_A t} - \lambda_B N_B$$

or $$dN_B + \lambda_B N_B dt = \lambda_A N_0 e^{-\lambda_A t}$$

Multiplying the equation by $e^{\lambda_B t}$, we have

$$e^{\lambda_B t} dN_B + e^{\lambda_B} \lambda_B N_B dt = \lambda_A N_0 e^{(\lambda_B - \lambda_A)t}$$

or $$d(N_B e^{\lambda_B t}) = \lambda_A N_0 e^{(\lambda_B - \lambda_A)t} dt$$

After integration, we get

$$N_B . e^{\lambda_B t} = \left(\frac{\lambda_A}{\lambda_B - \lambda_A}\right) N_0 e^{(\lambda_B - \lambda_A)t} + C \quad \text{... (i)}$$

At $t = 0, N_B = 0$, ∴ $$C = -\left(\frac{\lambda_A}{\lambda_B - \lambda_A}\right) N_0 .$$

Substituting the value of C in equation (i), we get

$$N_B = \left(\frac{\lambda_A N_0}{\lambda_B - \lambda_A}\right)(e^{-\lambda_A t} - e^{-\lambda_B t}) \quad \text{... (1)}$$

Special cases : If parent nuclide *A* is of long life than *B*, then $\lambda_A << \lambda_B$, and from equation (1), we have

$$N_B = \frac{\lambda_A N_B}{\lambda_B}(1 - e^{-\lambda_B t}) \quad \text{... (2)}$$

After time t which is longer than half-life of B but shorter than half life of A, then

$e^{-\lambda_B t} << 1$ and $N_A = N_0$ and so

$$N_B = \frac{\lambda_A N_A}{\lambda_B}$$

or $$\lambda_A N_A = \lambda_B N_B. \qquad ...(3)$$

This is the condition of **radioactive equilibrium** of parent and daughter nuclides.

6.10 NUCLEAR FISSION

Enrico Fermi observed that when neutrons bombard various elements, new radioactive elements are produced. According to him, neutron being uncharged would be a useful projectile; it experiences no repulsive coulomb force when it nears a nucleus. Even thermal neutrons which are slowly moving neutrons in thermal equilibrium with the surrounding matter at room temperature, with a mean kinetic energy of about 0.04 eV, are useful projectiles in nuclear studies.

Otto Frisch suggested that when a heavy nucleus like uranium is bombarded by a thermal neutron, the uranium nucleus absorbed the thermal neutron and splits into roughly two equal parts with the release of large amount of energy. This process is called **fission**. When slow neutrons are bombarded on $_{90}U^{235}$, the fission takes place according to the equation

$$_{92}U^{235} + {_0n^1} \longrightarrow {_{56}Ba^{141}} + {_{36}Kr^{92}} + 3(_0n^1) + 200 \text{ MeV}.$$

It should be remembered that it is not necessary that in each fission of uranium, the two fragments Ba^{141} and Kr^{92} are formed but they may be any stable isotopes into two fragments of about 40% and 60% of the original nucleus with the emission of 2 to 3 neutrons per fission.

In nuclear fission the sum of masses before fission is greater than the sum of masses after fission; the difference in mass may release in the form of energy.

Model for nuclear fission

After the discovery of fission, Niels Bohr and John wheeler proposed a fission model which is based on analogy between a nucleus and a charged liquid drop. Figure shows how the fission process proceeds from this point of view.

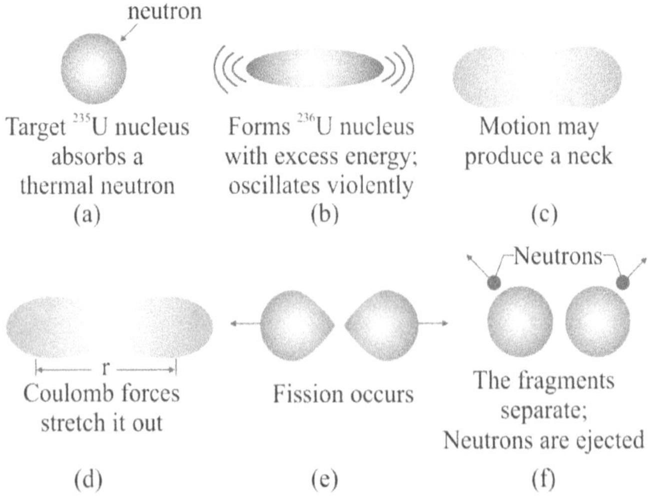

Fig. 6.6

Chain reaction

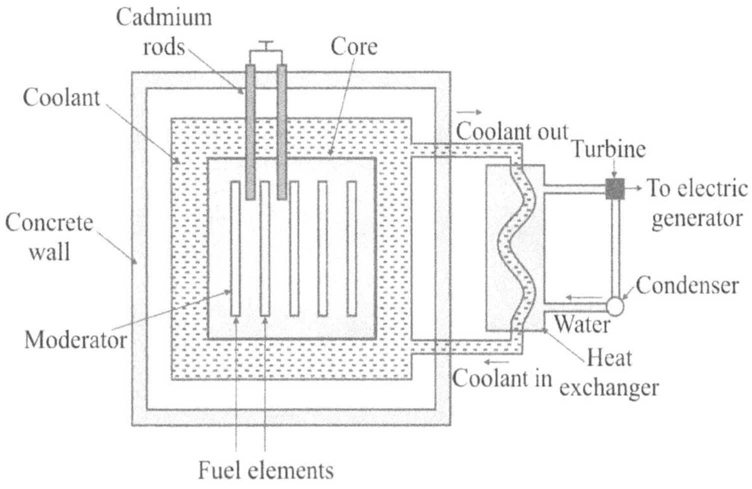

Fig.6.6 **Nuclear reactor.**

In the fission process , if on average more than one neutron are released and are capable of causing further fission, then number of fission taking place at successive stages goes on increasing at a rapid rate. This gives rise to self sustained sequence of fission known as **chain reaction**. The chain reaction takes place only if the size of the fissionable material is greater than a certain size called the **critical size**. There are two types of chain reactions. These are :

1. **Uncontrolled chain reaction**

   If the fission rate goes on increasing, then huge amount of energy continuously released and the system will have the explosive tendency. This forms the principle of **atom bomb**.

2. **Controlled chain reaction**

   In the fission process, if the released neutrons are limited by absorbing them, then fission rate can be maintained. This forms the principle of **nuclear reactor**.

Nuclear reactor

The fission nuclear reactor consists of following parts :

(i) **Fuel :** In nuclear reactor the fuel used is ; U^{235} or Pu^{239} or U^{233}.

(ii) **Moderator :** To slow down the neutrons released in the fission process, a moderator is used. The best choices as moderators are heavy water (D_2O) and graphite.

(iii) **Coolant :** Due to release of enormous energy in the fission process, the reactor shield gets heated . So suitable fluids, known as coolant are used. The usual coolants are water, carbon -dioxide, air etc.

(iv) **Reactor shield :** In the fission process, intense neutrons and gamma radiation are produced which are very harmful for human body. To protect the workers from these radiations, the reactor core is surrounded by concrete wall, which is called the reactor shield.

Ex. 4 **Find the disintegration energy Q for the fission event represented by equation**

$$_{92}U^{235} + {}_0n^1 \longrightarrow {}_{92}U^{236} \longrightarrow {}^{140}_{58}Ce + {}^{94}_{40}Zr + {}_0n^1$$

Some required data are :

Mass of $_{92}U^{235}$ = **235.0439 u**

$_0n^1$ = **1.00867 u**

$^{140}_{58}Ce$ = **139.9054 u**

$^{94}_{40}Zr$ = **93.9063 u**

Find energy released in the process.

Sol. The mass lost in the process

Δm = 235.0439 – (139.9054 + 93.9063 + 1.00867)

= 0.22353 u

The corresponding energy released

$= \Delta mc^2$

$= (0.22353)(3 \times 10^8)^2$ J

= 208 MeV *Ans.*

Note :

One kilogram of $_{92}U^{235}$ on complete fission generates about 3×10^4 MW of power

India's atomic energy programme (from NCERT)

The atomic energy programme in India was lanched around the time of independence under the leadership of Homi J. Bhabha (1909 - 1966). An early historic achievement was the design and construction of the first nuclear reactor in India (named Apsara) which went critical on August 4, 1956. It used enriched uranium as fuel and water as moderator. Following this was another notable landmark: the construction of the Canada India Reactor (CIRUS) in 1960. This 40 MW reactor used natural uranium as fuel and heavy water as moderator. Apsara and Cirus spurred research in a wide range of areas of basic and applied nuclear science. An important milestone in the first two decades of the programme was the indigenous design and construction of the plutonium plant at Trombay, which ushers in the technology of fuel reprocessing (separating useful fissile and fertile nuclear materials from the spent fuel of a reactor) in India. Research reactors that have been subsequently commissioned include EERLINA, PURNIMA (I, II and III), DHRUVA and KAMINI is the country is first large research reactor that uses U-233 as fuel. As the name suggests, the primary objective of a research reactor is not generation of power but to provide a facility for research on different aspects of nuclear science and technology. Research reactors are also an excellent source for production of a variety of isotopes that find application in diverse fields: industry, medicine and agriculture.

The main object of the programme from its inception has been to provide safe and reliable electric power for the country's social and economic progress and to be self-reliant in all aspects of nuclear technology. Exploration of atomic minerals in India undertaken since the early fifties has indicated that India has limited reserves in uranium but fairly abundant reserves in thorium. Accordingly, our country has adopted a three-stage strategy of nuclear power generation. The first stage involves the use of natural uranium as a fuel, with heavy water as moderator. The Plutonium-239 obtained from reprocessing of the discharged fuel from the reactors then serves as a fuel for the second stage — the fast breeder reactors. They are so called because they use fast neutrons for sustaining the chain reaction (hence no moderator needed) and , besides generating power, also breed more fissile species (plutonium) than they consume. The third stage, most significant in the long term, involves using fast breeder reactors to produce fissile Uranium-233 from Thorium-232 and to build power reactors based on them.

India is currently well into the second stage of the programme and considerable work has also been done on the third — the thorium utilisation – stage. The country has mastered the complex technologies of mineral exploration and mining, fuel fabrication, heavy water production, reactor design, construction and operation, fuel reprocessing, etc. Pressurised heavy water Reactors (PHWRs) built at different sites in the country mark the accomplishment of the first stage of the programme. India is now more than self-sufficient in heavy water production. Elaborate safety measures both in the design and operation of reactors, as also adhering to stringent standards of radiological protection are the hallmark of the Indian Atomic Energy Programme.

6.11 NUCLEAR FUSION

When two or more light nuclei combine to form a single larger nucleus, enormous amount of energy is released. This process is called **fusion**. The sum of masses after fusion is less than sum of masses before fusion; the difference in masses is appeared as fusion energy. The fusion of two deuterium nuclei into helium nucleus is expressed as :

$$_1H^2 + {}_1H^2 \longrightarrow {}_2He^4 + 21.6 \text{ MeV}.$$

For fusion to take place, extreme conditions of temperature and pressure are required, which are available only in the interiors of stars. The source of energy of sun and other stars is nuclear fusion. The principle of hydrogen bomb is also based on nuclear fusion.

Note:

For the fusion process, the component nuclei must be brought to within a distance of 10^{-14}m. For this they must be imparted high energies to overcome the repulsive force between nuclei. This is possible at a very high temperature order of 10^7 K.

Proton-proton cycle

The fusion reaction in the sun is a multi-step process in which hydrogen changes into helium. Hydrogen being the fuel and helium the ashes. The proton-proton cycle by which this occurs can be represented as follows :

$$_1H^1 + {_1H^1} \longrightarrow {_1H^2} + {_1\beta^0} + \nu + \text{energy}$$

$$_1H^1 + {_1H^2} \longrightarrow {_2He^3} + \text{energy}$$

$$_2He^3 + {_2He^3} \longrightarrow {_2He^4} + {_1H^1} + {_1H^1} + \text{energy}$$

The net result is :

$$4 {_1H^1} \longrightarrow {_2He^4} + 2 {_1\beta^0} + 2\nu + 26.7\,\text{MeV}$$

Thus four hydrogen atoms combine to form an ^4_2He atom with a release of 26.7 MeV of energy. Another set of reactions has also been suggested for energy of the sun, which is known as carbon cycle.

Ex. 5 **Two protons, each having a kinetic energy *K*, are fired at each other. What must *K* be if the particles are brought to rest by their mutual Coulomb repulsion ? Assume a proton to be a sphere of radius *R* = 1 fm.**

Sol. The initial energy of the protons is $E_i = 2K$. At the closest approach this kinetic energy changes into their potential energy. Thus

$$2K = U$$

$$= \frac{1}{4\pi \epsilon_0} \frac{e^2}{2R}$$

or

$$K = \frac{1}{4}\left(\frac{1}{4\pi \epsilon_0}\right)\frac{e^2}{R}$$

$$= \frac{1}{4} \times 9 \times 10^9 \times \frac{(1.6 \times 10^{-19})^2}{1 \times 10^{-15}}$$

$$= 5.75 \times 10^{-14}\,J$$

$$= 360\,keV$$

$$\simeq 400\,\text{keV}$$

This is approximately the Coulomb barrier between two protons.

The temperature at which protons is a proton gas would have enough energy to overcome the coulomb barrier between them can be calculated as :

$$\frac{3}{2}kT = K_{av}$$

$$T = \frac{2K_{av}}{3k}$$

$$= \frac{2 \times 5.75 \times 10^{-14}}{3 \times 1.38 \times 10^{-23}}$$

$$= 3 \times 10^9\,\text{K}.$$

The temperature of interior of the sun is about 1.5×10^7 K. Therefore, even in the sun if the fusion is to take place, only very high energy protons are involved.

Carbon cycle

$$_6C^{13} + {_1H^1} \longrightarrow {_7N^{13}} + \text{Energy}$$

$$_7N^{13} \longrightarrow {_6C^{13}} + {_1\beta^0} + \nu + \text{Energy}$$

$$_6C^{13} + {_1H^1} \longrightarrow {_7N^{14}} + \text{Energy}$$

$$_7N^{14} + {_1H^1} \longrightarrow {_8O^{15}} + \text{Energy}$$

$$_8O^{15} \longrightarrow {_7N^{15}} + {_1\beta^0} + \text{Energy}$$

$$_7N^{15} + {_1H^1} \longrightarrow {_6C^{12}} + {_2He^4} + \text{Energy}$$

The net result is :

$$4 {_1H^1} + {_6C^{12}} \longrightarrow {_2He^4} + 2 {_1\beta^0} + 2\nu + 24.8\,\text{MeV}$$

It may be noted that in the process carbon is not destroyed but acts only as a catalyst.

Note:

The proton-proton cycle occurs at relatively lower temperature as compared to carbon cycle which requires very high temperature. At the interior of sun where temperature is order of 10^7 K, the proton-proton cycle has more changes of occurrence.

6.12 PAIR PRODUCTION AND PAIR ANNIHILATION

When an energetic γ-photon falls on a heavy nucleus, it is absorbed by the nucleus and a pair of electron and positron is produced. This phenomenon is called **pair production** and can be represented by the following equation :

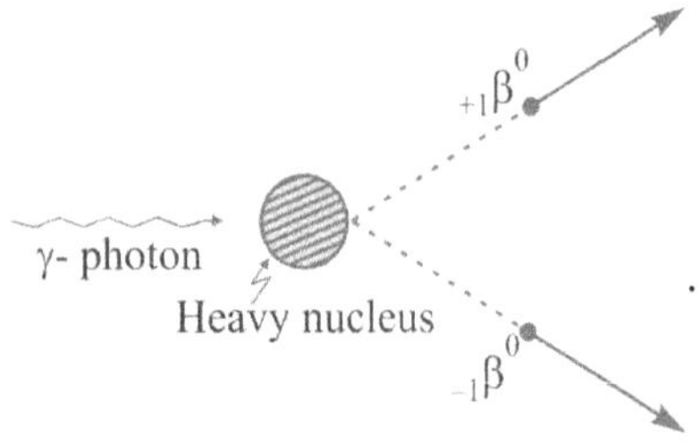

Fig. 6.8

$$\underset{(\gamma-\text{photon})}{h\nu} = \underset{(\text{Positron})}{_{+1}\beta^0} + \underset{(\text{electron})}{_{-1}\beta^0}$$

The rest mass energy of each of electron or positron is :

$$E_0 = m_0c^2$$
$$= (9.1\times10^{-31})\times(3\times10^8)^2$$
$$= 8.2\times10^{-14}\,\text{J}$$
$$\simeq 0.51\,\text{MeV.}$$

Hence for pair production, the minimum energy of γ-photon must be $2\times0.51 = 1.02$ MeV. If the energy of γ-photon is less than this, there may be Compton's effect. If energy of γ-photon is greater than E_0, then extra energy will become kinetic energy of the particles. If E is the energy of γ-photon, then kinetic energy of each particle will be,

$$K_{\text{electron}} = K_{\text{positron}} = \frac{E-2E_0}{2}.$$

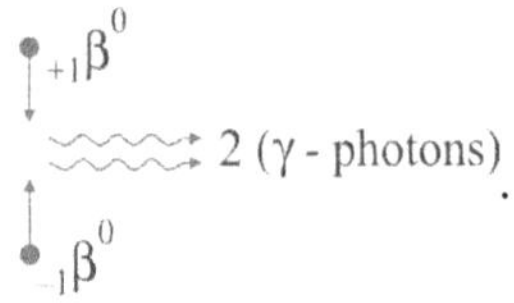

Fig. 6.9

The inverse process of pair production is called **pair annihilation**. According to it when electron and a positron come close to each other, they annihilate each other and produces two γ-photons. Thus

$$\underset{(\text{Positron})}{_{+1}\beta^0} + \underset{(\text{electron})}{_{-1}\beta^0} = \underset{(\gamma-\text{photon})}{2hf}$$

Ex. 6 A radioactive nucleus undergoes a series of decay according to the scheme

$$A \xrightarrow{\alpha} A_1 \xrightarrow{\beta^-} A_2 \xrightarrow{\alpha} A_3 \xrightarrow{\gamma} A_4.$$

If the mass number and atomic number of A are 180 and 72 respectively, what are these numbers for A_4?

Sol. The process can be expressed as :

$$_{72}A^{180} \xrightarrow{\alpha} {_{70}A_1^{176}} \xrightarrow{\beta^-} {_{71}A_2^{176}} \xrightarrow{\alpha} {_{69}A_3^{172}} \xrightarrow{\gamma} {_{69}A_4^{172}}$$

Thus, the mass number of A_4 is 172.

Ex. 7 Some amount of a radioactive substance (half life = 10 days) is spread inside a room and consequently the level of radiation becomes 50 times permissible level for normal occupancy of the room. After how many days the room will be safe for occupation?

Sol. If N_0 is the initial level of radiation and N is the permissible level, then

$$N = \frac{N_0}{50}.$$

We know that

$$N = N_0e^{-\lambda t} \quad \dots (1)$$

where

$$\lambda = \frac{0.693}{t_{1/2}}$$
$$= \frac{0.693}{10} = 0.0693\ \text{day}^{-1}$$

From equation (1), we have

$$\frac{N_0}{50} = N_0\,e^{-0.0693t}$$

or $t = 56.45$ days. ***Ans.***

Ex. 8 In an ore containing uranium, the ratio of U^{238} to Pb^{206} is 3. Calculate the age of the ore, assuming that all the lead present in the ore is the final stable product of U^{238}. Take the half life of U^{238} to be 4.5×10^9 years.

Sol. If M_0 is the initial mass of the uranium, then after time t, its mass can be calculated as :

$$M_u + M_{Pb} = M_0$$

and

$$\frac{M_u}{M_{Pb}} = 3$$

After solving, $M_u = \frac{3}{4}M_0.$

According to $N = N_0e^{-\lambda t}$, we can write $M = M_0e^{-\lambda t}$.

Thus

$$\frac{3}{4}M_0 = M_0e^{-\lambda t} \quad \dots (i)$$

also

$$\lambda = \frac{0.693}{t_{1/2}}$$

$$= \frac{0.693}{4.5\times10^9}\, year^{-1} \quad \ldots \text{(ii)}$$

On solving equations (i) & (ii), we get

$t = 1.867 \times 10^9$ years. *Ans.*

Ex. 9 **There is a stream of neutrons with a kinetic energy of 0.0327 eV. If the half life of neutrons is 700 seconds, what fraction of neutrons will decay before they travel a distance of 10 m? Given mass of neutron = 1.675×10^{-27} kg.**

Sol. If v is the velocity of electron, then

$$\frac{1}{2}mv^2 = 0.0327\text{ eV}$$

or $$\frac{1}{2}\times1.675\times10^{-27}v^2 = 0.0327 \times 1.6 \times 10^{-19}$$

$\therefore$ $$v = 2.5 \times 10^3 \text{ m/s.}$$

The time taken by neutron to travel a distance of 10 m,

$$t = \frac{10}{2.5\times10^3} = 4 \times 10^{-3}\text{s}$$

Given $t_{1/2}$ =700 s

$\therefore$ $$\lambda = \frac{0.693}{t_{1/2}} = \frac{0.693}{700} = 0.00099$$

Using $N = N_0e^{-\lambda t}$, we have

$$\frac{N}{N_0} = e^{-0.00099\times4\times10^{-3}}$$

$$= 0.999952$$

The fraction of neutron decayed

$$= 1 - 0.999952$$

$$= 0.000048.$$ *Ans.*

Ex. 10 **At a given instant there are 25% undecayed radioactive nuclei in a sample. After 10 second the number of undecayed nuclei reduces to 12.5 %. Calculate (i) mean life of the nuclei and (ii) the time in which the number of undecayed nuclei will further reduce to 6.25 % of the reduced number.**

Sol.

The half life of the sample = time taken to become 25% to 12.5 %

= 10 s

(i) Mean life $T = 1.44\, t_{1/2}$

$= 1.44 \times 10 = 14.4$ s

(ii) If N_0 are the total number of the reduced sample, then

$$\frac{N}{N_0} = \left(\frac{1}{2}\right)^n$$

or $$\frac{6.25}{100} = \left(\frac{1}{2}\right)^n$$

$\therefore$ $$n = 4$$

The time taken $t = nt_{1/2} = 4 \times 10$

$= 40$ s. *Ans.*

Ex. 11 **A rock is 1.5×10^9 years old. The rock contains ^{238}U which disintegrates to form ^{206}U. Assume that there was no ^{206}Pb in the rock initially and it is the only stable product formed by the decay. Calculate the ratio of number of nuclei of ^{238}U to that of ^{206}Pb in the rock. Half life of ^{238}U is 4.5×10^9 years.** $(2^{1/3} = 1.259)$.

Sol. The number of half lives are $= \frac{1.5\times10^9}{4.5\times10^9} = \frac{1}{3}$.

If N_0 was the initial and N_U is the present number of atoms of U-atoms, then

$$\frac{N_U}{N_0} = \left(\frac{1}{2}\right)^{1/3}$$

The number of Pb-atoms $N_{Pb} = N_0 - N_U$

$\therefore$ $$\text{Required ratio} = \frac{N_U}{N_{Pb}} = \frac{N_U}{N_0 - N_U}$$

$$= \frac{1}{\frac{N_0}{N_U} - 1} = \frac{1}{2^{1/3} - 1}$$

$$= \frac{1}{1.259 - 1} = 3.86.$$ *Ans.*

Ex. 12 **The half lives of a radioactive substance are 1620 and 405 years for α-emission and β-emission respectively. Find out the time during which three forth of a sample will decay if it is decaying both by α-emission and β-emission simultaneously.**

Sol. If λ_α and λ_β be the decay constants for α and β-emission respectively, then effective decay constant, $\lambda = \lambda_\alpha + \lambda_\beta$.

As $$\lambda = \frac{0.693}{t_{1/2}},$$

$$\frac{0.693}{t_e} = \frac{0.693}{t_1} + \frac{0.693}{t_2}$$

or $$t_e = \frac{t_1t_2}{t_1 + t_2} = \frac{1620 \times 405}{1620 + 405}$$

$$= 324 \text{ years.}$$

When $\frac{3}{4}$ of the sample has been decayed, the undecayed sample will be $\frac{1}{4}$. Thus

$$\frac{N}{N_0} = \frac{1}{4}$$

If t is the required time, then

$$\frac{N}{N_0} = e^{-\lambda t}$$

or $$\frac{1}{4} = e^{-\lambda t}$$

or $$\ell n(1/4) = -\lambda t$$

$\therefore$ $$t = -\frac{1}{\lambda}\ell n(1/4)$$

As $\frac{1}{\lambda} = t_e$,

$\therefore$ $$t = t_e \ell n 4$$

$$= 324 \ln 4 = 449.94 \text{ years.} \quad \textbf{\textit{Ans.}}$$

Ex. 13 **Count rate-meter is used to measured the activity of a given sample. At one instant the meter shows 4750 counts per minute. Five minute later it shows 2700 counts per minute. Find (a) the decay constant, and (b) the half life of the sample. ($\log_{10}$ 1.760 = 0.2455).**

Sol. (a) If A_0 is the initial activity, and A at any time t, then

$$A = A_0 e^{-\lambda t}$$

$$2700 = 4750\, e^{-\lambda \times 5}$$

$$e^{-5\lambda} = 1.76$$

or $$-5\lambda = \ell n\, 1.76$$

$\therefore$ $$\lambda = \frac{-\ell n 1.76}{5} = 0.113 \text{ minute}^{-1} \textbf{\textit{Ans.}}$$

(b) Half life $$t_{1/2} = \frac{0.693}{\lambda}$$

$$= \frac{0.693}{0.113} = 6.1 \text{ minute.} \quad \textbf{\textit{Ans.}}$$

Ex. 14 **In the chemical analysis of a rock, the mass ratio of two radioactive isotopes is found to be 100 : 1. The mean lives of two isotopes are 4 × 10⁹ years and 2 × 10⁹ years respectively. If it is assumed that at the time of formation the atoms of both the two isotopes were in equal proportion, calculate the age of the rock. Ratio of the atomic weights of two isotopes is 1.02 : 1.**

Sol. Given half lives of the isotopes; $t_1 = 4 \times 10^9$ years and $t_2 = 2 \times 10^9$ years. The ratio of their atoms at $t = 0$,

$$\frac{N_1}{N_2} = 1.$$

If m is the mass of the substance and M is its atomic mass, then number of atoms

$$n = \frac{m}{M}.$$

Thus at any time t,

$$\frac{N_1}{N_2} = \frac{m_1/M_1}{m_2/M_2} = \frac{m_1}{m_2} \times \frac{M_2}{M_1}$$

$$= \frac{100}{1} \times \frac{1}{1.02} = \frac{100}{1.02} \quad \text{... (i)}$$

We know that $$N = N_0 e^{-\lambda t}$$

$\therefore$ $$\left[\frac{N_1}{N_2}\right]_t = \frac{N_{01}\, e^{-\lambda_1 t}}{N_{02}\, e^{-\lambda_2 t}}$$

$$= 1 \times e^{-(\lambda_1 - \lambda_2)t}$$

or $$\ell n\left(\frac{N_1}{N_2}\right) = (\lambda_2 - \lambda_1)t$$

$\therefore$ $$t = \frac{\ell n\left(\frac{N_1}{N_2}\right)}{(\lambda_2 - \lambda_1)}$$

$$= \frac{\ell n\left(\frac{N_1}{N_2}\right)}{\frac{0.693}{t_1} - \frac{0.693}{t_2}}$$

On substituting the values of $\frac{N_1}{N_2}$, t_1 and t_2, we get

$$t = 18.34 \times 10^9 \text{ years} \quad \textbf{\textit{Ans.}}$$

Ex. 15 **A radioactive element decays by β-emission. A detector records n-beta particles in 2 seconds and in next 2 seconds it records 0.75 n beta particles. Find mean life correct to nearest whole number. Given ℓn 2 = 0.6931, ℓn 3 = 1.0986.**

Sol. Suppose N_0 be the initial number of particles. The number of undecayed particles is $N = N_0 e^{-\lambda t}$. Thus number of particles decayed in time t

$$n = N_0 - N = N_0 - N_0 e^{-\lambda t}$$

$$= N_0(1 - e^{-\lambda t}). \quad \text{... (i)}$$

If now N is the number of particles after t seconds over initial, then undecayed particles.

$$0.75\, n = N - N'$$

$$= N_0 e^{-\lambda t} - N e^{-\lambda t} = N_0 e^{-\lambda t} - (N_0 e^{-\lambda t})e^{-\lambda t}$$

$$= N_0 e^{-\lambda t}(1 - e^{-\lambda t}) \quad \text{... (ii)}$$

Dividing equation (ii) by (i), we get

$$0.75 = e^{-\lambda t}$$

or $$\ell n 0.75 = -\lambda t$$

$$\therefore \quad \lambda = -\frac{\ell n 0.75}{t} = -\frac{\ell n 4/3}{2}$$

$$= 0.1438 \text{ s}^{-1}$$

Mean life $\quad T = \frac{1}{\lambda} = \frac{1}{0.1438} = 7\text{s}$ ***Ans.***

Ex. 16 **A sample of uranium is a mixture of three isotopes $_{92}U^{234}$, $_{92}U^{235}$ and $_{92}U^{238}$ present in the ratio 0.006%, 0.71% and 99.284% respectively. The half lives of these isotopes are 2.5 × 10^5 years, 7.1 × 10^8 years and 4.5 × 10^9 years respectively. Calculate the contribution to activity (in %) of each isotope in the sample.**

Sol. Let m is the total mass of the uranium mixture. The masses of the isotopes $_{92}U^{234}$, $_{92}U^{235}$ and $_{92}U^{238}$ in the mixture are

$$m_1 = \frac{0.006}{100}m,$$

$$m_2 = \frac{0.71}{100}m,$$

and $$m_3 = \frac{99.284}{100}m.$$

If N_A is the Avogadro number, then number of atoms of three isotopes are ;

$$N_1 = \frac{m_1 N_A}{M_1},$$

$$N_2 = \frac{m_2 N_A}{M_2},$$

and $$N_3 = \frac{m_3 N_A}{M_3}$$

Activity of radioactive sample $A = \lambda N$.

As $\lambda = \frac{0.693}{t_{1/2}}$, $\therefore \quad A = \frac{0.693}{t_{1/2}}N.$

If t_1, t_2 and t_3 be the half lives, then

$$A_1 : A_2 : A_3 = \frac{N_1}{t_1} : \frac{N_2}{t_2} : \frac{N_3}{t_3}$$

or $$A_1 : A_2 : A_3 = \frac{m_1}{M_1 t_1} : \frac{m_2}{M_2 t_2} : \frac{m_3}{M_3 t_3}$$

$$= \frac{0.006}{234(2.5\times10^5)} : \frac{0.71}{235(7.5\times10^8)} : \frac{99.284}{238(4.5\times10^9)}$$

$$= 51.41\,\% : 2.13\,\% : 46.46\,\%.$$ ***Ans.***

Ex. 17 **Nuclei of radioactive element A are being produced at a constant rate α. The element has a decay constant λ. At time t = 0, there are N_0 nuclei of the element.**

(a) Calculate the number N of nuclei of A at time t.

(b) If $\alpha = 2N_0\lambda$, calculate the number of nuclei of A after one half life of A and also the limiting value of N at $t \to \infty$.

Sol.

(a) The rate of formation of nuclei is = α.

The rate of decay of nuclei = λN.

Thus net rate of formation of nuclei, $\frac{dN}{dt} = (\alpha - \lambda N)$

$$\therefore \quad \frac{dN}{(\alpha - \lambda N)} = dt.$$

On integrating, we have

$$\int_{N_0}^{N} \frac{dN}{(\alpha - \lambda N)} = \int_0^t dt$$

or $$\left|\frac{\ell n(\alpha - \lambda N)}{-\lambda}\right|_{N_0}^{N} = t$$

$$\ell n(\alpha - \lambda N) - \ell n(\alpha - \lambda N_0) = -\lambda t$$

or $$\ell n\left(\frac{\alpha - \lambda N}{\alpha - \lambda N_0}\right) = -\lambda t$$

or $$\frac{\alpha - \lambda N}{\alpha - \lambda N_0} = e^{-\lambda t}$$

$$\therefore \quad N = \frac{\alpha}{\lambda}(1 - e^{-\lambda t}) + N_0 e^{-\lambda t}$$ ***Ans.***

(b) For $\alpha = 2N_0\lambda$ and $t = t_{1/2}$, we have

$$N = \frac{\alpha}{\lambda}(1 - e^{-\lambda \times t_{1/2}}) + N_0 e^{-\lambda t_{1/2}}$$

As $t_{1/2} = 0.693/\lambda$,

$$\therefore \quad N = \frac{2N_0\lambda}{\lambda}(1 - e^{-0.693}) + N_0 e^{-0.693}$$

$$= N_0(2 - e^{-0.693}) = N_0(2 - 0.5)$$

$$= 1.5\,N_0.$$

For $t \to \infty$, $$N = \frac{\alpha}{\lambda}(1 - e^{-\infty}) + N_0 e^{-\infty}$$

$$= \frac{\alpha}{\lambda}.$$ ***Ans.***

Ex. 18 **Polonium ($_{84}Po^{210}$) emits $_2\alpha^4$ - particles and is converted into lead ($_{82}Pb^{206}$). This reaction is used for producing electric power in a space mission. Po^{210} has half life of 138.6 days. Assuming an efficiency of 10% of the thermoelectric machine, how much Po^{210} is required to produce 1.2 × 10^7 J of electrical energy per day at the end of 693 days ? Also find the initial activity of the material. (Given masses of the nuclei Po^{210} = 209.982.64 amu, Pb^{206} = 205.97440 amu, α^4 = 4.00260 amu, 1 amu = 931 MeV and Avogadro number = 6 × 10^{23} / mol).**

Sol. The nuclear reaction is according to ;

$$_{84}Po^{210} \longrightarrow {}_{82}Pb^{206} + {}_2He^4.$$

Mass defect per reaction

Δm = 209.98264 – (205.97440 + 4.00260)
= 0.00564 amu.

The energy produced per reaction

$$\Delta E = \Delta mc^2$$
$$= (0.00564) \times (1.66 \times 10^{-27}) \times (3 \times 10^8)^2$$
$$= 8.4 \times 10^{-13} \text{ J.}$$

Total amount of energy required = 1.2×10^7 J.

Given, efficiency of machine is 10%, so

$$\text{Input energy} = \frac{1.2\times10^7}{0.10} = 1.2 \times 10^8 \text{ J}$$

Thus number of reactions required per day

$$n = \frac{1.2\times10^8}{8.4\times10^{-13}} = \frac{1}{7}\times10^{21}$$

If N is the number of polonium atoms required, then

$$\left(-\frac{dN}{dt}\right) = \lambda N \text{ or } n = \lambda N$$

or

$$N = \frac{n}{\lambda} = n\times\frac{t_{1/2}}{0.693}$$
$$= \frac{1}{7}\times10^{21}\times\frac{138.6}{0.693}$$
$$= \frac{200}{7}\times10^{21}$$

Mass of each polonium atom=210 amu.

∴ Mass of polonium required after 693 days

$$m = \frac{200}{7}\times10^{21}\times210 \text{ amu}$$
$$= \frac{200}{7}\times10^{21}\times210\times1.66\times10^{-24} g$$
$$= 1g$$

If m_0 is the initial mass of the polonium atoms, then

$$\frac{m}{m_0} = \left(\frac{1}{2}\right)^{t/t_{1/2}}$$
$$= \left(\frac{1}{2}\right)^{\frac{693}{138.8}} = \left(\frac{1}{2}\right)^5$$

∴ $m_0 = 32$ g.

Initial number of polonium atoms required

$$N = N_0\left(\frac{1}{2}\right)^5$$

or

$$N_0 = 32N = 32\times\frac{200}{7}\times10^{21}$$
$$= \frac{64}{7}\times10^{23}.$$

Initial activity of polonium

$$A_0 = \lambda N_0$$
$$= \frac{0.693}{t_{1/2}}N_0$$
$$= \frac{0.693}{138.6}\times\frac{64}{7}\times10^{23}$$
$$= 4.57\times10^{21} \text{ days}^{-1}.$$ ***Ans.***

Ex. 19 **A nuclear explosion is designed to deliver 1 MW of heat energy, how many fission events must be required in a second to attain this power level. If this explosion is designed with a nuclear fuel consisting of uranium –235 to run a reactor at this power level for one year, then calculate the amount of fuel needed. You can assume that the amount of energy released per fission event is 200 MeV.**

Sol. If P is the power delivered, then energy delivered in one second

$$E = P\times t = P\times1 = P$$

If e is the energy released per fission, then number of fission per second

$$= \frac{E}{e} = \frac{P}{e}$$
$$= \frac{10^6}{200\times1.6\times10^{-13}} = 3.125\times10^{16}$$

Total energy required in 1 year

$$E = Pt = P \times 365 \times 24 \times 3600$$
$$= 3.15 \times 10^{13} \text{ J}$$

∴ Number of fission required

$$= \frac{3.15\times10^{13}}{200\times1.6\times10^{-13}} = 9.85\times10^{23}$$

$$\text{Mass of uranium required} = 9.85 \times 10^{23} \times \frac{235}{6.02\times10^{23}}$$
$$= 384.5 \text{ g.}$$ ***Ans.***

Review of Formulae & Important Points

1. Nucleus consists of protons (Rutherford) and neutrons (Chadwick). They held together by strong nuclear forces; which is same between p-p, n-n and p-n. Protons and neutrons combinedly called as nucleons.
2. Mass number A = no. of protons (Z) + no. of neutrons (N)
3. Radius of nucleus $R = R_0 A^{1/3}$
   * Size of nucleus is of the order of 10^{-15} m.
   * Size of atom is of the order of 10^{-10} m.
   * Nuclear density is of the order of 10^{17} kg/ m^3
4. Mass defects (ΔM) = Mass of nucleons (M) – Mass of nucleus (A).
5. 1 amu = 1.66×10^{-27} kg
   = 931 MeV.
6. Packing fraction $f = \dfrac{\text{Mass defect}}{\text{Mass number}} = \dfrac{M-A}{A}$
7. B. E = Δmc^2
8. Binding energy per nucleon $\simeq 8 MeV$
9. **Nuclear fission :** Breaking of heavy nucleus into two comparable nuclei.

   $${}_{92}U^{235} + {}_0n^1 \rightarrow {}_{56}Ba^{141} + {}_{36}Kr^{92} + 3({}_0n^1) + 200\,\text{MeV}$$

   * Atom bomb, nuclear reactor are based on fission.
10. **Nuclear fusion :** combining of lighter nuclei into heavier one at high temperature and pressure, is called nuclear fusion.
    * Hydrogen bomb, solar energy are based on fusion.
11. **Nuclear reactor : (i)** Fuel : U^{235}, U^{238} or Pu^{239}.
    (ii) Moderator : Graphite, heavy water.
    (iii) Controller : Cadmium or boron-steel.
    (iv) Coolant : Water, air and CO_2.
    (v) Reactor shield : Thick concrete walls.
12. **Pair annihilation :** ${}_{-1}e^0 + {}_{+1}e^0 \rightarrow$ γ- photons

Pair production : Rest mass energy of ${}_{-1}e^0$ or ${}_{+1}e^0$ is order of 0.51 MeV.

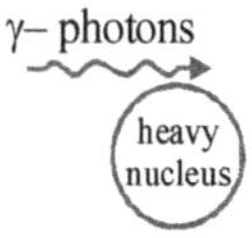

$\Rightarrow {}_{-1}e^0 + {}_{1}e^0$ electron & positorn

13. **Radioactivity**

(i) Spontaneous disintegration of nucleus is called radioactivity.

* It is matter of chance, for any atom to disintegrate first. The life time of radioactive atoms will therefore be from zero to infinite.

(ii) $N = N_0 e^{-\lambda t}$.

Also $N = N_0 (1/2)^n$, $n = \dfrac{t}{t_{1/2}}$.

(iii) Mean life $T = (1/\lambda) = 1.44 t_{1/2}$.

* β-particle is not initially present in nucleus, but is produced due to disintegration of neutron

$${}_0n^1 \rightarrow {}_1H^1 + {}_{-1}\beta^0 + \nu^-.$$

(iv) **Activity (A) :** $A = \left|\dfrac{dN}{dt}\right| = \lambda N$

Also $A = A_0 e^{-\lambda t}$.

S.I. unit of radioactivity is becquerel.

1 becquerel = 1 disintegration /s.

* 1 rutherford = 10^6 disintegration /s.

* 1 curie = 3.7×10^{10} disintegration /s.

☆☆☆

Modern Physics

MCQ Type 1

Exercise 6.1

LEVEL - 1

1. The mass number of a nucleus is
   (a) always less than its atomic number
   (b) always more than its atomic number
   (c) always equal to its atomic number
   (d) sometimes more than and sometimes equal to its atomic number

2. The average binding energy per nucleon in the nucleus of an atom is approximately
   (a) 8 eV (b) 8 KeV
   (c) 8 MeV (d) 8 J

3. Which of the following statement(s) is / (are) correct
   (a) the rest mass of a stable nucleus is less than the sum of rest masses of its separated nucleons
   (b) the rest mass of a stable nucleus is greater than the sum of the rest masses of its separated nucleons.
   (c) in nuclear fusion, energy is released by fusing two nuclei of medium mass (approximately 100 a.m.u.)
   (d) in nuclear fission, energy is released by fragmentation of a very heavy nucleus

4. Order of magnitude of density of uranium nucleus is $\left(m_p = 1.67\times10^{-27}\ kg\right)$
   (a) $10^{20}\ kg/m^3$ (b) $10^{17}\ kg/m^3$
   (c) $10^{14}\ kg/m^3$ (d) $10^{11}\ kg/m^3$

5. If the binding energy per nucleon in Li^7 and He^4 nuclei are respectively 5.60 MeV and 7.06 MeV, then energy of reaction $Li^7 + p \rightarrow 2\ {}_2He^4$ is
   (a) 19.6 MeV (b) 2.4 MeV
   (c) 8.4 MeV (d) 17.3 MeV

6. A nucleus ruptures into two nuclear parts which have their velocity ratio equal to 2 : 1. What will be the ratio of their nuclear size (nuclear radius)
   (a) $2^{1/3}:1$ (b) $1:2^{1/3}$
   (c) $3^{1/2}:1$ (d) $1:3^{1/2}$

7. Two nucleons are at a separation of 1×10^{-15}m. The net force between them is F_1, if both are neutrons, F_2 if both are protons and F_3 if one is a proton and other is a neutron. In such a case
   (a) $F_2 > F_1 > F_3$ (b) $F_1 = F_2 = F_3$
   (c) $F_1 = F_2 > F_3$ (d) $F_1 = F_3 > F_2$

8. The binding energy of deuteron ${}_1^2H$ is 1.112 MeV per nucleon and an α–particle He^4 has a binding energy of 7.047 MeV per nucleon. Then in the fusion reaction ${}_1^2H + {}_1^2H \rightarrow {}_2^4He + Q$, the energy Q released is
   (a) 1 MeV (b) 11.9 MeV
   (c) 23.8 MeV (d) 931 MeV

9. In nuclear reaction ${}_2He^4 + {}_zX^A \rightarrow {}_{z+2}Y^{A+3} + A$, A denotes
   (a) electron (b) positron
   (c) proton (d) neutron

10. If the binding energy per nucleon in Li^7 and He^4 nuclei are respectively 5.60 MeV and 7.06 MeV then energy of reaction $Li^7 + p \rightarrow 2\ {}_2He^4$ is
    (a) 19.6 MeV (b) 2.4 MeV
    (c) 8.4 MeV (d) 17.3 MeV

11. The binding energy per nucleon of deuterium and helium atom is 1.1 MeV and 7.0 MeV. If two deuterium nuclei fuse to form helium atom, the energy released is
    (a) 19.2 Mev (b) 23.6 MeV
    (c) 26.9 MeV (d) 13.9 MeV

12. Which of the following fusion reactions will not result in the net release of energy
    (a) ${}^6Li + {}^6Li$ (b) ${}^4He + {}^4He$
    (c) ${}^{12}C + {}^{12}C$ (d) ${}^{35}Cl + {}^{35}Cl$

13. Fusion reaction takes place at high temperature because
    (a) atoms are ionised at high temperature
    (b) molecules break-up at high temperature
    (c) nuclei break-up at high temperature
    (d) kinetic energy is high enough to overcome repulsion between nuclei

14. In nuclear reactions, we have the conservation of
    (a) mass only
    (b) energy only
    (c) momentum only
    (d) mass, energy and momentum

Answer Key	1	(d)	2	(c)	3	(a)	4	(b)	5	(d)	6	(b)	7	(b)
Sol. from page 330	8	(c)	9	(d)	10	(d)	11	(b)	12	(d)	13	(d)	14	(d)

15. A reaction between a proton and $_8O^{18}$ that produces $_9F^{18}$ must also liberate

(a) $_0n^1$ (b) $_1e^0$

(c) $_1n^0$ (d) $_0e^1$

16. The energy released in a typical nuclear fusion reaction is approximately

(a) 25 MeV (b) 200 MeV

(c) 800 MeV (d) 1050 MeV

17. Heavy water is used as moderator in a nuclear reactor. The function of the moderator is

(a) to control the energy released in the reactor

(b) to absorb neutrons and stop chain reaction

(c) to cool the reactor faster

(d) to slow down the neutrons to thermal energies

18. Half life of radioactive element depends upon

(a) amount of element present

(b) temperature

(c) pressure

(d) nature of element

19. During a negative beta decay

(a) an atomic electron is ejected

(b) an electron which is already present within the nucleus is ejected

(c) a neutron in the nucleus decays emitting an electron

(d) a part of the binding energy is converted into electron

20. Some radioactive nucleus may emit

(a) only one α, β or γ at a time

(b) all the three α, β and γ one after another

(c) all the three α, β and γ simultaneously

(d) only α and β simultaneously

21. Beta rays emitted by a radioactive material are

(a) electromagnetic radiation

(b) the electrons orbiting around the nucleus

(c) charged particles emitted by nucleus

(d) neutral particles

22. In the given reaction

$$_ZX^A \to {}_{Z+1}Y^A \to {}_{Z-1}K^{A-4} \to {}_{Z-1}K^{A-4}$$

Radioactive radiations are emitted in the sequence

(a) α, β, γ (b) β, α, γ

(c) γ, α, β (d) β, γ, α

23. If T is the half life of a radioactive material, then the fraction that would remain after a time $\frac{T}{2}$ is

(a) $\frac{1}{2}$ (b) $\frac{3}{4}$

(c) $\frac{1}{\sqrt{2}}$ (d) $\frac{\sqrt{2}-1}{\sqrt{2}}$

24. The half life period of radium is 1600 years. The fraction of a sample of radium that would remain after 6400 years is

(a) $\frac{1}{4}$ (b) $\frac{1}{2}$

(c) $\frac{1}{8}$ (d) $\frac{1}{16}$

25. Three α–particles and β–particle decaying takes place in series from an isotope $_{88}Ra^{238}$. Finally the isotope obtained will be

(a) $_{84}X^{220}$ (b) $_{86}X^{222}$

(c) $_{83}X^{226}$ (d) $_{83}X^{215}$

26. What is the respective number of α and β particles emitted in the following radioactive decay

$$_{90}X^{200} \to {}_{80}Y^{168}$$

(a) 6 and 8 (b) 8 and 8

(c) 6 and 6 (d) 8 and 6

27. A radioactive reaction is $_{92}U^{238} \to {}_{82}Pb^{206}$. How many α and β particles are emitted

(a) $10\,\alpha$, 6β (b) 4 protons, 8 neutrons

(c) 6 electrons, 8 protons (d) 6β, 8α

28. After two hours, one-sixteenth of the starting amount of a certain radioactive isotope remained undecayed. The half life of the isotope is

(a) 15 minutes (b) 30 minutes

(c) 45 minutes (d) 4 hour

Answer Key	15	(a)	16	(a)	17	(d)	18	(d)	19	(c)	20	(a)	21	(c)
Sol. from page 330	22	(b)	23	(c)	24	(d)	25	(c)	26	(d)	27	(d)	28	(b)

29. Which of the following is a correct statement

(a) beta rays are same as cathode rays

(b) gamma rays are high energy neutrons

(c) alpha particles are singly ionized helium atoms

(d) protons and neutrons have exactly the same mass

30. ^{22}Ne nucleus after absorbing energy decays into two α – particles and an unknown nucleus. The unknown nucleus is

(a) nitrogen (b) carbon

(c) boron (d) oxygen

31. An element A decays into element C by a two step process :

$A \to B + {}_2He^4; \quad B \to C + 2e^-$. Then

(a) A and C are isotopes (b) A and C are isobars

(c) A and B are isotopes (d) A and B are isobars

32. Consider the following two statements

A. Energy spectrum of α-particles emitted in radioactive decay is discrete

B. Energy spectrum of β-particles emitted in radioactive decay is continuous

(a) only A is correct

(b) only B is correct

(c) a is correct but B is wrong

(d) both A and B are correct

33. Which of the following processes represents a gamma-decay

(a) $^AX_Z + \gamma \to {}^AX_{Z-1} + a + b$

(b) $^AX_Z + {}^1n_0 \to {}^{A-3}X_{Z-2} + c$

(c) $^AX_Z \to {}^AX_Z + f$

(d) $^AX_Z + e_{-1} \to {}^AX_{Z-1} + \gamma$

34. A nucleus with Z = 92 emits the following in a sequence :
$\alpha, \beta^-, \beta^-, \alpha, \alpha, \alpha, \alpha, \alpha, \beta^-, \beta^-, \alpha, \beta^+, \beta^+, \alpha$. The Z of the resulting nucleus is

(a) 74 (b) 76

(c) 78 (d) 82

35. Radioactive nuclei that are injected into a patient collect at certain sites within its body, undergoing radioactive decay and emitting electromagnetic radiation. These radiations can then be recorded by a detector. This procedure provides an important diagnostic tool called

(a) gamma camera (b) CAT scan

(c) radiotracer technique (d) gamma ray spectroscopy

36. Starting with a sample of pure ^{66}Cu, $\frac{7}{8}$ of it decays into Zn in 15 min. The corresponding half-life is

(a) 5 min (b) $7\frac{1}{2}$ min

(c) 10 min (d) 15 min

37. From a newly formed radioactive substance (half life 2 hours), the intensity of radiation is 64 times the permissible safe level. The minimum time after which work can be done safely from this source is

(a) 6 hours (b) 12 hours

(c) 24 hours (d) 128 hours

38. Binding energy per nucleon plot against the mass number for stable nuclei is shown in the figure. Which curve is correct

(a) A

(b) B

(c) C

(d) D

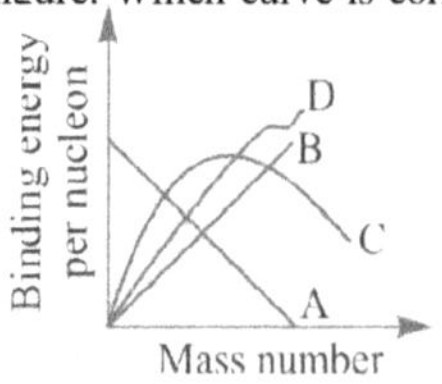

39. A radioactive sample consists of two distinct species having equal number of atoms initially. The mean life time of one species is τ and that of the other is 5τ. The decay products in both cases are stable. A plot is made of the total number of radioactive nuclei as a function of time. Which of the following figures best represents the form of this plot

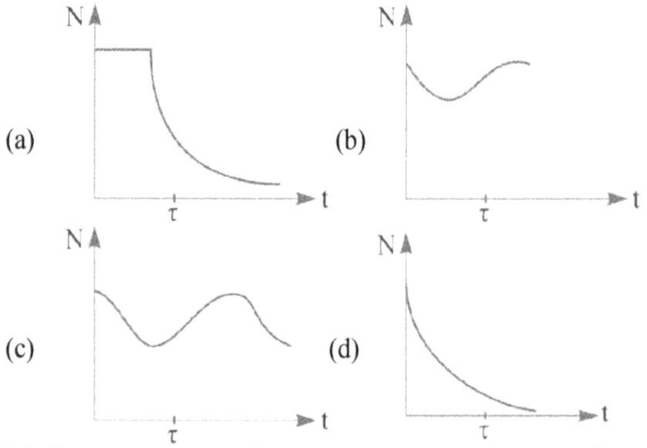

40. Binding energy per nucleon versus mass number curve for nuclei is shown in the figure. W, X, Y and Z are four nuclei indicated on the curve. The process that would release energy is

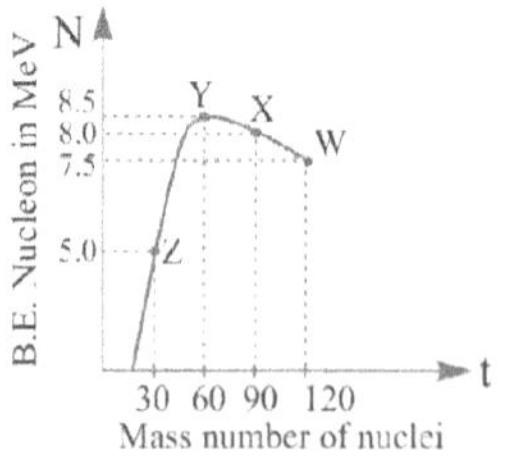

(a) $Y \to 2Z$ (b) $W \to X + Z$

(c) $W \to 2Y$ (d) $X \to Y + Z$

Answer Key	**29**	(a)	**30**	(b)	**31**	(a)	**32**	(b)	**33**	(c)	**34**	(c)
Sol. from page 330	**35**	(c)	**36**	(a)	**37**	(b)	**38**	(c)	**39**	(d)	**40**	(c)

41. In the nuclear fusion reaction ${}_1^2H + {}_1^3H \rightarrow {}_2^4He + x$, given that the repulsive potential energy between the two nuclei is -7.7×10^{-14} *J*, the temperature at which the gases must be heated to initiate the reaction is nearly : [Boltzmann's constant $k = 1.38 \times 10^{-23}$ *J/K*]

(a) 10^9 *K* (b) 10^7 *K*
(c) 10^5 *K* (d) 10^3 *K*

42. The energy spectrum of β - particles [number N (E) as a function of β- energy E] emitted from a radioactive source is :

(a)
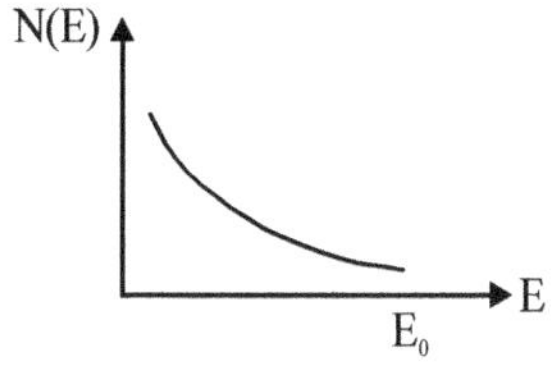

(b)
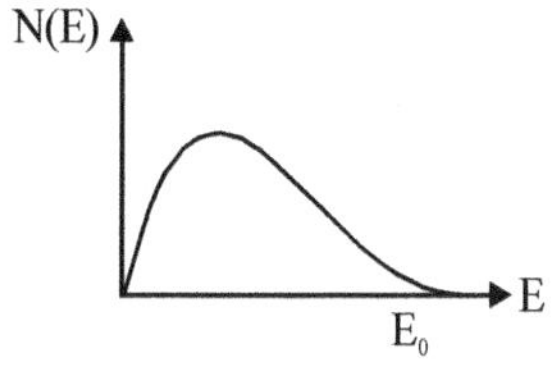

(c)
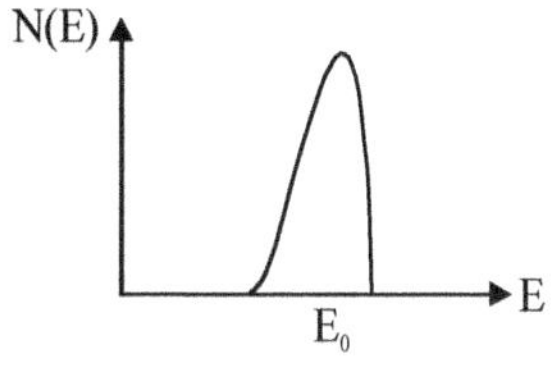

(d)
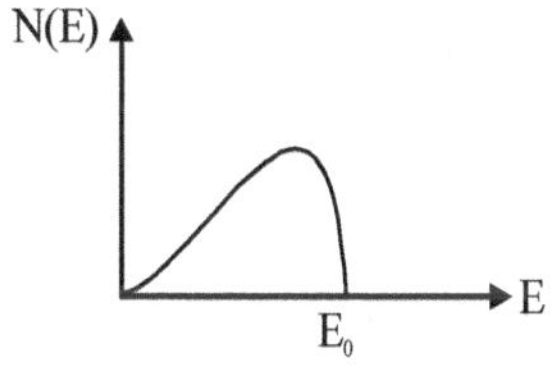

43. If radius of the ${}_{13}^{27}Al$ nucleus is estimated to be 3.6 *fermi* then radius of ${}_{52}^{125}Te$ nucleus be nearly

(a) 4 *fermi* (b) 5 *fermi*
(c) 6 *fermi* (d) 8 *fermi*

44. Consider a radioactive material of half-life 1.0 minute. If one of the nuclei decays now, the next one will decay

(a) after 1 minute
(b) after $\frac{1}{\log_e 2}$ minute
(c) after $\frac{1}{N}$ minute, where N is the number of nuclei present at that moment
(d) after any time

45. If the decay or disintegration constant of a radioactive substance is λ, then its half life and mean life are respectively

(a) $\frac{1}{\lambda}$ and $\frac{\log_e 2}{\lambda}$ (b) $\frac{\log_e 2}{\lambda}$ and $\frac{1}{\lambda}$
(c) $\lambda \log_e 2$ and $\frac{1}{\lambda}$ (d) $\frac{\lambda}{\log_e 2}$ and $\frac{1}{\lambda}$

46. Which one of the following nuclear reactions is a source of energy in the sun

(a) ${}_4^9Be + {}_2^4He \rightarrow {}_2^{16}C + {}_0^{-1}n$
(b) ${}_2^3He + {}_2^3He \rightarrow {}_2^4He + {}_1^1H + {}_1^1H$
(c) ${}_{56}^{144}Ba + {}_{56}^{92}Kr \rightarrow {}_{92}^{235}U + {}_0^{-1}n$
(d) ${}_{26}^{56}Fe + {}_{48}^{112}Ca \rightarrow {}_{74}^{167}W + {}_0^{-1}n$

47. The half-life of ${}^{215}At$ is 100μs. The time taken for the radioactivity of a sample of ${}^{215}At$ to decay to $1/16^{th}$ of its initial value is

(a) 400 μs (b) 6.3 μs
(c) 40 μs (d) 300 μs

Answer Key								
Sol. from page 330	41	(a)	42	(b)	43	(c)	44	(d)
	45	(b)	46	(b)	47	(a)		

LEVEL -2

1. When $_{92}U^{235}$ undergoes fission, 0.1% of its original mass is changed into energy. How much energy is released if 1 kg of $_{92}U^{235}$ undergoes fission
(a) 9×10^{10} J (b) 9×10^{11} J
(c) 9×10^{12} J (d) 9×10^{13} J

2. If the energy released in the fission of one nucleus is 200 MeV. Then the number of nuclei required per second in a power plant of 16 kW will be
(a) 0.5×10^{14} (b) 0.5×10^{12}
(c) 5×10^{12} (d) 5×10^{14}

3. M_p denotes the mass of a proton and M_n that of a neutron. A given nucleus, of binding energy *B*, contains *Z* protons and *N* neutrons. The mass M(N, Z) of the nucleus is given by (c is the velocity of light)
(a) $M(N, Z) = NM_n + ZM_p - Bc^2$
(b) $M(N, Z) = NM_n + ZM_p + Bc^2$
(c) $M(N, Z) = NM_n + ZM_p - B/c^2$
(d) $M(N, Z) = NM_n + ZM_p + B/c^2$

4. A sample contains 16 gm of a radioactive material, the half life of which is two days. After 32 days, the amount of radioactive material left in the sample is
(a) less than 1 mg (b) $\frac{1}{4}$gm
(c) $\frac{1}{2}$gm (d) 1 gm

5. N atoms of a radioactive element emit n alpha particles per second. The half life of the element is
(a) $\frac{n}{N}$sec (b) $\frac{N}{n}$ sec.
(c) $\frac{0.693\,N}{n}$ sec (d) $\frac{0.693}{N}$ sec.

6. The counting rate observed from a radioactive source at $t = 0$ second was 1600 counts per second and at $t = 8$ seconds it was 100 counts per second. The counting rate observed, as counts per second at $t = 6$ seconds, will be
(a) 400 (b) 300
(c) 200 (d) 150

7. A star initially has 10^{40} deuterons. It produces energy via the processes
$$_1H^2 + {_1H^2} \rightarrow {_1H^3} + p$$
$$_1H^2 + {_1H^3} \rightarrow {_2He^4} + n$$
The masses of the nuclei are as follows :
$$M(H^2) = 2.014 \text{ amu}; M(p) = 1.007 \text{ amu};$$
$$M(n) = 1.008 \text{ amu}; M(He^4) = 4.001 \text{ amu}$$
If the average power radiated by the star is 10^{16}W, the deuteron supply of the star is exhausted in a time of the order of
(a) 10^6 sec (b) 10^8 sec
(c) 10^{12} sec (d) 10^{16} sec

8. A nucleus with mass number 220 initially at rest emits an α-particle. If the Q value of the reaction is 5.5 MeV, calculate the kinetic energy of the α-particle
(a) 4.4 MeV (b) 5.4 MeV
(c) 5.6 MeV (d) 6.5 MeV

9. A radioactive material decays by simultaneous emission of two particles with respective half lives 1620 and 810 years. The time (in years) after which one-fourth of the material remains is
(a) 1080 (b) 2430
(c) 3240 (d) 4860

10. Two radioactive materials X_1 and X_2 have decay constants 10λ and λ respectively. If initially they have the same number of nuclei, then the ratio of the number of nuclei of X_1 to that of X_2 will be 1/e after a time
(a) $1/(10\lambda)$ (b) $1/(11\lambda)$
(c) $11/(10\lambda)$ (d) $1/(9\lambda)$

11. After 280 days, the activity of a radioactive sample is 6000 dps. The activity reduces to 3000 dps after another14 days. The initial activity of the sample in dps is
(a) 6000 (b) 9000
(c) 3000 (d) 24000

12. A radioactive sample of U^{238} decay to Pb through a process for which half life is 4.5×10^9 years. The ratio of number of nuclei of Pb to U^{238} after a time of 1.5×10^9 years (given $2^{1/3} = 1.26$)
(a) 0.12 (b) 0.26
(c) 1.2 (d) 0.37

13. The given below is a plot of binding energy per nucleon E_b, against the nuclear mass M; A, B, C, D, E, E correspond to different nuclei. Consider four reactions :

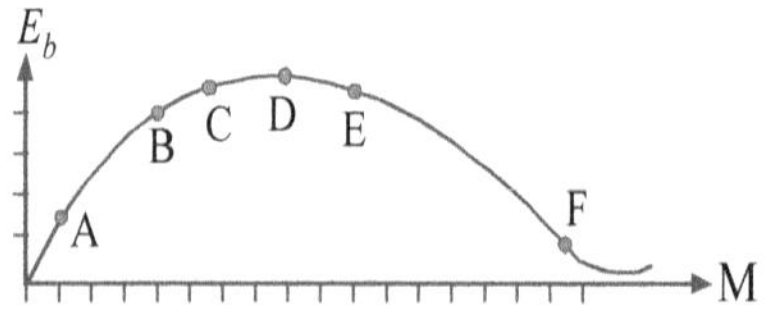

(i) $A + B \rightarrow C + \varepsilon$ (ii) $C \rightarrow A + B + \varepsilon$
(iii) $D + E \rightarrow F + \varepsilon$ (iv) $F \rightarrow D + E + \varepsilon$
where E is the energy released ? In which reactions is *E* positive :
(a) (i) and (iv) (b) (i) and (iii)
(c) (ii) and (iv) (d) (ii) and (iii)

Answer Key	1	(d)	2	(d)	3	(c)	4	(a)	5	(c)	6	(c)	7	(c)
Sol. from page 331	8	(b)	9	(a)	10	(d)	11	(d)	12	(b)	13	(d)		

Modern Physics

MCQ Type 2

Exercise 6.2

1. From the following equations, pick out the possible nuclear reaction

(a) ${}_6C^{13} + {}_1H^1 \rightarrow {}_6C^{14} + 4.3\ MeV$

(b) ${}_6C^{12} + {}_1H^1 \rightarrow {}_7N^{13} + 2\ MeV$

(c) ${}_7N^{14} + {}_1H^1 \rightarrow {}_8O^{15} + 7.3\ MeV$

(d) ${}_{92}U^{235} + {}_0n^1 \rightarrow {}_{54}X^{140} + {}_{38}Si^{94} + 2{}_0n^1 + \gamma + 200MeV$

2. A generic fission event is

$^{235}U + n \rightarrow x + y + 2n.$

Which of the following pairs cannot represent x and y ?

(a) ^{141}Xe and ^{93}Sr (b) ^{139}Cs and ^{95}Rb

(c) ^{156}Nd and ^{79}Ge (d) ^{121}In and ^{113}Ru

3. After 1α and 2β emissions

(a) mass number reduces by 3

(b) mass number reduces by 4

(c) mass number reduces by 6

(d) atomic number remains unchanged

4. Let m_p be the mass of a proton, m_n the mass of a neutron, M_1 the mass of a ${}^{20}_{10}Ne$ nucleus and M_2 the mass of a ${}^{40}_{20}Ca$ nucleus. Then

(a) $M_2 = 2\ M_1$ (b) $M_2 > 2M_1$

(c) $M_2 < 2\ M_1$ (d) $M_1 < 10\ (m_n + m_p)$

Answer Key	1	(b, c)	2	(c, d)	3	(b, d)	4	(c, d)
Sol. from page 332								

Modern Physics

Statement Questions

Exercise 6.3

Read the two statements carefully to mark the correct option out of the options given below. Select the right choice.

(a) If both the statements are true and the ***Statement* - 2** is the correct explanation of ***Statement* - 1**.

(b) If both the statements are true but ***Statement* - 2** is not the correct explanation of the ***Statement* - 1**.

(c) If ***Statement* - 1** true but ***Statement* - 2** is false.

(d) If ***Statement* - 1** is false but ***Statement* - 2** is true.

1. ***Statement* -1 :** The binding energy per nucleon, for nuclei with atomic number A > 100, decreases with A.
***Statement* - 2 :** The nuclear forces are weak for heavier nuclei.

2. ***Statement* - 1 :** Density of all the nuclei is same.
***Statement* - 2 :** Radius of nucleus is directly proportional to the cube root of mass number.

3. ***Statement* - 1 :** Neutrons penetrate mater more readily as compared to protons.
***Statement* -2 :** Neutrons are slightly more massive than protons.

4. ***Statement* - 1 :** Radioactive nuclei emit β^{-1} particles.
***Statement* - 2 :** Electrons exist inside the nucleus.

5. ***Statement* - 1 :** ${}_ZX^A$ undergoes 2α, 2β- particles and 2γ-rays, the daughter product is ${}_{Z-2}Y^{A-8}$.
***Statement* - 2 :** In α- decay the mass number decreases by 4 and atomic number decreases by 2. In β-decay the mass number remains unchanged, but atomic number increases by 1.

6. ***Statement* - 1 :** The heavier nuclei tend to have larger N/Z ratio because neutron does not exert electric force.
***Statement* - 2 :** Coulomb forces have longer range compared to the nuclear force.

7. ***Statement* - 1 :** A free neutron decays to a proton but a free proton does not decay to a neutron. This is because neutron is an uncharged particle and proton is a charged particle.
***Statement* - 2 :** Neutron has larger rest mass than the proton.

8. ***Statement* - 1 :** The mass number of a nucleus is always less than its atomic number.
***Statement* - 2 :** Mass number of a nucleus may be equal to its atomic number.

9. ***Statement* - 1 :** It is not possible to use ^{35}Cl as the fuel for fusion energy.
***Statement* - 2 :** The binding energy of ^{35}Cl is to small.

10. ***Statement* - 1 :** Cobalt-60 is useful in cancer therapy.
***Statement* - 2 :** Cobalt -60 is source of γ- radiations capable of killing cancerous cells.

Answer Key	1	(a)	2	(a)	3	(b)	4	(c)	5	(a)
Sol. from page 332	6	(a)	7	(d)	8	(d)	9	(c)	10	(a)

Modern Physics

Passage & Matrix

Exercise 6.4

PASSAGES

Passage for (Qs. 1 - 3) :

^{238}U decays to ^{206}Pb with a half life of 4.47×10^9y. Although the decay occurs in many individual steps, the first step has by far the longest half-life; therefore one can often consider the decay to go directly to lead. That is,

$$^{238}U \longrightarrow {}^{206}Pb + \text{various decay products}$$

A rock is found to contain 4.20 mg of ^{238}U and 2.135 mg of ^{206}Pb. Assume that the rock contained no lead at formation, so all the lead now present arose from the decay of uranium.

1. The number of atoms of ^{238}U the rock now contains
   (a) 1.06×10^{19} (b) 2.2×10^{18}
   (c) 2.12×10^{19} (d) none of these
2. The number of atoms of ^{238}U did the rock contain at formation
   (a) 1.06×10^{19} (b) 1.69×10^{19}
   (c) 0.624×10^{19} (d) none of these
3. The age of the rock is
   (a) 2.50×10^9 y (b) 2.80×10^9 y
   (c) 2.98×10^9 y (d) 4.80×10^9 y

Passage for (Qs. 4 - 6) :

Scientists are working hard to develop nuclear fusion reactor. Nuclei of heavy hydrogen, ^2_1H, known as deuteron and denoted by D can be thought of as a candidate for fusion reactor. The D-D reaction is $^2_1H + ^2_1H \rightarrow ^3_2He + n + \text{energy}$. In the core of fusion reactor, a gas of heavy hydrogen is fully ionized into deuteron nuclei and electrons. This collection of ^2_1H nuclei and electrons is known as plasma. The nuclei move randomly in the reactor core and occasionally come close enough for nuclear fusion to take place. Usually, the temperatures in the reactor core are too high and no material wall can be used to confine the plasma. Special techniques are used which confine the plasma for a time t_0 before the particles fly away from the core. If n is the density (number/ volume) of deuterons, the product nt_0 is called Lawson number. In one of the criteria, a reactor is termed successful if Lawson number is greater than 5×10^{14} s/cm^3.

It may be helpful to use the following : Boltzman constant $k = 8.6 \times 10^{-5}$ eV/K ; $\frac{e^2}{4\pi\varepsilon_0} = 1.44 \times 10^{-9}$ eVm.

4. In the core of nuclear fusion reactor, the gas becomes plasma because of
   (a) strong nuclear force acting between the deuterons
   (b) Coulomb force acting between the deuterons
   (c) Coulomb force acting between deuterons-electrons pairs
   (d) the high temperature maintained inside the reactor core
5. Assume that two deuteron nuclei in the core of fusion reactor at temperature T are moving towards each other, each with kinetic energy 1.5kT, when the separation between them is large enough to neglect Coulomb potential energy. Also neglect any interaction from other particles in the core. The minimum temperature T required for them to reach a separation of 4×10^{-15} m in the range.
   (a) $1.0 \times 10^9 K < T < 2.0 \times 10^9 K$
   (b) $2.0 \times 10^9 K < T < 3.0 \times 10^9 K$
   (c) $3.0 \times 10^9 K < T < 4.0 \times 10^9 K$
   (d) $4.0 \times 10^9 K < T < 5.0 \times 10^9 K$
6. Results of calculations for four different designs of a fusion reactor using D-D reaction are given below. Which of these is most promising based on Lawson criterion?
   (a) deuteron density = 2.0×10^{12} cm^{-3}, confinement time = 5.0×10^{-3}s
   (b) deuteron density = 8.0×10^{14} cm^{-3}, confinement time = 9.0×10^{-1} s
   (c) deuteron density = 4.0×10^{23} cm^{-3}, confinement time = 1.0×10^{-11}s
   (d) deuteron density = 1.0×10^{24} cm^{-3}, confinement time = 4.0×10^{-12} s

Passage for (Qs. 7 - 9) :

In a mixture of He – He$^+$ gas (He$^+$ is singly ionised He atom), H atoms and He$^+$ ions are excited to their respective first excited states. Subsequently, H atoms transfer their total excitation energy to He$^+$ ions are excited to their respective first excited staes. Subsequently, H atoms transfer their total excitation energy to He$^+$ ions (by collisions). Assume that the Bohr model of atoms is exactly valid.

7. The quantum number n of the state finally populated in He$^+$ ions is
   (a) 2 (b) 3
   (c) 4 (d) 5
8. The wavelength of light emitted in the visible region by He$^+$ ions after collisions with H atoms is
   (a) 6.5×10^{-7}m (b) 5.6×10^{-7}m
   (c) 4.8×10^{-7}m (d) 4.0×10^{-7}m
9. The ratio of the kinetic energy of the $n = 2$ electron for the H atom to that of He$^+$ ion is
   (a) $\frac{1}{4}$ (b) $\frac{1}{2}$
   (c) 1 (d) 2

Answer Key	1	(a)	2	(b)	3	(c)	4	(d)	5	(a)
Sol. from page 332	6	(b)	7	(c)	8	(c)	9	(a)		

Passage for (Qs. 10 & 11)

The β-decay process, discovered around 1900, is basically the decay of a neutron (n). In the laboratory, a proton (p) and an electron (e^-) are observed as the decay products of the neutron, therefore, considering the decay of a neutron as a tro-body decay process, it was predicted theoretically that the kinetic energy of the electron should be a constant. But experimentally, It was observed that the electron kinetic energy has a continuous spectrum. Considering a three-body decay process, i.e., $n \rightarrow p + e^- + \overline{v}_e$, around 1930, Pauli explained the observed electron energy spectrum. Assuming the anti-neutron ($\overline{v}_e$) to be massless and processing negligible energy, and neutron to be at rest, momentum and energy conservation principles are applied. From this calculation, the maximum kinetic energy of the electron is 0.8×10^6 eV. The kinetic energy carried by the proton is only the recoil energy.

10. What is the maximum energy of the anti-neutrino?

(a) Zero

(b) Much less than 0.8×10^6eV

(c) Nearly 0.8×10^6eV

(d) Much larger than 0.8×10^6eV

11. If the anti-neutrino had a mass of 3eV/c^2 (where c is the speed of light) instead of zero mass, what should be the range of the kinetic energy, K, of the electron?

(a) $0 \le K \le 0.8 \times 10^3 eV$

(b) $3\, 3.0eV \le K \le 0.8 \times 10^6 eV$

(c) $3.0eV \le K < 0.8 \times 10^6 eV$

(d) $0 \le K < 0.8 \times 10^6 eV$

MATRIX MATCHING

12. Given below are certain matching type questions, where two columns (each having 4 items) are given. Immediately after the columns the matching grid is given, where each item of **Column I** has to be matched with the items of **Column II**, by encircling the correct match(es). Note that an item of **Column I** can match with more than one item of **Column II**. All the items of **Column II** must be matched.

Match the following :

Column – I	**Column – II**
A. Nuclear fusion	(p) Converts some matter into energy
B. Nuclear fission	(q) Generally possible for nuclei with low atomic number
C. β-decay	(r) Generally possible for nuclei with higher atomic number
D. Exothermic nuclear reaction	(s) Essentially proceeds by weak nuclear forces

13. Match the following

Column – I	**Column – II**
A. Hydrogen bomb	(p) Fission
B. Atom bomb	(q) Fusion
C. Stellar energy	(r) Critical mass
D. Nuclear reactor	(s) Controlled chain reaction
	(t) High temperature and pressure

14. Match the following

Column – I	**Column – II**
A. Isobars	(p) Saturation
B. Isotones	(q) Same mass number
C. Isotopes	(r) Different chemical properties
D. Nuclear force	(s) Same atomic number
	(t) Non-central

Answer Key	10	(c)	11	(d)	12	A-(p, q);B-(p, r);C-(p,s) ; D - (p, q, r)
Sol. from page 332	13	A - (q,s) ; B-(p, t) ; C - (q,s) ; D - (r)			14	A-(r) ; B-(r,s,t) ; C-(s) ; D-(p, q, r)

Modern Physics

Subjective Integer Type

Exercise 6.5

Solution from page 333

1. x- alpha and y-beta particles are emitted when uranium $({}_{92}U^{238})$ decays to lead ${}_{82}Pb^{206}$. The value of x and y are ?

Ans. 8 and 6.

2. The table that follows shows some measurements of the decay rate of a sample of ^{128}I, a radionuclide often used medically as a tracer to measure the rate at which iodine is absorbed by the thyroid gland.

Time (min)	A (counts/s)	Time (min)	A (counts/s)
4	392.2	132	10.9
36	161.4	164	4.56
68	65.5	196	1.86
100	26.8	218	1.00

Find the disintegration constant λ and the half life $t_{1/2}$ for this radionuclide.

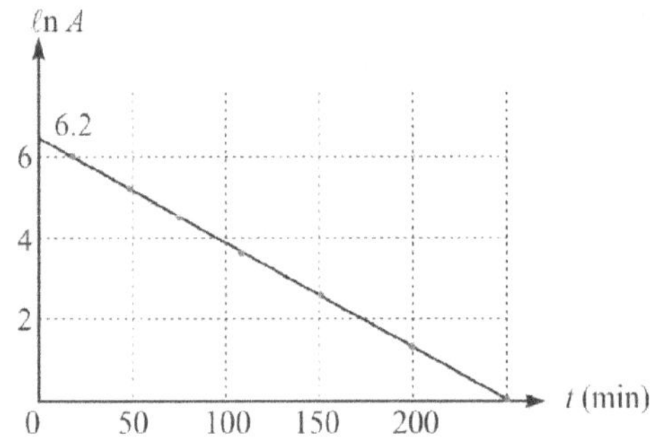

Ans. $t_{1/2} \simeq 25\,\text{min}$

3. It is proposed to use the nuclear fusion reaction

$$_1H^2 +_1 H^2 \rightarrow 2He^4$$

in a nuclear reactor of 200 MW rating. If the energy from the above reaction is used with 25% efficiency in the reactor, how many gram of deuterium fuel will be needed per day. (The masses of ${}_1H^2$ and ${}_2He^4$ are 2.0141 amu and 4.0026 amu respectively).

Ans. 120 g.

Modern Physics

Subjective

Exercise 6.6

Solution from page 334

1. A radioactive element decays by β emission. A detector records n beta particles in 2 second and in next 2 seconds it records 0.75 n beta particles. Find mean life corrected to nearest whole number. Given $\ell n2 = 0.6931$ and $\ell n3 = 1.0986$.

Ans. 6.9 seconds

2. The half life of radon is 3.8 days. After how many days will only one twentieth of radon sample be left over?

Ans. 16.45 days.

3. A ^7Li target is bombarded with a proton beam current of 10^{-4} A for 1 hour to produce ^7Be of activity 1.8×10^8 disintegrations per second. Assuming that one ^7Be radioactive nucleus is produced by bombarding 1000 protons, determine its half life.

Ans. 8.63×10^6 s.

4. A nucleus at rest undergoes a decay emitting an α-particle of de-Broglie wavelength $\lambda = 5.76 \times 10^{-15} m$. If the mass of the daughter nucleus is 223.610 amu and that of the α-particle is 4.002 amu, determine the total kinetic energy in the final state. Hence obtain the mass of the parent nucleus in amu. (1 amu = 931.470 MeV/c^2]

Ans. 6.25 MeV, 227.62 amu.

5. The count rate from a radioactive sample falls from 4.0×10^6 per second to 1×10^6 per second in 20 hour. What will be the count rate, 100 hour after the beginning?

Ans. 3.91×10^3 per second.

6. The disintegration rate of a certain radioactive sample at any instant is 4750 disintegrations per minute. Five minutes later the rate becomes 2700 disintegrations per minute. Calculate half life of the sample.

Ans. 6.1 minute.

7. In an ore containing uranium, the ratio of U^{238} to Pb^{206} nuclei is 3. Calculate the age of the ore, assuming that all the lead present in the ore in the final stable product of U^{238}. Take the half life of U^{238} to be 4.5×10^9 year.

Ans. 1.868×10^9 year.

8. In a nuclear reactor U^{235} undergoes fission liberating 200 MeV of energy. The reactor has 10% efficiency and produces 1000 MW power. If the reactor is to function for 10 year, find the total mass of the uranium required .

Ans. 3.8×10^4 kg.

9. A radioactive nucleus X decays to a nucleus Y with a decay constant $\lambda_x = 0.1 s^{-1}$. Y further decays to a stable nucleus Z with a decay constant $\lambda_y = \frac{1}{30} s^{-1}$. Initially, there are only X nuclei and their number is $N_0 = 10^{20}$. Set up the rate equations for the populations of X, Y and Z. The population of the Y nucleus as a function of time is given by

$N_y(t) = \{N_0\lambda_x/(\lambda_x - \lambda_y)\}\ [e^{(-\lambda yt)} - e^{(-\lambda xt)}]$. Find the time at which N_y is maximum and determine the populations X and Z at that instant.

Ans. $t = 16.48$ s, $N_x(t) = 1.924 \times 10^{19}$, $N_y = 5.76 \times 10^{19}$, $N_z = 2.32 \times 10^{19}$.

10. A radioactive source, in the form of a metallic sphere of radius 10^{-2} m emits β-particles at the rate of 5×10^{10} particles per second. The source is electrically insulated. How long will it take for its potential to be raised by 2V, assuming that 40% of the emitted β-particles escapes the sources.

Ans. 6.94×10^{-4}s..

11. The ratio of ^{235}U to ^{238}U in natural uranium deposits today is 0.0072. What was this ratio 2.0×10^9 year ago ? The half-lives of the two isotopes are 7.04×10^8 year and 44.7×10^8 year, respectively.

Ans. $\simeq 3.8\%$

12. The proton -proton mechanism that accounts for energy production in the sun releases 26.7 MeV energy for each event. In this process, protons fuse to form an alpha particle (^{4}He). At what rate $\frac{dm}{dt}$ is hydrogen being consumed in the core of the sun by the p-p cycle? Power of sun is 3.90×10^{26} W.

Ans. 6.2×10^{11} kg/s.

13. The binding energies per nucleons for deuteron $_1H^2$ and helium $_2He^4$ are 1.1 MeV and 7.0 MeV respectively. Calculate the energy released when two deuterons fuse to form a helium nucleus ($_2He^4$).

Ans. 23.6 MeV.

14. Find the kinetic energy of the α-particle emitted in the decay

$$^{238}Pu \rightarrow {}^{234}U + \alpha$$

The atomic masses needed are as follows :

$$^{238}Pu = 238.04955u$$

$$^{234}U = 234.04095u$$

$$^{4}He = 4.002603u$$

Neglect any residual nucleus ***Ans.*** 5.58 MeV

15. Calculate the Q-value in the following decays :

(a) $^{19}O \rightarrow {}^{19}F + e + \bar{\nu}$

(b) $^{25}Al \rightarrow {}^{25}Mg + e^+ + \nu$

The atomic masses needed are as follows :

$$^{19}O = 19.003576u$$

$$^{19}F = 18.998403u,$$

$$^{25}Al = 24.990432u,$$

$$^{25}Mg = 24.985839u.$$

Ans. (a) 4.816 MeV (b) 3.254 MeV

16. What is the power output of a $_{92}U^{235}$ reactor if it takes 30 days to use up 2 kg of fuel, and if each fission gives 185 MeV of usable energy?

Ans. 6.06×10^7 W.

17. Polonium $_{84}Po^{210}$ emits $_2He^4$ particles and is converted into lead $_{82}Pb^{206}$ This reaction is used for producing electric power in a space mission. Po^{210} has half life of 138.6 days. Assuming an efficiency of 10% for the thermoelectric machine, how much Po^{210} is required to produce 1.2×10^7 J of electric energy per day at the end of 693 days. Also find the initial activity of the material. (Given : masses of nuclei Po^{210} = 209.98264 amu, Pb^{206} = 205.97440 amu, $_2He^4$ = 4.00260 amu. 1 amu = 931 MeV and Avagadro number = 6×10^{23} / mol).

Ans. 4.57×10^7 per day.

18. A nuclear reactor generates power at 50% efficiency by fission of $_{92}U^{235}$ into two equal fragments of $_{46}Pd^{116}$ with the emission of two gamma rays of 5.2 MeV each and three neutrons. The average binding energies per particle of $_{92}U^{235}$ and $_{46}Pd^{116}$ are 7.2 MeV and 8.2 MeV respectively. Calculate the energy released in one fission event. Also estimate the amount of U^{235} consumed per hour to produce 1600 MW power.

Ans. 200 MeV, 140.5 g.

19. The element curium $_{96}Cm^{248}$ has a mean life of 10^{13} s. Its primary decay modes are spontaneous fission and α- decay, the former with a probability of 8% and the later with a probability of 92 %. Each fission releases 200 MeV of energy. The masses involved in α decay are as follows:

$$_{96}Cm^{248} = 248.072220\,u,$$

$$_{94}Pu^{244} = 244.064100\,u$$

and $\quad _2He^4 = 4.002603\,u$

Calculate the power output from a sample of 10^{20} Cm atoms. ($1u = 931$ MeV/c^2).

Ans. 3.3×10^{-5}W.

☆☆☆

Hints & Solutions

Solutions EXERCISE 6.1 LEVEL -1

1. (d) 2. (c) 3. (a) 4. (b)
5. (d) Energy of reaction $= 8 \times 7.06 - 7 \times 560$
$= 17.3$ MeV.
6. (b) $0 = m_1 v_1 + m_2 v_2$

$$\therefore \quad \frac{m_1}{m_2} = -\frac{v_2}{v_1} = \frac{1}{2}$$

The ratio of their nuclear size

$$\frac{r_1}{r_2} = \frac{r_0 A_1^{1/3}}{r_0 A_2^{1/3}} = \left(\frac{A_1}{A_2}\right)^{1/3} = \left(\frac{1}{2}\right)^{1/3} = \frac{1}{2^{1/3}}.$$

7. (b)
8. (c) Total binding energy of deuterons,
$= 4 \times 1.112 = 4.448$ MeV
Total binding energy of helium atom
$= 4 \times 7.047 = 28.188$ MeV
Q-energy value $= 28.188 - 4.448$
$= 23.8$ MeV
9. (d) A should have zero atomic number and one mass number, so it will be neutron.
10. (d) Energy of reaction $= 2 \times 4 \times 7.06 - 7 \times 5.60$
$= 17.3$ MeV
11. (b) Energy released. $= 4 \times 7.0 - 2 \times 2 \times 1.1$
$= 23.6$ MeV.
12. (d) 13. (d) 14. (d) 15. (a) 16. (a)
17. (d) Heavy water is used as moderator to slow down the neutrons.
18. (d)
19. (c) Neutron inside nucleus decays and produces a proton and an electron;

$${}_0n^1 \longrightarrow {}_1\text{H}^1 + {}_{-1}\beta^0.$$

20. (a) 21. (c)
22. (b) The atomic number of Y is one greater than X, X will emit β - particle. The atomic number of K is two less than Y, so it emits α – particle.
23. (c)

$$N = N_0\left(\frac{1}{2}\right)^n = N_0\left(\frac{1}{2}\right)^{\frac{1}{2}} = N_0\frac{1}{\sqrt{2}}.$$

24. (d) Number of half life, $n = \frac{6400}{1600} = 4$

Now $$N = N_0\left(\frac{1}{2}\right)^n = N_0\left(\frac{1}{2}\right)^4 = \frac{N_0}{16}.$$

25. (c) The atomic number and mass number of resulting atom will be,
$Z = 88 - 3 \times 2 + 1 = 83$
and $A = 238 - 3 \times 4 = 226$
26. (d) The number of α - particles
$= \frac{200 - 168}{4} = 8$
If n be the number of β-particles emitted , then
$90 - 8 \times 2 + n \times 1 = 80$
$\therefore \quad n = 6$
27. (d) The number of α-particles
$= \frac{238 - 206}{4} = 8$
If n be the number of β-particles emitted then
$92 - 8 \times 2 + n \times 1 = 82$
$\therefore \quad n = 6.$
28. (b)

$$N = N_0\left(\frac{1}{2}\right)^n$$

or $$\frac{N_0}{16} = N_0\left(\frac{1}{2}\right)^n$$

or $n = 4$

Half life $$t_{1/2} = \frac{t}{n} = \frac{2}{4} = \frac{1}{2}h.$$

29. (a) Beta rays and cathode rays both are made of electrons.
30. (d) The atomic number of resulting nucleus,
$Z = 10 - 2 \times 2 = 6$
So the unknown nucleus should be carbon.
31. (a) Atomic number of A and C will be equal and so they are isotopes.
32. (b) 33. (c)
34. (c) $Z = 92 - 8 \times 2 + 4 - 2$
$= 78.$
35. (c)
36. (a) The present amount $= 1 - \frac{7}{8} = \frac{1}{8}$

So $N = N_0\left(\frac{1}{2}\right)^n$

or $\frac{N_0}{8} = N_0\left(\frac{1}{2}\right)^n$

$\therefore$ $n = 3$

Now $t = n\,t_{1/2}$

or $t_{1/2} = \frac{t}{n} = \frac{15}{3}$

$= 5$ min.

37. (b) $N = N_0\left(\frac{1}{2}\right)^n$

or $\frac{N_0}{64} = N_0\left(\frac{1}{2}\right)^n$

$\therefore$ $n = 6$

Now $t = n\,t_{1/2}$

$= 6 \times 2$

$= 12$ h.

38. (c) 39. (d)

40. (c) Energy is released in a process when total binding energy (BE) of products is more than the reactants. By calculations we can see that this happens in option (c).

Given $W = 2Y$

BE of reactants = 120 × 7.5 = 900 MeV

BE of products = 2 × (60 × 8.5) = 1020 MeV.

41. (a) $E = \frac{3}{2}KT$

or $7.7 \times 10^{-14} = \frac{3}{2} \times 1.38 \times 10^{-23} \times T$

$\therefore$ $T = 3.72 \times 10^9$ K

42. (b)

43. (c) $r = r_0 A^{1/3}$

$\therefore$ $\frac{r_1}{r_2} = \left[\frac{A_1}{A_2}\right]^{1/3}$

or $r_2 = \left[\frac{A_1}{A_2}\right]^{1/3} r_1$

$= \left[\frac{125}{27}\right]^{1/3} \times 3.6$

$= 6$ fermi

44. (d) 45. (b) 46. (b)

47. (a) $N = N_0\left(\frac{1}{2}\right)^n$

or $\frac{N_0}{16} = N_0\left(\frac{1}{2}\right)^n$

or $n = 4$

$\therefore$ $t = nt_{1/2} = 4 \times 100 = 400\ \mu s.$

Solutions EXERCISE 6.1 LEVEL -2

1. (d) Mass of uranium changed into energy

$= \frac{0.1}{100} \times 1$

$= 10^{-3}$ kg.

The energy released $= mC^2$

$= 10^{-3} \times (3 \times 10^8)^2$

$= 9 \times 10^{13}$ J.

2. (d) The number of nuclei required

$= \frac{16 \times 10^3 \times 1}{200 \times 1.6 \times 10^{-13}} = 5 \times 10^{14}$

3. (c)

4. (a) $n = \frac{t}{t_{1/2}} = \frac{32}{2} = 16$

Now $N = N_0\left(\frac{1}{2}\right)^n$

or $N = 16\left(\frac{1}{2}\right)^{16}$

< 1 *mg*.

5. (c) Rate of disintegration,

$\frac{dN}{dt} = \lambda N$

or $n = \lambda N$

$\therefore$ $\lambda = \frac{n}{N}$.

Now half life,

$t_{1/2} = \frac{0.693}{\lambda}$

$= \frac{0.693}{n/N} = \frac{0.693N}{n}$.

6. (c) $N = N_0 e^{-\lambda t}$

or $100 = 1600e^{-\lambda \times 8}$ ... (i)

and $N = 1600e^{-\lambda \times 6}$ ... (ii)

(ii)/(i), we have

$\frac{N}{100} = e^{(-6\lambda + 9\lambda)}$

$= e^{+2\lambda}$ ... (iii)

Now from equation (i) and (iii), we get

$\frac{N}{100} = 2$

$N = 200.$

7. (c) Mass defect, $\Delta M = 3 \times 2.014 - 0\ 4.001 - 1.007 - 1.008$
$= 0.026$ amu
$= 0.026 \times 931 \times 10^6 \times 1.6 \times 10^{-19}$
$= 3.82 \times 10^{-12}$ J
Power of star $= 10^{16}$ W

Number of deuterons used $= \dfrac{10^{16}}{\Delta M} = 0.26 \times 10^{28}$

$$\text{Time} = \frac{10^{40}}{0.26 \times 10^{28}} \simeq 10^{12}\, s.$$

8. (b)

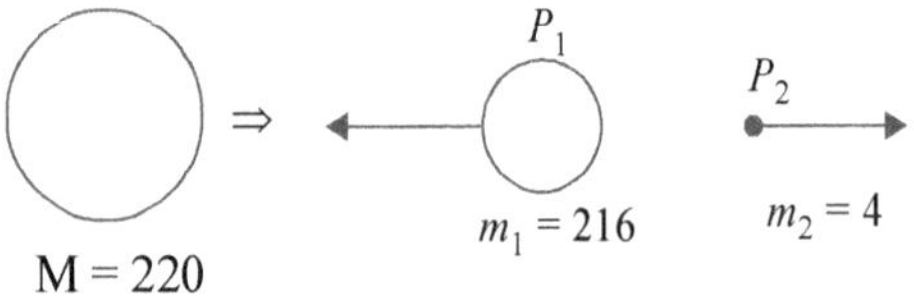

$K_1 + K_2 = 5.5 MeV$ ... (i)

and $P_1 = P_2 = \sqrt{2 \times 216 K_1} = \sqrt{2 \times 4 K_2}$ ... (ii)

On solving equation (i) and (ii), we get
$K_2 = 5.4$ MeV.

9. (a) $\lambda = \lambda_1 + \lambda_2 \Rightarrow \dfrac{1}{t} = \dfrac{1}{t_1} + \dfrac{1}{t_2}$

$$\therefore \quad t = \frac{t_1 t_2}{t_1 + t_2} = \frac{810 \times 1620}{810 + 1620} = 540 \text{ year}$$

Thus it takes two half life to remains $\dfrac{1}{4}th$ of the sample. So the time
$= 2 \times 540 = 1080$ year.

10. (d) $N_1 = N_0 e^{-10\lambda}$ and $N_2 = N_0 e^{-\lambda t}$

$$\therefore \frac{N_1}{N_2} = e^{(-10\lambda + \lambda t)} = e^{-9\lambda t}$$

So $\dfrac{1}{e} = e^{-9\lambda t}$

or $t = \dfrac{1}{9\lambda}$.

11. (d) The activity of the radioactive sample reduces to half in 140 days. Therefore the half life of the sample is 140 days. Before two half lives its activity was
$= 2^2 \times 6000 = 24000$ dps.

12. (b) $\dfrac{N}{N_0} = \left(\dfrac{1}{2}\right)^n = \left(\dfrac{1}{2}\right)^{1/3} = \dfrac{1}{1.26}$

Also $\dfrac{N}{N_0} = \dfrac{1}{1.26} \Rightarrow \dfrac{Nu}{N_{Pb} + N_0} = \dfrac{1}{2.26}$

$$\Rightarrow N_{Pb} = 0.26 N_0 \Rightarrow \frac{N_{Pb}}{N_0} = 0.26.$$

13. (a)

Solutions EXERCISE 6.2

1. (b, c) 2. (c, d) 3. (c, d) 4. (c, d)

Solutions EXERCISE 6.3

1. (a)

2. (a) $\rho = \dfrac{M}{V} = \dfrac{A}{\frac{4}{3}\pi r^3}$

$$= \frac{A}{\frac{4}{3}\pi (r_0 A^{1/3})^3} = \frac{1}{\left(\frac{4}{3}\pi r_0^3\right)} = \text{constant}$$

3. (b) Both statements are separately correct.
4. (c) Electrons are not inside nucleus.
5. (a)
6. (a)
7. (d)
8. (d) In case of hydrogen atom mass number and atomic number are equal.
9. (c)
10. (d)

Solutions EXERCISE 6.4

1. (a)
2. (b)
3. (c)
4. (d) The collection of ${}^2_1$H nuclei and electron is known as plasma which is formed due to high temperature inside the reactor core.
5. (a) Applying conservation of mechanical energy we get
Loss of kinetic energy of two deuteron nuclei
= Gain in their potential energy.

$$2 \times 1.5 kT = \frac{1}{4\pi\varepsilon_0} \frac{e \times e}{r}$$

$$\Rightarrow 2 \times 1.5 \times \left(8.6 \times 10^{-5} \frac{eV}{k}\right) \times T = \frac{(1.44 \times 10^{-9} eVm)}{4 \times 10^{-15} m}$$

$$\Rightarrow T = \frac{1.44 \times 10^{-9}}{2 \times 1.5 \times 8.6 \times 10^{-5} \times 4 \times 10^{-15}}$$

$= 0.0139 \times 10^{11} = 1.4 \times 10^9$K

6. (b) For the reading B we get $nt_o > 5 \times 10^{14}$ which is the Lawson criterion for a reactor to work successfully.

7. (c) For hydrogen like atoms $E_n = \frac{-13.6 Z^2}{n^2}$ eV/atom

For hydrogen atom (Z = 1) $E_1 = -13.6 eV$

$E_2 = -3.4$eV

$\therefore \Delta E = E_2 - E_1 = -3.4 - (-13.6) = 10.2$ eV

i.e., when hydrogen comes to ground state it will release 10.2 eV of energy.

For He^+ ion $(Z = 2)$ $E_1 = -13.6 \times 4$ eV $= -54.4$ eV

$E_2 = -13.6$ eV

$E_3 = -6.04$ eV

$E_4 = -3.4$eV

Here He^+ ion is in the first excited state i.e., possessing energy – 13.6 eV. After receiving energy of + 10.2 eV from excited hydrogen atom on collision, the energy of electron will be (–13.6 + 10.2) eV = –3.4 eV. This means that the electron will jump to $n = 4$.

8. (c) After collision with hydrogen atom the He^+ ion is in its third excited state (n = 4). After that the electron can jump into n = 3.

$$\Delta E = h\nu = \frac{hc}{\lambda} = E_4 - E_3$$

$$= \left[\frac{-13.6\times4}{16} - \left(\frac{-13.6\times4}{9}\right)\right]\times1.6\times10^{-19}$$

$$\therefore \frac{6.6\times10^{-34}\times3\times10^8}{\lambda} = -13.6\times4\left[\frac{1}{16}-\frac{1}{9}\right]$$

$$\lambda = \frac{6.6\times10^{-34}\times3\times10^8\times9\times16}{7\times13.6\times4\times1.6\times10^{-19}} = 4.68\times10^{-7}\,m$$

Since only one option is correct, we need not work out the case of electron jumping from n = 4 to n = 2 .

9. (a) K. E. for hydrogen atom (for n = 2) = $\frac{+13.6\times1^2}{4} eV$

K. E for He^+ (for $n = 2$) = $\frac{13.6\times2^2}{2^2} = 13.6\ eV$

$\therefore$Ratio $= \frac{1}{4}$

10. (c) KE_{max} of β^-

$Q = 0.8 \times 10^6$eV

$KE_p + KE_{\beta^-} + KE_{\bar{\nu}} = Q$

KE_p is almost zero

When $KE_{\beta^-} = 0$

Then $KE_{\bar{\nu}} = Q - KE_p$

$\cong Q$

11. (d) $0 \le KE_{\beta^-} \le Q - KE_p - KE_{\bar{\nu}}$

$0 \le KE_{\beta^-} < Q$

12. A-(p, q) ; B-(p, r) ; C- (p, s) ; D - (p, q, r)
13. A- (q, s) ; B- (p, t) ; C- (q, s) ; D- (r)
14. A-(r) ; B-(r, s, t) ; C-(s) ; D-(p, q, r)

Solutions EXERCISE 6.5

1. The equation of decay process is

$${}_{92}U^{238} \rightarrow {}_{82}Pb^{206} + n({}_2He^4) + m({}_{-1}\beta^o)$$

Here n and m are the numbers of α and β particles respectively. By conservation of mass

$206 + n(4) = 238$

$\therefore\ n = 8$

Also $82 + 2n + m(-1) = 92$

or $82 + 2\times8 - m = 92$

$\therefore\ m = 6$ ***Ans.***

2. We have $A = A_0 e^{-\lambda t}$

or $\ln A = \ln A_0 - \lambda t$

It represents a straight line with negative slope

From above equation, we have

$$\lambda = \frac{\ln A_0 - \ln A}{t}$$

$$= \frac{6.2-0}{225} = 0.0275\ \text{min}^{-1}$$

The half life $t_{1/2} = \frac{0.695}{0.0275} = 25$ minute ***Ans.***

3. Total energy used in nuclear reactor per day

$E = Pt$

$= (200\times10^6)\times(24\times3600)$

$= 1.72 \times 10^{12}$ J

Energy used in reactor per reaction

$$= \frac{25}{100}(2\times2.0141 - 4.0026)\times931\ MeV$$

$= 5.9584$ MeV

$= 9.5334 \times 10^{-13}$ J

The mass of deuterium used per reaction

$= 2 \times 2.0141 = 4.0282$ amu

$$= \frac{4.0282}{6.02\times10^{23}} g = 0.6691\times10^{-23} g$$

Thus mass of deuterium required to produce 1.72×10^{12} J of energy

$$= \frac{(0.6691\times10^{-23})\times(1.72\times10^{12})}{9.5334\times10^{-13}}$$

$= 120$ g. ***Ans.***

Solutions EXERCISE 6.6

1. We know that,

$$N = N_0 e^{-\lambda t}$$

After 2 second, $N_1 = N_0 e^{-\lambda \times 2}$

After (2 + 2) second, $N_2 = N_0 e^{-\lambda \times 4}$

According to given conditions,

$$N_0 - N_1 = n$$

$$\text{or} \quad N_0 - N_0 e^{-2\lambda} = n \quad \text{... (i)}$$

$$\text{and} \quad N_0 e^{-2\lambda} - N_0 e^{-4\lambda} = 0.75\, n \quad \text{... (ii)}$$

After solving above equations, we get

$$\lambda = 0.145 \text{ s}$$

$$\text{Mean life} \quad T = 1/\lambda = 6.9 \text{ s}. \quad \textbf{Ans.}$$

2. Disintegration constant

$$\lambda = \frac{0.693}{t_{1/2}} = \frac{0.693}{3.8} = 0.182 \text{ per day}$$

The number of particles left after time t

$$N = N_0 e^{-\lambda t}$$

$$\text{or} \quad \frac{N_0}{20} = N_o e^{-\lambda t}$$

$$\text{or} \quad e^{\lambda t} = 20$$

$$\text{or} \quad t = \frac{\ln 20}{\lambda}$$

$$= \frac{\ln 20}{0.182} = 16.45 \text{ days} \quad \textit{Ans.}$$

3. The total number of protons bombarded

$$= \frac{it}{\lambda} = \frac{10^{-4} \times 3600}{1.6 \times 10^{-19}} = 22.5 \times 10^{17}$$

Number of ^{7}Be produced

$$N = \frac{22.5 \times 10^{17}}{1000} = 22.5 \times 10^{14}$$

We know that activity

$$A = \lambda N$$

$$\text{or} \quad A = \left(\frac{0.693}{t_{1/2}}\right) N$$

$$\therefore \quad t_{1/2} = 0.693 \frac{N}{A}$$

$$= 0.693 \times \frac{22.5 \times 10^{14}}{1.8 \times 10^{8}}$$

$$= 8.63 \times 10^6 \text{ s} \quad \textbf{Ans.}$$

4. By conservation of momentum, we have

$$0 = \vec{P}_\alpha + \vec{P}_d$$

$$\Rightarrow \quad \vec{P}_\alpha = -\vec{P}_d$$

$$\text{or} \quad P_\alpha = P_d = P$$

The kinetic energy released in the process

$$K = K_\alpha + K_p$$

$$= \frac{p^2}{2m_\alpha} + \frac{p^2}{2m_d}$$

$$= \frac{P^2}{2m_\alpha}\left(1 + \frac{m_\alpha}{m_d}\right)$$

$$= \frac{(h/\lambda)^2}{2m_\alpha}\left(1 + \frac{m_\alpha}{m_d}\right)$$

After substituting the given values, we get

$$K = 6.25 \text{ MeV}$$

If m_p is the mass of the parent nucleus, then

$$K + (m_\alpha + m_d)c^2 = m_p c^2$$

$$\text{or} \quad 6.25 + (223.61 + 4.002)c^2 = m_p c^2$$

After simplifying, we get

$$m_p = 227.62 \text{ amu}. \quad \textbf{Ans.}$$

5. If A_0 is the initial activity of radioactive sample, then activity at any time

$$A = A_0 e^{-\lambda t}$$

$$\text{or} \quad 1 \times 10^6 = 4 \times 10^6 e^{-\lambda \times 20}$$

$$\text{or} \quad e^{-20\lambda} = \frac{1}{4}$$

The count rate after 100 hour is given by

$$A' = A_0 e^{-\lambda \times 100} = A_0 e^{-100\lambda}$$

$$= A_0 [e^{-20\lambda}]^5$$

$$= 4 \times 10^6 \left[\frac{1}{4}\right]^5$$

$$= 3.91 \times 10^3 \text{ per second} \quad \textit{Ans.}$$

6. We know that the rate of integration $\left|-\frac{dN}{dt}\right| = A$

$$\therefore \quad A = A_0 e^{-\lambda t}$$

$$\text{or} \quad 2700 = 4750 e^{-\lambda \times 5}$$

$$\text{or} \quad \lambda = 0.1131 \text{ per minute}$$

$$\text{Half life} \quad t_{1/2} = \frac{0.693}{\lambda}$$

$$= \frac{0.693}{0.1131} = 6.1 \text{ minute} \quad \textbf{Ans.}$$

7. Suppose x is the number of Pb^{206} nulei. The number of U^{238} nuclei will be 3x, Thus

$$3x + x = N_0$$

$$\text{We know that} \quad N = N_0 e^{-\lambda t}$$

$$\text{or} \quad 3x = 4x e^{-\lambda t}$$

$$\therefore \quad e^{\lambda t} = \frac{4}{3}$$

$$\text{or} \quad t = \frac{\ln 4/3}{\lambda} = \frac{\ln 4/3}{(0.693/t_{1/2})}$$

$$= \frac{\ln 4/3}{(0.693/4.5 \times 10^9)}$$

$$= 1.868 \times 10^9 \text{ year}. \quad \textbf{Ans.}$$

8. If m kg is the required mass of the uranium, then number of nuclei

$$= \frac{(m \times 1000) \times 6.02 \times 10^{23}}{235}$$

Each U^{235} nucleus releases energy 200 MeV,

∴ total energy released in 10 years

$$E_{in} = \frac{m \times 6.02 \times 10^{26}}{235} \times 200$$

Energy required in 10 years, E_{our} = Pt

=(1000 × 10^6) × (10 ×365× 24 ×3600)

Efficiency $\eta = \frac{E_{out}}{E_{in}}$

Substituting the values, we get

$$m = 3.8 \times 10^4\ kg.$$ **Ans.**

9. For radioactive nucleus X, we have

$$\frac{dN_x}{dt} = -\lambda_x N_x$$

or $$\frac{dN_x}{N_x} = -\lambda_x dt$$

∴ $$N_x(t) = N_0 e^{-\lambda_x t}$$

For radioactive nucleus Y, we have

$$\frac{dNy}{dt} = \lambda_x N_x - \lambda_y N_y$$

$$= 0.1\,N_x - \frac{N_y}{30}$$

For radioactive nucleus Z, we have

$$\frac{dN_z}{dt} = \lambda_y N_y = \frac{N_y}{30}$$

Given $$N_y(t) = \frac{N_0\lambda_x}{(\lambda_x - \lambda_y)}\left[e^{-\lambda_y t} - e^{-\lambda_x t}\right]$$

For $N_y(t)$ to be maximum, $\frac{dN_y(t)}{dt} = 0$

or $$\frac{N_0\lambda_x}{(\lambda_x - \lambda_y)}\left[e^{-\lambda yt}(-\lambda y) - e^{-\lambda xt}(-\lambda_x)\right] = 0$$

or $$\lambda x e^{-\lambda_x t} = \lambda_y e^{-\lambda_y t}$$

or $$0.1e^{-0.1t} = \frac{e^{-t/30}}{30}$$

After solving, we get

$$t = 16.48\ \text{s}$$

At this time ; $N_x = N_0 e^{-\lambda_x t}$

$= 10^{20}\ e^{-0.1 \times 16.48}$

$= 1.924 \times 10^{19}$ **Ans.**

Similarly, Y and Z can be calculated.

10. In time t, the total number of β-particles emitted = 5 × 10^{10} t. As only 40% escape from the surface, so N = 0.40 × (5 × 10^{10})t = 2 × 10^{10}t. The charge develops due to escape of each β- particle is 1.6 × 10^{-19} C, so total charge escapes in time t, $q = (2 \times 10^{10})t \times (1.6 \times 10^{-19})C$. Thus we can write,

$$V = \frac{1}{4\pi \epsilon_0}\frac{q}{R}$$

or $$2 = \frac{1}{4\pi \epsilon_0}\frac{(2 \times 10^{10})t \times (1.6 \times 10^{-19})}{10^{-2}}$$

∴ $t = 6.94 \times 10^{-4}$s *Ans.*

11. If N_{01} and N_{02} are initial numbers of ^{235}U and ^{238}U respectively, then after time t.

$$N_1 = N_{01}e^{-\lambda_1 t}$$

and $$N_2 = N_{02}e^{-\lambda_2 t}$$

∴ $$\frac{N_1}{N_2} = \frac{N_{01}}{N_{02}}e^{-(\lambda_1 - \lambda_2)t}$$

or $$\frac{N_{01}}{N_{02}} = \frac{N_1}{N_2}e^{(\lambda_1 - \lambda_2)t} \quad \text{... (i)}$$

Where $$\lambda_1 = \frac{0.693}{t_{1/2}} = \frac{0.693}{7.04 \times 10^8}$$

$$= 9.85 \times 10^{-10}\ year^{-1}$$

and $$\lambda_2 = \frac{0.693}{t_{1/2}} = 1.55 \times 10^{-10}\ \text{year}$$

∴ $$(\lambda_1 - \lambda_2)t = \left[(9.85 - 1.55) \times 10^{-10}\right] \times (2 \times 10^9)$$

$$= 1.66$$

Substituting this value in equation (i), and $\frac{N_1}{N_2} = 0.0072$, we get

$$\frac{N_{01}}{N_{02}} = 0.0072 \times e^{1.66} = 0.0379$$

$\simeq$ 3.8 % *Ans.*

12. The rate dm/dt can be calculate as ;

Power, $$P = \frac{dE}{dt}$$

$$= \frac{dE}{dm} \times \frac{dm}{dt} = \frac{\Delta E}{\Delta m} \times \frac{dm}{dt}$$

∴ $$\frac{dm}{dt} = \frac{\Delta m}{\Delta E}P \quad \text{... (i)}$$

We known that 26.2 MeV = 4.20 × 10^{-12} J of thermal energy is produced when four protons are consumed. This is ΔE = 4.20× 10^{-12} J for Δm = 4 × (1.67 × 10^{-27} kg). Substituting these values in equation (i), we have

$$\frac{dm}{dt} = \frac{\Delta m}{\Delta E}P$$

$$= \frac{4(1.67 \times 10^{-27})}{4.20 \times 10^{-12}} \times (3.90 \times 10^{26})$$

$= 6.2 \times 10^{11}$ kg /s **Ans.**

13. The fusion of deutrons can be written as :

$${}_1H^2 + {}_1H^2 \rightarrow {}_2He^4 + Energy$$

The binding energy per nucleon of deutrons is 1.1 MeV, ∴ net binding energy of deutrons will 4 × 1.1 = 4.4 MeV.

The binding energy per nucleon of ${}_2He^4$ is 7.0 MeV. The binding energy of helium nucleus is 4 × 7.0 = 28.0 MeV.

The energy released = 28.0 MeV – 4.4 MeV = 23.6 MeV

Ans.

14. The mass defect in the process

$\Delta m = m(^{238}Pu) - m(^{234}U) - m(^{4}He)$
$= 238.04955\text{ u} - 234.04095\text{ u} - 4.002603\text{ u}$
$= 0.005997\text{ u}$

The kinetic energy of α- particle

$K = \Delta mc^2$
$= 0.005997 \times 931\text{ MeV/u}$
$= 5.58\text{ MeV}$. *Ans.*

15. (a) Q - Value of β - decay is

$Q = [m(^{19}O) - m(^{19}F)]c^2$
$=[19.003576\text{ u} - 18.998403\text{ u}] \times (931\text{ MeV/u})$
$= 4.816\text{ MeV}$. **Ans.**

(b) The Q-value of β-decay is

$Q = [m(^{25}Al) - m(^{25}Mg) - 2me]C^2$

$= [24.990432u - 24.985939u - 2\times 0.511\frac{MeV}{c^2}]c^2$

$=(0.004593\text{u}) \times (931\text{ MeV/u}) = 1.022\text{ MeV}$
$= 3.254\text{ MeV}$ **Ans.**

16. The number of ${}_{92}U^{235}$ in 2 kg,

$N = \frac{(2\times 1000)}{235}\times 6.02\times 10^{23}$
$= 5.12 \times 10^{24}$

The fission of each ${}_{92}U^{235}$ produces energy

$= 185\text{ MeV}$

$\therefore$ Total energy produces,

$E = (5.12\times 10)^{24}\times(185\times 1.6\times 10^{-13})J$
$= 1572.3 \times 10^{11}\text{ J}$

The power output $P = \frac{E}{t} = \frac{1572.3\times 10^{11}}{30\times 24\times 3600}$
$= 6.06 \times 10^{7}\text{ W}$ **Ans.**

17. The nuclear reaction for the process is

${}_{84}Po^{210} \rightarrow {}_{82}Pb^{206} + {}_{2}He^{4}$

Mass converted into electric power per reaction

$\Delta m = 209.98264 - (205.91440 + 4.00260)$
$= 0.00564\text{ amu}$

The energy process per reaction

$= 0.00564 \times (931 \times 1.6 \times 10^{-13})$
$= 8.4 \times 10^{-13}\text{ J}$

Let m gm Po^{210} is required to produce 1.2×10^{7} J per day, then numbers of nuclei are

$N = \frac{m}{210}\times(6\times 10^{23})$

The decay rate is given by

$\left(-\frac{dN}{dt}\right) = \lambda N$

$=\left(\frac{0.693}{138.6}\right)\times\frac{m}{210}\times(6\times 10^{23})$ per day ... (i)

Energy produce per day

$=\left(\frac{0.693}{138.6}\right)\times\frac{m}{210}\times(6\times 10^{23})\times 8.4\times 10^{-13}$

As efficiency of the machine is 10%, so

$=\frac{10}{100}\left[\left(\frac{0.693}{138.6}\right)\times\frac{m}{210}\times(6\times 10^{23})\times 8.4\times 10^{-13}\right]$
$= 1.2 \times 10^{7}$

On solving, $m = 10$ gm **Ans.**

From equation (i), the activity

$A = \lambda N$

$= \left(\frac{0.693}{138.6}\right)\times\left(\frac{6\times 10^{23}}{210}\times 10\right)$

$= \frac{10^{21}}{7}$ per day

If A_0 is the initial activity, then

$A = A_0\left(\frac{1}{2}\right)^{\frac{t}{t_{1/2}}}$

$= A_0\left(\frac{1}{2}\right)^{(693/138.6)}$

$= A_0\left(\frac{1}{2}\right)^{5}$

$\therefore A_0 = 32\,A$

$=\frac{32}{7}\times 10^{21} = 4.57\times 10^{21}$ per day

Ans.

18. The nuclear reaction for the process is

${}_{92}U^{235} \rightarrow 2\,{}_{46}Pd^{116} + 2\gamma$

The binding energy of ${}_{92}U^{235}$ nucleus

$= 7.2 \times 235 = 1692\text{ MeV}$

Binding energy of two ${}_{46}Pd^{116}$ nuclei

$= 2 \times 8.2 \times 116 = 1902.4\text{ MeV}$

Energy of two γ rays $= 2 \times 5.2 = 10.4$ MeV

$\therefore$ Energy released $= 1902.4 - (1692 + 10.4)$
$= 200\text{ MeV}$
$=200 \times 1.6 \times 10^{-13} = 3.2 \times 10^{-11}$

The required energy $= Pt = (1600 \times 10^{6}) \times 3600$
$= 5.76 \times 10^{12}\text{ J}$

If m is the required amount of ${}_{92}U^{235}$, then for 50% efficiency, we have

$\left(\frac{50}{100}\right)\left[\frac{m}{235}\times 6.02\times 10^{23}\times 3.2\times 10^{-11}\right]$
$= 5.76 \times 10^{12}$

$\therefore m = 740.5$ gm. **Ans.**

19. The total energy released

E =Energy released in fission process
+ energy released in α- decay process
$= N_F \times 200 + N_\alpha \times (0.005517 \times 931)$

$=\left(\frac{8}{100}\times 10^{20}\right)\times 200+\left(\frac{92}{100}\times 10^{20}\right)\times(0.005517\times 931)$

$= 20.725\times 10^{20}$ MeV

Power output $P = E/t$

$= \frac{20.725\times 10^{20}\times 1.6\times 10^{-13}}{10^{13}}$

$= 3.3 \times 10^{-5}$ W. **Ans.**

★★★

7 Electronics & Communication

(337- 382)

7.1 ENERGY LEVELS AND ENERGY BANDS

We know that, in an atom electrons revolve in different orbit around nucleus and each orbit has its fixed amount of energy which is called **energy level**. The electrons moving in a particular orbit possess the energy of that orbit. The larger the orbit, the greater is its energy. The electrons revolving around the nucleus of an isolated atom possess definite energy level. However, an atom in a solid is in the influence of neighboring atoms. Due to which the energy levels of an individual atom lose their validity. In a crystal of N-atoms each energy level is in influence of all the atoms and so splits into N-close sub levels. As N is very large and the separation between the sub levels is very small so that these dense levels are almost continuous and are said to form an **energy band**. These energy bands are in general separated by regions called **band gaps** or forbidden gaps.

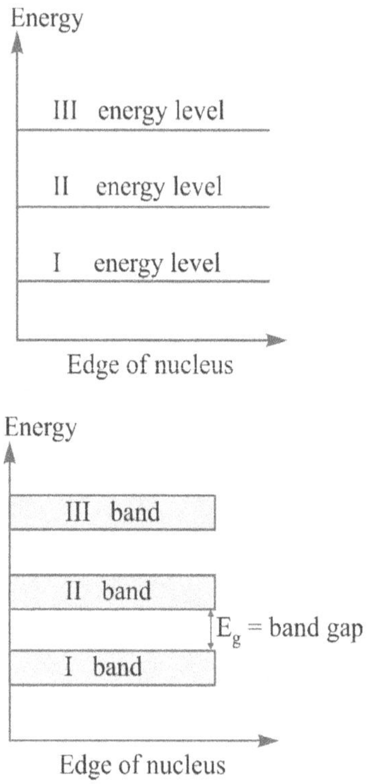

Fig. 7.1

7.2 VALENCE BAND AND CONDUCTION BAND

According to Pauli exclusion principle, each energy level can have two electrons with opposite spins. So normally only lower energy bands are filled with electrons. The highest energy band containing electrons is called **valence band**. This band may be completely or partially filled with electrons. In inert gases, it is completely filled whereas for other material, it is partially filled. The next higher band to valence band is called **conduction band**. All electrons in the conduction band are free electrons. The conduction band is partially filled for conductors and is empty for insulators.

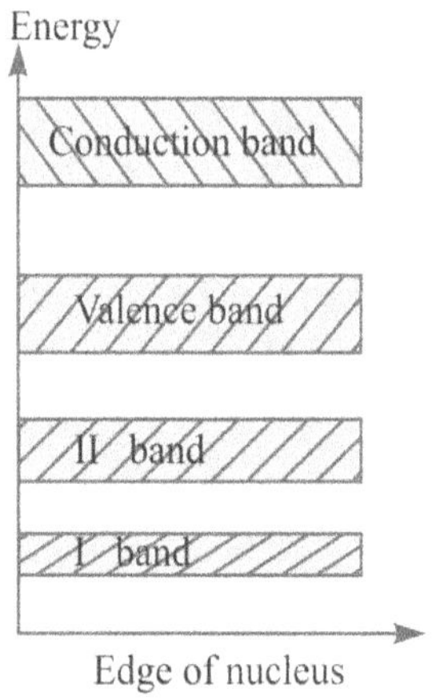

Fig. 7.2

Conductor, insulator and semiconductor on the basis of band theory

If the valence band and the conduction band overlap, the substance is called **conductor.** If the forbidden gap between valence band and conduction band is very large (more than 3 eV), the substance will be insulator. In such material a very high electric field is required to push the electron from balance band to conduction band. If the forbidden gap between valence band and conduction bands is less than 3 eV, the substance is called **semi-conductor.** Germanium (Ge) and silicon (Si) are the well known semiconductors. In germanium forbidden gap is, $E_g = 0.7$ eV and in silicon it is, $E_g = 1.1$ eV. At 0 K, semiconductor behaves like an insulator.

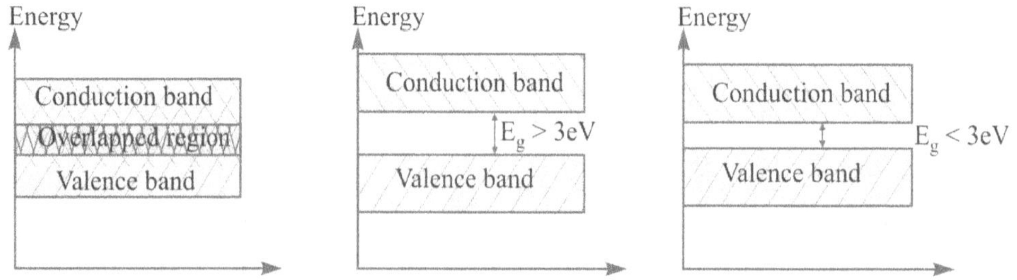

(a) Conductor (b) Insulator (c) Semi-conductor

Fig. 7.3

7.3 INTRINSIC AND EXTRINSIC SEMICONDUCTORS

Intrinsic semiconductor

The pure state of semiconducting material is called intrinsic semiconductor. In pure Ge there are four electrons in valence band, and so they make covalent bonds with the electrons of four other Ge-atoms; thereby leaving no free electrons for conduction. When such a semiconductor is given energy, some covalent bonds break due to thermal agitation and some electrons get separated for conduction. As soon as one electron gets separated, there becomes a deficiency on that place which acts as region of positive charge and is called a **hole**. Thus in this type of semiconductor, the number of free electrons and holes are same. Also both take part in conduction. At room temperature only 1 out of 10^9 covalent bonds breaks, and therefore produces very few charge carriers. Due to very few charge carriers, they can not be used for practical purposes.

Extrinsic semiconductor

Experiments show that when trivalent or pentavalent impurity is mixed in pure semiconductor crystal, its conductivity increases appreciably. The mixing of impurity in semiconductor is called doping and the resulting semiconductor is called extrinsic semiconductor. Extrinsic semiconductors are of two types :

n-type semiconductor

When pentavalent impurity like phosphorus or antimony is mixed in pure semiconductor, the conductivity of resulting crystal increases due to surplus electron associated with each impurity atom. Such a crystal is called n-type semiconding crystal and the impurity atom is called donor. In each impurity atom there are five electrons in valence band; four of which make covalent bond with four semiconducting atoms, leaving one surplus electron. This electron is free for conduction. Therefore in n-type semiconductor the free-electrons become the majority charge carriers, and holes are the minority carries. These holes are produced due to thermal energy. In an n-type semiconductor the donor level of impurity atom is close to the conduction band.

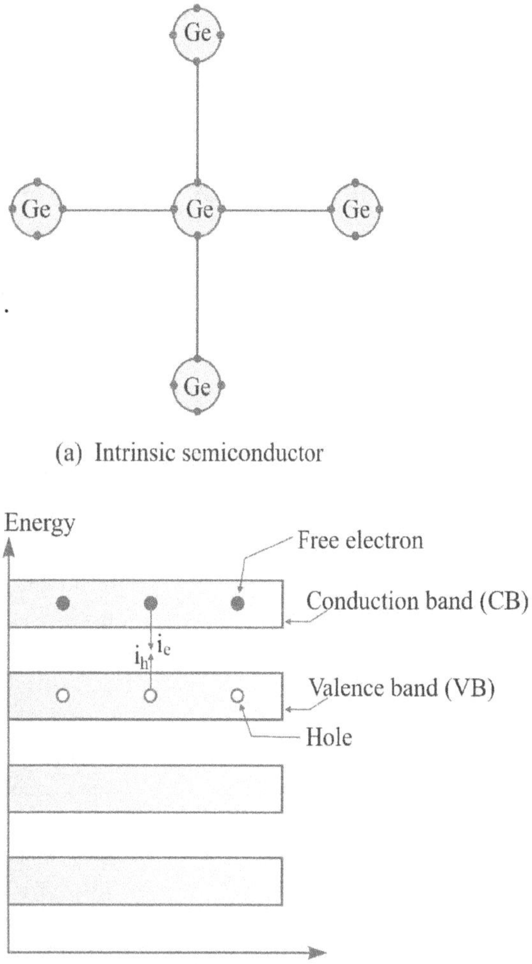

(a) Intrinsic semiconductor
(b) Edge of nucleus

Fig. 7.4

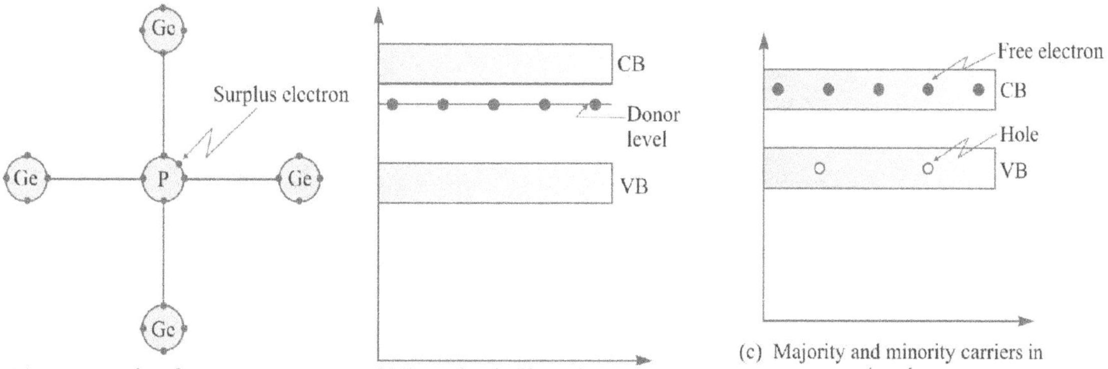

(a) n- type semiconductor atom.
(b) Donor level of impurity atom
(c) Majority and minority carriers in n-type semiconductors.

Fig. 7.5

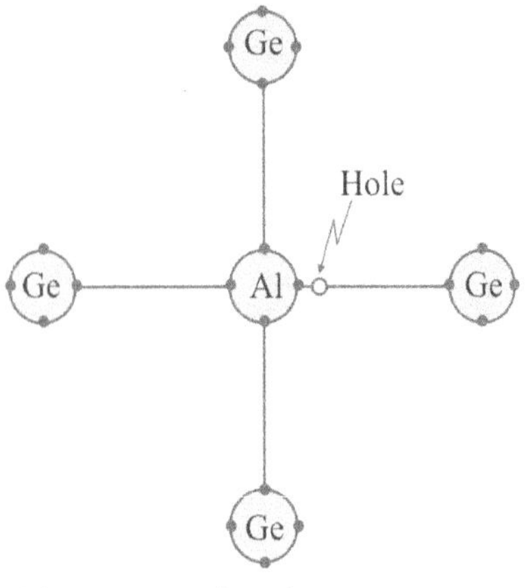

(a) p- type semiconductor.

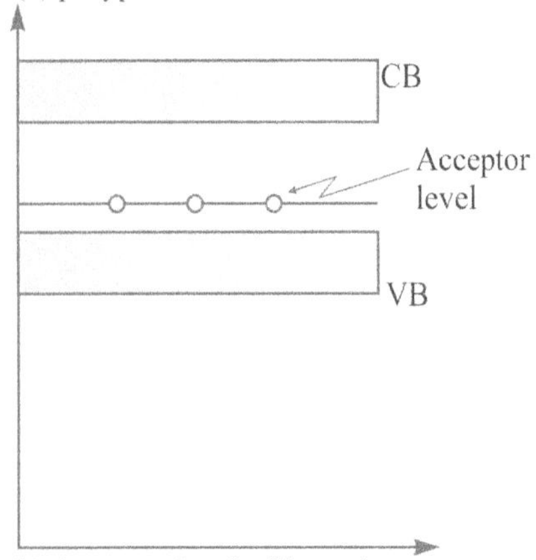

(b) Acceptor level of impurity atom

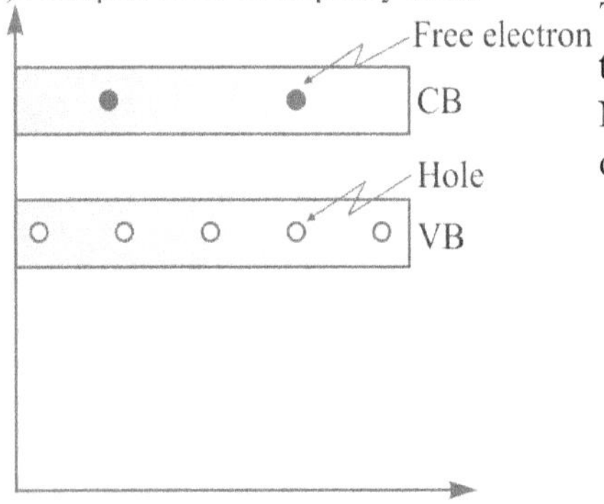

(c) Majority and minority carriers in p-type semiconductors

Fig. 7.6

p-type semiconductor

When a trivalent impurity like aluminium or indium is mixed with pure semiconductor, the conductivity of the resulting crystal increases due to deficiency of electron associated with each impurity atom. Such a crystal is called p-type semiconductor and impurity atom is called **acceptor.**

In each impurity, atom, there are three electrons in valence band; having deficiency of one electron to make covalent bonds with four semiconducting atoms. This deficiency of electron acts as a positive charge carrier called a hole. Thus in p-type semiconductor holes are the majority charge carrier and electrons are the minority carriers.

***Note* :**

Semiconductors, either intrinsic or extrinsic : n-type are p-type has no net charge. n-type semiconductor is so called because negatively charged free electrons are the charge carriers, similarly in p-type semiconductor holes are charge carriers.

7.4 ELECTRON CURRENT AND HOLE CURRENT

In metals, the current flows due to movement of the free electrons. While in semiconductors it is due to both types of charge carriers; free electrons and holes. We have studied about electron current. Here question arises; what is hole current? Hole current is due to the movement of valence electrons from one co-valent bond to another bond. In this case also electrons take part in conduction. When electron moves from one bond to other, the hole thus appears to move oppositely, and causes **hole current**. Suppose the valence electron at L shell gets free due to thermal energy. This creates a hole in the covalent bond at L. As the hole is a strong centre of attraction for the electron, so a valence electron from neighboring atom (say at M) fills in the hole at L. This will create the hole at M. Another valence electron from N in turn may leave its bond to fill the hole at M, thus creating a hole at N. This shows that hole has moved from L to N. This constitutes hole current. This current is in addition to current due to movement of free electrons. Thus total current $i = i_h + i_e$.

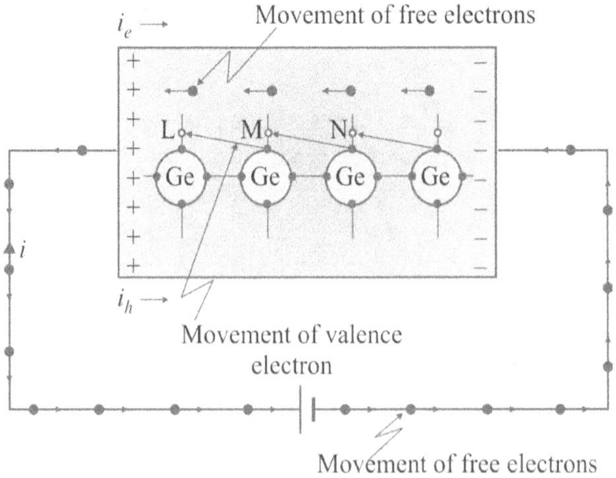

Fig. 7.7

Conductivity of semiconductor

We have studied that the resistivity of a metal is given by

$$\rho = \frac{E}{j}.$$

Here E is electric field and j is the current density which is equal to nev_d. If σ is the conductivity, then

$$\sigma = \frac{1}{\rho} = \frac{j}{E}$$

$$= \frac{nev_d}{E}.$$

Here n is the free electron density, and $\frac{v_d}{E} = \mu$, is called **mobility** of free electrons. Thus we can write

$$\sigma = ne\mu. \quad ...(1)$$

In semiconductor, the charge carriers are free electrons and holes. If n_e and n_h are the charge densities of free electrons and holes respectively, then

$$\sigma = n_e e\mu_e + n_h e\mu_h \quad ...(2)$$

In intrinsic semiconductor, $n_e = n_h$ and in extrinsic semiconductors; *n*-type, $n_e > n_h$ and in p-type, $n_h > n_e$.

If n_i is the charge density of either type of charge carrier (in intrinsic semiconductor), then

$$n_i^2 = n_e n_h \quad ...(3)$$

Ex. 1 **An intrinsic sample of germanium crystal has a hole of density 10^{13}cm^{-3} at the room temperature. When doped with antimony the hole density is decreased to 10^{11}cm^{-3} at the same temperature. Find the number density of majority charge carriers.**

Sol. We know that

$$n_e n_h = n_i^2$$

$$\therefore \quad n_e = \frac{n_i^2}{n_h}$$

$$= \frac{(10^{13})^2}{10^{11}} = 10^{15}\,\text{cm}^{-3}. \quad \textit{Ans.}$$

Ex. 2 **Find the current produced at a room temperature in a pure germanium plate of area 2 × 10^{-4} m^2 and of thickness 1.2 × 10^{-3}m when a potential of 5V is applied across the faces. Concentration of carriers in germanium at room temperature is 1.6 × 10^6 per cubic metre. The mobilities of electrons and holes are 0.4 m^2 V^{-1} s^{-1} and 0.2 m^2 V^{-1} s^{-1} respectively. How much heat is generated in the plate in 100 second?**

Sol. Electric field

$$E = \frac{V}{d} = \frac{5}{1.2\times10^{-3}} = \frac{5}{12}\times10^4 \text{ V/m}$$

Electric current across the plate : We know that

$$\mu = \frac{v_d}{E}, \therefore \quad v_d = \mu E$$

Thus $i = neAE\mu = neAE\,(\mu_e + \mu_h)$

$$= 1.6 \times 10^6 \times 1.6 \times 10^{-19} \times 2 \times 10^{-4} \times \frac{5}{12} \times 10^4 \times 2\,(0.4 + 0.2)$$

$$= 1.28 \times 10^{-13} A.$$

Heat produced in the plate in 100 second

$$H = Vit$$

$$= 5 \times 1.28 \times 10^{-13} \times 100$$

$$= 6.4 \times 10^{-11}\ \text{J}. \quad \textit{Ans.}$$

Ex. 3 **If resistivity of pure silicon is 3000 ohm-metre and the mobilities of electrons and holes are 0.12 m^2/V-s and 0.025 m^2/V-s respectively, find**

(i) the resistivity of a specimen of the material when 10^{19} atoms of phosphorous are added per ms,

(ii) the resistivity of specimen if further 2 × 10^{19} boron atoms per m^3 are also added.

Sol. The resistivity of semiconductor is given by

$$\rho = \frac{1}{\sigma} = \frac{1}{n_i e(\mu_e + \mu_h)}$$

$$\therefore \quad n_i = \frac{1}{\rho e(\mu_e + \mu_h)}$$

$$= \frac{1}{3000\times1.6\times10^{-19}(0.12+0.025)}$$

$$= 1.437 \times 10^{16}\ \text{m}^{-3}$$

(i) When 10^{19} atoms of phosphorous (donor atoms) are added per m^3, we have

$$n_e >> n_h$$

$$\therefore \quad \rho \simeq \frac{1}{n_e e \mu_e}$$

$$= \frac{1}{10^{19} \times 1.6 \times 10^{-19} \times 0.12}$$

$$= 5.21 \text{ ohm-m}$$

(ii) When 2×10^{19} boron (acceptor atoms) are also added, we have

$$n_h - n_e \simeq n_{acceptor} - n_{donor}$$

$$= 2 \times 10^{19} - 10^{19}$$

Since $n_h > h_e$, hence $n_h \simeq 10^{19}$

$$\therefore \quad \rho = \frac{1}{n_h e \mu_h}$$

$$= \frac{1}{10^{19} \times 1.6 \times 10^{-19} \times 0.025}$$

$$= 25 \text{ ohm-m.} \qquad \textbf{\textit{Ans.}}$$

7.5 p-n JUNCTION DIODE

When a p-type semiconductor is joined with a n-type semiconductor by appropriate method, the resulting device is called **p-n junction diode**.

Symbol of p-n junction diode is 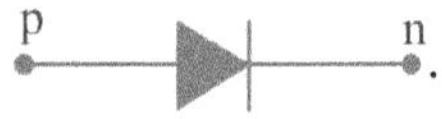

.

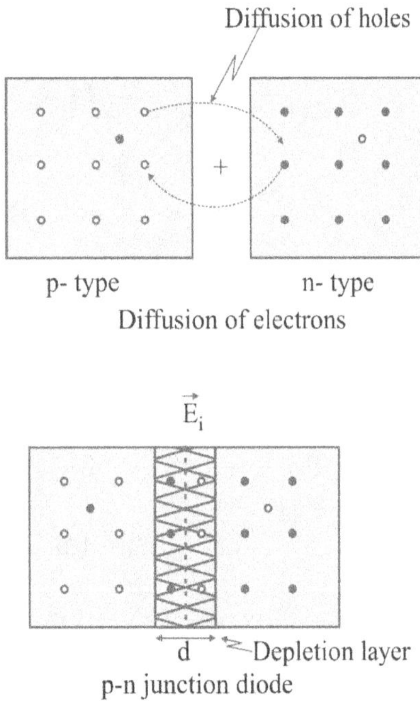

Fig. 7.8

Diffusion and drift current

In p-type crystal, the majority carriers are the holes and in n-type crystal, the majority carriers are the electrons. Due to difference in concentration of charge carriers, hole / electron start diffusing from their side to other side. Only those holes / electrons cross the junction which have high kinetic energy. Due to which the diffusion current takes place from the p-side to n-side of the crystal.

Because of the thermal energy, the collision occur in each part of the material of the diode. Because of these collisions a covalent bond breaks and the electron jumps to the conduction band. An electron-hole pair is created. Also a conduction electron fills up a vacant bond and so destroying an electron-hole pair. If an electron-hole pair is created in the depletion layer, they are send to their regions by the electric field inside depletion layer. This constitutes drift current from the n-side to p-side of the crystal. Thus drift current and the diffusion current are in opposite directions. In steady state both the currents are equal in magnitude and so there is no net transfer of charge across the junction diode.

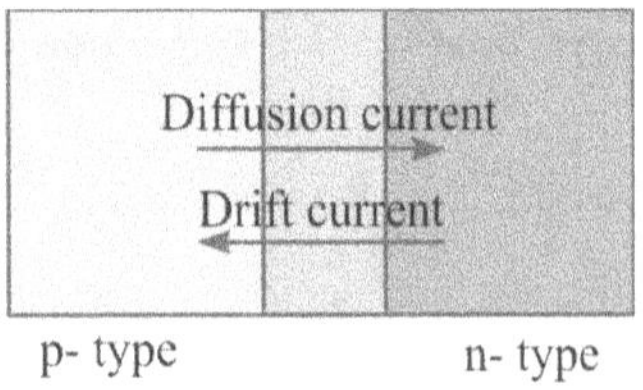

Fig. 7.9

Depletion layer

Initially, due to diffusion of charge carriers, a thin layer is formed on both sides of the junction. In this layer the charge carriers become static due to mutual attraction force between the opposite charges. This layer is called **depletion layer**. The thickness of depletion layer is of the order of 10^{-6} m.

Potential barrier

In equilibrium, the opposite charge carriers accumulate on both sides of the junction. This produces an electric field E_i from hole side to electron side. The corresponding potential difference across the junction is called **potential barrier**. It can be denoted by V_0 and equal to Ed. It is 0.3 V for Ge and 0.7 V for Si.

7.6 BIASING OF JUNCTION DIODE

The junction diode can be connected across the battery in following two ways :

(i) Forward bias

In forward bias (FB), the positive terminal of the battery is connected to p-side and negative terminal to n-side of the diode. If external electric field produced by the battery exceeds the internal electric field E_i, then hole move from p-region to n-region and electrons from n-region to p-region. A current is thus set-up across the junction diode due to the diffusion of charge carriers. This results decrease in the thickness of depletion layer, and so potential barrier decreases. If d_1 is the thickness of depletion layer, then potential barrier $V = E_i d_1$. The following are the important points regarding with the forward bias:

1. The forward current is of the order of mA.
2. Within the junction diode the current flows due to both types of charge carriers, while in external circuit (connecting metallic wires) the current flows due to free electrons.
3. The variation of current is not proportional to V; the graph between i and V is non linear.

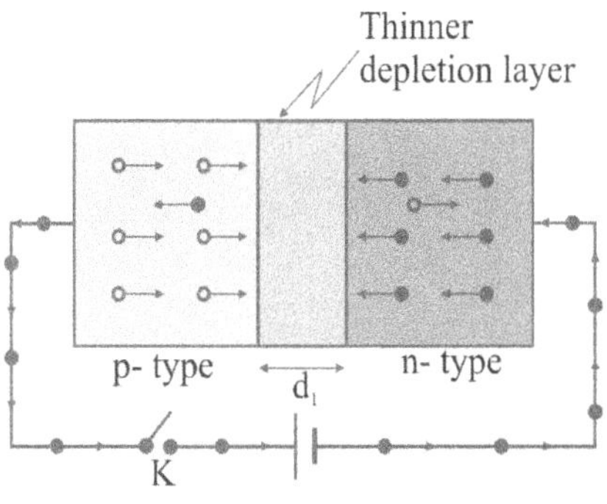

(a) Forward biasing

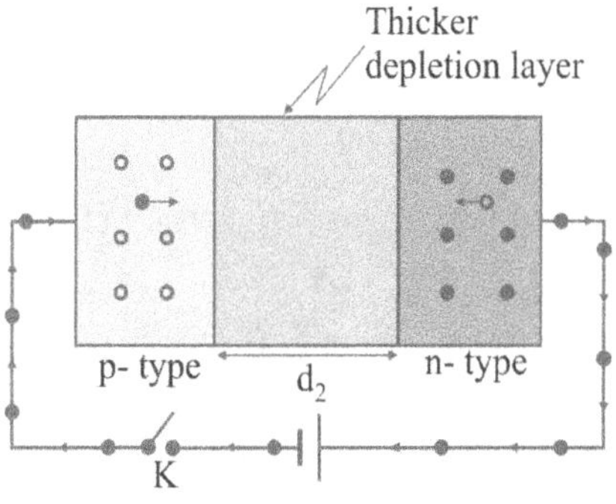

(b) Reverse biasing.

Fig. **7.10**

(ii) Reverse bias

In reverse bias (RB), the positive terminal of the battery is connected to n-side and negative terminal of the p-side of the diode. The external electric field produced by the battery is established to help the internal electric field $\vec{E}_i$. Because of this, majority charge carriers are prevented to cross the junction while minority carriers are pushed to cross the junction, which constitutes a very small reverse current. The thickness of the depletion layer increases and so potential barrier increases. If d_2 is the thickness of the depletion layer, then potential barrier $V = E_i d_2$. The following are the important points regarding with reverse bias :

1. The reverse current is order of μA and due to drift of minority charge carriers.
2. Within the junction diode the current is due to the both types of minority charge carriers but in external circuit it is due to electrons only.
3. The graph between i and V is non-linear.

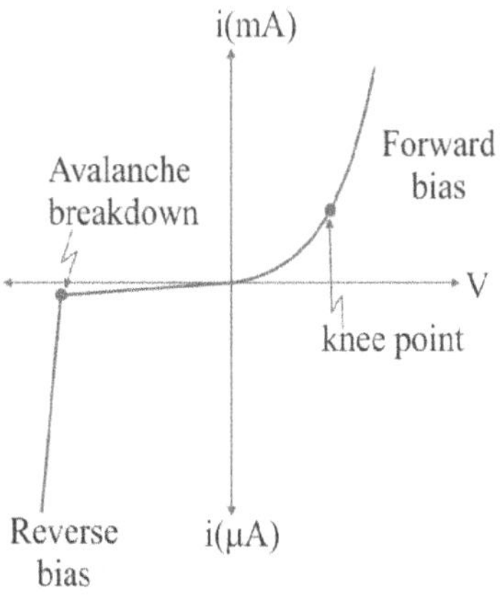

(a) Variation of i with V.

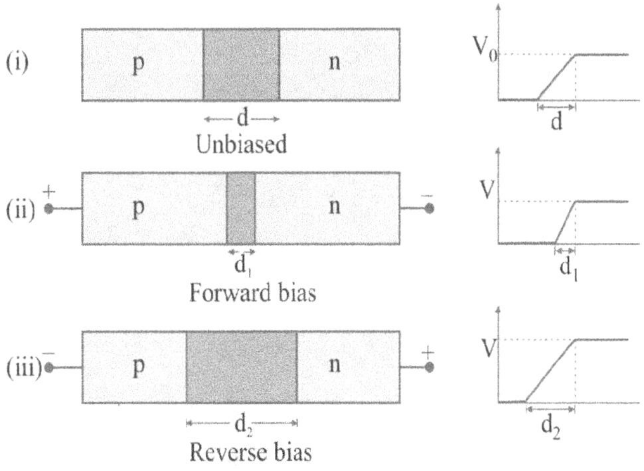

(b) Potential barrier.

Fig. **7.11**

Avalanche breakdown

If the reverse bias voltage is made sufficiently high, the covalent bonds near the junction break down and so large number of charge carriers are produced. Which then increases the reverse current abruptly. This is called avalanche breakdown which was explained by **Zener.**

Forward and reverse resistance

The resistance offered by diode in forward bias is called forward resistance R_f. The resistance offered by diode in reverse bias is called reverse resistance R_r. For an ideal diode $R_f = 0$ and $R_r = \infty$ also $V_0 = 0$. But for practical diode the ratio of $\frac{R_r}{R_f} \simeq 40000$ for Ge and 100000 for Si.

Ex. 4 **Diodes are connected in the circuits as shown. Find their biasing with the data given.**

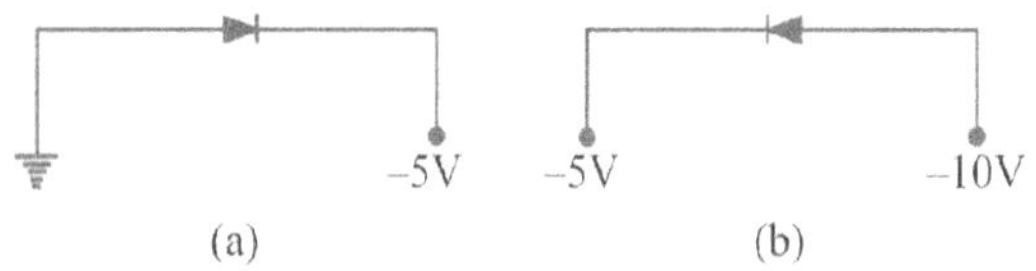

Fig. 7.12

Sol.

(a) p-side of the diode is at higher potential and so it is in FB.

(b) RB.

Ex. 5 **Determine the current i in the circuit shown in *fig.* 7.13. Assume diodes are made of silicon (V_0 = 0.7 V).**

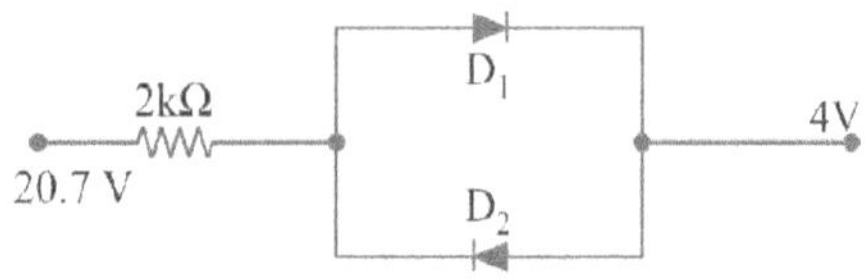

Fig. 7.13

Sol. In the given circuit, D_1 is in FB and D_2 is in RB and so current will pass through D_1. The equivalent circuit is :

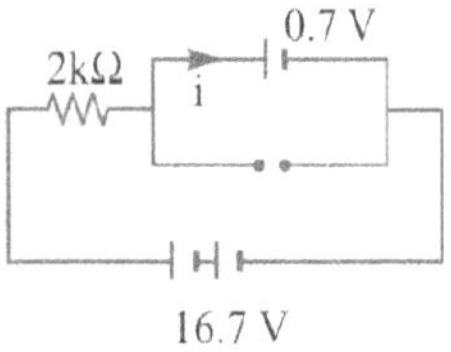

Fig. 7.14

Current $\quad i = \dfrac{16.7 - 0.7}{2 \times 10^3} = 8 \times 10^{-3}\,A = 8\,mA$ ***Ans.***

Ex. 6 **Find the voltage V_A in the circuit shown in figure. The potential barrier for Ge is 0.3 V and for Si is 0.7 V.**

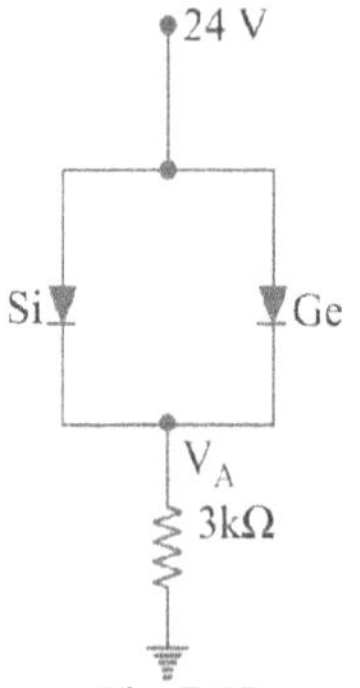

Fig. 7.15

Sol. In the situation given, germanium diode will turn on first because potential barrier for germanium is smaller. The silicon diode will not get the opportunity to flow the current and so remains in open circuit. The equivalent circuit is as in figure.

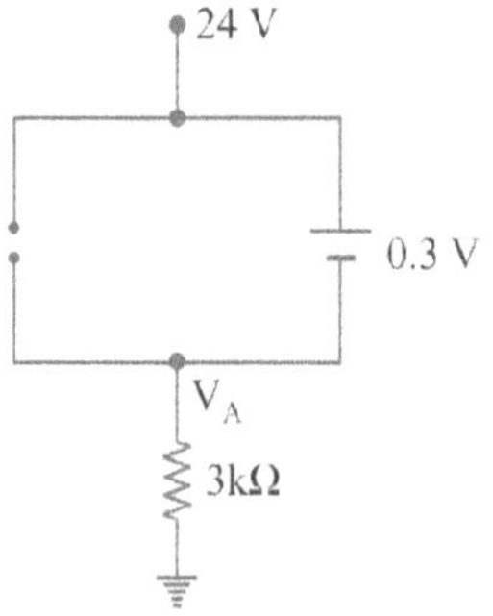

Fig. 7.16

$$V_A = 24 - 0.3$$
$$= 23.7\,V. \qquad \textit{Ans.}$$

7.7 ZENER DIODE

It is the highly doped diode in which reverse current increases very sharply. It can operate continuously without damaging the junction. The symbol of zener diode is

The following points should be noted about zener diode:

1. A zener diode is like an ordinary diode except that it is heavily doped so as to have a sharp breakdown voltage called zener voltage (see figure).
2. Zener diode is always used in reverse bias.
3. It is used for voltage stabilisation.

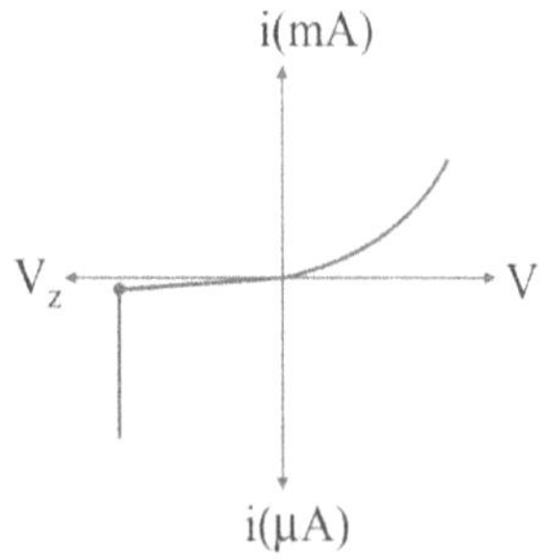

Fig. 7.17

Zener diode as voltage stabiliser

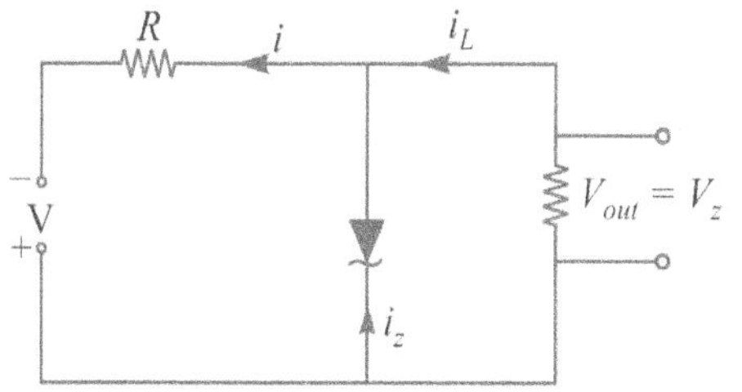

*Fig.*7.18. Circuit diagram of voltage stabiliser.

A zener diode can be used to get a constant voltage output from a source whose voltage may vary over a wide range. In the circuit arrangement a zener diode of zener voltage V_Z (output voltage) is connected across the load resistance R_L across which constant voltage is desired. When imput voltage varies, the zener diode change its resistance by creating charge carriers inside and keep voltage constant. In the circuit R_L is connected parallel to diode and so output voltage will equal to V_Z which is constant.

7.8 LIGHT EMITTING DIODE

When a conduction electron falls into a hole in valence band, the energy may be emitted as a photon. For usual diodes the wavelength of photon emitted lies in infrared region. If the wavelength of the photons is in visible range (4000 Å to 7000 Å), the emitted photon will cause visual effect. Such a diode is known as light emitting diode and abbreviated as **LED**. The LED's are usually made from gallium arsenide (GaAs) or indium phosphide. LED's are used in electronic gadgets and indicator lights. The symbol of LED is shown in fig:

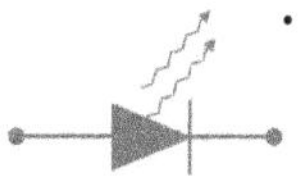
.

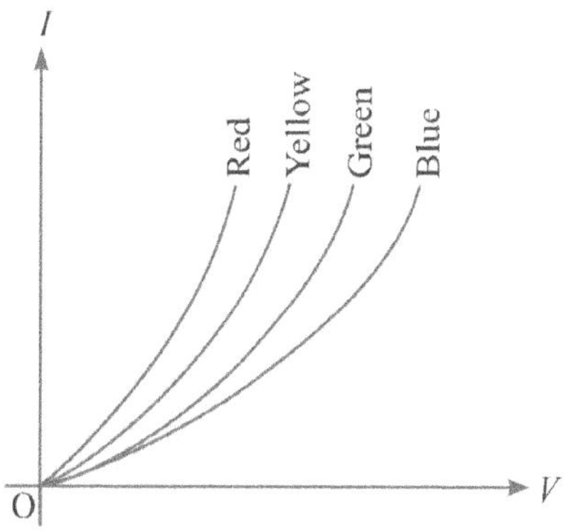

Fig 7.18 (a) I –V characteristic of an LED

7.9 PHOTO DIODE

Photodiode is a diode whose function is controlled by the light falling on it. Suppose the light of wavelength λ is sufficient to break the valence bond. When such a light falls on the junction of the diode, new hole-electron pairs are created. If such a diode is connected in the circuit, then the circuit current can be controlled by incident light. This type of diode is called **photodiode**. The symbol of photo diode is shown in fig:

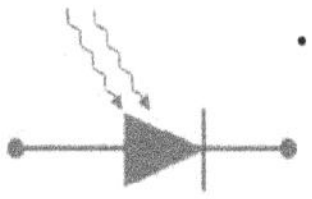
.

7.10 RECTIFICATION BY JUNCTION DIODE

In many electrical applications, there need direct current. It can be obtained from alternating current by rectification. The conversion of alternating current into direct current is called rectification. It may be of two types.

(i) Half wave rectification

In half wave rectification, the current will flow in the load resistor R_L during positive half cycle of the input of ac. Therefore current always flows in one direction and so dc output is obtained.

Consider an ideal diode connected in the circuit and input ac with a transformer as shown in the figure. During the positive half cycle of input ac, end A of the transformer binding becomes positive with respect to B. This makes the diode in forward bias, and so it allows current.

During the negative half cycle, end A becomes negative with respect to end B, and diode be in reverse bias. Under reverse bias condition diode will not pass any current. Therefore current flows in the load resistance during each positive half cycle.

The current through load resistor during half cycle is given by

$$i = \frac{V_0 \sin(\omega t + \phi)}{R_L + R_{diode}}.$$

The efficiency of half wave rectification can be obtained by :

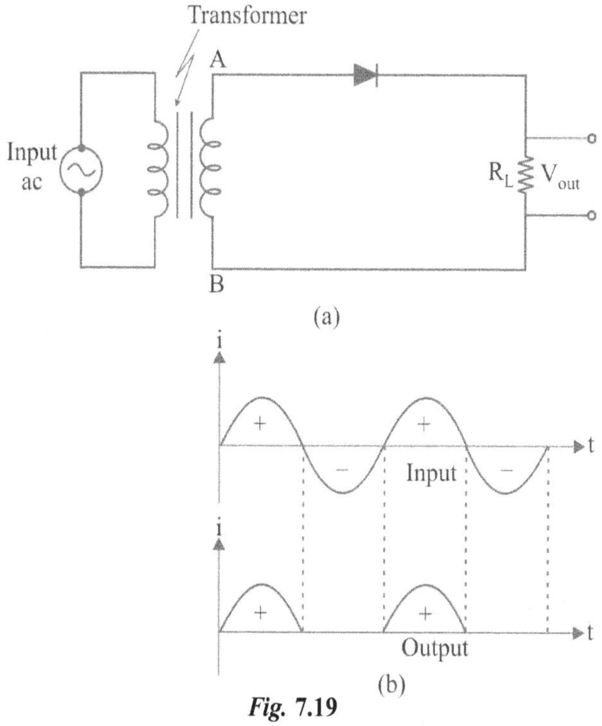

Fig. 7.19

$$\eta(\%) = \frac{40.6}{1+\frac{R_f}{R_L}}.$$

Here R_f is the forward resistance of the diode and R_L is the load resistance. The maximum efficiency becomes 40.6% when $\frac{R_f}{R_L} \to 0$.

(ii) Full wave rectification

In full wave rectification, current in the load resistor R_L in the same direction for both half-cycles of input of ac. This may be achieved by using two diodes working alternately. The following two methods are commonly used for full-wave rectification.

(a) Centre-tap full wave rectifier

The circuit consists of two diodes D_1 and D_2. These are connected across two ends of the secondary winding of the transformer. A load resistor R_L is connected by a centre tap at O (see *fig.* 7.20).

During the positive half cycle of ac the end A of the secondary winding becomes positive and end B negative. This makes the diode D_1 in forward bias and D_2 in reverse bias. Therefore D_1 allows current while D_2 does not. Thus current in load resistor R_L will come through diode D_1. During the negative half-cycle of ac, end A of the secondary winding becomes negative and end B positive. This makes diode D_1 in reverse bias and D_2 in forward bias. Thus current in load resistor will pass through D_2. Therefore the current in the load resistor is in the same direction for both half-cycles of input ac. The efficiency of full wave rectification can be obtained by :

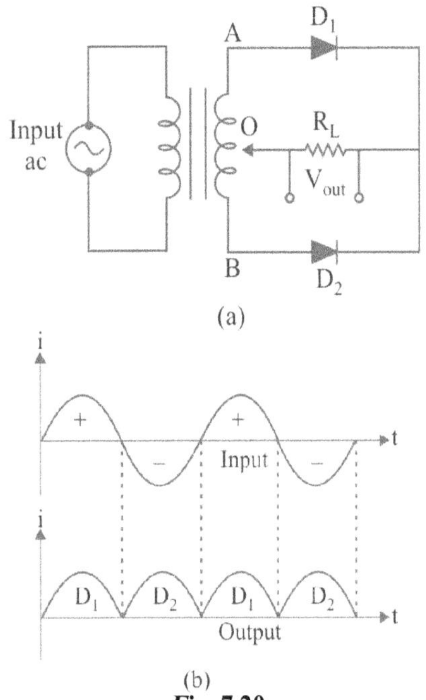

Fig. 7.20

$$\eta(\%) = \frac{81.2}{1+\frac{R_f}{R_L}}.$$

The maximum efficiency becomes 81.2% when $\frac{R_f}{R_L} \to 0$.

(b) Full wave bridge rectifier

It consists of four diodes D_1, D_2, D_3 and D_4 connected in the form of bridge (see figure). Between two ends of bridge load resistor R_L is connected.

During the positive half-cycle of input ac, the end A of the secondary winding becomes positive and end B negative. This makes diodes D_1 and D_3 in forward bias while D_2 and D_4 in reverse bias. In this situation, current will pass in load resistor through D_1 and D_3. During the negative half-cycle end B of the secondary winding becomes positive. This makes the diodes D_2 and D_4 in forward bias while D_1 and D_3 in reverse bias and so current will pass through D_2 and D_4. Thus in load resistor , the current will flow in the same direction (see dotted path).

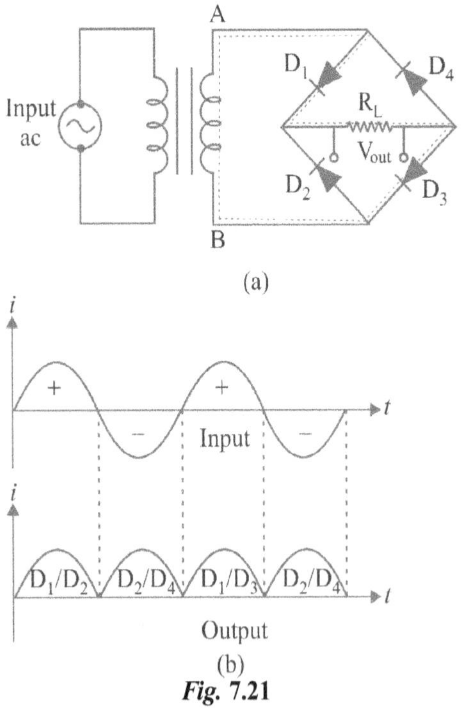

Fig. 7.21

Ex. 7 **An ac voltage of peak value 20 V is connected in series with silicon diode and a load resistance of 500 Ω. The forward resistance of the diode is 10 Ω and the barrier voltage is 0.7 V. Find the peak current through diode and the peak voltage across the load. What will happen to these values if the diode is assumed to be ideal.**

Sol.

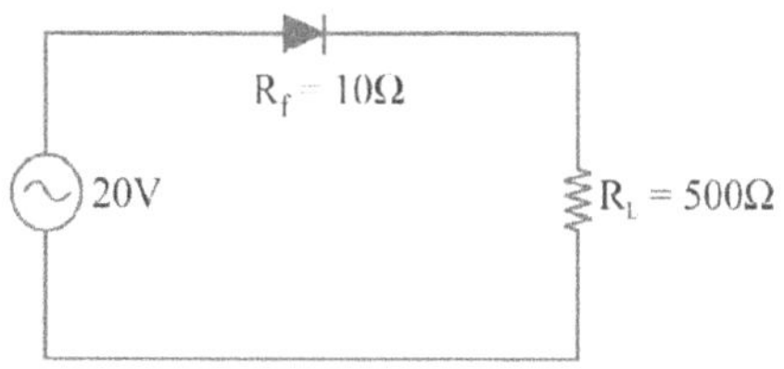

Fig. 7.22

The diode will be in forward bias only in positive half cycle of ac. As potential barrier of diode is 0.7 V and so net peak potential of the circuit becomes 20 – 0.7 V = 19.3 V. Given load resistance $R_L = 500\ \Omega$, and $R_f = 10\Omega$

$$\therefore \quad \text{Peak current} \quad i = \frac{\text{net peak potential}}{\text{total resistance}}$$

$$= \frac{19.3}{500+10}$$

$$\simeq 0.038\text{ A} \qquad \textit{Ans.}$$

The peak voltage across the load resistor

$$= iR_L = 0.038 \times 500$$

$$= 18.9\text{ V.}$$

For ideal diode R_f becomes zero and so barrier potential also becomes zero. Thus

$$\text{peak current} \quad i' = \frac{20}{500} = 0.04\ A$$

and $\quad$ peak potential = 20 V. $\qquad$ ***Ans.***

7.11 TRANSISTOR

Transistor is the modern electronic device which is capable of doing anything in the electronics. Transistor can does, rectification, amplification, oscillation etc. Transistor was discovered by J. Bardeen and W.H. Brattain of USA in 1948. A transistor consists of a p-type crystal sandwiching between two n-type crystals or a n-type crystal sandwiching between two p-type crystals. Accordingly there are two types of transistors : p-n-p and n-p-n. These are :

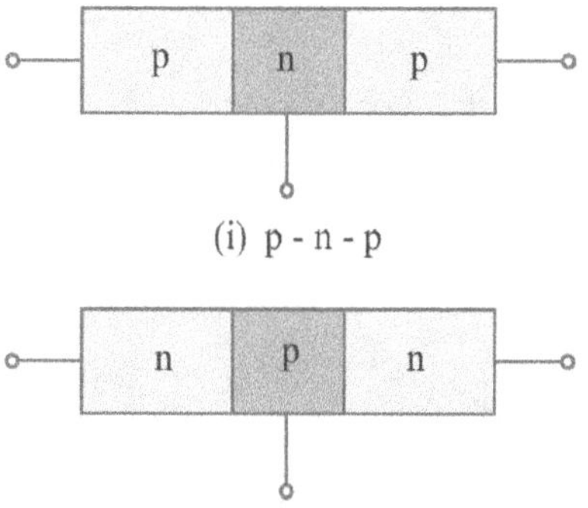

(i) p - n - p

(ii) n - p - n

Fig. 7.23

Transistor symbols

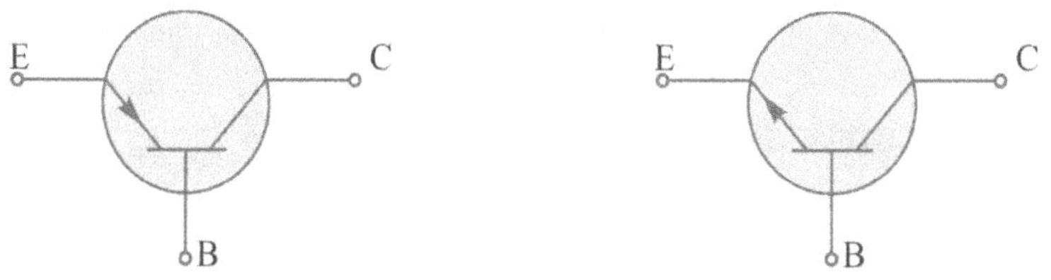

(i) Symbol of p-n-p transistor. (ii) Symbol of n-p-n transistor.

Fig. 7.24

Parts of a transistor

(i) **Emitter :** It is the heavily doped crystal which supplies the majority charge carriers. It is made thinner than collector and thicker than base

(ii) **Base :** The base is the lightly doped crystal and made very thin. It passes most of the emitter injected charge carriers to the collector.

(iii) **Collector :** It is the moderately doped crystal and made thickest one. Its function is to remove charges from its junction with the base. For the sake of convenience, it is customary to show emitter and collector to be of equal size.

Working of p-n-p transistor

Consider a p-n-p transistor connected in the circuit in such a way that base is common with emitter and collector. Thus there are two loops in the circuit. The emitter-base junction is given small forward bias, while collector-base junction is given large reverse bias. Because of the forward bias of emitter-base region, holes move from emitter towards base. Most of them (nearly 98%) cross base and enter into collector region, while very few (nearly 2%) combine with the electrons in base. As soon as a hole combines with the electron, an electron leaves the negative terminal of battery V_E and enters

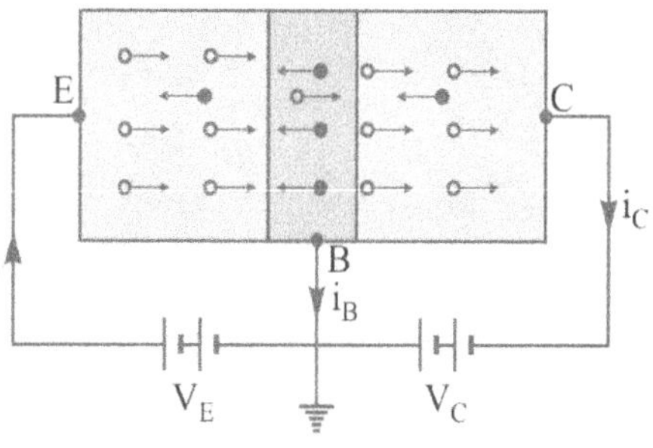

Fig. 7.25

into base. This causes a small base current i_B. The holes entering into the collector region combine with the electrons coming from the negative terminal of V_C. This causes collector current i_C. Both the currents together constitute emitter current i_E. Thus

$$i_E = i_B + i_C.$$

It should be remembered that :

(i) The base current may be nearly 2 to 10% of the emitter current depending on the dopping level. Similarly collector current may be nearly 90 to 98% of the emitter current.

(ii) The holes are the charge carriers within the transistor while electrons are charge carriers in external circuit.

Working of n-p-n transistor

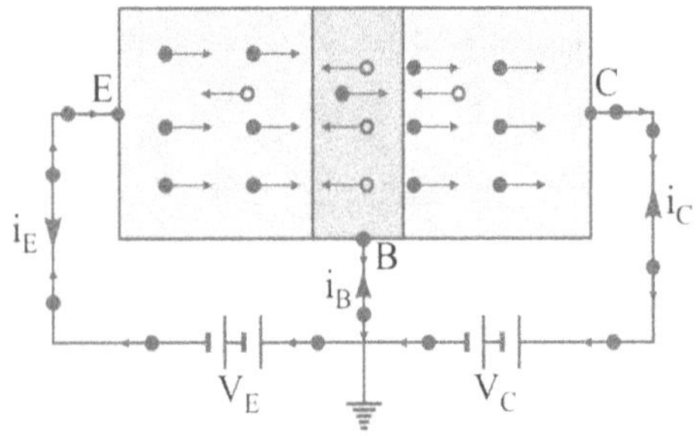

Fig. 7.26

Consider a n-p-n transistor connected in a circuit in such a way that base is common with emitter and collector. The emitter-base junction is given a small forward bias V_E while collection base junction is given large reverse bias. Because of forward bias in emitter-base region, electrons from emitter region move towards base. Most of them (nearly 98%) cross the base and enter into collector region while very few (nearly 2%) combine with the holes in base. As soon as an electron combines with the hole, a bond break in base region and produces a pair of hole and electron.

This electron is captured by positive terminal of the battery V_E and send it towards emitter region. This causes a small base current i_B. The electrons entering into collector region are attracted by the positive terminal of V_C. This causes collector current i_C. These two currents combine together constitute emitter current i_E. Thus

$$i_E = i_B + i_C.$$

It should be remembered that :

(i) The base current may be 2 to 10% of the emitter current depending on the doping level. Similarly collector current may be 90 to 98% of the emitter current.

(ii) The electrons are the charge carriers within the transistor as well as in external circuit.

7.12 TRANSISTOR CONNECTIONS OR CONFIGURATIONS

There are three terminals in a transistor; emitter, base and collector. However for connection, there need four terminals; two for input and two for output. This difficulty can be overcome by making one terminal of the transistor common to both input and output terminals. Accordingly a transistor can be connected in the circuit in the following three ways :

(i) Common base (CB) connection,

(ii) Common emitter (CE) connection,

(iii) Common collector (CC) connection.

Out of these three, first two are commonly used in practice. Each circuit connection has specific advantage and disadvantage. In all the transistor connections, the emitter is always connected with small forward bias, while the collector always has a large reverse bias. In each connection there are two types of characteristic curves. These are :

Input characteristic curve and output characteristic curve.

CB connection

Figure shows a p-n-p transistor in common base connection. The input is applied between emitter and base and output is taken from collector base.

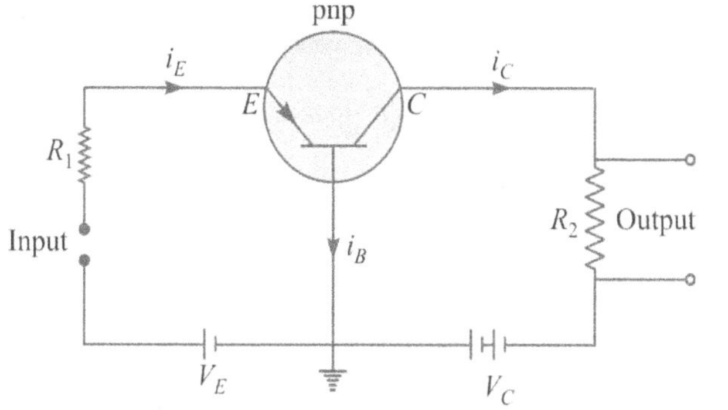

*Fig.*7.27 **pnp transistor in CB connection.**

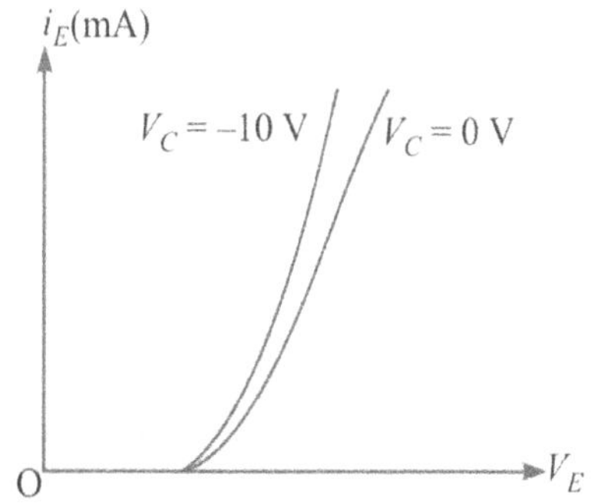

(a) Input characteristics.

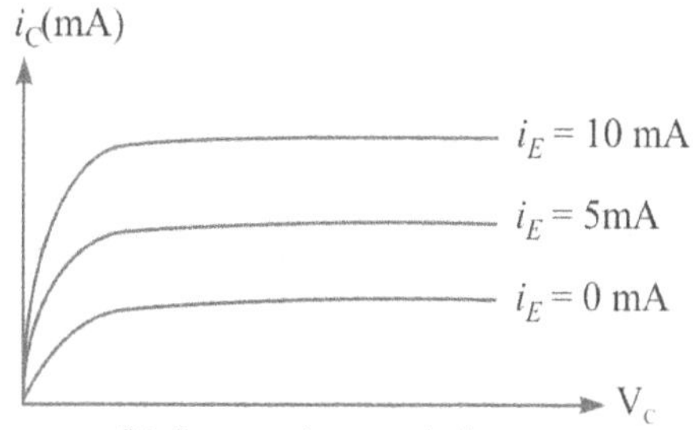

(b) Output characteristics

Fig. 7.28

Input characteristics

It represents variation of emitter current (i_E) with emitter voltage (V_E) at constant collector voltage (V_C).

Output characteristics

It represents the variation of collector current (i_C) with collector voltage (V_C) at constant emitter current (i_E).

CE connection

Figure shows a pnp transistor in common emitter connection. The input is applied between base and emitter and output is taken from collector and emitter.

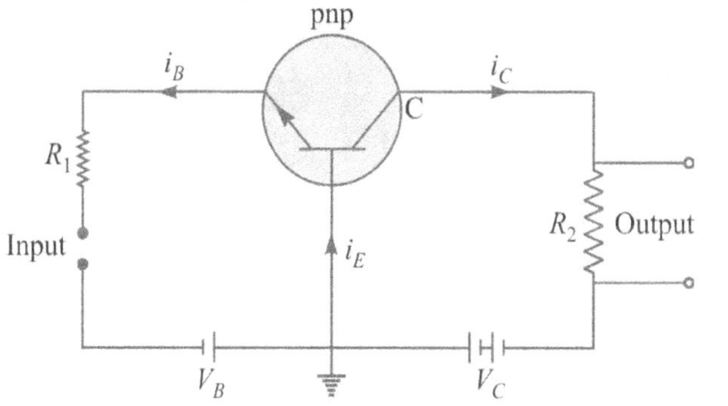

*Fig.*7.29 pnp transistor in CE connection.

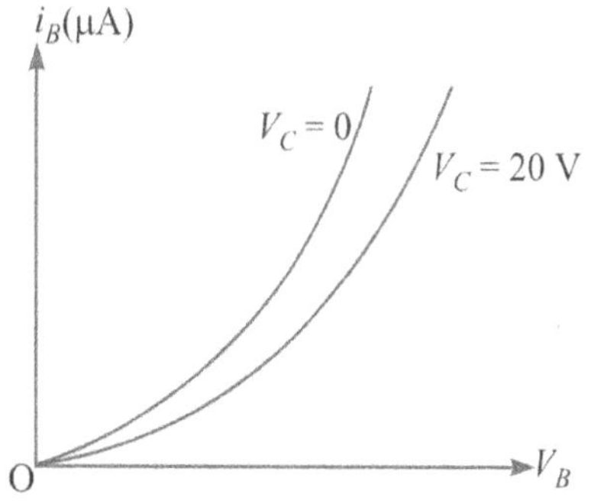

(a) Input characteristics.

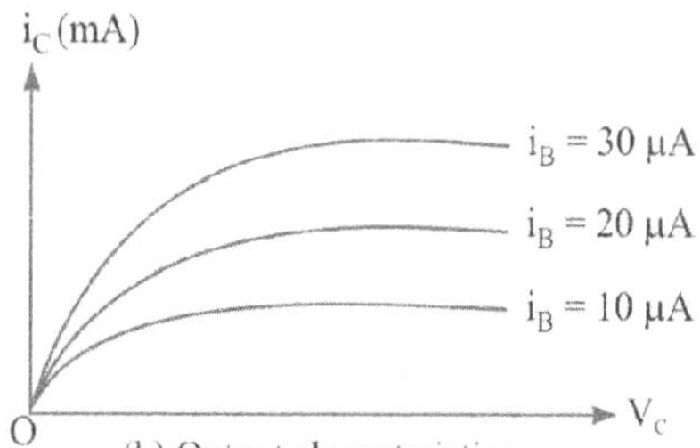

(b) Output characteristics.

Fig. 7.30

Input characteristics

It represents the variation of base current (i_B) with base voltage (V_B) at constant collector voltage (V_C).

Output characteristics

It represents the variation of collector current i_C with collector voltage (V_C) at constant base current i_B.

7.13 TRANSISTOR AS AN AMPLIFIER

A transistor can be used for amplification in which strength of output signal is more than input signal. The transistor can be used as an amplifier in the following three configurations.

(i) CB amplifier,
(ii) CE amplifier,
(iii) CC amplifier.

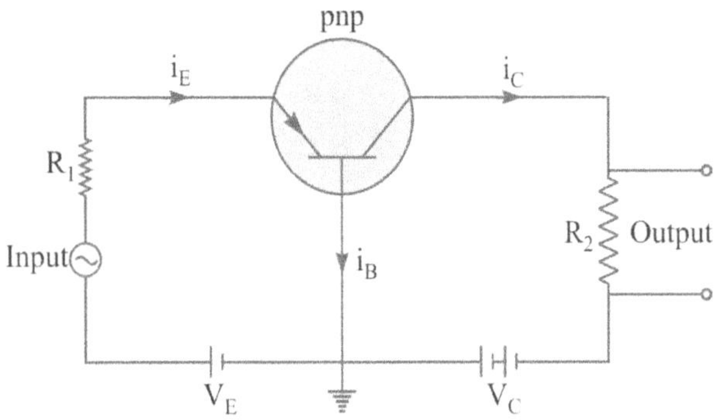

(a) pnp transistor in an amplifier.

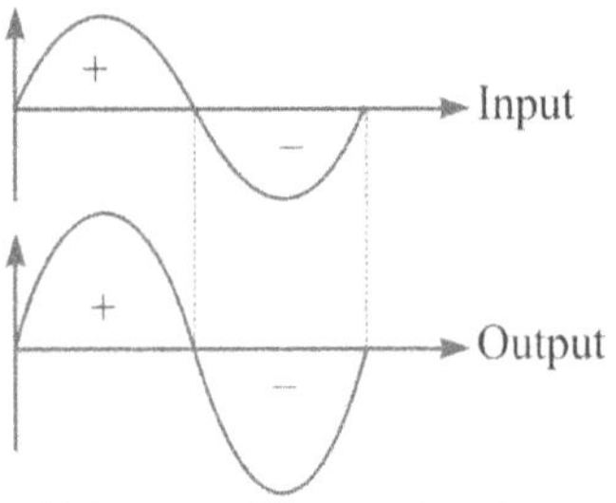

(b) Input and output signals.

Fig. **7.31**

CB transistor amplifier

Figure represents a pnp transistor in common-base-connection. The signal to be amplified is fed between the emitter and base. If resistance of input circuit is R_1, then corresponding to emitter current i_E at any time, the input voltage becomes $i_E R_1$. The output is taken from load resistor R_2 connected between collector and base. If i_C is the collector current then output voltage becomes $i_C R_2$. Thus

voltage gain $= \dfrac{\text{output voltage}}{\text{input voltage}} = \dfrac{i_C R_2}{i_E R_1}$. The output signal is in phase with input signal.

CE transistor amplifier

The figure represents a pnp transistor in common emitter connection. The signal to be amplified is fed between base and emitter. If base current is i_B, in resistor R_1, then input voltage becomes $i_B R_1$. The output is taken from load resistor R_2, connected between collector and emitter. If I_C is the collector current, at any time, then output voltage becomes $I_C R_2$. Thus voltage gain $= \dfrac{\text{output voltage}}{\text{input voltage}} = \dfrac{i_C R_2}{i_B R_1}$.

The output signal is out of phase with the input signal.

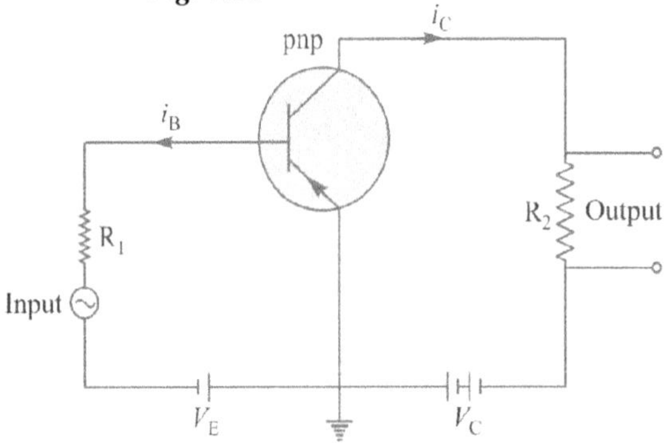

(a) pnp as an amplifier.

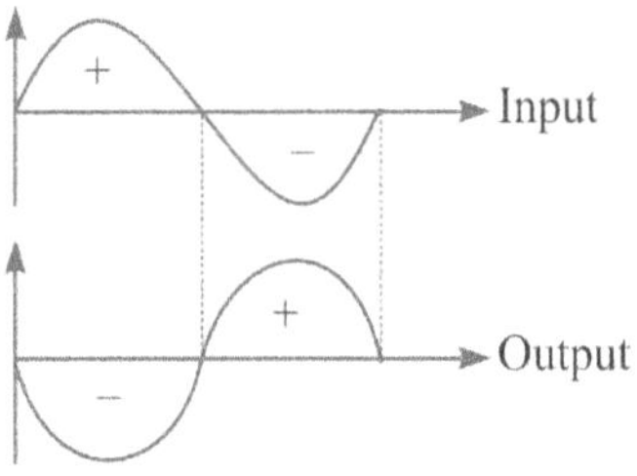

(b) Input and output signals.

Fig. **7.30**

Amplification factors of a transistor

The current gain α :

In common base connection, α is defined as :

$$\alpha = \left[\frac{\text{change in collector current}}{\text{change in emitter current}}\right]_{V_C \text{ constant}}$$

or
$$\alpha = \left(\frac{\Delta i_C}{\Delta i_E}\right)_{V_C \text{ constant}}$$

For dc signal,
$$\alpha = \frac{i_C}{i_E}.$$

The value of α ranges from 0.9 to 0.99.

The current gain β :

In common emitter connection β is defined as :

$$\beta = \left[\frac{\text{change in collector current}}{\text{change in base current}}\right]_{V_C \text{ constant}}$$

or $\beta = \left(\frac{\Delta i_C}{\Delta i_B}\right)_{V_C \text{ constant}}$

For dc signal, $\beta = \frac{i_C}{i_B}$.

The value of β ranges from 20 to 200.

Relationship between α and β

We know that $i_E = i_B + i_C$

or $\Delta i_E = \Delta i_B + \Delta i_C$

Dividing above equation by Δi_C, we have

$$\frac{\Delta i_E}{\Delta i_C} = \frac{\Delta i_B}{\Delta i_C} + 1$$

or $$\frac{1}{\alpha} = \frac{1}{\beta} + 1$$

∴ $$\beta = \left[\frac{\alpha}{1-\alpha}\right] \quad ...(1)$$

and $$\alpha = \left[\frac{\beta}{1+\beta}\right]. \quad ...(2)$$

NCERT BASED

Transistor as anAmplifier (CE - Configuration)

In general amplifier are used to amplify alternating signals. Now let us we have to superimpose an ac input signal V_i on the dc signal as shown and the output is taken between the collecter and the ground.

When no input ac signal ($V_i = 0$), we can write by Kirchhoff's rule input loop

or $V_{AB} - i_0 R_A - V_{CC} = 0$

And in output loop, we have

$$V_{CC} = V_C + i_C R \quad ...(i)$$

when output is taken through R_L, then

$$V_{CC} = V_{CE} + i_C R_L \quad ...(ii)$$

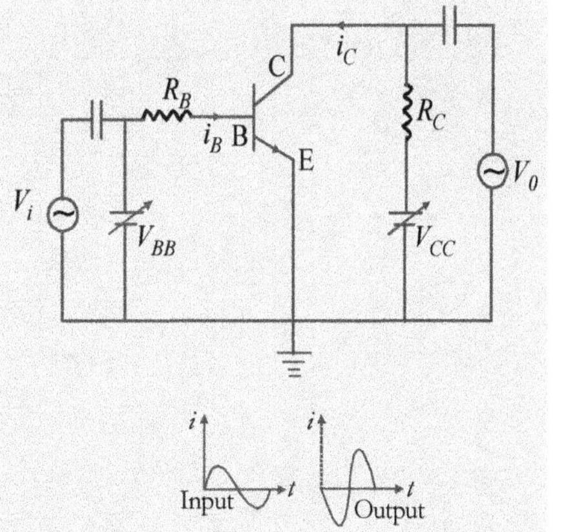

For input voltage V, we can write

$$V = V_{BE} + i_B (R_B + r_i)$$

or $\Delta V = \Delta V_{BE} + \Delta i_B (r)$

Putting $\Delta V \rightarrow V_i$ and ΔV_{BE} is very small in comparision to $\Delta i_B R_B$, so

$$V_i = \Delta i_B r \quad ...(iii)$$

From equation (ii), for small change Δi_c

$$\Delta V_{CC} = \Delta V_{CE} + \Delta i_C R_L$$

As V_{CC} is fixed and so $\Delta V_{CC} = 0$

∴ $$\Delta V_{CE} = -\Delta i_C R_L \quad ...(iv)$$

The voltage gain of the amplifier

$$A_v = \frac{V_0}{V_i} = -\frac{\Delta i_C R_L}{\Delta i_B r}$$

As $$\frac{\Delta i_C}{\Delta i_B} = \beta_{ac}$$

so $$A_v = -\beta_{ac} \frac{R_L}{r}$$

The negative sign represents that output voltage is opposite phase with the input.

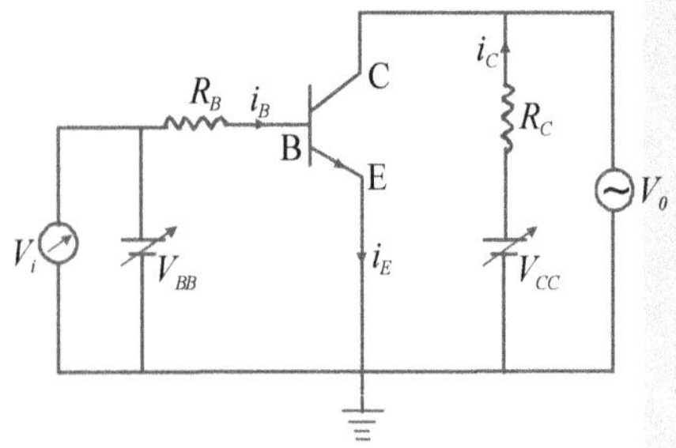

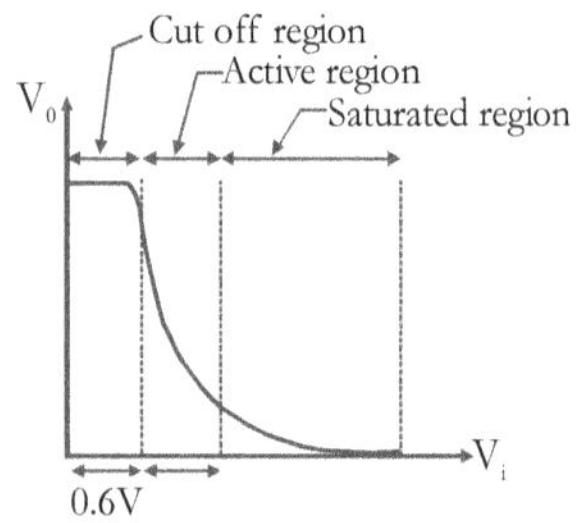

TRANSISTOR AS A SWITCH

Let us try to understand the operation of the transistor as a switch analysing the base-bised transistor in CE configuration (see figure).

Applying Kirchhoff's law in input and output sides of the circuit, we have

$$V_{RB} = V_i$$

$$= i_B R_B + V_{RE} \quad \ldots \text{(i)}$$

and $$V_{CE} = V_{cc} - i_c R_c$$

or $$V_0 = V_{CC} - i_c R_c \quad \ldots \text{(ii)}$$

For Si transistor V_0 vs V_i graph as ;

For Si transistor less than 0.6 V, the transistor willbe in cut off state and current i_c will be zero.

Hence $$V_0 = V_{cc}.$$

When V_i becomes greater than 0.6 V the transistor is in active state with some value of current i_c and so V_0 decreases. With increase of V_i, i_c increases and so V_0 decreases almost linearily till its value becomes less than about 1.0 V.

Beyond this the change becomes non-linear and transistor goes into saturation state.

Let us see now how the transistor is operated as a switch.

As long as V_i is low and unable to forward bias the transistor V_0 is high. If V_i high enough to derive the transistor into saturation the V_0 is low, very near to zero. When the transistor is not conducting it is said to be **switched off** and when it is driven into saturation it is said to be **switched on**.

7.14 TRANSISTOR AS AN OSCILLATOR

An oscillator is a device which converts dc into ac. It consists of mainly three parts. These are :

(i) LC circuit :

It is also known as tank circuit. It converts dc of low voltage into ac of low voltage. [This we have studied in chapter *AC* and *Em*-wave (vol 3) under the head *LC*-oscillations]. If *L* and *C* are the inductance and capacitance used in the circuit, then frequency of ac output will be

$$f = \frac{1}{2\pi}\sqrt{\frac{1}{LC}}.$$

(ii) Transistor amplifier : It amplifies the low voltage ac into high voltage ac

(iii) Positive feed back circuit : Due to the resistance of the circuit, some electrical energy will be converted into heat energy. To compensate this loss a fraction of output fed back into input circuit by using an inducting coil. If the feed back is in phase with the input, then it is known as positive feed back.

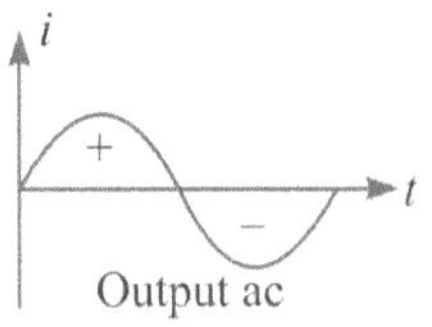

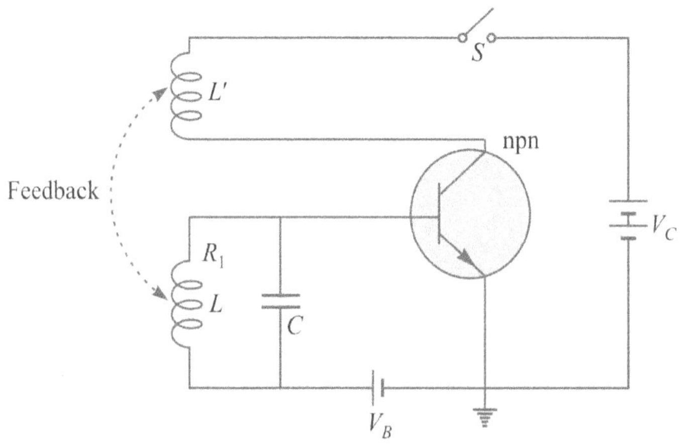

Fig. **7.33. Transistor as an oscillator.**

Ex. 8 **Find the value of β if (i) α = 0.9 (ii) α = 0.99.**

Sol.(i) We known that $\beta = \frac{\alpha}{1-\alpha} = \frac{0.9}{1-0.9} = 9.$

(ii) $\beta = \frac{\alpha}{1-\alpha} = \frac{0.99}{1-0.99} = 99.$ ***Ans.***

Ex. 9 **Calculate the emitter current i_E in a transistor for which β = 50 and i_B = 20 μA.**

Sol. We know that $\beta = \frac{i_C}{i_B}$

∴ $i_C = \beta\, i_B = 50 \times 0.02 = 1$ mA

Emitter current $i_E = i_B + i_C$

$= 0.02 + 1 = 1.02$ mA ***Ans.***

Ex. 10 **Find the value of i_C and α from the data given in the figure.**

Sol. We know that $i_E = i_B + i_C$

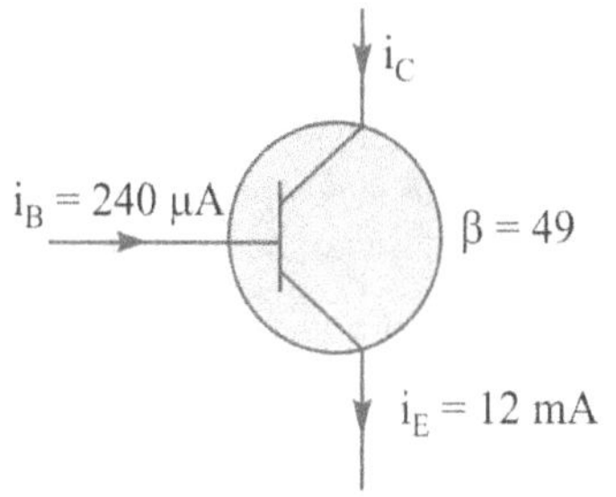

Fig. 7.34

$i_C = i_E - i_B$

$= 12 - 0.24 = 11.76$ mA ***Ans.***

Current gain $\alpha = \frac{\beta}{1+\beta}$

$= \frac{49}{1+49} = 0.98$ ***Ans.***

Ex. 11 **For a transistor, β = 45 and voltage drop across 1kΩ which is connected in the collector circuit is 1 volt. Find the base current for common emitter connection.**

Sol.

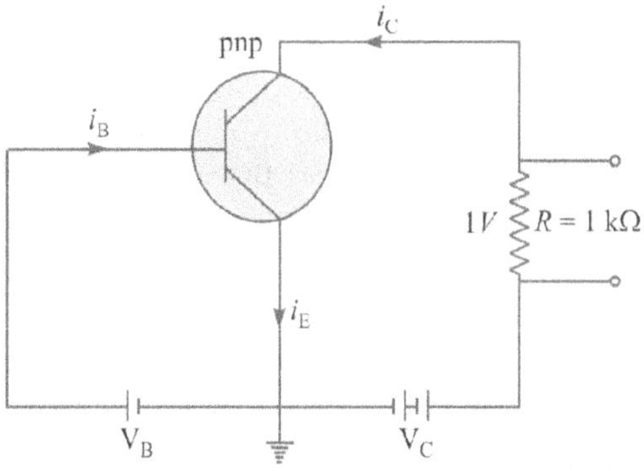

Fig. 7.35

From the data given,

$i_C = \frac{1}{1\times10^3} = 10^{-3} A$

$= 1$ mA.

We know that, $\beta = \frac{i_C}{i_B}$

∴ $i_B = \frac{i_C}{\beta} = \frac{1}{45} = 0.022$ mA. ***Ans.***

Ex. 12 **A silicon transistor amplifier circuit is given below: If the current amplification factor β = 100, determine :**

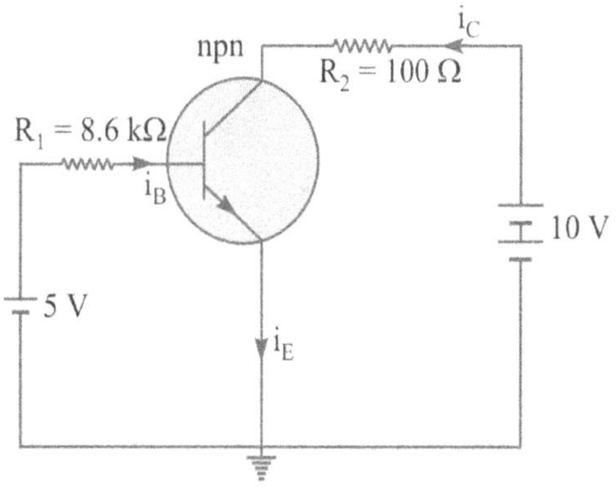

Fig. 7.36

(a) **base current i_B,**

(b) **collector current i_C,**

(c) **collector-emitter voltage**

(d) **collector base-voltage.**

Take the voltage drop between base and emitter as 0.7 V.

Sol.

(a) Figure represents npn transistor in common emitter connection. Applying Kirchhoff's loop rule in base-emitter circuit.

$+5 - i_B R_1 - V_{barrier} = 0$

∴ $i_B = \frac{5 - V_{barrier}}{R_1} = \frac{5-0.7}{8.6\times10^3}$

$= 0.5$ mA

(b) We know that $\beta = \frac{i_C}{i_B}$

∴ $i_C = \beta\, i_B$

$= 100 \times 0.5 = 50$ mA

(c) Applying Kirchhoff's loop rule in collector-emitter circuit, we have

$i_C R_2 - 10 + V_{CE} = 0$

∴ $V_{CE} = 10 - i_C R_2$

$= 10 - 50 \times 10^{-3} \times 100$

$= 5\text{ V}$

(d) For collector-base voltage, we can write

$$V_{CE} = V_{CB} + V_{BE}$$

$$\therefore \quad V_{CB} = V_{CE} - V_{BE}$$

$$= 5 - 0.7$$

$$= 4.3\text{ V} \qquad \textit{Ans.}$$

Ex. 13 **Find voltage gain and power gain in common-base amplifier.**

Sol. If input and output resistances are R_1 and R_2 respectively, then

$$\text{Voltage gain } A_v = \frac{\text{output voltage}}{\text{input voltage}}$$

$$= \frac{i_C R_2}{i_E R_1} = \alpha \frac{R_2}{R_1}.$$

$$\text{Power gain} = \frac{\text{output power}}{\text{input power}}$$

$$= \frac{i_C^2 R_2}{i_E^2 R_1} = \alpha^2 \frac{R_2}{R_1}. \qquad \textit{Ans.}$$

7.15 LOGIC GATES

An electronic circuit based on some logic and connected between input and output, is called a **logic gate**. The logic gates are based on Boolean algebra, which has two digits; 0 and 1, and three operators; OR, AND, and NOT. The meaning of 0 (zero) is; OFF, false, no, open, low and the meaning of 1 (one) is : ON, true, yes, close high.

OR operator

In Boolean algebra, OR operator is used for addition symbolically, it is represented by sign +. For addition of A and B, one can write A + B = Y, and reads as; A OR B is equal to Y. The expression like A + B = Y is called Boolean expression. The electrical circuit for OR operator is as follows :

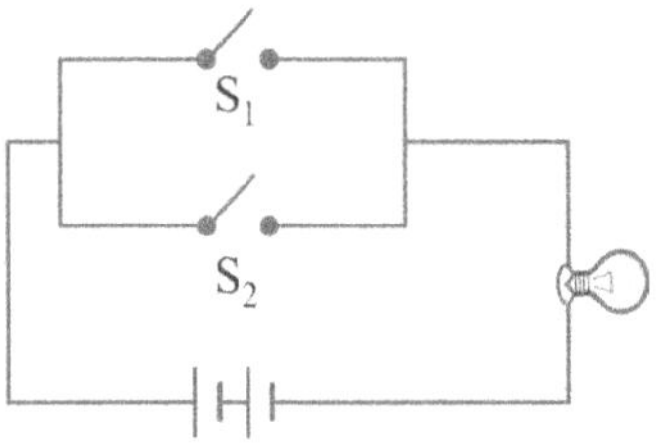

Fig. 7.37

Truth table

Truth table represents the all possible inputs and outputs. For the OR operator it is :

Inputs		Outputs
Switch S_1	Switch S_2	Bulb glows
Open	Open	No
Open	Close	Yes
Close	Open	Yes
Close	Close	Yes

In Boolean digits, it can be represented as follows :

A	B	A + B = Y
0	0	0
1	0	1
0	1	1
1	1	1

AND operator

In Boolean algebra, AND operator is used for multiplication. Symbolically it is represented by sign dot (.). For the multiplication of A and B, one can write, A.B = Y, and reads as; A AND B is equal to Y. The electrical circuit for AND operator is as follows :

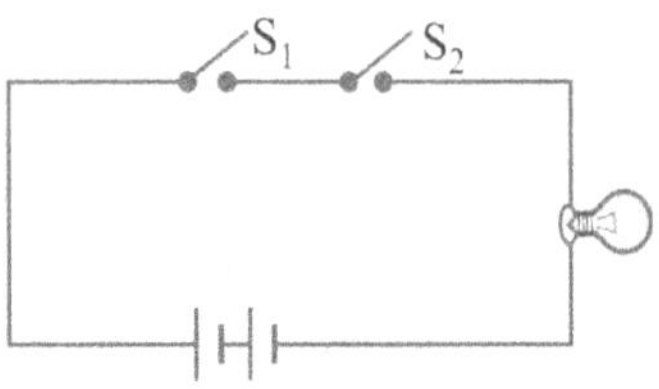

Fig. 7.38

Truth table

Inputs		Outputs
Switch S_1	Switch S_2	Bulb glows
Open	Open	No
Open	Close	No
Close	Open	No
Close	Close	Yes

In Boolean digits, it can be represented as follows :

A	B	A • B = Y
0	0	0
0	1	0
1	0	0
1	1	1

NOT operators

In Boolean algebra, NOT operator is used for inversion. Symbolically, it is represented by a sign bar over the input (–). For inversion of A, one can write $\overline{A} = Y$, and reads as; A NOT is equal to Y. The electrical circuit for NOT operator is as follows :

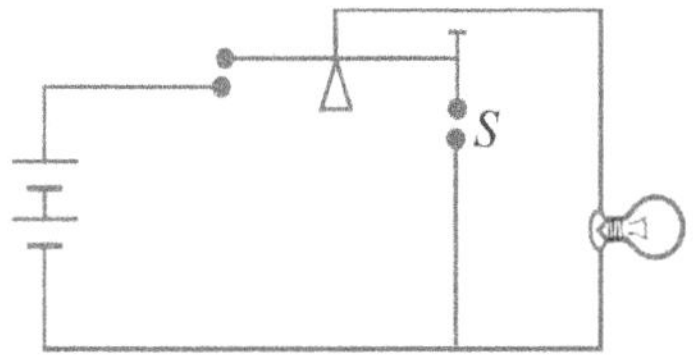

Fig. 7.39

Truth table

Switch S	Bulb glows
Open	Yes
Close	No

In Boolean digits, it can be represented as follows :

A	$\overline{A} = Y$
0	1
1	0

Some basic Boolean laws

1. Boolean postulates :

$$A + 0 = A, \quad 1.A = A$$
$$1 + A = 1, \quad 0.A = 0$$
$$A + \overline{A} = 1$$

2. Identity law : $A + A = A, \quad A.A = A$

3. Negation law : $\overline{\overline{A}} = A$

4. Absorption laws :

$$A + A.B = A,$$
$$A.(A + B) = A$$
$$\overline{A}.(A + B) = \overline{A}.B$$

5. Boolean identities : $A + \overline{A}B = A + B,$

$$A(\overline{A} + B) = AB$$
$$A + BC = (A + B)(A + C),$$
$$(\overline{A} + B).(A + C) = \overline{A}C + AB.$$

7.16 OR, AND AND NOT GATES

OR gate

There are two or more input signals in OR gate and one output signal. The output signal is high if any or all of the inputs are high. The Boolean expression of OR gate is : $A + B = Y$.

The symbol of OR gate is shown in figure :

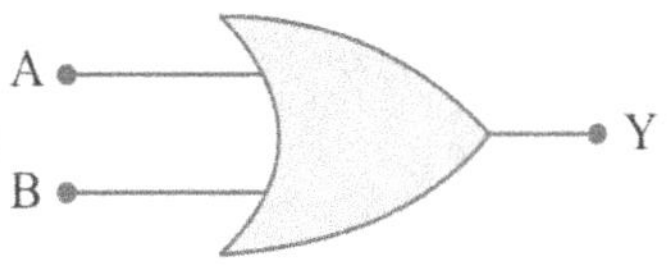

Truth table

A	B	A + B = Y
0	0	0
0	1	1
1	0	1
1	1	1

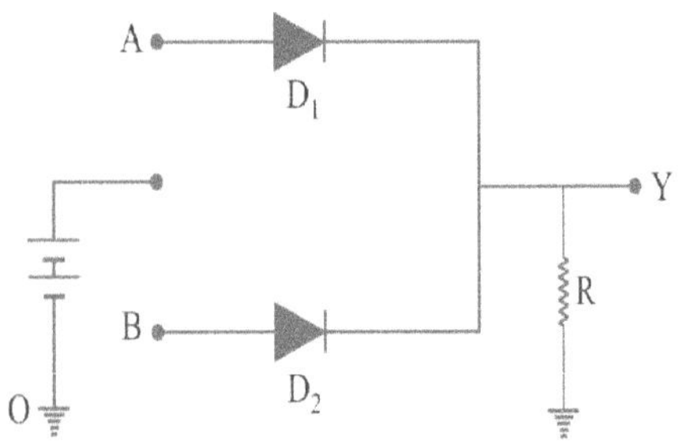

Fig. 7.40

Realization of OR gate

In practice the realization of OR gate can be understand by the following circuit. Based on the logic of OR gate, we have three algebraic laws. These are :

$$A+1 = 1, \; A+0=A, \; A+A=A.$$

AND gate

There are two or more input signals in AND gate and one output signal. The output signal is high only when all the input signals are high. The Boolean expression of AND gate is :

$$A.B = Y.$$

The symbol of AND gate is shown in figure :

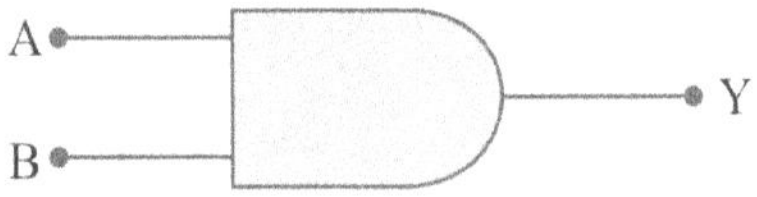

Truth table

A	B	A. B = Y
0	0	0
0	1	0
1	0	0
1	1	1

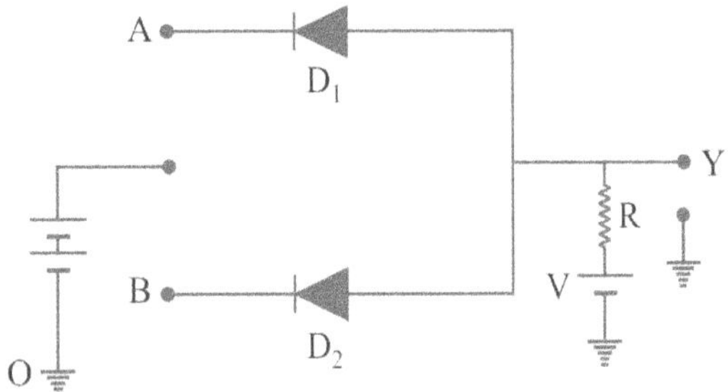

Fig. 7.41

Realization of AND gate

In practice the realization of AND gate can be understand by the following circuit.

Based on the logic of OR gate, we have three laws.

These are : $A.0 = 0, \; A.1=A, \; A.A=A.$

NOT gate

There is one input and one output in NOT gate. The output signal is high when input signal is low and vice-versa. The Boolean expression of NOT gate is :

$$\overline{A} = Y.$$

The symbol of NOT gate is shown in figure:

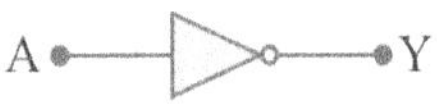

Truth table

A	$\overline{A}$ = Y
0	1
1	0

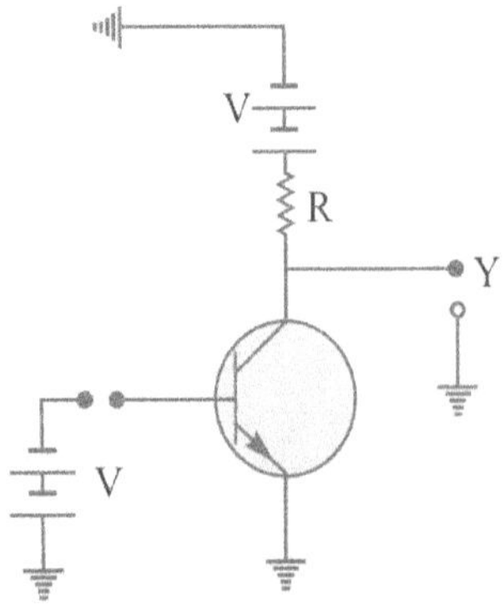

Fig. 7.42

Realization of NOT gate

In practice the realization of NOT gate can be understand by the following circuit. Based on the logic of NOT gate, we have

$$\overline{0} = 1, \; \overline{1} = 0. \qquad \text{Also } \; \overline{A} = A.$$

7.17 COMBINATION OF GATES

By combing any two or all the three basic gates, we can get new logic gates.

NAND gate

When output of AND gate becomes the input of NOT gate, this results in a new gate, which is called NAND gate. Therefore we can have;

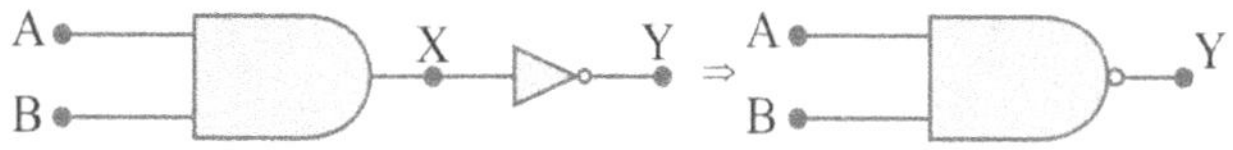

Fig. 7.43

The Boolean expression of NAND gate is :

$$\overline{A.B} = Y$$

Truth table

A	B	A.B	$\overline{A.B} = Y$
0	0	0	1
0	1	0	1
1	0	0	1
1	1	1	0

NOR gate

When output of OR gate becomes the input of NOT gate, this results in a new gate, which is called NOR gate. Therefore we can have;

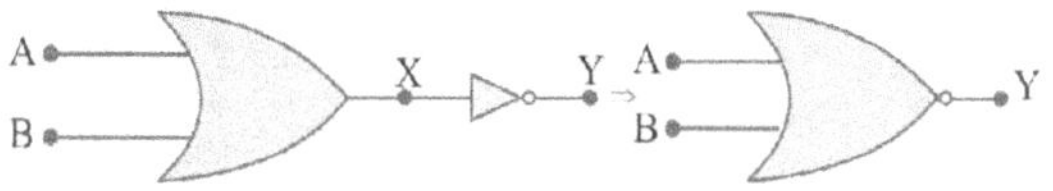

Fig. 7.44

The Boolean expression of NOR gate is :

$$\overline{A+B} = Y$$

Truth table

A	B	A + B	$\overline{A+B}$
0	0	0	1
0	1	1	0
1	0	1	0
1	1	1	0

Exclusive OR or XOR gate

It consists of two NOT gates, two AND gates and one OR gate. The output signal is high if either input A or input B but not when both are high. The XOR gate may be expressed as :

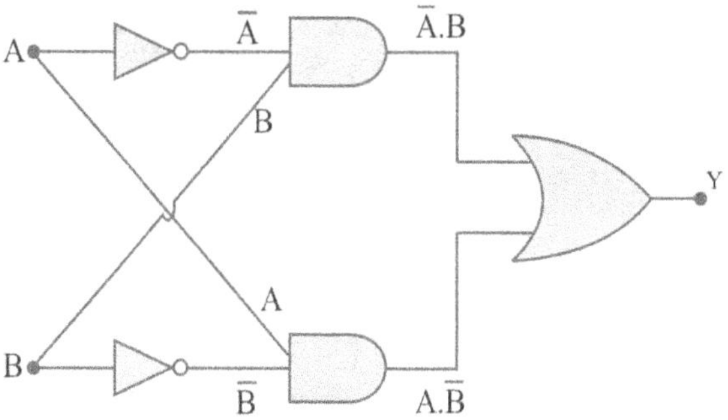

Fig. 7.45

The Boolean expression of XOR gate is :

$$\overline{A}B + A\overline{B} = Y$$

The symbol of XOR gate is shown in figure :

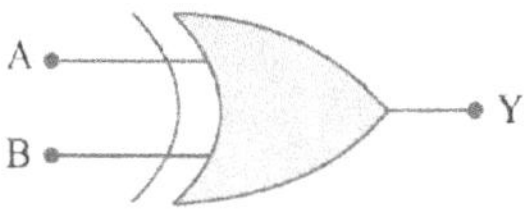

Truth table

A	B	$\overline{A}$	$\overline{B}$	$\overline{A}B$	$A\overline{B}$	$\overline{A}B + A\overline{B} = Y$
0	0	1	1	0	0	0
0	1	1	0	1	0	1
1	0	0	1	0	1	1
1	1	0	0	0	0	0

Exclusive NOR or XNOR gate

When output of XOR becomes the input of NOT gate, this results in a new gate, which is called XNOR gate. Thus

$$XOR + NOT \rightarrow XNOR.$$

The Boolean expression of XNOR gate is :

$$\overline{\bar{A}\,B + A\bar{B}} = Y.$$

The symbol of X NOR is :

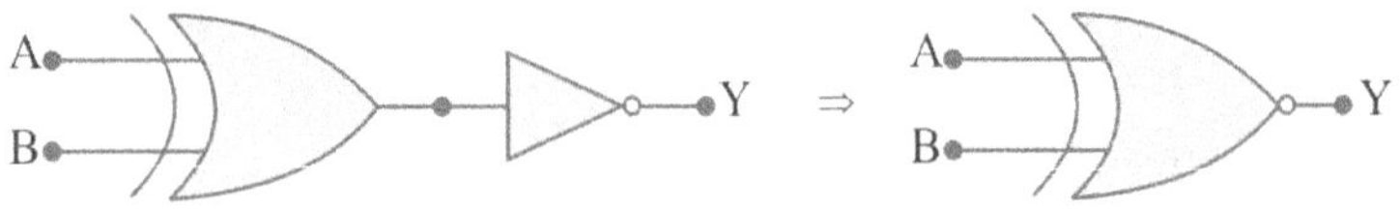

Fig. **7.46**

Building blocks

The NAND gate is known as universal building block; with the help of it, we can get basic gates. The other universal building block is NOR gate.

NOT from NAND gate

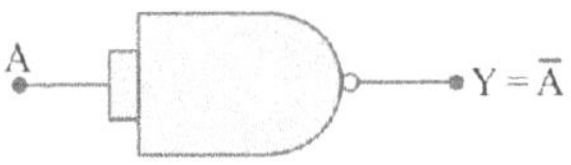

Fig. **7.47**

When both the inputs A and B of the NAND gate are joined together then it works as the NOT gate. Thus we have;

$$\overline{A.A} = \bar{A}$$

Truth table

Input	Output
A = B	Y
0	1
1	0

AND from NAND gate

When two NAND gates are connected in series, the output is equivalent to AND gate. That is;

$$NAND + NAND = (AND + NOT) + (AND + NOT) \Rightarrow AND$$

Fig. **7.48**

Truth table

A	B	$\overline{A.B}$	$\left(\overline{\overline{A.B}}\right) = Y$	
0	0	1	0	
0	1	1	0	→ NOT
1	0	1	0	
1	1	0	1	

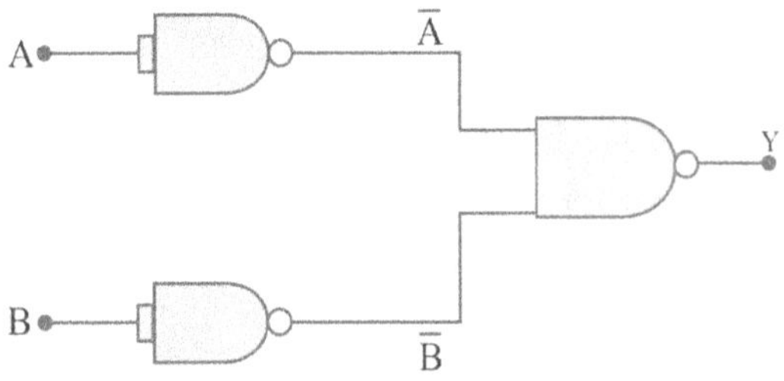

Fig. **7.49**

OR from NAND gate

When the outputs of two NOT gates (which are obtained from NAND gates) is given to the input of the another NAND gate, the resultant gate works as the OR gate.

Truth table

A	B	$\bar{A}$	$\bar{B}$	$\left(\overline{\bar{A}\,\bar{B}}\right) = Y$	
0	0	1	1	0	
0	1	1	0	1	→ OR
1	0	0	1	1	
1	1	0	0	1	

Ex. 14 **By using NOR gate, construct OR gate.**

Sol. If output signal of NOR is sent into NOT gate, then final Output is equivalent to OR gate. Thus

$$\text{NOR} + \text{NOT} = \text{OR} + \text{NOT} + \text{NOT} \Rightarrow \text{OR}$$

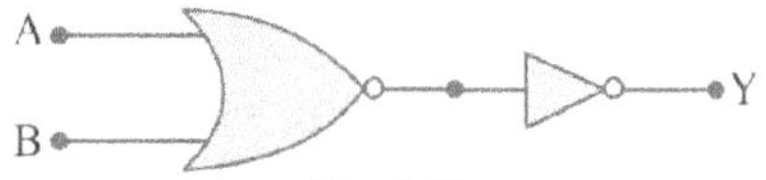

Fig. 7.50

Ex. 15 **Write the truth table for the combination of gates as shown in figures.**

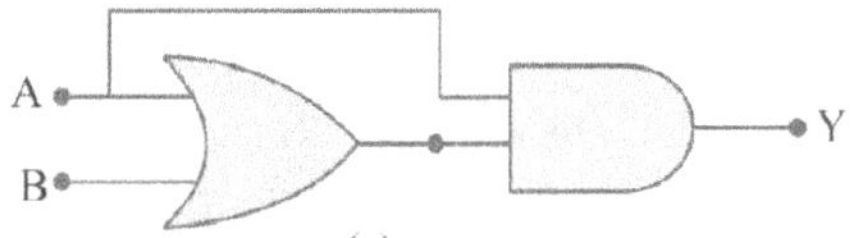

(a)

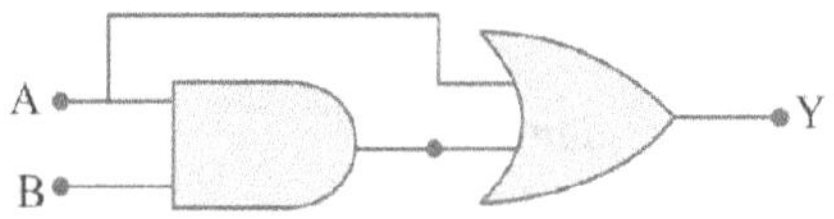

(b)

Fig. 7.51

Sol.

(a)

A	B	A + B	A.(A + B) = Y
0	0	0	0
0	1	1	0
1	0	1	1
1	1	1	1

(b)

A	B	A.B	A + (A.B)
0	0	0	0
0	1	0	0
1	0	0	1
1	1	1	1

Ex. 16 **The output of an OR gate is connected to both the inputs of a NOR gate. Draw the logic circuit for this combination and write the truth table.**

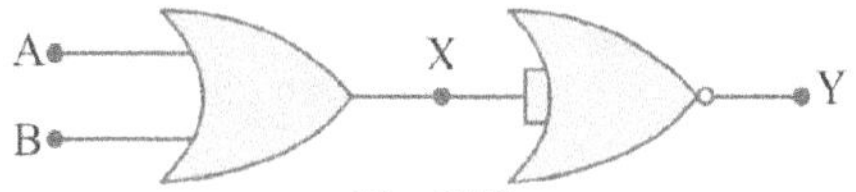

Fig. 7.52

Sol. $A + B = X$,

$$\overline{(A+B)+(A+B)} = \overline{A+B} = Y$$

Truth table :

A	B	X	Y
0	0	0	1
0	1	1	0
1	0	1	0
1	1	1	0

COMMUNICATION SYSTEMS

7.18 Communication

1. Communication as we all know is the act of transmission and reception of information.
2. For successful communication, sender and receiver must understand some common language.
3. Radio and television provide us audio and visual information.
4. Videophones, voice mails and satellite conferences enable us to see live images instantly and how us to communicate directly with people of different parts of the globe.
5. Marconi was the first to establish radio transmission in 1901.
6. J.C. Bose made significant contribution in this field.
7. Satellite communication started in 1962 with the launching of Telestar in USA.
8. Optical fibre communication started in USA in the year 1970.
9. The present day communication systems are electrical, electronic or optical in nature.
10. Every communication system has the following three essential elements :
    1. Transmitter 2. communication channel
    3. Receiver

Basically, the transmitter is located at one place, and the receiver at the other place, the channel is the physical medium that connects the transmitterand receiver.

The block diagram of generalised communication system is shown in figure.

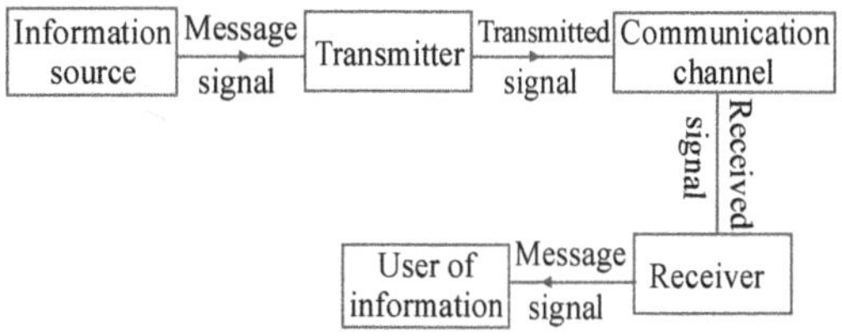

The communication channel carries the modulated wave from the transmitter to receiver.

There are two basic modes of communication :

(i) Point to point and **(ii)** Broadcast.

In point to point communication mode, message is transmitted over a link between a single transmitter and a receiver. For **Ex.** Telephone.

In broadcast mode : There are large number of receivers corresponding to a single transmitter. Radio and TV are the common examples of broadcast mode.

Basic terminology used in electronic communication system :

In communication frequently used terms are :

1. **Signal :** It is a single valued function of time that carries the information. It is usually in electrical form and is suitable for transmission.

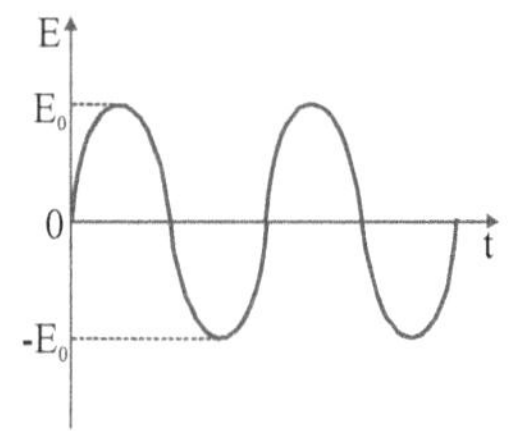

(a) **Analog signal** : is that in which current or voltage value varies continuously with time.

Ex.: $E = E_0 \sin(\omega t + \phi)$

Speech, music, sound produced by tuning fork.

For speech signal, frequency range is form 300 Hz to 3100 Hz. Thus band width of speech signal = 3100 Hz – 300 Hz = 2800 Hz.

For video signals require a bandwidth of 4.2 MHz.

The frequency produced by musical instruments are high therefore approximate bandwidth for music is 20 kHz.

TV signals contains both voice/music and picture signals. Therefore band width alocated for transmission of TV is 6 MHz.

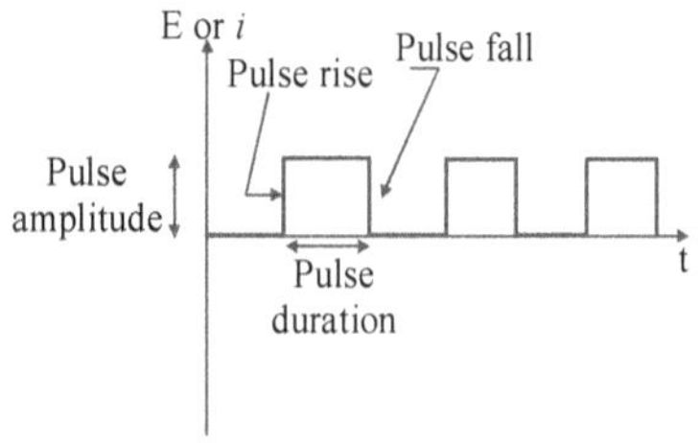

(b) **Digital signal :** It is the discontinuous function of time. Ex. letters printed on books, output of digital computer, Fax etc.

A digital signal is in the form of pulses.

2. **Transducer :** A device / arrangement which converts one form of energy into another. For example

Microphone converts speech sound signals into electrical signals

Piezoelectric sensor converts pressure variation into electrical signals.

Photo detector converts light signals into electrical signals. Loud speaker converts electrical signal into sound signal.

3. **Noise :** It refers to the disturbance or distortion in the transmission. The noise may be due to channel imperfection or some sources inside or outside the system.

4. **Transmitter :** It is an arrangement that converts the message signals into a form suitable for transmission and then transmits it through some communication channel.

5. **Receiver :** A receiver is an arrangement that picks up the transmitted signal at the channel output and processes it to reproduce the message signal in the suitable form.

6. **Attenuation :** refers to the loss of strength of a signal during its propagation through the commnication channel.

7. **Amplification :** It is the process of increasing the strength of the transmitted signals using some suitable electronic circuit, It can be done anywhere between the transmitter and receiver when signal strength becomes weaker than required strength. The energy required for additional signal strength is obtained from a dc power source.

8. **Range :** It is the largest distance between transmitter and receiver where the signal is received in due strength.

9. **Band width :** Band width refers usually to the range of frequencies over which the communication system works.

10. **Modulation :** It is the phenomenon of superimposing the low frequency message signal to a high frequency wave (called the carrier wave). The resulting wave is called modulated wave.
11. **Demodulation :** It is the reverse process of modulation. Demodulation is the phenomenon of retrival of information from the modulated wave at the receiver.
12. **Repeater :** Repeaters are erected at suitable locations in between the transmitter and the receiver. Each repeater receives the transmitted signal, amplifies it properly keeping its original form intact, and then relays it to the next repeater.

Transmission medium or Communication channel

Communication Channel is a link through which informations/ message signal may propagate from the source to the destination without any noise ordistortion.
Transmission medium divided into two types :

1. **Guided transmission medium :**
   It is that communication medium which is used in point to point communication between a single transmitter and a receiver. For example, parallel wire lines, twisted pair and co-axial cable are guided transmission media **optical fibres** are other example of guided transmission medium.
2. **Unguided transmission medium :**
   There are large number of receiver corresponding to a single transmitter. It is used in space communication and satellite communication, such as in radio and TV.

7.19 BAND WIDTH OF TRANSMISSION MEDIUM

The commonly used transmission media are wire, free space and optical fibre cable. Co-axial cable is a widely used wire medium. It offers a band width of 750 MHz. These cables are generally operated below 18 GHz.
Communication through free space using radiowaves occurs at frequencies from 10^5 to 10^8 Hz. This range is subdivided further into table given below. Optical fibre communication is used in the frequency range of 1 THz to 1000 THz (microwaves to ultraviolet). An optical fibre can offer a transmission band width in excess of 100 GHz.

Services	Frequency bands	Remarks
Standard AM broadcast	540 - 1600 kHz	
FM broadcast	88 - 108 MHz	
Television	54 - 72 MHz	VHF TV
	76 - 88 MHz	
	174 - 216 MHz	UHF TV
	420 - 890 MHz	
Collector, Mobile, Radio	896 - 901 MHz	Mobile to base station
	840 - 935 MHz	Base station to mobile
Satellite	5.925-6.425GHz	Uplink
Communication	3.7 - 4.2 GHz	Downlink

7.20 ANTENNA

Antenna : An antenna plays a vital role in a communication system. It is used in both, the transmission and reception of radio frequency signals.
An antenna is a structure that is capable of radiating electromagnetic waves or receiving them as the case may be. Basically, an antenna is generally a metallie object, often a wire or collection of wires.

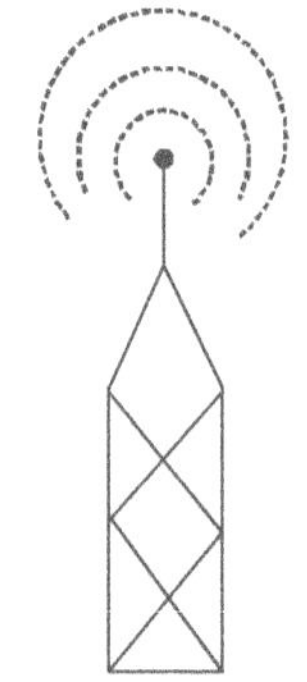

When a transmitting antenna is held vertically, the EM-waves produced are polarised vertically. When the same antenna held horizontally, the EM-waves produced are polarised horizontally.

A **Hertz antenna** is a straight conductor of length equal to the half the wavelength of radio signals to be transmitted or received i.e., $\boxed{l = \lambda / 4}$. This antenna is not grounded.

A **Marconi antenna** is a straight conductor of length equal to the quarter of the wavelength of radio signals to be transmitted or received i.e., $\boxed{l = \lambda / 4}$. It held vertically with its lower end touching the ground. The electromagnetic waves emitted from Marconi antenna are the same as those emitted from Hertz antenna.

The design of an antenna depends on frequency of carrier wave and directivity of the beam etc.

Two common types of antenna are

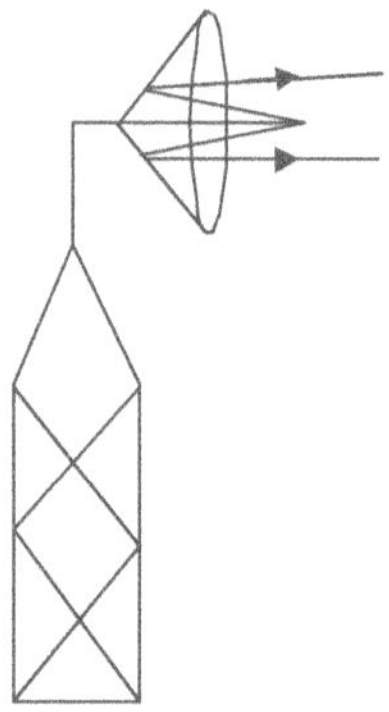

1. **Dipole antenna :** It is used for transmission of radio waves.
2. **Dish type antenna :** Such an antenna has a parabolic reflector with an active element called dipole or horn feed at the focus of reflector. Dish antenna can transmits waves in particular direction. Dish antenna is commonly used in radar and satellite communication.

Modulation and its Necessity : A message signal usually spread over a range of frequencies, called the signal band width. That is why message signals are also called base band signals, representing the band of frequencies of the original signal.

Suppose we wish to transmit an electrical signal in the audio frequency (AF) range (20 Hz to 20 kHz) over a long distance. We cannot do it because of the following reasons.

1. **Size of the antenna or aerial :** An antenna or aerial is needed for both transmission and reception. Each antenna should have a size comparable to the wavelength of the signal, (atleast $\frac{\lambda}{4}$ in size), so that time variation of the signal is properly sensed by the antenna. For an audio frequency f = 15 kHz,

   $$\lambda = \frac{c}{f} = \frac{3 \times 10^8}{15 \times 10^3} = 20000 \text{ m}.$$

   The length of antenna $= \frac{\lambda}{4} = \frac{20000}{4} = 5000$ m.

   To set up an antenna of height 5000 m is practically impossible.

   If transmission frequency were raised to 1 MHz, then $\lambda = \frac{c}{f} = \frac{3 \times 10^8}{10^6} = 300$ m,

   and $\frac{\lambda}{4} = \frac{300}{4} = 75$ m

   which is reasonable. Therefore there is a need of converting the information contained in our low frequency base-band signal to high frequencies before transmission.
2. **Effective power radiated by antenna :**

   Studied revals that power P radiated from a linear antenna of length l is $P \propto \left(\frac{l}{\lambda}\right)^2$

   As high powers are needed for good transmission,therefore, for given antenna length wavelength λ should be small or frequency should be high.
3. **Mixing up of signals from different transmitters :**

   When many people are talking at the same time, we just cannot make out who is talking what. Similarly when many transmitters are transmitting baseband information signals simultaneously, they get mixed up and there is no way to distinguish between them. The possible solution is communication at high frequencies and a band of frequencies to each transmitter so that there is no mixing. This is what is being done for different radio and TV broadcast stations.

Ex. 17 **Find the minimum length of antenna required to transmit a radio signal of frequency 10 MHz.**

Sol. $f = 10\text{ MHz} = 10^7\text{ Hz}$

$$\lambda = \frac{c}{f} = \frac{3 \times 10^8}{10^7} = 30\text{ m}$$

Minimum length of antenna $= \frac{\lambda}{4} = 30/4 = 7.5$ m.

7.21 MODULATION AND ITS TYPES

Modulation : Modulation is the phenomenon of superimposing the low audio frequency baseband message or information signals on a high frequency wave (called the carrier wave). The resultant wave is called modulated wave, which is to be transmitted.

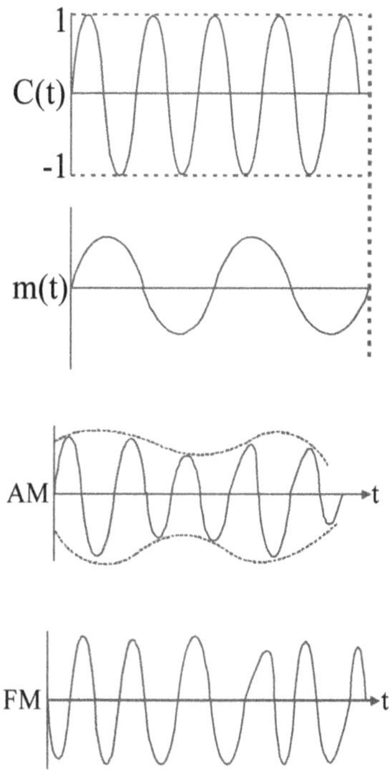

Types of Modulation

Three types of modulation

1. Amplitude modulation (AM)
2. Frequency modulation (FM)
3. Phase modulation (PM)

Amplitude Modulation : In amplitude modulation, the amplitude of carrier wave is varied in accordance with the amplitude of the modulating signal.
However frequency of the amplitude modulated wave remains the same as that of the carrier wave.
Let us take a sinusoidal modulating signal, represented by

$$m(t) = A_m \sin\omega_m t \qquad \ldots(i)$$

and carrier wave is represented by

$$C(t) = A_c \sin\omega_c t \qquad \ldots(ii)$$

In amplitude modulation, the amplitude of modulated wave is given by,
$C_m(t) = (A_c + A_m \sin\omega_m t)$, as its frequency is that of carrier wave and so, we can write

$$C_m(t) = (A_c + A_m \sin\omega_m t) \sin\omega_c t$$

$$= A_c \left(1 + \frac{A_m}{A_c} \sin\omega_m t\right) \sin\omega_c t \qquad \ldots(iii)$$

Put, $\frac{A_m}{A_c} = \mu$, amptitude modulation index, we get

$$C_m(t) = A_c \sin\omega_c t + \mu A_c \sin\omega_m t \sin\omega_c t \qquad \ldots(iv)$$

$$= A_c \sin\omega_c t + \frac{\mu A_c}{2}\left[\cos(\omega_c - \omega_m)t - \cos(\omega_c + \omega_m)t\right] \qquad \ldots(v)$$

Above equation shows the amplitude modulated wave constant of the carrier wave of frequency ω_c plus two sinusoidal waves, one of frequency $(\omega_c - \omega_m)$ and other of frequency $(\omega_c + \omega_m)$. These two additional waves are called **side bands.**
Their frequencies are called side band frequencies $\omega_{SB} = \omega_c \pm \omega_m$
Frequency of lower side, $\omega_{LSB} = \omega_c - \omega_m$
and frequency of upper side, $\omega_{USB} = \omega_c + \omega_m$
Band width of amplitude modulated wave is $\Delta\omega = \omega_{USB} - \omega_{LSB} = 2\omega_m$

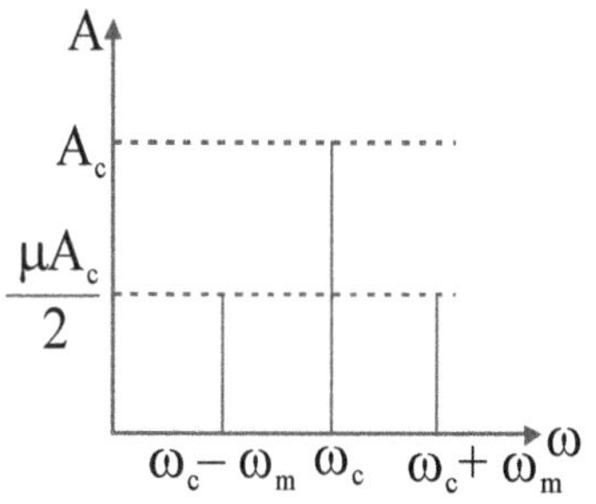

Ex. 18 **An audio signal of amplitude 0.1 V is used in amplitude modulation of a carrier wave of amplitude 0.2 V. Calculate the modulation index.**

Sol. : $\mu = \frac{A_m}{A_c} = \frac{0.1}{0.2} = 0.5$

Ex. 19 **A message signal of frequency 10 kHz and peak voltage of 10 volt is used to modulate a carrier of frequency 1 MHz and peak voltage 20 V. Determine (i) modulation index (ii) the side bands produced.**

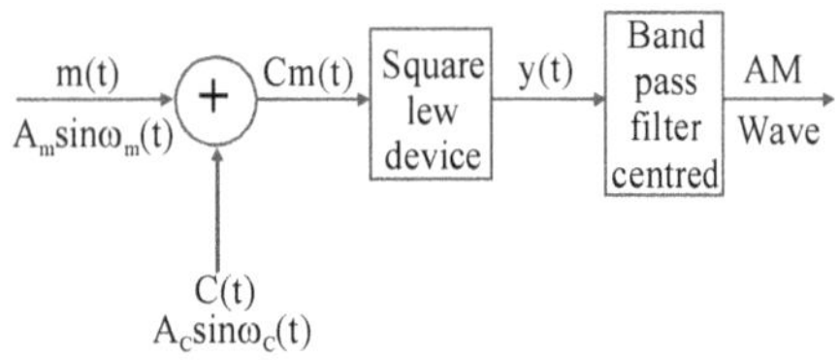

Block diagram of a simple modulator

Sol. (i) $\mu = \frac{A_m}{A_c} = \frac{10}{20} = 0.5$.

(ii) Side bands are $= \omega_c \pm \omega_m = 1000 + 10 = 1010$ Hz and $1000 - 10 = 990$ Hz.

Production of Amplitude Modulated Wave :

Amplitude modulated wave can be obtained by various methods. A conceptually simple method is shown in the block diagram.

Block diagram of a simple modulator for obtaining an AM signal

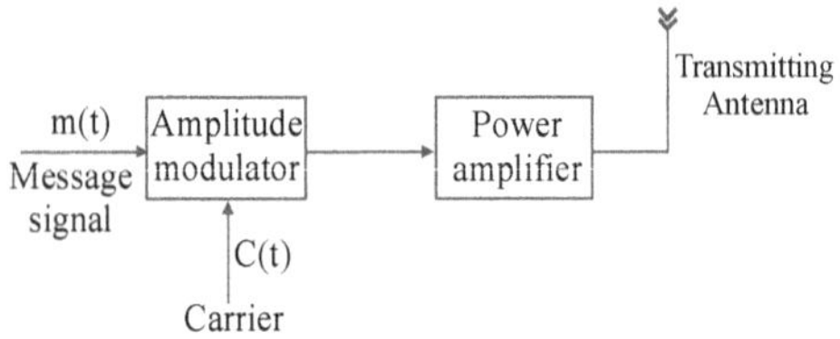

Block diagram of a transmitter

Demodulation : Detection of Amplitude Modulated Wave Demodulation is the reverse process of modulation, which is performed in a receiver to recover the original modulating signals.

Block diagram of a Receiver :

IF = Intermediate frequency

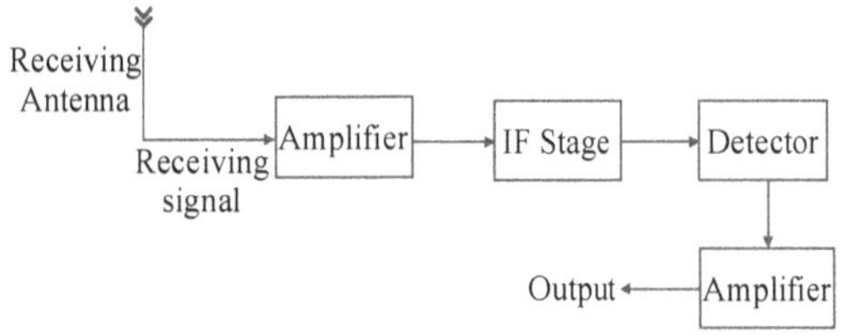

7.22 VARIOUS MODES OF PROPAGATION OF EM-WAVES

Sky Waves : 30 MHz to 40 MHz

In the frequency range from 30 MHz to 40 MHz, Long distance communication can be acheived by ionosphere reflection of **radio waves** back towards the earth. This mode of propagation is called **sky wave** propagation and is used by **short wave broadcast services**. The ionosphere is so called because of presence of large number of ions or charged particles. It extends from a height of ~ 65 km to 400 km above the earth's surface.

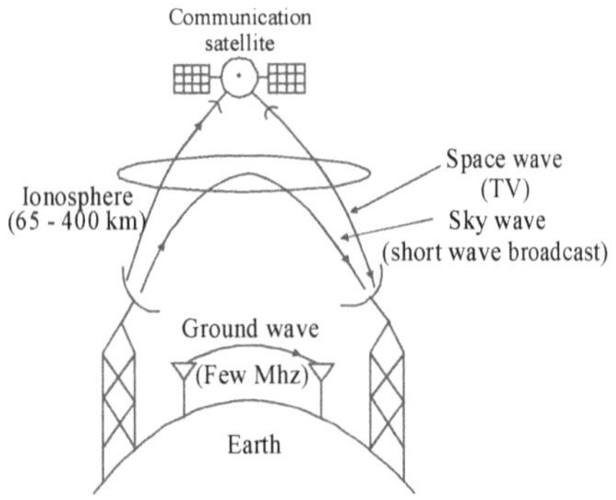

Space Wave : > (40 MHz)

A space wave travels in a straight line from transmitting antenna to the receiving antenna. Space waves are used for line-of-sight (LOS) communication as well as satellite communication. At frequency above 40 MHz communication is essentially limited to line-of sight paths. At these frequencies, the antennas are relatively smaller and can be placed at heights of many wavelengths above the ground. Because of line of sight nature of propagation, direct waves get bocked at some point by the curvature of the earth. If the signal is to be received beyond the horizon the receiving antenna must be high enough to intercept the line of sight waves.

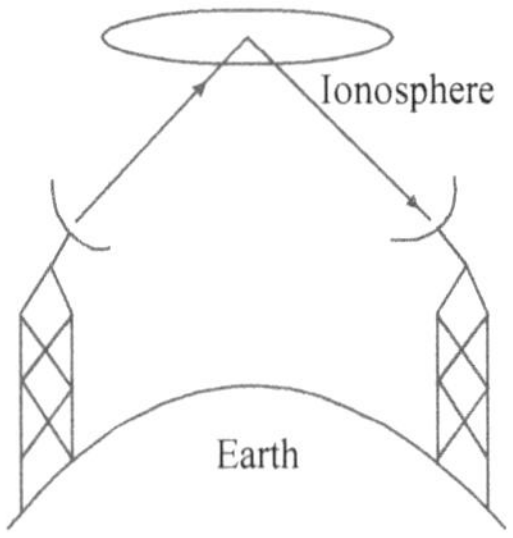

Height of Transmitting Antenna :

If h is the height of antenna, then by geometry we get $\boxed{d = \sqrt{2Rh}}$ R is radius of earth.

$$(R + h)^2 = R^2 + d^2 + h^2$$

or $$R^2 + h^2 + 2Rh = R^2 + d^2 + h^2$$

$$\therefore \quad d = \sqrt{2Rh}$$

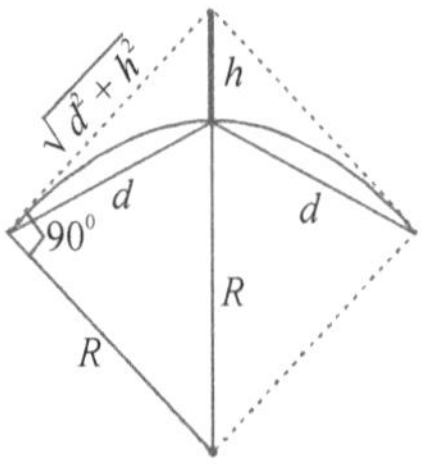

The maximum line of sight distance dm between the two antenna having heights hT and hR above the earth is given by

$$d_m = \sqrt{2Rh_T} + \sqrt{2Rh_R}$$

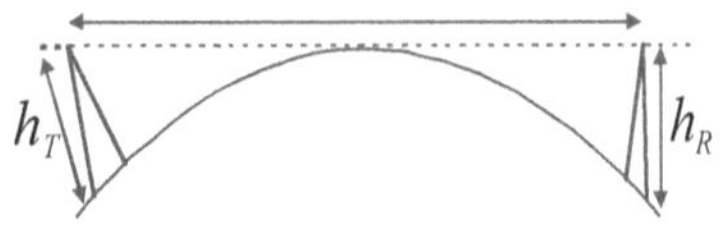

Ex. 20 A transmitting antenna at the top of a tower has a height 32 m and the height of the receiving antenna is 50 m. What is the maximum distance between them for satisfactory communication in LOS mode ? Given radius of earth 6.4×10^6 m.

Sol. $d_m = \sqrt{2Rh_T} + \sqrt{2Rh_R}$

$= \sqrt{2 \times 64 \times 10^5 \times 32} + \sqrt{2 \times 64 \times 10^5 \times 50}$

$= 45.5 \times 10^3$ m $= 45.5$ km

Review of Formulae & Important Points

1. According to band theory, the substance is a semi conductor if forbidden gap is order of 1 eV.

   * For Ge, $E_g = 0.7 eV$ and for Si, $E_g = 1.1\ eV$.

2. Conductivity of a semiconductor

$$\sigma = e(n_e\mu_e + n_h\mu_h)$$

for intrinsic semiconductor $n_e = n_h$

for extrinsic semiconductor

(a) N-type, $n_e > n_h$

(b) P-type $n_h > n_e$

* In N-type semiconductor, impurity added is pentavalent, (Antimony, Arsenic etc.)
* In P-type semiconductor, impurity added is trivalent, (Aluminium, Boron, Indium etc)

3. Forward bias

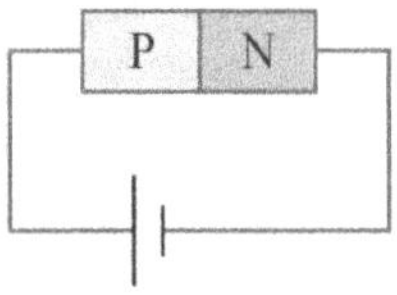

Reverse bias

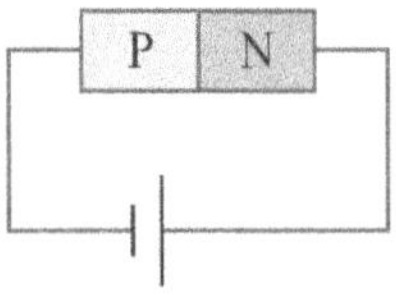

* For an ideal junction diode, forward resistance $R_f = 0$ and reverse resistance $R_r = \infty$.

4. Current in p-n junction

$$i = i_0 e^{(ev/\eta^{kt})} - 1;\ \eta = 1 \text{ for Ge and } \eta = 2 \text{ for Si.}$$

5. **Rectification (A.C. → D.C) by diode :**

(a) Half wave : $i_{dc} = i_0/\pi,\ i_{rms} = i_0/\sqrt{2}$

$$P_{DC} = i_{dc}^2 R_L.$$

$$P_{AC} = i^2_{rms}(R_L + R_f).$$

$$\eta_{rec} = \frac{P_{dc}}{P_{ac}} \times 100\% = \frac{40.6}{1 + \frac{R_f}{R_L}}$$

(b) Full wave : $i_{dc} = 2i_0/\pi,\ i_{rms} = i_0/2$

$$P_{DC} = i_{dc}^2 R_L$$

$$P_{AC} = i^2_{rms}(R_L + R_f)$$

$$\eta_{rec} = \frac{P_{dc}}{P_{ac}} \times 100\% = \frac{81.2}{1 + \frac{R_f}{R_L}}.$$

6. **Transistor : (Willium Shockley) :**

Function : Amplification, oscillation (A.C → D.C) and modulation

For any transistor, $i_e = i_b + i_c$.

7. **Current gain :** $\alpha = \frac{\Delta I_c}{\Delta I_e}$ in common base

$\beta = \frac{\Delta I_c}{\Delta I_b}$ in common emitter

$\alpha = \frac{\beta}{1+\beta}$ and

$\beta = \frac{\alpha}{1-\alpha}$.

8. **Voltage gain :** $A_v = \alpha\frac{R_2}{R_1}$ in common base

$A_v = \beta\frac{R_2}{R_1}$ in common emitter

9. **Power gain :** $A_p = \alpha^2\frac{R_2}{R_1}$ in common base

$A_p = \beta^2\frac{R_2}{R_1}$ in common emitter

10. **Transistor as Oscillator :** It consists of :

(i) LC Circuit

(ii) Transistor Amplifier

(iii) Positive feed back circuit, $f = \frac{1}{2\pi\sqrt{LC}}$.

* Negative feed back is used in amplification to reduce distortions.
* Positive feedback is used in oscillators.

11. Transmitter, transmission channel and receiver are three basic units of a communication system.

12. Two important forms of communication system are: Analog and Digital.The information to be transmitted is generally in continuous waveform for the former while for the latter it has only discrete or quantised levels.

13. Every message signal occupies a range of frequencies. The bandwidth of a message signal refers to the band of frequencies,

which are necessary for satisfactory transmission of the information contained in the signal. Similarly, any parctical communication system permits transmission of a range of frequencies only, which is referred to as the bandwidth of the system.

Services	**Frequency bands**	**Comments**
Standard AM broadcast	540 - 1600 kHz	
FM broadcast	88 - 108 MHz	
Television	54 - 72 MHz	VHF (very high
	76 - 88 MHz	
frequencies) TV		
	174 - 216 MHz	UHF (ultra high
	420 - 890 MHz	frequencies) TV

14. Low frequencies cannot be transmitted to long distances. Therefore, they are superimposed on a high frequency carrier signal by a process known as modulation.

15. In modulation, some characteristic of the carrier signal like amplitude, frequency or phase varies in accordance with the modulating or message signal. Correspondingly, they are called Amplitude Modulated (AM), Frequency Modulated (FM) or Phase Modulated (PM) waves.

16. For transmission over long distances, signals are radiated into space using devices called antennas. The radiated signals propagate as electromagnetic waves and the mode of propagation is influenced by the presence of the earth and its atmosphere. Near the surface of the earth, electromagnetic waves propagate as surface waves. **Surface waves** propagation is useful up to a **few MHz** frequencies.

17. Long distance communication between two points on the earth is achieved through reflection of electromagnetic waves by ionosphere. Such waves are called sky waves. **Sky wave** propagation takes place up to frequency of about **30 MHz**. Above this frequency, electromagnetic waves essentially propagate as space waves. **Space waves** are used for line-of-sight (LOS) communication and satellite communication.

18. If an antenna radiates electromagnetic waves from a height h_T, then the range d_T is given by $\sqrt{2Rh_T}$ where R is the radius of the earth.

Line-of-sight distance, $d_m = \sqrt{2Rh_T} + \sqrt{2Rh_R}$

19. Amplitude modulated signal contains frequencies $(\omega_c - \omega_m)$, ω_c and $(\omega_c + \omega_m)$.

20. Amplitude modulated waves can be produced by application of the message signal and the carrier wave to a non-linear device, followed by a band pass filter.

Amplitude modulation index, $\mu = \frac{A_m}{A_c}$; $\mu \leq 1$.

★★★

Modern Physics

MCQ Type 1

Exercise 7.1

LEVEL - 1

1. A piece of copper and the other of germanium are cooled from the room temperature to 80 K, then which of the following would be a correct statement
   (a) resistance of each increases
   (b) resistance of each decreases
   (c) resistance of copper increases while that of germanium decreases
   (d) resistance of copper decreases while that of germanium increases

2. The forbidden energy band gap in conductors, semiconductors and insulators are EG_1, EG_2 and EG_3 respectively. The relation among them is
   (a) $EG_1 = EG_2 = EG_3$
   (b) $EG_1 < EG_2 < EG_3$
   (c) $EG_1 > EG_2 > EG_3$
   (d) $EG_1 < EG_2 > EG_3$

3. P-type semiconductor is formed when
   A. as impurity is mixed in Si
   B. Al impurity is mixed in Si
   C. B impurity is mixed in Ge
   D. P impurity is mixed in Ge
   (a) A and C (b) A and D
   (c) B and C (d) B and D

4. In a P-type semiconductor
   (a) current is mainly carried by holes
   (b) current is mainly carried by electrons
   (c) the material is always positively charged
   (d) doping is done by pentavalent material

5. In a semiconductor
   (a) there are no free electrons at any temperature
   (b) the number of free electrons is more than that in a conductor
   (c) there are no free electrons at 0 K
   (d) none of these

6. In a semiconducting material the mobilities of electrons and holes are μ_e and μ_h respectively. Which of the following is true
   (a) $\mu_e > \mu_h$ (b) $\mu_e < \mu_h$
   (c) $\mu_e = \mu_h$ (d) $\mu_e < 0; \mu_h > 0$

7. The reverse biasing in a PN junction diode
   (a) decreases the potential barrier
   (b) increases the potential barrier
   (c) increases the number of minority charge carriers
   (d) increases the number of majority charge carriers

8. The PN junction diode is used as
   (a) an amplifier (b) a rectifier
   (c) an oscillator (d) a modulator

9. The potential barrier, in the depletion layer, is due to
   (a) ions (b) holes
   (c) electrons (d) both (b) and (c)

10. In a PN-junction diode not connected to any circuit
    (a) the potential is the same everywhere
    (b) the P-type is a higher potential than the N-type side
    (c) there is an electric field at the junction directed from the N-type side to the P-type side
    (d) there is an electric field at the junction directed from the P-type side to the N-type side

11. Which of the following statements is not true
    (a) the resistance of intrinsic semiconductors decrease with increase of temperature
    (b) doping pure Si with trivalent impurities give P-type semiconductors
    (c) the majority carriers in N-type semiconductors are holes
    (d) a PN-junction can act as a semiconductors diode

12. The dominant mechanisms for motion of charge carriers in forward and reverse biased silicon P-N junctions are
    (a) drift in forward bias, diffusion in reverse bias
    (b) diffusion in forward bias, drift in reverse bias
    (c) diffusion in both forward and reverse bias
    (d) drift in both forward and reverse bias

13. The probability of electrons to be found in the conduction band of an intrinsic semiconductor at a finite temperature
    (a) decreases exponentially with increasing band gap
    (b) increases exponentially with increasing band gap
    (c) decreases with increasing temperature
    (d) is independent of the temperature and the band gap

14. Which one is reverse-biased

(a)
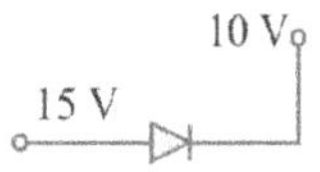

(b)
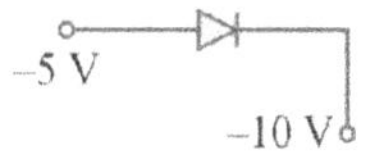

(c)
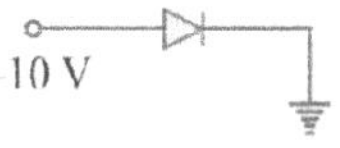

(d)
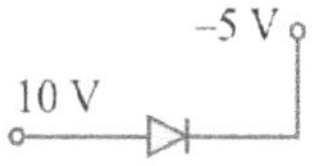

Answer Key	1	(d)	2	(b)	3	(c)	4	(a)	5	(c)	6	(a)	7	(b)
Sol. from page 368	8	(b)	9	(a)	10	(c)	11	(c)	12	(b)	13	(a)	14	(c)

15. Two PN-junctions can be connected in series by three different methods as shown in the figure. If the potential difference in the junctions is the same, then the correct connections will be

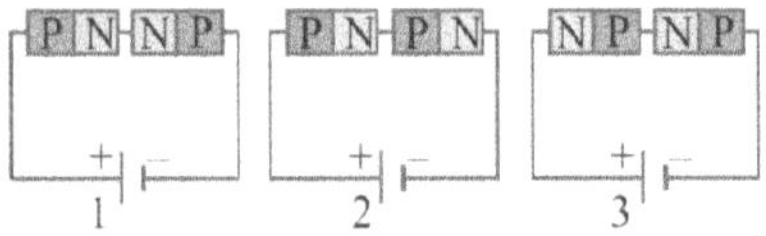

(a) in the circuit (1) and (2)
(b) in the circuit (2) and (3)
(c) in the circuit (1) and (3)
(d) only in the circuit (1)

16. Of the diodes shown in the following diagrams, which one is reverse biased

(a) 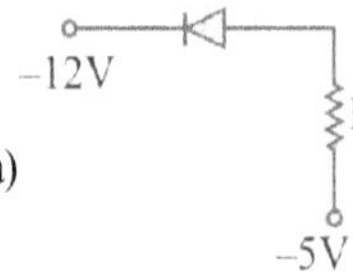

(b) 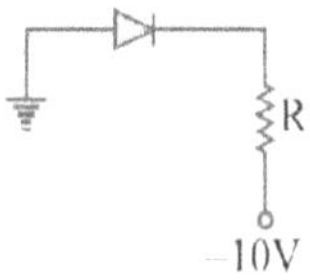

(c) 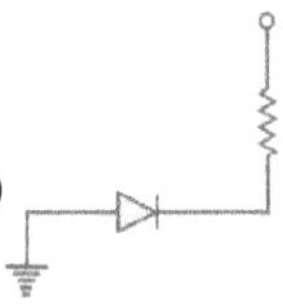

(d) 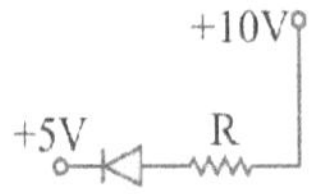

17. Which is the correct diagram of a half-wave rectifier

(a) 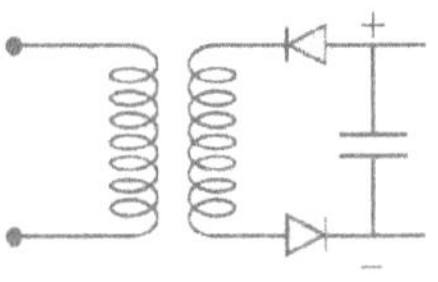
(b) 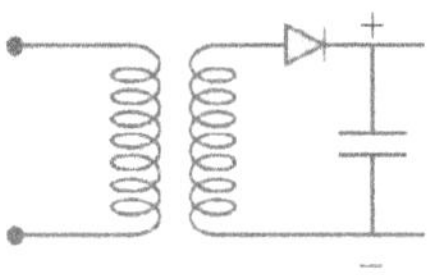
(c) 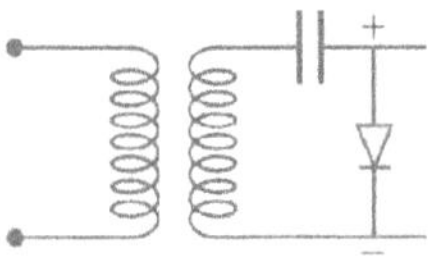
(d) 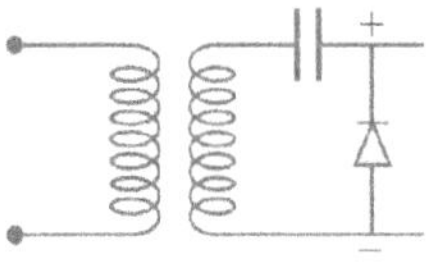

18. If a full wave rectifier circuit is operating from 50 Hz mains, the fundamental frequency in the ripple will be
(a) 50 Hz (b) 70.7 Hz
(c) 100 Hz (d) 25 Hz

19. When NPN transistor is used as an amplifier
(a) electrons move from base to collector
(b) holes move from emitter to base
(c) electrons move from collector to base
(d) holes move from base to emitter

20. In the case of constants a and β of a transistor
(a) $\alpha = \beta$ (b) $\beta < 1\ \alpha > 1$
(c) $\alpha\beta = 1$ (d) $\beta > 1\ \alpha < 1$

21. An NPN-transistor circuit is arranged as shown in figure. It is

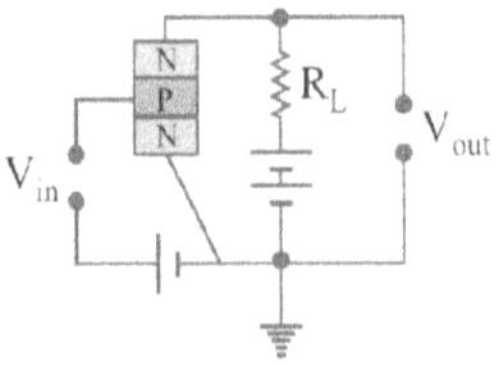

(a) a common base amplifier circuit
(b) a common emitter amplifier circuit
(c) a common collector amplifier circuit
(d) neither of the above

22. In case of NPN-transistors the collector current is always less than the emitter current because
(a) collector side is reverse biased and emitter side is forward biased
(b) after electrons are lost in the base and only remaining ones reach the collector
(c) collector side is forward biased and emitter side is reverse biased
(d) collector being reverse biased attracts less electrons

23. In a common base amplifier the phase difference between the input signal voltage and the output voltage is
(a) 0 (b) $\pi / 4$
(c) $\pi / 2$ (d) π

24. In the study of transistor as an amplifier, if $\alpha = I_c / I_e$ and $\beta = I_c / I_b$, where I_c, I_b and I_e are the collector, base and emitter currents then
(a) $\beta = \frac{1-\alpha}{\alpha}$ (b) $\beta = \frac{\alpha}{1-\alpha}$
(c) $\beta = \frac{\alpha}{1+\alpha}$ (d) $\beta = \frac{1+\alpha}{\alpha}$

25. The circuit shown in following figure contains two diode D_1 and D_2 each with a forward resistance of 50 ohms and with infinite backward resistance. If the battery voltage is 6 V, the current through the 100 ohm resistance (in amperes) is

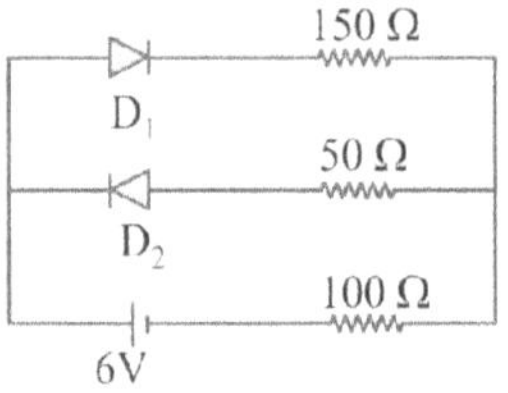

(a) zero (b) 0.02
(c) 0.03 (d) 0.036

26. The temperature (T) dependence of resistivity (ρ) of a semiconductor is represented by

(a) 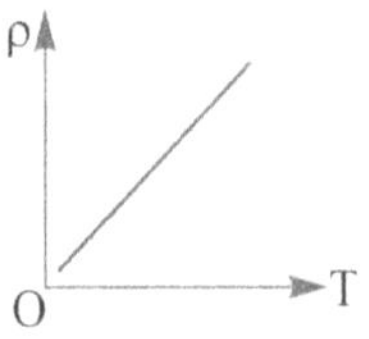

(b) 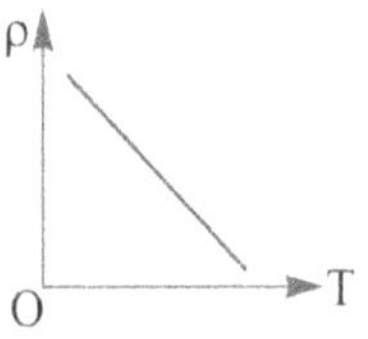

(c) 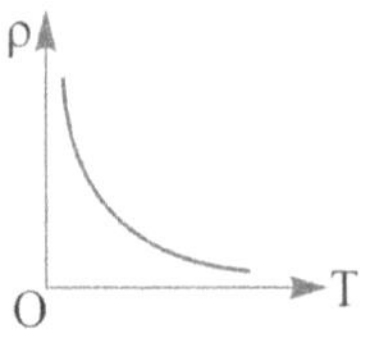

(d) 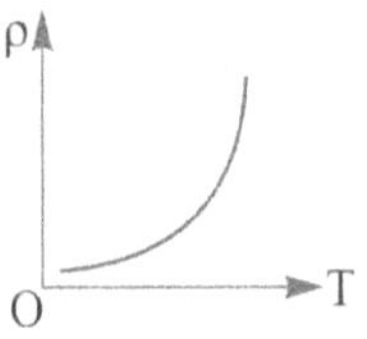

Answer Key Sol. from page 368	15	(a)	16	(c)	17	(b)	18	(c)	19	(a)	20	(d)
	21	(b)	22	(b)	23	(a)	24	(b)	25	(b)	26	(c)

27. Different voltages are applied across a P-N junction and the currents are measured for each value. Which of the following graphs is obtained between voltage and current

(a) 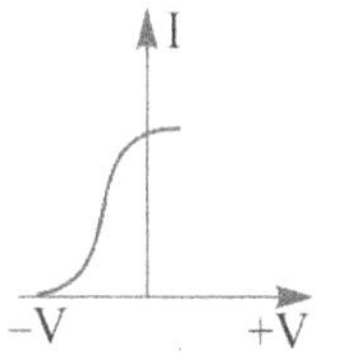

(b) 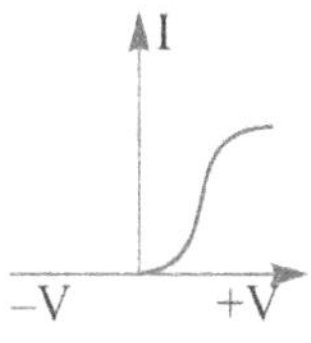

(c) 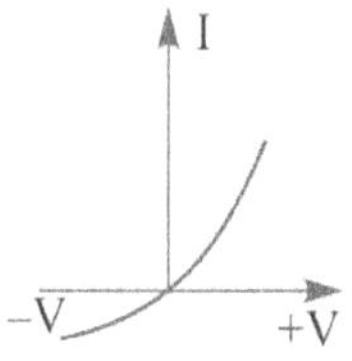

(d) 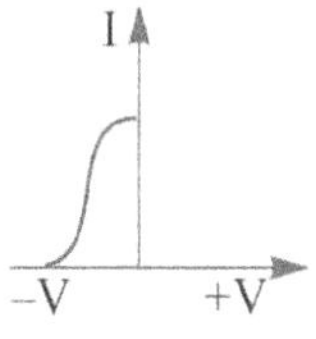

28. Which circuit will not show current in ammeter?

(a) 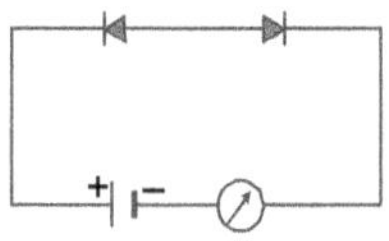

(b) 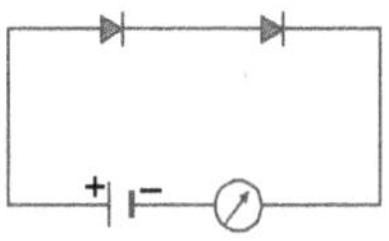

(c) 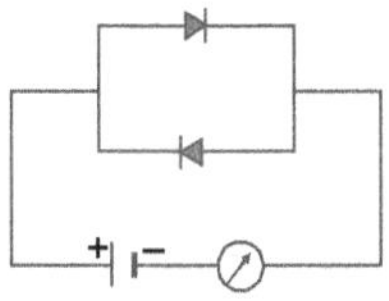

(d) 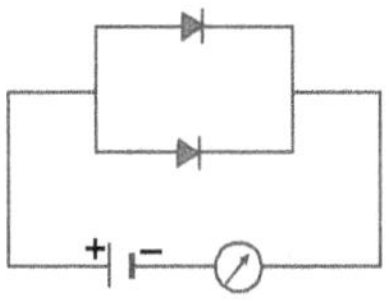

29. Given below are four logic gate symbol (figure). Those for OR, NOR and NAND are respectively

(1) 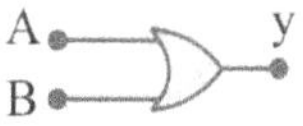

(2) 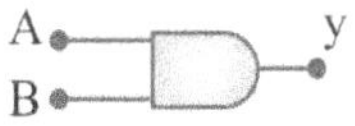

(3) 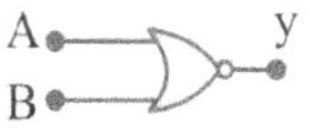

(4) 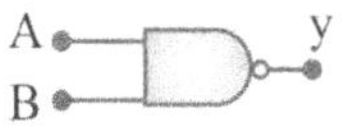

(a) 1, 4, 3
(b) 4, 1, 2
(c) 1, 3, 4
(d) 4, 2, 1

30. A truth table is given below. Which of the following has this type of truth table

A	0	1	0	1
B	0	0	1	1
y	1	0	0	0

(a) XOR gate
(b) NOR gate
(c) AND gate
(d) OR gate

31. For the given combination of gates, if the logic states of inputs A, B, C are as follows A = B = C = 0 and A = B = 1, C = 0 then the logic states of output D are

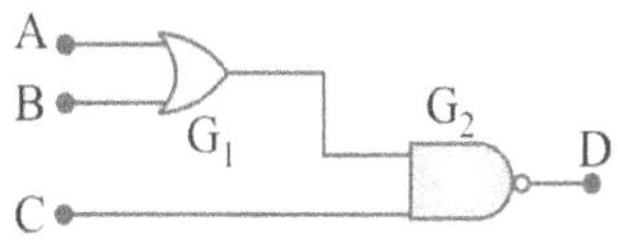

(a) 0, 0
(b) 0, 1
(c) 1, 0
(d) 1, 1

32. Which of the following gates will have an output of 1

(a) 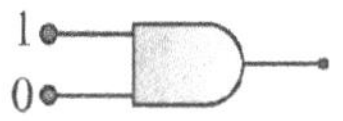

(b) 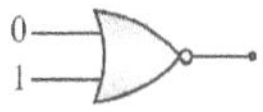

(c) 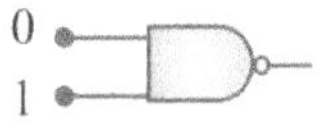

(d) 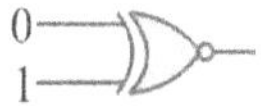

33. The given truth table is of

A	X
0	1
1	0

(a) OR gate
(b) AND gate
(c) NOT gate
(d) None of above

34. To get an output 1 from the circuit shown in the figure, the input must be

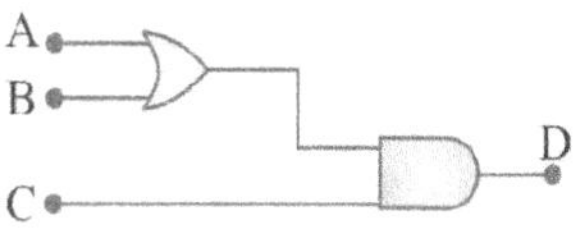

(a) A = 0, B = 1, C = 0
(b) A = 1, B = 0, C = 0
(c) A = 1, B = 0, C = 1
(d) A = 1, B = 1, C = 0

35. Which logic gate is represented by the following combination of logic gates

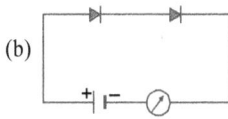

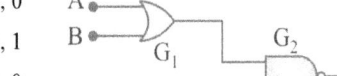

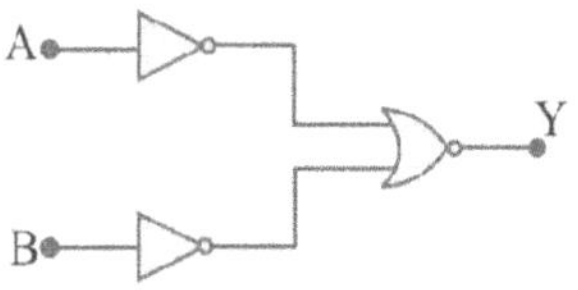

(a) OR
(b) NAND
(c) AND
(d) NOR

36. The truth-table given below is for which gate

A	0	0	1	1
B	0	1	0	1
C	1	1	1	0

(a) XOR
(b) OR
(c) AND
(d) NAND

Answer Key	27	(c)	28	(a)	29	(c)	30	(b)	31	(d)
Sol. from page 368	32	(c)	33	(c)	34	(c)	35	(c)	36	(d)

Communication

37. A carrier wave of peak voltage 12 V is used to transmit a message signal. The modulation index is 75%. The peak value of voltage of modulation index is:

(a) 3 V (b) 6 V (c) 9 V (d) 12 V

38. For an amplitude modulated wave, the maximum amplitude is found to be 10 V while the minimum is found to be 2V. The modulation index is:

(a) 1/3 (b) 2/3 (c) 3/2 (d) 1/4

39. A transmitting antenna at the top of a tower has height 32 m and the height of the receiving antenna is 50 m. The maximum distance between them for satisfactory communication in LOS mode is: (Given radius of earth 6400 km).

(a) 30 km (b) 40 km (c) 42 km (d) 45.5 km

40. A message signal of frequency 10 kHz and peak voltage of 10 volts is used to modulate a carrier of frequency 1 MHz and peak voltage of 20 volts. The side bands are:

(a) 1010 kHz and 990 kHz (b) 1000 kHz and 900 kHz

(c) 10 kHz and 1 MHz (d) 505 kHz and 445 kHz

41. Which of the following four alternatives is not correct ? We need modulation :

(a) to reduce the time lag between transmission and reception of the information signal

(b) to reduce the size of antenna

(c) to reduce the fractional band width, that is the ratio of the signal band width to the centre frequency

(d) to increase the selectivity

42. A 10 kW transmitter emits radio waves of wavelength 500 m. The number of photons emitted per second by the transmitter is of the order of

(a) 10^{37} (b) 10^{31} (c) 10^{25} (d) 10^{43}

43. Given the electric field of a complete amplitude modulated wave as

$$\vec{E} = \hat{i}E_c\left(1+\frac{E_m}{E_c}\cos\omega_m t\right)\cos\omega_c t.$$

Where the subscript c stands for the carrier wave and m for the modulating signal. The frequencies present in the modulated wave are

(a) ω_c and $\sqrt{\omega_c^2+\omega_m^2}$

(b) $\omega_c, \omega_c+\omega_m$ and $\omega_c-\omega_m$

(c) ω_c and ω_m

(d) ω_c and $\sqrt{\omega_c\omega_m}$

44. If a carrier wave $c(t) = A\sin\omega_c t$ is amplitude modulated by a modulator signal $m(t) = A\sin\omega_m t$ then the equation of modulated signal $[C_m(t)]$ and its modulation index are respectively

(a) $C_m(t) = A(1+\sin\omega_m t)\sin\omega_c t$ and 2

(b) $C_m(t) = A(1+\sin\omega_m t)\sin\omega_m t$ and 1

(c) $C_m(t) = A(1+\sin\omega_m t)\sin\omega_c t$ and 1

(d) $C_m(t) = A(1+\sin\omega_c t)\sin\omega_m t$ and 2

45. Which of the following statement is NOT correct?

(a) Ground wave signals are more stable than the sky wave signals.

(b) The critical frequency of an ionospheric layer is the highest frequency that will be reflected back by the layer when it is vertically incident.

(c) Electromagnetic waves of frequencies higher than about 30 MHz cannot penetrate the ionosphere.

(d) Sky wave signals in the broadcast frequency range are stronger at night than in the day time.

46. Which of the following modulated signal has the best noise-tolerance ?

(a) Long-wave (b) Short-wave

(c) Medium-wave (d) Amplitude-modulated

47. A transmitting antenna at the top of a tower has height 32 m and height of the receiving antenna is 50 m. What is the maximum distance between them for satisfactory communication in line of sight (LOS) mode?

(a) 55.4 km (b) 45.5 km (c) 54.5 km (d) 455 km

48. For sky wave propagation, the radio waves must have a frequency range in between:

(a) 1 MHz to 2 MHz (b) 5 MHz to 25 MHz

(c) 35 MHz to 40 MHz (d) 45 MHz to 50 MHz

49. Long range radio transmission is possible when the radio waves are reflected from the ionosphere. For this to happen the frequency of the radio waves must be in the range:

(a) 80 - 150 MHz (b) 8 - 25 MHz

(c) 1 - 3 MHz (d) 150 - 1500 kHz

50. Choose the correct statement :

(a) In frequency modulation the amplitude of the high frequency carrier wave is made to vary in proportion to the amplitude of the audio signal.

(b) In frequency modulation the amplitude of the high frequency carrier wave is made to vary in proportion to the frequency of the audio signal.

(c) In amplitude modulation the amplitude of the high frequency carrier wave is made to vary in proportion to the amplitude of the audio signal.

(d) In amplitude modulation the frequency of the high frequency carrier wave is made to vary in proportion to the amplitude of the audio signal.

Answer Key														
Sol. from page 368	37	(c)	38	(b)	39	(d)	40	(a)	41	(a)	42	(b)	43	(b)
	44	(c)	45	(c)	46	(b)	47	(b)	48	(b)	49	(b)	50	(c)

LEVEL - 2

1. In the given figure, which of the diodes are forward biased ?

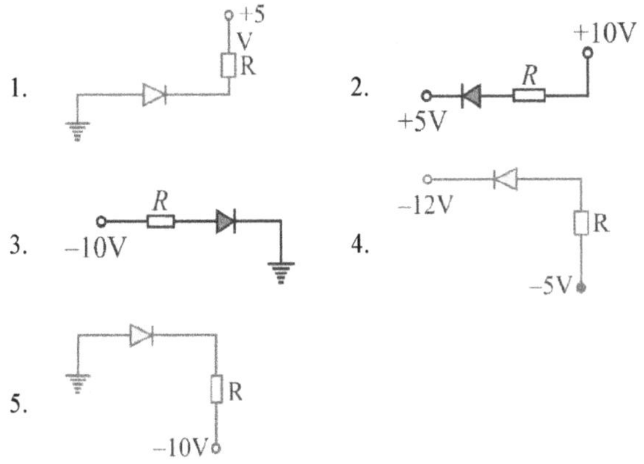

(a) 1, 2, 3 (b) 2, 4, 5
(c) 1, 3, 4 (d) 2, 3, 4

2. In the diagram, the input is across the terminals A and C and the output is across the terminals B and D, then the output is

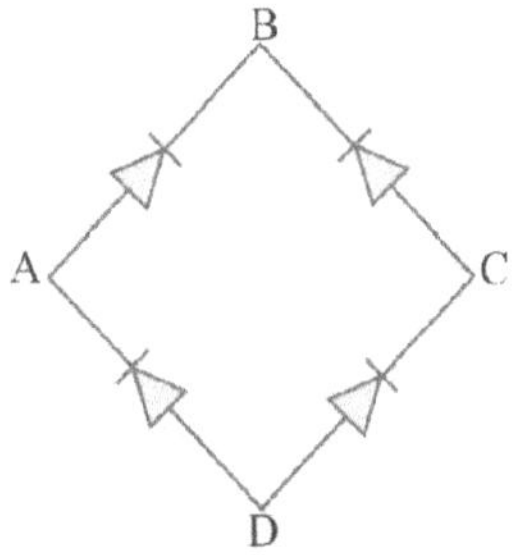

(a) zero (b) same as input
(c) full wave rectifier (d) half wave rectifier

3. The current through an ideal PN-junction shown in the following circuit diagram will be

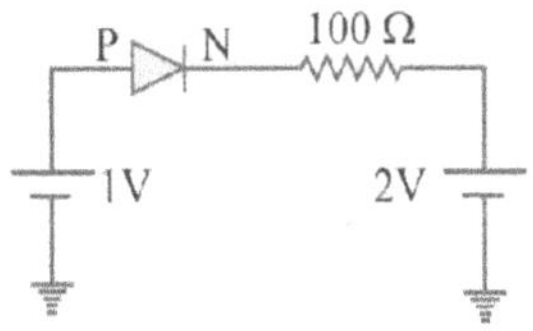

(a) zero (b) 1 mA
(c) 10 mA (d) 30 mA

4. What will be the input of A and B for the Boolean expression

$\overline{(A+B)}.\overline{(A.B)}=1$

(a) 0, 0 (b) 0, 1
(c) 1, 0 (d) 1, 1

5. The transfer ratio β of transistor is 50. The input resistance of a transistor when used in C.E. (common emitter) configuration is 1kΩ. The peak value of the collector A.C. current for an A.C. input voltage of 0.01V peak is

(a) 100 μA (b) .01 mA
(c) 500 μA (d) 25 mA

6. In the following common emitter configuration an NPN transistor with current gain β = 100 is used. The output voltage of the amplifier will be

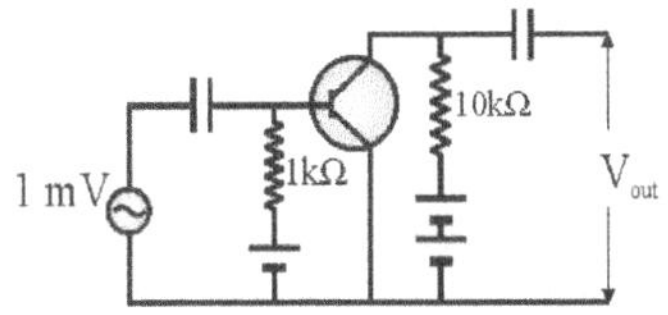

(a) 10 mV (b) 0.1 V
(c) 1.0 V (d) 10 V

7. In the circuit given below, V(t) is the sinusoidal voltage source, voltage drop $V_{AB}(t)$ across the resistance R is

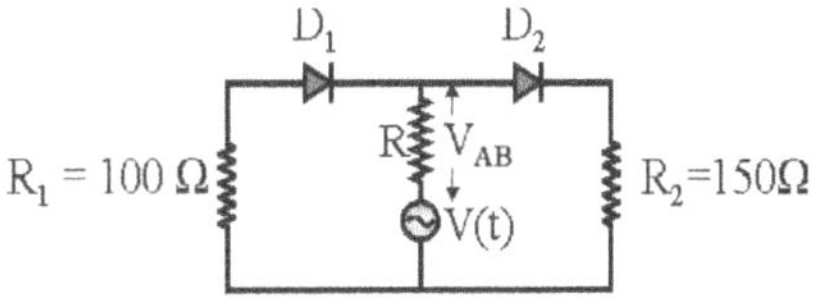

(a) is half wave rectified
(b) is full wave rectified
(c) has the same peak value in the positive and negative half cycles
(d) has different peak values during positive and negative half cycle

8. Ge and Si diodes conduct at 0.3 V and 0.7 V respectively. In the following figure if Ge diode connection are reversed, the value of V_0 changes by

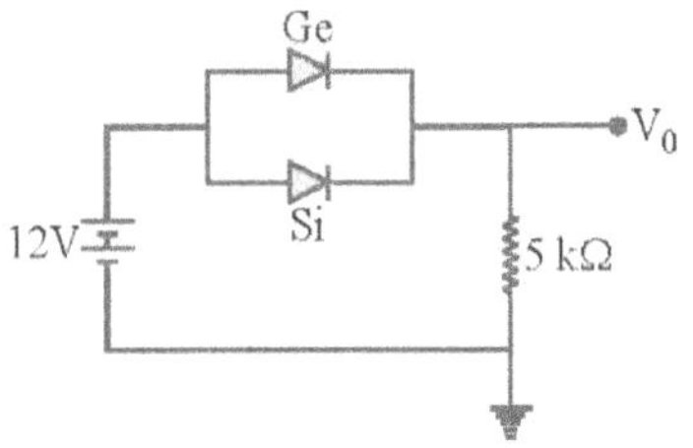

(a) 0.2 V (b) 0.4 V
(c) 0.6 V (d) 0.8 V

9. Currents flowing in each of the circuits A and B respectively are

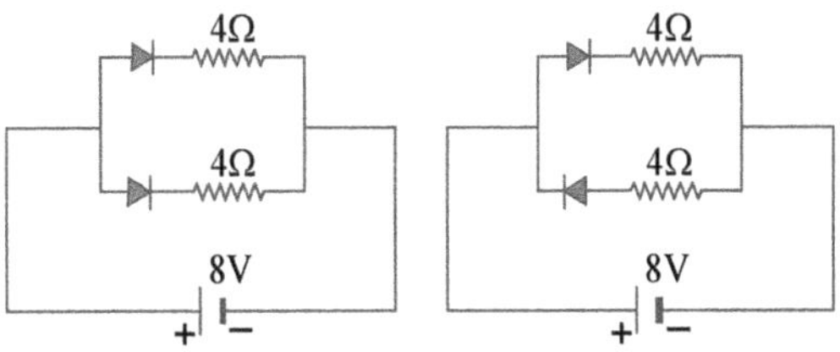

(Circuit A) (Circuit B)

(a) 1 A, 2A (b) 2A, 1A
(c) 4A, 2A (d) 2A, 4A

Answer Key	1	(b)	2	(c)	3	(a)	4	(a)	5	(c)
Sol. from page 368	6	(c)	7	(d)	8	(b)	9	(c)		

10. Assuming the diodes to be of silicon with forward resistance zero, the current I in the following circuit is

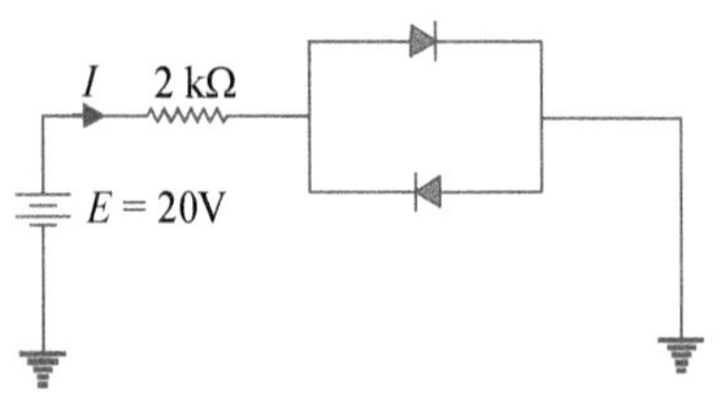

(a) 0 (b) 9.65 mA

(c) 10 mA (d) 10.36 mA

11. The following configuration of gate is equivalent to

(a) NAND

(b) XOR

(c) OR

(d) None of these

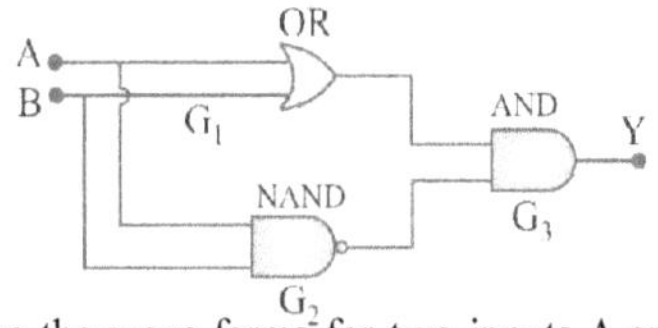

12. The given figure shows the wave forms for two inputs A and B and that for the output Y of a logic circuit. The logic circuit is

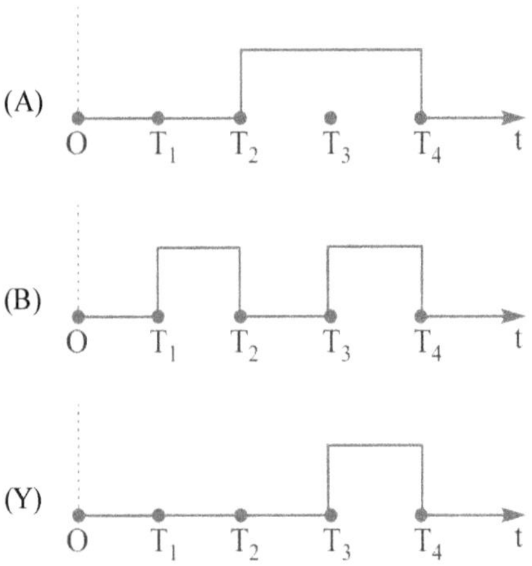

(a) an AND gate (b) an OR gate

(c) a NAND gate (d) an NOT gate

13. The logic circuit shown below has the input waveforms 'A' and 'B' as shown. Pick out the correct output waveform.

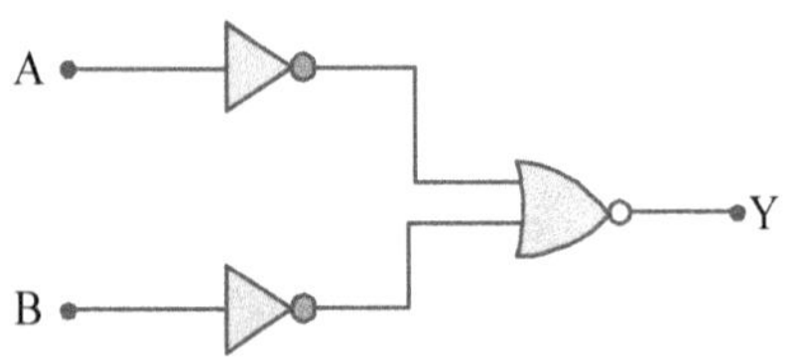

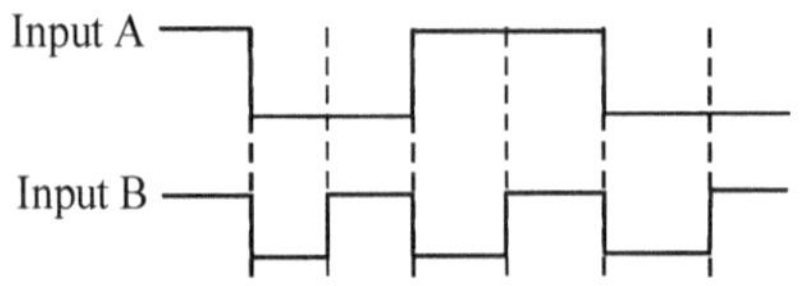

Output is :

(a)

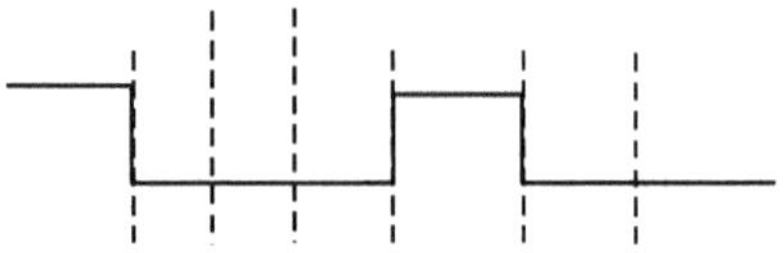

(b)

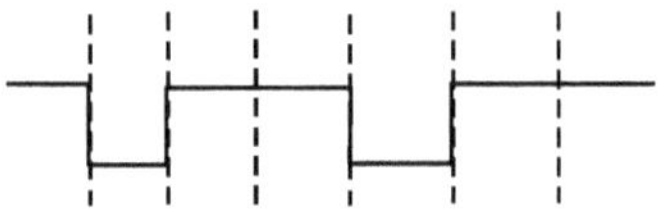

(c)

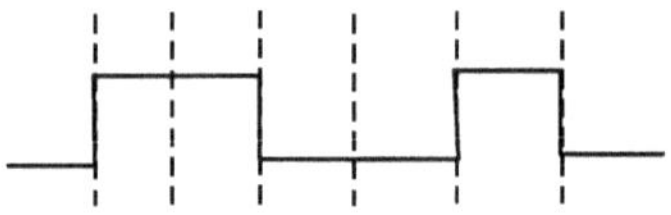

(d)

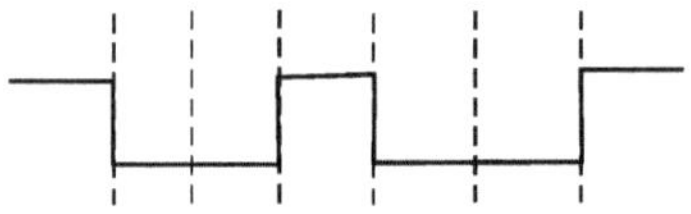

14. If in a p-n junction diode, a square input signal of 10V is applied as shown

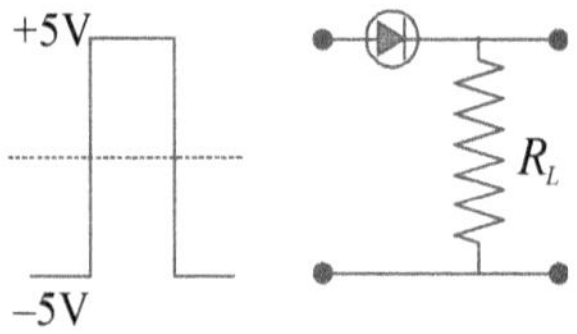

Then the output signal across R_L will be

(a)

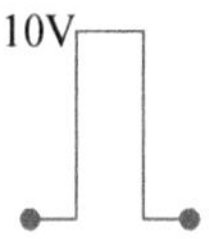

(b)

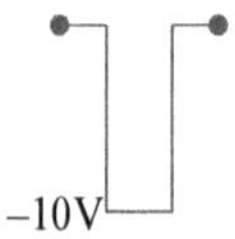

(c)

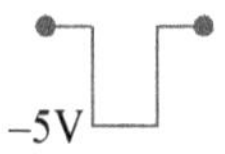

(d)

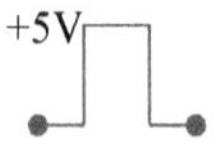

15. In the circuit shown below, an input of 1V is fed into the inverting input of an ideal OP-amplifier. The output signal V_{out} will be

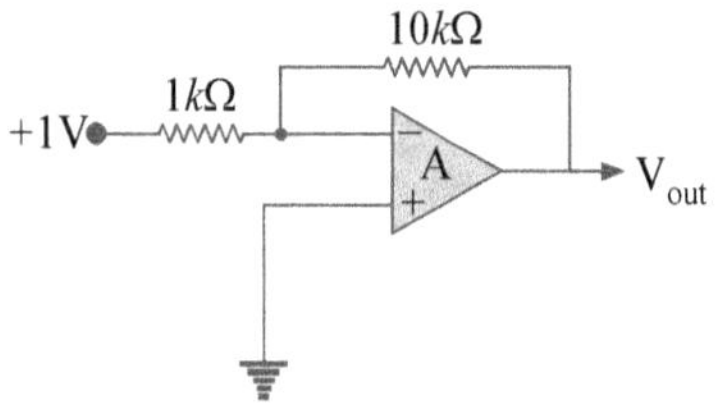

(a) +10 V (b) –10 V

(c) 0 V (d) Infinity

16. The circuit is equivalent to

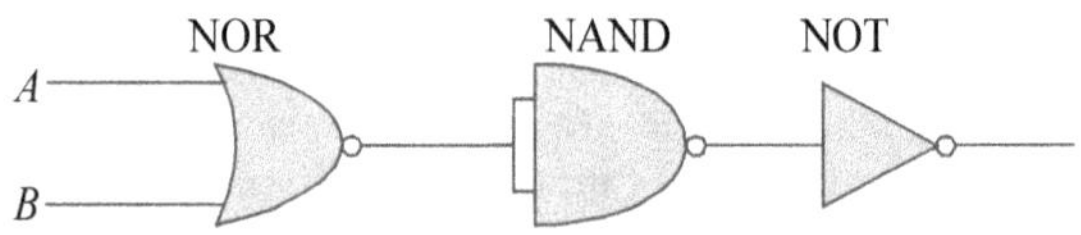

(a) NOR gate (b) OR gate

(c) AND gate (d) NAND gate

Answer Key	10	(c)	11	(b)	12	(a)	13	(a)
Sol. from page 368	14	(a)	15	(b)	16	(a)		

17. The truth table for the following logic circuit is

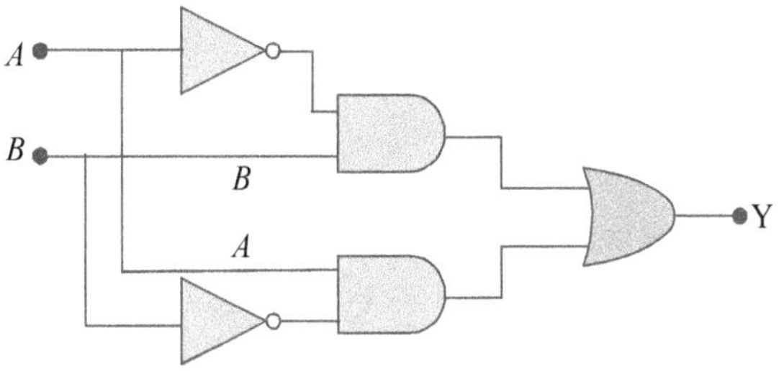

(a)

A	B	Y
0	0	0
0	1	1
1	0	1
1	1	0

(b)

A	B	Y
0	0	0
0	1	1
1	0	1
1	1	1

(c)

A	B	Y
0	0	1
0	1	0
1	0	1
1	1	0

(d)

A	B	Y
0	0	1
0	1	1
1	0	0
1	1	1

(e)

A	B	Y
0	0	1
0	1	1
1	0	1
1	1	0

18. In the following combinations of logic gates, the outputs of A, B and C are respectively

(A)
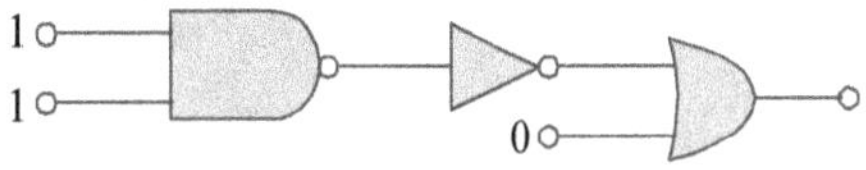

(B)
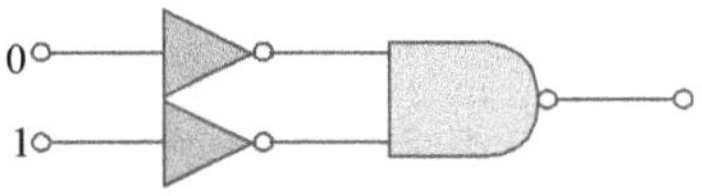

(C)
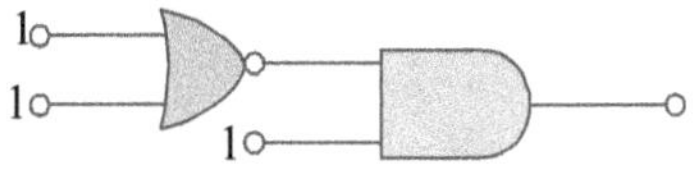

(a) 0, 1, 1 (b) 0, 1, 0
(c) 1, 1, 0 (d) 1, 0, 1

19. Select the outputs Y of the combination of gates shown below for inputs A = 1, B = 0; A = 1, B = 1 and A = 0, B = 0 respectively.

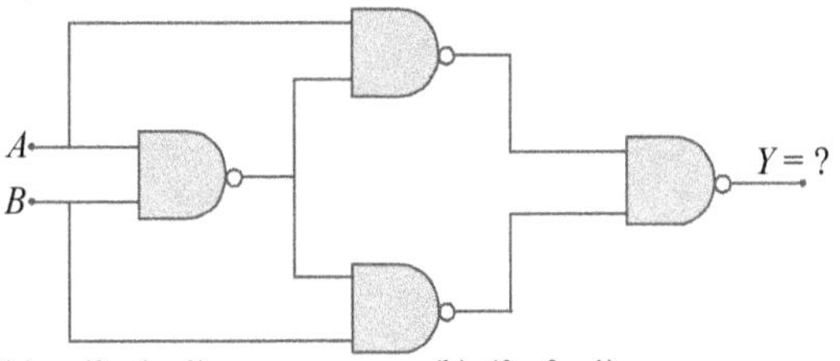

(a) (0 1 1) (b) (0 0 1)
(c) (1 0 0) (d) (1 1 1)

20. The following configuration of gate is equivalent to

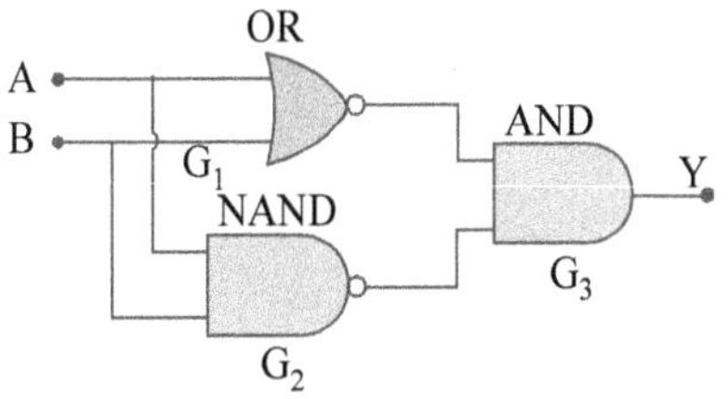

(a) NAND (b) XOR
(c) OR (d) None of these

21. The voltage gain of the following amplifier is

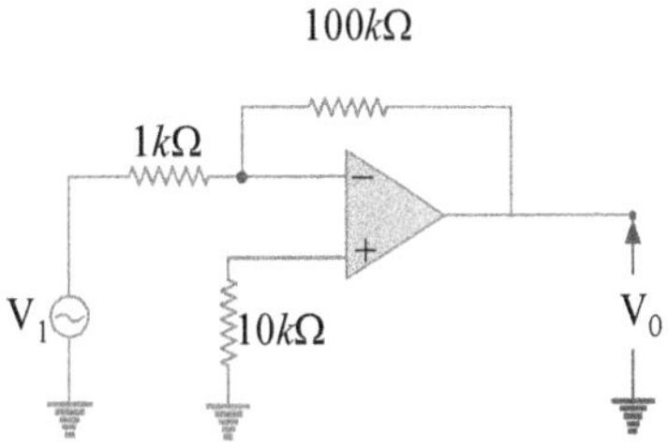

(a) 10 (b) 100
(c) 1000 (d) 9.9

22. A radar has a power of 1kW and is operating at a frequency of 10 GHz. It is located on a mountain top of height 500 m. The maximum distance upto which it can detect object located on the surface of the earth (Radius of earth = 6.4×10^6m) is :
(a) 80 km (b) 16 km (c) 40 km (d) 64 km

23. A radio transmitter transmits at 830 kHz. At a certain distance from the transmitter magnetic field has amplitude 4.82×10^{-11}T. The electric field and the wavelength are respectively
(a) 0.014 N/C, 36 m (b) 0.14 N/C, 36 m
(c) 0.14 N/C, 360 m (d) 0.014 N/C, 360 m

24. A diode detector is used to detect an amplitudemodulated wave of 60% modulation by using a condenser of capacity 250 picofarad in parallel with a load resistance 100 kilo ohm. Find the maximum modulated frequency which could be detected by it.

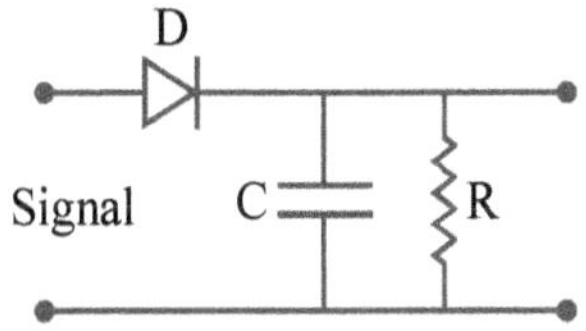

(a) 10.62 MHz (b) 10.62 kHz
(c) 5.31 MHz (d) 5.31 kHz

25. A modulated signal $C_m(t)$ has the form $C_m(t) = 30 \sin 300\pi t + 10 (\cos 200\pi t - \cos 400\pi t)$. The carrier frequency f_c, the modulating frequency (message frequency) f_ω and the modulation index μ are respectively given by :

(a) $f_c = 200$ Hz; $f_w = 50$ Hz; $\mu = \frac{1}{2}$

(b) $f_c = 150$ Hz; $f_w = 50$ Hz; $\mu = \frac{2}{3}$

(c) $f_c = 150$ Hz; $f_w = 30$ Hz; $\mu = \frac{1}{3}$

(d) $f_c = 200$ Hz; $f_w = 30$ Hz; $\mu = \frac{1}{2}$

26. An audio signal consists of two distinct sounds: one a human speech signal in the frequency band of 200 Hz to 2700 Hz, while the other is a high frequency music signal in the frequency band of 10200 Hz to 15200 Hz. The ratio of the AM signal bandwidth required to send both the signals together to the AM signal bandwidth requried to send just the human speech is :
(a) 2 (b) 5
(c) 6 (d) 3

Answer Key												
	17	(a)	18	(c)	19	(c)	20	(b)	21	(b)	22	(a)
Sol. from page 368	23	(d)	24	(b)	25	(b)	26	(c)				

Modern Physics

MCQ Type 2

Exercise 7.2

1. Holes are charge carriers in
   (a) intrinsic semiconductors (b) ionic solids
   (c) p-type semiconductors (d) metals
2. Which of the following statements concerning the depletion zone of an unbiased PN junction is (are) true
   (a) the width of the zone is independent of the densities of the dopants (impurities)
   (b) the width of the zone is dependent on the densities of the dopants
   (c) the electric field in the zone is produced by the ionized dopant atoms
   (d) the electric field in the zone is provided by the electrons in the conductor band and the holes in the valence band
3. A transistor is used in common emitter mode as an amplifier. Then
   (a) the base-emitter junction is forward biased
   (b) the base-emitter junction is reverse biased
   (c) the input signal is connected in series with the voltage applied to the base-emitter junction
   (d) the input signal is connected in series with the voltage applied to bias the base collector junction
4. When a potential difference is applied across, the current passing through
   (a) an insulator at 0K is zero
   (b) a semiconductor at 0K is zero
   (c) a metal at 0K is finite
   (d) a P-N diode at 300K is finite, if it is reverse biased
5. The following logic circuit represents

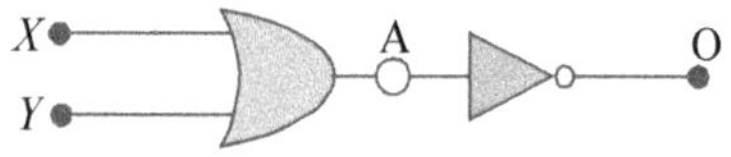

   (a) NAND gate with output $O = \overline{X} + \overline{Y}$
   (b) NOR gate with output $O = \overline{X + Y}$
   (c) NAND gate with output $O = \overline{XY}$
   (d) NOR gate with output $O = \overline{X}.\overline{Y}$

Answer Key	1	(a, c)	2	(b, c)	3	(a, c)	4	(a, b, d)
Sol. from page 369	5	(b, d)						

Modern Physics

Statement Questions

Exercise 7.3

Read the two statements carefully to mark the correct option out of the options given below. Select the right choice.

(a) If both the statements are true and the ***Statement* - 2** is the correct explanation of ***Statement* - 1**.

(b) If both the statements are true but ***Statement* - 2** is not the correct explanation of the ***Statement* - 1**.

(c) If ***Statement* - 1** true but ***Statement* - 2** is false.

(d) If ***Statement* - 1** is false but ***Statement* - 2** is true.

1. **Statement -1 :** If the temperature of a semiconductor is increased, then its resistance decreases.

Statement - 2 : The energy gap between conduction band and valence band in semiconductor is very small.

2. **Statement -1 :** In semiconductors, thermal collisions are respossible for taking a valence electron to the conduction band.

Statement -2 : The number of conduction electrons go on increasing with time as thermal collisions continuously take place.

3. **Statement - 1 :** A p-type semiconductors is a positive type crystal.

Statement - 2 : A p- type semiconductor is an uncharged crystal.

4. **Statement - 1 :** The diffusion current in a p-n junction is from the p-side to the n-side.

Statement - 2 : The diffusion current in a p-n junction is greater than the drift current when the junction is in forward biased.

5. **Statement - 1 :** The drift current in a p-n junction is from the n-side to the p-side.

Statement - 2 : It is due to free electrons only.

6. **Statement - 1 :** Silicon is preferred over germanium for making semiconductor devices.

Statement - 2 : The energy gap in germanium is more than the energy gap in silicon.

7. **Statement - 1 :** Electron has higher mobility than hole in a semiconductor.

Statement 2 : The mass of electron is less than the mass of the hole.

8. **Statement - 1 :** A p-n junction with reverse bias can be used as a photo-diode to measure light intensity.

Statement - 2 : In a reverse bias condition the current is small but it is more sensitive to changes in incident light intensity.

9. **Statement -1 :** The number of electrons in a p-type silicon semiconductor is less than the number of electrons in a pure silicon semiconductor at room temperature.

Statement - 2 : It is due to law of mass action.

10. **Statement - 1 :** A transistor amplifier in common emitter configuration has a low input impedance.

Statement - 2 : The base to emitter region is forward biased.

11. **Statement – 1 :** Sky wave signals are used for long distance radio communication. These signals are in general, less stable than ground wave signals.

Statement – 2 : The state of ionosphere varies from hour to hour, day to day and season to season.

Answer Key	**1**	(a)	**2**	(c)	**3**	(d)	**4**	(b)	**5**	(a)	**6**	(c)
Sol. from page 369	7	(a)	**8**	(a)	**9**	(a)	**10**	(a)	**11**	(b)		

Modern Physics

Subjective

Exercise 7.4

Solution from page 381

1. Copper, a monovalent, has molar mass 63.54 g/mol and density 8.96 g/cm^3. What is the number density n of conduction electron in copper? ***Ans.*** 8.49×10^{28} m^{-1}.

2. An LED is constructed from a p-n junction based on a certain Ga-As -P semiconducting material whose energy gap is 1.9 eV. What is the wavelength of the emitted light? ***Ans.*** 650 nm.

3. In a photodiode, the conductivity increases when the material is exposed to light. It is found that the conductivity changes only if the wavelength is less than 620 nm. What is the band gap? ***Ans.*** 2.0 eV.

4. A potential barrier of 0.3 V exists across a p-n junction.
   (a) If the depletion region is 1 μm wide, what is the intensity of electric field in this region?
   (b) An electron with speed 5×10^5 m/s approaches this p-n junction from n-side, what will be its speed on entering the p-side? ***Ans.*** (a) 3×10^5 V/m (b) 3.8×10^5 m/s

5. The number density n_0 of conduction electrons in pure silicon at room temperature is about 10^{16}m^{-3}. Assume that, by doping the silicon lattice with phosphorus, we want to increase this number by a factor of a million (10^6). What fraction of silicon atoms must we replace with phosphorus atoms ? (Recall that at room temperature, thermal agitation is so effective that essentially every phosphorus atom donates its "extra" electron to the conduction band) given density of silicon = 2.33×10^3.

   Ans. $\dfrac{n_p}{n_{Si}} = \dfrac{1}{5 \times 10^6}$.

6. Calculate the value of V_0 and i if the Si diode and the Ge diode conduct at 0.7V and 0.3V respectively, in the circuit given below:

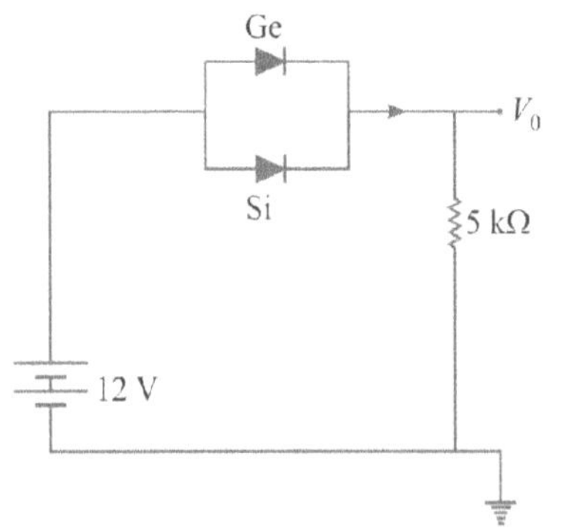

If now the Ge diode connection are reversed, what will be the new values of V_0 and i ? ***Ans.*** 11.7 V, 2.34 mA ; 11.3 V, 2.26 mA

7. A 5V battery may be connected across the points A and B as shown in figure. Assume that the resistance of each diode is zero in forward bias and infinity in reverse bias. Find the current supplied by the battery if the positive terminal of the battery is connected to (a) the point A (b) the point B.

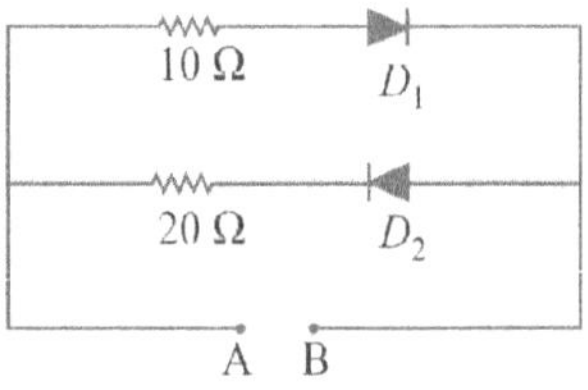

Ans. (a) 0.5 A (b) 0.25 A.

8. Find the current through the resistance in the circuit shown in figure (Assuming ideal diode).

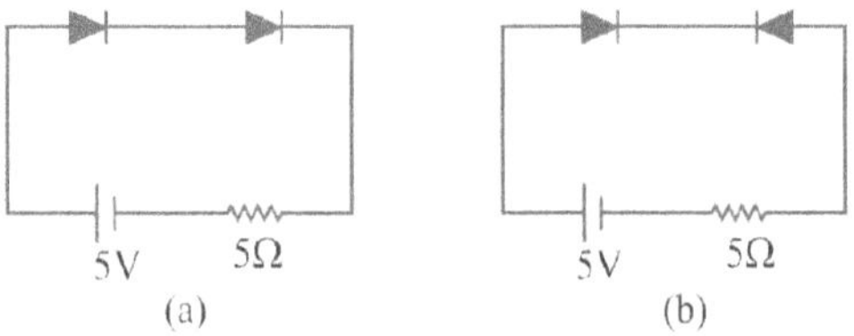

Ans. (a) 1 A (b) Zero.

9. What are the reading of the ammeters A_1 and A_2 shown in figure (Assuming diodes and ammeters are ideal)

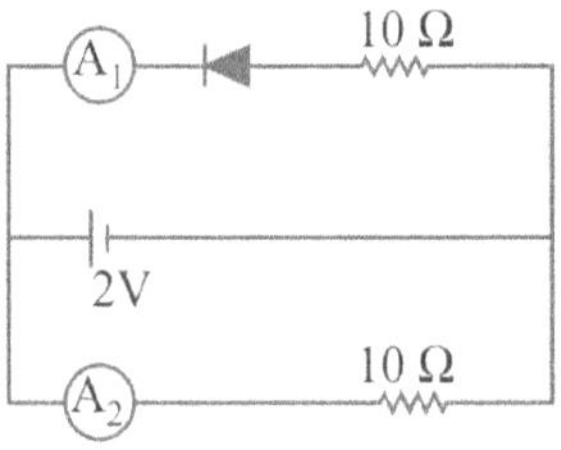

Ans. Zero, 0.2 A

10. The current-voltage characteristic of an ideal p-n junction diode is given by $i = i_0(e^{ev/kT} - 1)$ where the drift current i_0 equal 10 μA. Take the temperature T to be 300 K.
    (a) Find the voltage V_0 for which $e^{eV/KT} = 100$. One can neglect the term 1 for voltages greater than this value
    (b) Find an expression for the dynamic resistance of the diode as a function of V For $V > V_0$.
    (c) Find the voltage for which the dynamic resistance is 0.2 Ω.

    Ans. (a) 0.12 V (b) $\dfrac{kT}{ei_0}e^{-eV/kT}$ (c) 0.25 V.

11. When the base current in a transistor is changed from 30 μA to 80 μA, the collector current is changed from 1.0 mA to 3.5 mA. Find the current gain β. ***Ans.*** 50

12. A transistor is connected in common -emitter configuration. The collector supply is 8V and the voltage drop across a resistor of 800 W in the collector is 0.5 V. If the current gain factor α is 0.96. Find the base current. ***Ans.*** 26 μA.

13. A pnp transistor is used in common-emitter mode in an amplifier circuit. A change of 40 μA in the base current brings a change of 2 mA in collector current and 0.04 V in base emitter voltage. Find the

(i) input resistor R_{in} and

(ii) the base current amplification factor β.

(iii) If a load of 6 kΩ is used, then also find the voltage gain of the amplifier. ***Ans.*** (i) 1 kΩ (ii) 50 (iii) 300.

14. A npn transistor in a common emitter mode is used as a simple voltage amplifier with a collector current of 4mA. the terminal of a 8V battery is connected to the collector through a load resistance R_L and to the base through a resistance R_B. The collector emitter voltage $V_{CE} = 4V$, base-emitter voltage $V_{BE} = 0.6$ and the base current amplification factor $\beta_{dc} = 100$, calculate the value of R_L and R_B. ***Ans.*** 185 kΩ, 1 kΩ.

15. Construct the truth table for the function Y of A and B represented by figure.

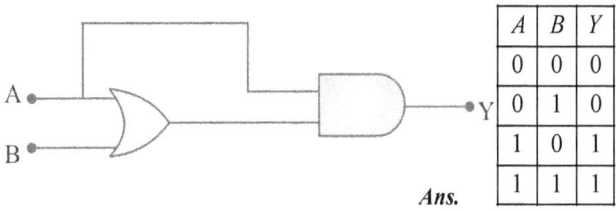

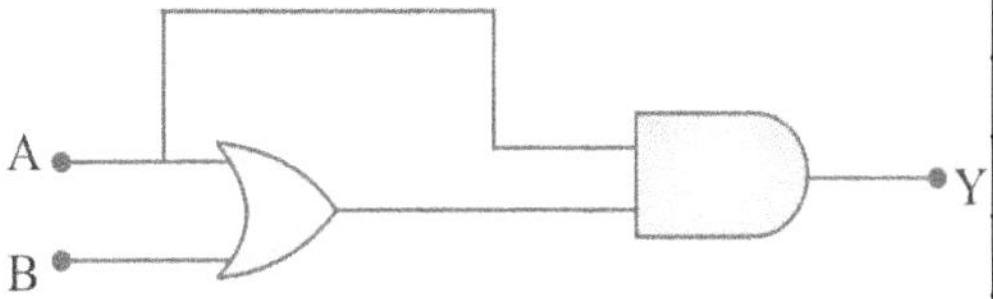

Ans.

A	*B*	*Y*
0	0	0
0	1	0
1	0	1
1	1	1

★★★

Hints & Solutions

Solutions EXERCISE 7.1 LEVEL -1

1. (d) Resistance of metals decreases with decrease in temperature while resistance of non-metals increases with decrease in temperature.
2. (b)
3. (c) P-type semiconductor is formed when trivalent impurities like Al or B is mixed with Si or Ge.
4. (a)
5. (c) At 0 K, the motion of free electrons ceases.
6. (a) 7. (b) 8. (b)
9. (a) Potential barrier is due to positive and negative ions on both sides of junction.
10. (c)
11. (c) Majority carriers in N-type semiconductors are electrons.
12. (b) 13. (a)
14. (c) In this case the p.d. across the diode in negative, so the diode will be in reverse bias.
15. (b) In first circuit, two diodes are oppositely connected, which are not possible.
16. (c) 17. (b)
18. (c) One full wave after rectification constitutes two ripples.
19. (a)
20. (d) The value of α is always less than 1 and that of β always be greater than 1 (20 – 200).
21. (b) In the circuit emitter is common.
22. (b) 23. (a) 24. (b)
25. (b) The current will flow through diode D_1 and so

$$i = \frac{6}{(150+50+100)} = 0.02A$$

26. (c) 27. (c)
28. (a) In this case diodes are oppositely connected and so they will not allow any current in the circuit.
29. (c) 30. (b)
31. (d) Truth table of the gate is as follows :

A	B	C	$A+B$	$Y=(A+B).C$	$\overline{Y}$
0	0	0	0	0	1
1	1	0	1	0	1

32. (c) 33. (c)
34. (c) $(A+B).C$. For $A = 1$, B = 0 and C = 1 will give 1.
35. (c)

A	B	$\overline{A}$	$\overline{B}$	$\overline{Y}=\overline{A}+\overline{B}$	Y
0	0	1	1	1	0
0	1	1	0	1	0
1	0	0	1	1	0
1	1	0	0	0	1

This table is of AND gate.

36. (d)
37. (c) $\frac{A_m}{A_c} = 0.75$

$\therefore$ $A_m = 0.75\, A_c = 0.75 \times 12 = 9$ V.

38. (b) $M = \frac{A_m}{A_c} = \frac{M_1 - M_2}{M_1 + M_2} = \frac{10-2}{10+2} = \frac{2}{3}$
39. (d) $d_m = \sqrt{2Rh_T} + \sqrt{2Rh_R}$
40. (a)
41. (a) Low frequencies cannot be transmitted to long distances. Therefore, they are super imposed on a high frequency carrier signal by a process known as modulation.

    Speed of electro-magnetic waves will not change due to modulation. So there will be time lag between transmission and reception of the information signal.
42. (b) Power = $\frac{nhc}{\lambda}$

    (where, n = no. of photons per second)

$$\Rightarrow n = \frac{10\times10^3\times500}{6.6\times10^{-34}\times3\times10^8} \approx 10^{31}$$

43. (b) The frequencies present in amplitude modulated wave are :

    Carrier frequency = ω_c

    Upper side band frequency = $\omega_c + \omega_m$

    Lower side band frequency = $\omega_c - \omega_m$.
44. (c) Modulation index

$$m_a = \frac{E_m}{E_c} = \frac{A}{A} = 1$$

Equation of modulated signal $[C_m(t)]$

$= E_{(C)} + m_a E_{(C)} \sin \omega_m t$

$= A\,(1 + \sin w_C t) \sin \omega_m t$

(As $E_{(C)} = A \sin\omega_C t$)

45. (c) Above critical frequency (f_c), an electromagnetic wave penetrates the ionosphere and is not reflected by it.
46. (b) Short-wave has the best noise tolerance.
47. (b) **Given :** $h_R = 32$ m

    $h_T = 50$ m

    Maximum distance, d_M = ?

    Applying, $d_M = \sqrt{2Rh_T} + \sqrt{2Rh_R}$

    $= \sqrt{2\times6.4\times10^6\times50} + \sqrt{2\times6.4\times10^6\times32} = 45.5$ km
48. (b) Sky wave propagation is suitable for frequency range 5 MHz to 25 MHz.

49. (b) Frequency of radio waves for sky wave propagation is 2 MHZ to 30 MHZ.

50. (c) In amplitude modulation, the amplitude of the high frequency carrier wave made to vary in proportional to the amplitude of audio signal.

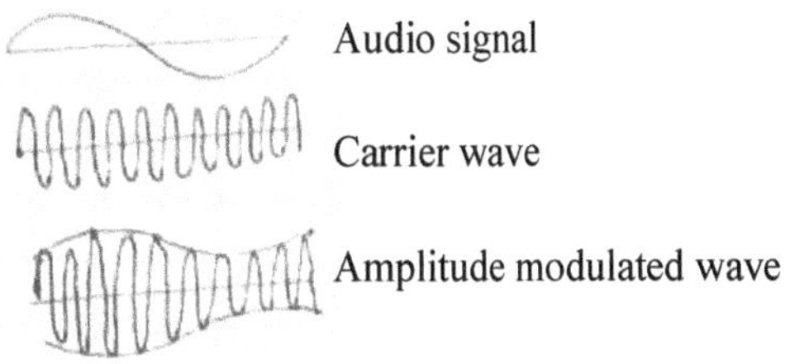

Solutions EXERCISE 7.1 LEVEL - 2

1. (b) If figure, 2, 4, 5 the potential difference across diode is greater than zero (V > 0) and so these are in forward bias.

2. (c)

3. (a) In the circuit the diode is in reverse bias and so no current in the circuit.

4. (a) For $A = 0$, $B = 0$,

$\overline{A+B} = 1$ and $\overline{A.B} = 1$

So $\overline{(A+B)}.\overline{(A.B)} = 1$.

5. (c) $i_b = \frac{V}{R_1} = \frac{0.01}{1\times10^2} = 10^{-5}\ A$

We know that, $\beta = \frac{i_c}{i_b}$

$\therefore \quad i_c = \beta\times i_b = 50\times10^{-5} = 500\mu A$

6. (c) Voltage gain,

$$\frac{V_0}{V_i} = \beta\frac{R_2}{R_1}$$

or $$V_0 = \left[\beta\frac{R_2}{R_1}\right]\times V_i = \left[100\times\frac{10}{1}\right]\times1\times10^{-3}$$

$= 1$ V.

7. (d) During the operation, either of D_1 and D_2 be in forward bias. Also R_1 and R_2 are different, so output across R will have different peaks.

8. (b) In case the circuit will be completed through Ge diode and so

$V_i = 12 - 0.3 = 11.7$ V

When Ge diode gets reverse, the Si diode will be in forward bias and so

$V_f = 12 - 0.7 = 11.3$ V.

Now $\Delta V = V_f \sim V_i = 11.3 \sim 11.7$

$= 0.4$ V

9. (c) In circuit A, both the diodes are in forward bias and in parallel, so

$R = 2\ \Omega$

Current, $i = \frac{V}{R} = \frac{8}{2} = 4A.$

In circuit B, only one diode is in forward bias,

so current, $i = \frac{8}{4} = 2$A.

10. (c) $i = \frac{V}{R} = \frac{20}{2\times10^3} = 10\ mA.$

11. (b)

12. (a) The truth table of the wave forms are as follows :

A	B	Y
0	0	0
0	1	0
1	0	0
1	1	1
0		0

The truth table is corresponding to AND gate.

13. (a) The truth table of the output is as follows :

A	B	$\overline{A}$	$\overline{B}$	$\overline{A}+\overline{B}$	$\overline{\overline{A}+B}$
1	1	0	0	0	1
0	0	1	1	1	0
0	1	1	0	1	0
1	0	0	1	1	0
1	1	0	0	0	1
0	1	1	0	1	0

So option (a) is the correct option.

14. (a)

15. (b) $\frac{V_0}{V_i} = \frac{R_2}{R_1}$

$\therefore \quad V_0 = \frac{R_2}{R_1}V_i$

$= -1\times\frac{10}{1} = -10V,$

16. (a) NOR + (NAND = NOT) + NOT

$\Rightarrow$ NOR.

17. (a) $Y = \overline{A}.B + A.\overline{B}$

The truth table for the given logic circuit is as follows :

A	B	$\overline{A}$	$\overline{B}$	$\overline{A}.B$	$A.\overline{B}$	Y
0	0	1	1	0	0	0
0	1	1	0	1	0	1
1	0	0	1	0	1	1
1	1	0	0	0	0	0

18. (c) (A)

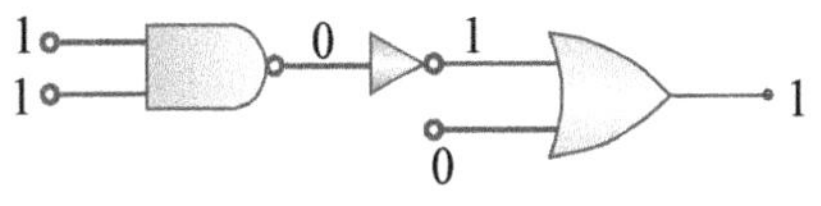

(B)

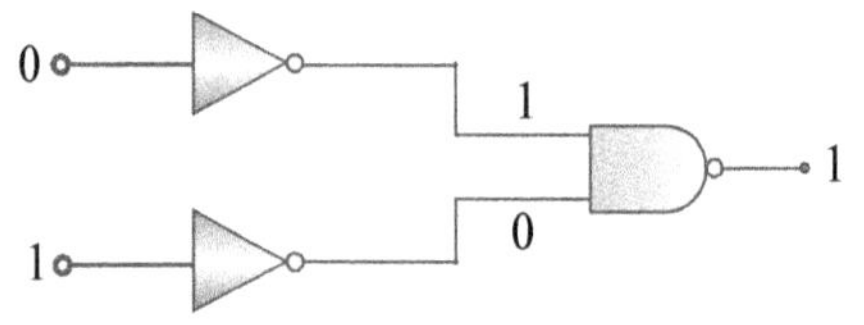

(C)

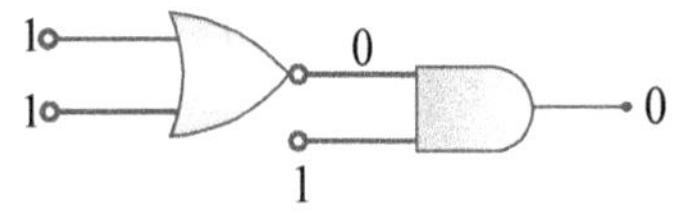

19. (c)

20. (b) $Y = (A+B).\overline{AB}$

The given output equation can be written as ;

$$Y = (A+B).(\overline{A}+\overline{B})$$

$$= A\overline{A} + A\overline{B} + B\overline{A} + B\overline{B} = 0 + A\overline{B} + \overline{A}B + 0$$

$$= \overline{A}B + A\overline{B} \Rightarrow XOR \text{ gate.}$$

21. (b) Voltage gain

$$\frac{V_0}{V_i} = \frac{R_f}{R_i} = \frac{100}{1} = 100$$

22. (a) Let d is the maximum distance, upto which it can detect the objects

From ΔAOC

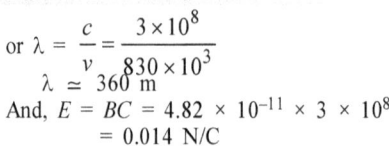

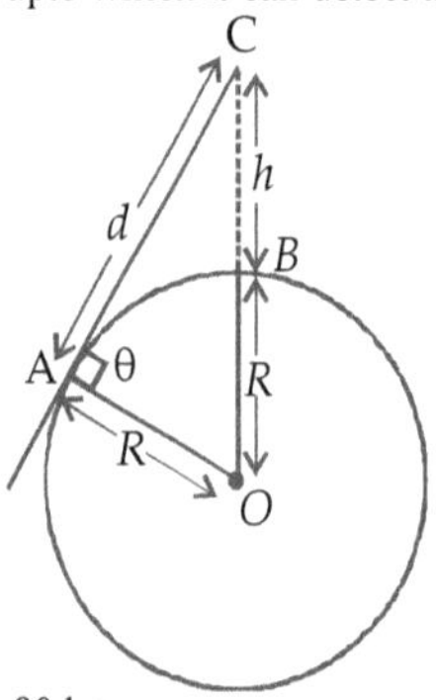

$$OC^2 = AC^2 + AO^2$$

$$(h+R)^2 = d^2 + R^2$$

$$\Rightarrow d^2 = (h+R)^2 - R^2$$

$$d = \sqrt{(h+R)^2 - R^2}$$

$$d = \sqrt{h^2 + 2hR}$$

$$d = \sqrt{500^2 + 2 \times 6.4 \times 10^6} = 80 \text{ km}$$

23. (d) Frequency of EM wave υ = 830 KHz
= 830×10^3 Hz.
Magnetic field, $B = 4.82 \times 10^{-11}$ T

As we know, frequency, $\upsilon = \frac{c}{\lambda}$

or $\lambda = \frac{c}{v} = \frac{3 \times 10^8}{830 \times 10^3}$

$\lambda \simeq 360$ m

And, $E = BC = 4.82 \times 10^{-11} \times 3 \times 10^8$
$= 0.014$ N/C

24. (b) **Given :** Resistance R = 100 kilo ohm
$= 100 \times 10^3\ \Omega$
Capacitance C = 250 picofarad
$= 250 \times 10^{-12}$F
$\tau = RC = 100 \times 10^3 \times 250 \times 10^{-12}$ sec
$= 2.5 \times 10^7 \times 10^{-12}$ sec
$= 2.5 \times 10^{-5}$ sec

The higher frequency whcih can be detected with tolerable distortion is

$$f = \frac{1}{2\pi m_a RC} = \frac{1}{2\pi \times 0.6 \times 2.5 \times 10^{-5}} Hz$$

$$= \frac{100 \times 10^4}{25 \times 1.2\pi} Hz = \frac{4}{1.2\pi} \times 10^4 \, Hz$$

= 10.61 KHz

This condition is obtained by applying the condition that rate of decay of capacitor voltage must be equal or less than the rate of decay modulated singnal voltage for proper detection of mdoulated signal.

25. (b) Comparing the given equation with standard modulated

signal wave equation, $m = A_c \sin \omega_c t + \frac{\mu A_c}{2} \cos(\omega_c - \omega_s)$

$t - \frac{\mu A_c}{2} \cos(\omega_c + \omega_s)\, t$

$$\mu \frac{A_c}{2} = 10 \Rightarrow \mu = \frac{2}{3} \text{ (modulation index)}$$

$A_c = 30$
$\omega_c - \omega_s = 200\pi$
$\omega_c + \omega_s = 400\pi$

$$\Rightarrow f_c = 150,\ f_s = 50 \text{ Hz}.$$

26. (c) Ratio of AM signal Bandwidths

$$= \frac{15200 - 200}{2700 - 200} = \frac{15000}{2500} = 6.$$

Solutions EXERCISE 7.2

1. (a, c) 2. (b, c) 3. (a, c)

4. (a, b, d)
At 0 K, the motion of electrons cease and so electric current becomes zero.

5. (b, d) The given logic current is

$OR + NOT \rightarrow NOR$

Also $\overline{X+Y} = \overline{X}.\overline{Y}$

Solutions EXERCISE 7.3

1. (a) 2. (c)

3. (d) There is no charge on P-type semiconductor, because each atom of semiconductor is itself neutral.

4. (b) Diffusion current is due to the migration of holes and electrons into opposite regions, so it will be from p-side to n-side. Also in forward bias it will increases.

5. (a)

6. (c) Silicon is cheaper than germanium, so it is preferred over germanium. But energy gap in germanium is smaller than silicon.

7. (a) 8. (a) 9. (a) 10. (a)

11. (b) For long distance communication, sky wave signals are used.
Also, the state of ionosphere varies every time.
So, both statements are correct.

Solutions EXERCISE 7.4

1. If M is the molar mass and ρ is the density then volume of one mole

$$V = \frac{M}{\rho}.$$

The number of atoms per unit volume

$$= \frac{N_A}{V} = \frac{N_A}{M/\rho} = \frac{N_A\rho}{M}$$

$$= \frac{(6.02\times10^{23})\times(8.96)}{63.54}$$

$$= 8.49\times10^{22}\ \text{cm}^{-3}$$

$$= 8.49\times10^{28}\ \text{m}^{-3}$$

As each copper (monovalent) atom has one electron, so number of electrons per unit volume

$$= 8.49\times10^{26}\ \text{m}^{-3}$$ *Ans.*

2. If λ is the wavelength of emitted light, then

$$E_g = \frac{hc}{\lambda}$$

or

$$\lambda = \frac{hc}{E_g}$$

$$= \frac{(6.63\times10^{-34})\times(3\times10^8)}{(1.9)\times(1.60\times10^{-19})}$$

$$= 6.5\times10^{-7}\ \text{m} = 650\ \text{nm}$$

3. The band gap $E_g = \dfrac{hc}{\lambda} = \dfrac{(6.63\times10^{-34})\times(3\times10^8)}{620\times10^{-9}}$

$$= 3.2\times10^{-19}\ \text{J}$$

$$= 2.0\ \text{eV}.$$ *Ans.*

4. (a) The intensity of electric field

$$E = \frac{V}{d} = \frac{0.3}{1\times10^{-6}} = 3\times10^5\ V/m$$

(b) The electric field retarded the electron. The retardation

$$a = \frac{Ee}{m}.$$

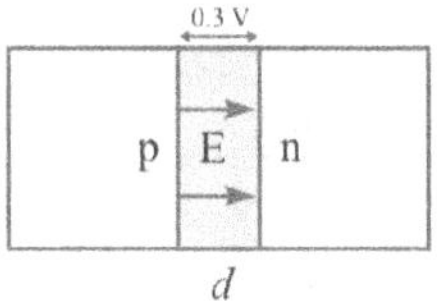

The speed of the electron on entering p-side

$$v^2 = u^2 - 2as = u^2 - 2\frac{eE}{m}.d$$

$$= (5\times10^5)^2 - \frac{2\times1.6\times10^{-19}\times3\times10^5}{9.1\times10^{-31}}\times(1\times10^{-6})$$

$$= 3.8\times10^5\ \text{m/s}$$ *Ans.*

5. As each phosphorus atom contributes one electron and we want total number density of conduction electrons to be $10^6\ n_0$, so the number density of phosphorus atoms n_p must be given by

$$10^6 n_0 = n_0 + n_p$$

Then

$$n_p = 10^6 n_0 - n_0 \simeq 10^6 n_0$$

$$= 10^6\times10^{16} = 10^{22}\ \text{m}^{-3}$$

This gives us an ideal that we must add 10^{22} atoms of phosphorus per cubic metre.

The number of silicon atoms per unit volume is given by

$$n_{Si} = \frac{\rho N_A}{M_{si}} = \frac{(2330)\times(6.02\times10^{23})}{0.0281}$$

$$= 5\times10^{28}\ \text{m}^{-3}.$$

The fraction we want

$$\frac{n_p}{n_{Si}} = \frac{10^{22}}{5\times10^{28}} = \frac{1}{5\times10^6}$$ *Ans.*

6. The potential barrier of Ge is 0.3 V, which is less than the potential barrier of Si (0.7 V). So Ge diode will conduct, therefore

$$i = \frac{V_{net}}{R} = \frac{12-0.3}{5\times10^3} = 2.34\ mA$$

$$V_0 = iR = 2.34\times10^{-3}\times5\times10^3$$

$$= 11.7\ \text{V}.$$ *Ans.*

When Ge diode is reversed, it offers infinite resistance, and now Si diode will conduct . Thus

$$V_0 = 12 - 0.7 = 11.3\ \text{V}$$

$$i = \frac{11.3}{5\times10^3} = 2.26\ mA$$ *Ans.*

7. (a) When positive terminal of battery is connected to terminal A, D_1 be in forward bias while D_2 be in reverse bias. Therefore the current will pass through D_1. Thus

$$i = \frac{5}{10} = 0.5\ A$$ *Ans.*

(b) In this case D_2 be in forward bias and so current will pass through it. Thus

$$i = \frac{5}{20} = 0.25A$$ *Ans.*

8. (a) Both the diodes are in forwards bias and so they offer zero resistance. Therefore

$$i = \frac{5}{5} = 1\ A.$$ *Ans.*

(b) In this case one diode is in reverse bias, and so it offers infinite resistance. Therefore

$$i = 0.$$ *Ans.*

9. The diode is in reverse bias, so it will conduct. Therefore

$$i_1 = 0 \text{ and } i_2 = \frac{2}{10} = 0.2A$$ *Ans.*

10. (a) Given $e^{ev/kT} = 100$

or

$$\frac{ev}{kT} = \ln 100$$

$$\therefore\quad V = \frac{kT\ln 100}{e}$$

$$= \frac{1.38\times10^{-23}\times300\times\ln100}{1.6\times10^{19}} = 0.12V$$

(b) Given $i = i_0(e^{eV/kT} - 1)$

On differentiating, we get

$$di = i_0\, e^{eV/kT} \times \frac{e}{kT} dV$$

$$\therefore \quad \frac{dV}{di} = \frac{kT}{ei_0} e^{-eV/kT}$$

$\frac{dV}{di}$ is the dynamic resistance R. Thus

$$R = \frac{kT}{ei_0} e^{-eV/kT}. \qquad \textit{Ans.}$$

11. We know that $\beta = \frac{\Delta i_c}{\Delta i_B}$

$$= \frac{(3.5-1.0)\times10^{-3}}{(80-30)\times10^{-6}} = 50 \quad \textit{Ans.}$$

12. We know that

$$\beta = \frac{\alpha}{1-\alpha} = \frac{0.96}{1-0.96} = 24.$$

The collector current is

$$i_C = \frac{V_C}{R} = \frac{0.5}{800} = 0.625\times10^{-3}A$$

Base current $i_B = \frac{i_C}{\beta} = \frac{0.625\times10^{-3}}{24}$

$$= 26 \times 10^{-6}\,A = 26\ \mu A. \quad \textit{Ans.}$$

13. (i) Input resistance

$$R_{in} = \frac{\Delta V_{BE}}{\Delta i_B} = \frac{0.04}{40\times10^{-6}} = 1k\Omega \quad \textit{Ans.}$$

(ii) Current amplification factor

$$\beta = \frac{2\times10^{-3}}{40\times10^{-6}} = 50 \qquad \textit{Ans.}$$

(iii) Voltage gain in common-emitter configuration is given by

$$A_v = \beta\frac{R_L}{R_{in}}$$

$$= 50\times\frac{6\times10^3}{1\times10^3} = 300 \qquad \textit{Ans.}$$

14. By the definition

$$\beta_{dc} = \frac{i_C}{i_B}$$

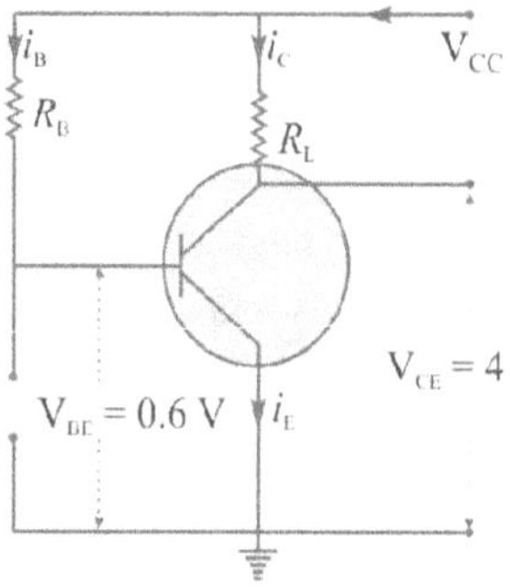

$$\therefore \quad i_B = \frac{i_C}{\beta_{dc}}$$

$$= \frac{4mA}{100}$$

$$= 0.04\ \text{mA}$$

From figure

$$i_B R_B + V_{BE} = V_{CC}$$

$$\therefore \quad R_B = \frac{V_{CC}-V_{BE}}{i_B} = \frac{(8-0.6)}{0.04\times10^{-3}}$$

$$= 185\ \text{k}\Omega \qquad \textit{Ans.}$$

Also $R_L i_C + V_{CE} = V_{CC}$

$$\therefore \quad R_L = \frac{V_{CC}-V_{CE}}{i_C}$$

$$= \frac{8-4}{8\times10^3} = 1k\Omega \qquad \textit{Ans.}$$

15. The output of OR gate is (A + B) and input of AND gate are A and (A + B). The following table evaluate Y for all combinations of A and B.

A	B	$X = A + B$	$Y = A(A+B)$
0	0	0	0
0	1	1	0
1	0	1	1
1	1	1	1

www.ingramcontent.com/pod-product-compliance
Lightning Source LLC
LaVergne TN
LVHW061936070526
838199LV00060B/3847
* 9 7 8 9 3 8 6 3 2 0 1 2 4 *